Handbook of Firearms and Ballistics

Second Edition

Handbook of Firearms and Ballistics

Examining and Interpreting Forensic Evidence

Second Edition

Brian J. Heard

A John Wiley & Sons, Ltd., Publication

This edition first published 2008, © 2008 by John Wiley & Sons Ltd

Wiley-Blackwell is an imprint of John Wiley & Sons, formed by the merger of Wiley's global Scientific, Technical and Medical business with Blackwell Publishing.

Registered office: John Wiley & Sons Ltd, The Atrium, Southern Gate, Chichester, West Sussex, PO19 8SQ, UK

Other Editorial Offices:
9600 Garsington Road, Oxford, OX4 2DQ, UK
111 River Street, Hoboken, NJ 07030-5774, USA

For details of our global editorial offices, for customer services and for information about how to apply for permission to reuse the copyright material in this book please see our website at www.wiley.com/wiley-blackwell

Library of Congress Cataloguing-in-Publication Data
Heard, Brian J.
  Handbook of firearms and ballistics : examining and interpreting forensic evidence / by Brian J. Heard.
      p. cm.
  Includes index.
  ISBN 978-0-470-69460-2
  1. Forensic ballistics. 2. Firearms. 3. Firearms–Identification. I. Title.
  HV8077.H43 2008
  363.25′62–dc 22

                                                                                    2008029101

ISBN: 978-0-470-69460-2

A catalogue record for this book is available from the British Library.

First Impression   2008

FSC
Mixed Sources
Product group from well-managed
forests and other controlled sources
Cert no. SGS-COC-2953
www.fsc.org
© 1996 Forest Stewardship Council

Contents

Developments in Forensic Science

The world of forensic science is changing at a very fast pace. This is in terms of the provision of forensic science services, the development of technologies and knowledge and the interpretation of analytical and other data as it is applied within forensic practice. Practicing forensic scientists are constantly striving to deliver the very best for the judicial process and as such need a reliable and robust knowledge base within their diverse disciplines. It is hoped that this book series will be a valuable resource for forensic science practitioners in the pursuit of such knowledge.

The Forensic Science Society is the professional body for forensic practitioners in the United Kingdom. The Society was founded in 1959 and gained professional body status in 2006. The Society is committed to the development of the forensic sciences in all of its many facets and in particular to the delivery of highly professional and worthwhile publications within these disciplines through ventures such as this book series.

Dr. Niamh Nic Daéid
Series editor.

Acknowledgements

In writing the second edition of this book I have been assisted by more people than I could begin to recount. Of these, a few deserve special mention.

Quenten Ford not only for his invaluable help in formulating the outline of the original book, but also for his assistance in correcting the many typos that crept in.

Barbara Scott for her help with the statistics and various formulae used in both editions.

Dr James Hamby, Evan Thompson and Chris Trumble for all their help and advice in so many ways.

And last, but not least Barbara, Edward and Emily, my wife and children, for all their support and understanding without which I could never have written this book.

Foreword

Medico-legal analysis forms, perhaps beyond all other branches, the most important work undertaken by the Analyst . . . its responsibility and importance lies in the fact that, as the term itself suggests, questions of health, or even of life or death are involved, and secondly, that the work performed will usually result in an action at law, either civil or criminal . . . For these reasons the work demands the greatest skill and experience that can be brought to bear upon it the best instrumental equipment that can be procured, the utmost patience, the most rigidly exact work, and, lastly, a sufficiency of time. . . .

Stirring and eminently appropriate sentiments which would do justice to any modern forensic laboratory administrator. The fact that these words were spoken by E.R. Dovey, Government Analyst of Hong Kong, in an address in 1917, is both a remarkable testament to that scientist and a realization that even 80 years ago, the profession he represented fully appreciated the vital role that forensic science can play in the justice system.

Incredible advances have been made in the sciences over the last few decades, and modern forensic laboratories are now staffed by teams of specialists, all experts in their own particular fields. The days are past when a forensic scientist appeared in the witness box one day as an expert in blood grouping, the next as a questioned document examiner and a third day as a suspicious fire investigator. Such 'generalists' do still present themselves from time to time, but informed courts now afford them a level of credence bordering on ridicule, and rightly so!

Increasing specialization and sophistication of scientific method has, however, widened the gulf of knowledge between the scientist, the lawyer and the jury. With a poor level of scientific literacy in the population at large, frequent criticism of the capacity of scientists to express themselves intelligibly to a lay audience, and a predominance of barristers who are unable or unwilling to help bridge the comprehension gap, that gulf is in danger of widening further.

The Select Committee on Science and Technology (House of Lords 5th Report 1992/3) has constructively, and to some, controversially, pointed the way forward with recommendations for pre-trial conferences between counsel and own experts as a norm rather than an occasion; pre-trial review between experts of both sides to define disagreements; encouragement for concluding statements by experts before leaving the witness box; increasing use of visual aids; and finally, for forensic science to feature more prominently in a lawyer's training.

To satisfy the last recommendation, however, there is a need for instructional and informational textbooks on the specialist areas of the forensic sciences written with the practising criminal lawyer in mind, which bridge the gap between the handbooks for the expert and a 'good read' for the lay reader of scientific bent. It is to be hoped that this book fills that purpose in the ballistics field.

BRYCE N. DAILLY BSc, PhD, JP
Government Chemist, Hong Kong, (retired)

1

Firearms

1.1 A Brief History of Firearms

1.1.1 Early hand cannons

The earliest type of handgun was simply a small cannon of wrought iron or bronze, fitted to a frame or stock with metal bands or leather thongs. These weapons were loaded from the muzzle end of the barrel with powder, wad and ball. A small hole at the breech end of the barrel, the *touch hole*, was provided with a pan into which *a priming charge* of powder was placed. On igniting this priming charge, either with a hot iron or lighted match, fire flashed through the touch hole and into the main powder charge to discharge the weapon.

These early weapons could have been little more than psychological deterrents being clumsy, slow to fire and difficult to aim. In addition, rain or damp weather had an adverse effect on the priming charge making it impossible to ignite.

Their first reported use is difficult to ascertain with any degree of certainty, but a number of instances are reported in Spain between 1247 and 1311. In the records for the Belgian city of Ghent, there are confirmed sightings of the use of hand cannons in Germany in 1313. One of the earliest illustrations concerning the use of hand cannons appears in the fifteenth century fresco in the Palazzo Publico, Sienna, Italy.

The first recorded use of the hand cannon as a cavalry weapon appeared in 1449 in the manuscripts of Marianus Jacobus. This shows a mounted soldier with such a weapon resting on a fork attached to the pommel of the saddle. It is interesting to note that the use of the saddle pommel to either carry or aim

Handbook of Firearms and Ballistics: Second Edition   Brian J. Heard
© 2008 John Wiley & Sons, Ltd.

Figure 1.1 Early hand cannon.

the hand guns could be the origin of the word 'pistol', the early cavalry word for the pommel of the saddle being 'pistallo'.

Combinations of the battle axe and hand cannon were used in the sixteenth century, and a number of these can be found in the Tower of London. One English development of this consisted of a large mace, the head of which had a number of separate barrels. At the rear of the barrels, a concealed chamber containing priming powder led to all the barrels. When the priming compound was ignited, all the barrels discharged at once.

1.1.2 The matchlock

This was really the first major advance in pistols as it enabled the weapon to be fired in one hand and also gave some opportunity to aim it as well.

The construction of the matchlock was exactly the same as the hand cannon in that it was muzzle loaded and had a touch hole covered with a priming charge. The only difference was that the *match*, a slow-burning piece of cord used to ignite the priming charge, was held in a curved hook screwed to the side of the frame. To fire the gun, the hook was merely pushed forward to drop

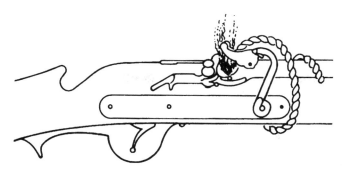

Figure 1.2 Matchlock (by courtesy of the Association of Firearms and Toolmark Examiners).

the burning end of the match into the priming charge. As these weapons became more sophisticated, the curved hook was embellished and took on the form of a snake and became known as the weapon's *serpentine*.

Eventually, the tail of the serpentine was lengthened and became the forerunner of the modern trigger. Further refinements included the use of a spring to hold the head back into a safety position. The final refinement consisted of a system whereby when the tail of the serpentine was pulled, the match rapidly fell into the priming compound under spring pressure. This refinement, a true trigger mechanism, provided better ignition and assisted aiming considerably (Figure 1.2).

It was during the era of the matchlock that reliable English records appeared, and it is recorded that Henry VIII, who reigned from 1509 until 1547, armed many of his cavalry with matchlocks. The first true revolving weapon is also attributed to the period of Henry VIII and is on show in the Tower of London. This weapon consists of a single barrel and four revolving chambers. Each chamber is provided with its own touch hole and priming chamber which has a sliding cover. Although the actual lock is missing from the Tower of London weapon, its construction strongly suggests a single matchlock was used.

The major defect with the matchlock design was that it required a slow-burning 'match' for ignition. As a result, it was of little use for surprise attack or in damp or rainy conditions.

1.1.3 The wheel lock

With the advent of the wheel lock the lighted match used in the matchlock was no longer necessary. This important innovation in the field of firearms design made ambush possible as well as making the firearm a practical weapon for hunting.

When fired from the shoulder, the wheel lock was often referred to as an *arquebus* from the shape of the butt which was often curved to fit the shoulder.

Another name, strictly only for much heavier calibre weapons, was the *hacque-but*, which literally means 'gun with a hook'. This referred to a hook projecting from the bottom of the barrel. This hook was placed over a wall, or some other object, to help take up the recoil of firing.

In its simplest form, the wheel lock consisted of a serrated steel wheel, mounted on the side of the weapon at the rear of the barrel. The wheel was spring-loaded via a chain round its axle with a small key or spanner similar to a watch drum (Figure 1.3). When the wheel was turned with a spanner, the chain wound round the axle and the spring was tensioned. A simple bar inside the lockwork kept the wheel from unwinding until released with the trigger. Part of the wheel protruded into a small pan, the *flash pan or priming pan*, which contained the priming charge for the touch hole. The serpentine, instead of containing a slow-burning match, had a piece of iron pyrite fixed in its jaws. This was kept in tight contact with the serrated wheel by means of a strong spring. On pressing the trigger, the bar was withdrawn from the grooved wheel which then turned on its axle. Sparks produced from the friction of the pyrite on the serrated wheel ignited the priming charge which in turn ignited the main powder charge and fired the weapon.

The wheel lock was a tremendous advance over the slow and cumbersome matchlock. It could be carried ready to fire and with a small cover over the flash pan, it was relatively impervious to all but the heaviest rain. The mechanism was, however, complicated and expensive, and if the spanner to tension the spring was lost, the gun was useless.

There is some dispute as to who originally invented the wheel lock, but it has been ascribed to Johann Kiefuss of Nuremberg, Germany in 1517.

Whilst the wheel lock reached an advanced stage of development in Germany, France, Belgium and Italy towards the close of the sixteenth century, England showed little interest in this type of weapon.

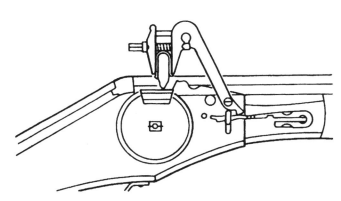

Figure 1.3 Wheel lock (by courtesy of the Association of Firearms and Toolmark Examiners).

Records show that the wheel lock was still being widely manufactured in Europe as late as 1640, but by the turn of the century, it was making way for its successor.

1.1.4 The snaphaunce

The snaphaunce first appeared around 1570, and was really an early form of the flintlock. This mechanism worked by attaching the flint to a spring-loaded arm. When the trigger is pressed, the cover slides off the flash pan, then the arm snaps forward striking the flint against a metal plate over the flash pan producing sparks to ignite the powder.

Whilst this mechanism was much simpler and less expensive than the wheel lock, the German gunsmiths, who tended to ignore the technical advances of other nationalities, continued to produce and improve upon the wheel lock up until the early eighteenth century.

1.1.5 The flintlock

The ignition system which superseded that of the wheel lock was a simple mechanism which provided a spark by striking a piece of flint against a steel plate. The flint was held in the jaws of a small vice on a pivoted arm, called the *cock*. This was where the term to 'cock the hammer' originated.

The steel, which was called the frizzen, was placed on another pivoting arm opposite the cock, and the pan containing the priming compound was placed directly below the frizzen. When the trigger was pulled, a strong spring swung the cock in an arc so that the flint struck the steel a glancing blow. The glancing blow produced a shower of sparks which dropped into the priming pan igniting the priming powder. The flash produced by the ignited priming powder travelled through the touch hole, thus igniting the main charge and discharging the weapon.

The flintlock represented a great advance in weapon design. It was cheap, reliable and not overly susceptible to damp or rainy conditions. Unlike the complicated and expensive wheel lock, this was a weapon which could be issued in large numbers to foot soldiers and cavalry alike.

As is the case with most weapon systems, it is very difficult to pinpoint an exact date for the introduction of the flintlock ignition system. There are indications of it being used in the middle of the sixteenth century, although its first wide use cannot be established with acceptable proof until the beginning of the seventeenth century (Figure 1.4).

Three basic types of flintlock were made:

- *Snaphaunce* – a weapon with the mainspring inside the lock plate and a priming pan cover which had to be manually pushed back before firing.

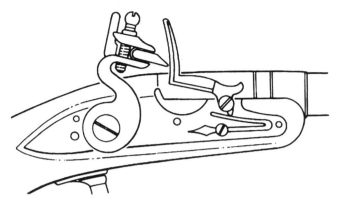

Figure 1.4 Flintlock (by courtesy of the Association of Firearms and Toolmark Examiners).

- *Miquelet* – a weapon with the mainspring outside the lockplate, but with a frizzen and priming pan cover all in one piece. In this lock type, the pan cover was automatically pushed out of the way as the flint struck the frizzen.
- *True flintlock* – a weapon with a mainspring inside the lock plate and with the frizzen and priming pan cover in one piece. This also had a half-cock safety position enabling the weapon to be carried safely with the barrel loaded and the priming pan primed with powder. This system was probably invented by Mann Le Bourgeoys, a gunmaker for Louis XIII of France, in about 1615.

Flintlock pistols, muskets (long-barrelled weapons with a smooth bore) and shotguns were produced with the flintlock mechanism. There was even a patent for flintlock revolvers issued in 1661.

1.1.6   The percussion system

The flintlock continued to be used for almost 200 years and it was not until 1807 that a Scottish minister, Alexander John Forsyth, revolutionized the ignition of gunpowder by using a highly sensitive compound which exploded on being struck. This compound, *mercury fulminate*, when struck by a hammer, produced a flash strong enough to ignite the main charge of powder in the barrel. A separate priming powder and sparking system was now no longer required (Figure 1.5). With this invention, the basis for the self-contained cartridge was laid and a whole new field of possibilities was opened up.

Once this type of ignition, known as *percussion priming*, had been invented, it still took some time to perfect ways of applying it. From 1807 until 1814, a wide range of systems were invented for the application of the percussion

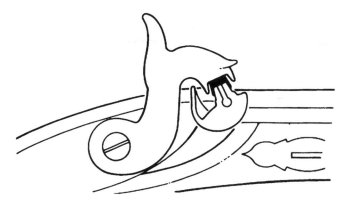

Figure 1.5 Percussion cap system (by courtesy of the Association of Firearms and Toolmark Examiners).

priming system including the Forsyth scent bottle, pill locks, tube locks and the Pauly paper cap.

The final form, the percussion cup, was claimed by a large number of inventors. It is probably attributable to Joshua Shaw, an Anglo-American living in Philadelphia in 1814. Shaw employed a small iron cup into which was placed a small quantity of mercury fulminate. This was placed over a small tube, called *a nipple*, projecting from the rear of the barrel. The hammer striking the mercury fulminate in the cup caused it to detonate and so send a flame down the nipple tube igniting the main charge in the barrel.

1.1.7 The pinfire system

Introduced to the United Kingdom at the Great Exhibition in London in 1851 by Lefaucheux, the pinfire weapon was one of the earliest true breech-loading weapons using a self-contained cartridge in which the propellant, missile and primer were all held together in a brass case.

In this system, the percussion cup was inside the cartridge case whilst a pin, which rested on the percussion cup, protruded through the side of the cartridge case. Striking the pin with the weapon's hammer drove the pin into the priming compound causing it to detonate and so ignite the main propellant charge (Figure 1.6).

The pin, which protruded through the weapon's chamber, not only served to locate the round in its correct position, but also aided extraction of the fired cartridge case.

The pinfire was at its most popular between 1890 and 1910 and was still readily available in Europe until 1940. It had, however, fallen out of favour in England by 1914 and was virtually unobtainable by 1935.

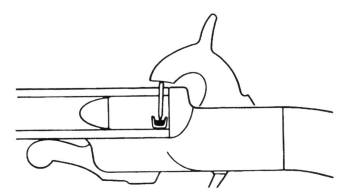

Figure 1.6 Pinfire system (by courtesy of the Association of Firearms and Toolmark Examiners).

Calibres available in the pinfire revolvers were 5, 7, 9, 12 and 15 mm, whilst shotgun and rifle ammunition in 9 mm, 12 bore and various other calibres was also available.

The really great advance of the pinfire system was, however, not just the concept of a self-contained cartridge, but obturation, the ability of the cartridge case under pressure to swell and so seal the chamber preventing the rearward escape of gases.

1.1.8   The rimfire system

Whilst the pinfire system was a significant step forward, it did have a number of drawbacks, not least of which was the propensity of the cartridge to discharge if dropped onto its pin. This problem was all but eliminated by the rimfire which, like the pinfire, was exhibited at the Great Exhibition in 1851.

The rimfire cartridge is a thin-walled cartridge with a hollow flanged rim. Into this rim is spun a small quantity of a priming compound. Crushing the rim with the firing pin causes the priming compound to explode, thus igniting the propellant inside the case.

The initial development of this system was made by a Paris gunsmith, Flobert, who had working examples of it as early as 1847 (Figure 1.7).

It was, however, some time before it gained acceptance, and it was not until 1855 that Smith and Wesson manufactured the first revolver to fire rimfire cartridges. This was a hinged-frame 0.22″ calibre weapon in which the barrel tipped up by means of a hinge on the top of the frame. This enabled the cylinder to be removed when loading and unloading the weapon.

Although a great step forward, the rimfire was only suitable for high-pressure weapons in small calibre. Anything above 0.22″ and the soft rim necessary for the ignition system resulted in cartridge case failures.

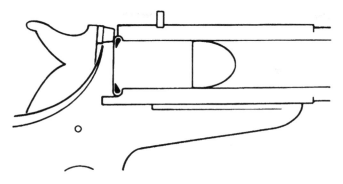

Figure 1.7 Rimfire system.

1.1.9 The Dreyse needle fire rifle

The Dreyse needle gun was a military breech-loading rifle, famous as the main infantry weapon of the Prussians, who adopted it for service in 1848 as the Dreyse Prussian Model 1848.

Its name, the needle gun, comes from its needle-like firing pin, which passed through the cartridge case to impact a percussion cap glued to the base of the bullet.

The Dreyse rifle was the first breech-loading rifle to use the bolt action to open and close the chamber, executed by turning and pulling a bolt handle.

The Dreyse rifle was invented by the gunsmith Johann Nikolaus von Dreyse (1787–1867) and was first produced as a fully working rifle in 1836. From 1848 onwards, the new weapon was gradually introduced into the Prussian service, then later into the military forces of many other German states. The employment of the needle gun radically changed military tactics in the nineteenth century.

The cartridge used with this rifle was a self-contained paper case containing the bullet, priming cap and black powder charge. The bullet, which was glued into the paper case, had the primer attached to its base. The upper end of the paper case was rolled up and tied together. Before the needle could strike the primer, its point had to pass through the powder and hit the primer ahead. The theory behind this placement of the primer is that it would give more complete combustion of the charge. Unfortunately, this led to severe corrosion of the needle which then either stuck in the bolt or broke off rendering the rifle useless. It was, however, a major step forward in the production of the modern rifle (Figure 1.8).

1.1.10 The centre fire system

This was the great milestone in weapon and ammunition development. In centre fire ammunition, only the primer cup needed to be soft enough to be crushed

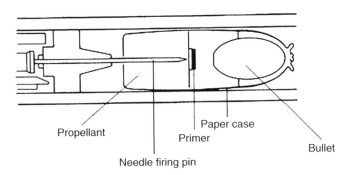

Figure 1.8 Dreyse needle fire system.

by the firing pin. The cartridge case could thus be made of a more substantial material which would act as a gas seal for much higher pressures than could be obtained with rimfire ammunition.

Once again the precise date for the invention of the first centre fire weapon is difficult to ascertain, although there is a patent issued in 1861 for a Daws centre fire system (Figure 1.9).

Probably no invention connected with firearms has had as much effect on the principles of firearms development as the obturating centre fire cartridge case. Although invented around 1860, the principles are still the same and are utilized in every type of weapon from the smallest handgun up to some of the largest artillery pieces.

Rocket-propelled bullets (the Gyrojet), caseless ammunition, hot air ignition and many other esoterica have come and gone. However, for simplicity, reliability and ease of manufacture, the centre fire ignition system in an obturating cartridge case has not been excelled.

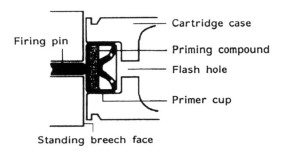

Figure 1.9 Centre fire system.

1.1.11   Rifling

Rifling is the term given to the spiral grooves cut into the bore of a barrel which impart a stabilizing spin to the bullet. This spin keeps the bullet travelling in a point-first direction and lessens any tendency for it to depart from its straight line of flight. As such, this was a very significant event in the evolution of firearms.

Some writers assign the invention of spiral-grooved barrels to Gaspard Kollner, a gunmaker of Vienna, in the fifteenth century. Others fix the date at 1520 and attribute it to Augustus Kotter of Nuremberg.

German weapons bearing the coat of arms of the Emperor Maximilian I and made between 1450 and 1500 have spiral-grooved barrels and are in fact the earliest identifiable rifled guns.

Both straight and spiral forms of rifling are encountered in early weapons, although it is generally accepted that the straight form of rifling was to accommodate the fouling produced in these early black powder weapons.

The number of grooves encountered can be anything from a single deeply cut rifling right up to 12 in number. The form of the groove also varies with square, round, triangular, ratchet and even comma shapes being encountered. The actual number of grooves appears to have little effect on the stabilizing effect of the rifling.

One of the problems encountered with the muzzle-loading rifle was the difficulty experienced in loading the projectile. If it was of sufficient diameter to take up the rifling, a large mallet was required to force it down the bore. If, on the other hand, it was of reduced diameter to assist in its insertion, the gases produced on firing would escape past the bullet leading to reduced velocity. In addition, the bullet took up little of the rifling and thus became unstable in flight. The Brunswick rifle overcame this problem by having a belted bullet and a barrel with two grooves to exactly match the rib on the bullet.

Several other designs were tried in which the bullet was rammed down onto various projections inside the breech end of the barrel. These projections deformed the bullet, thus filling out the bore. Unfortunately, the deformation was irregular and led to erratic behaviour of the bullet.

Greener in 1835 produced the first expansive bullet, the rear of which contained a steel plug. On firing, this was forced up into the bullet expanding it uniformly.

In 1852, Minie, a Frenchman, was awarded a British government contract for the production of an expanding bullet using a steel plug in the base very similar to the Greener design. This resulted in some acrimonious legal action by Mr Greener who was awarded a sum of money recognizing his as the earliest form of expanding bullet.

Lancaster, at about the same time as Minie invented his expanding bullet, produced a rifle with a spiral oval bore. This permitted easy loading of the bullet, did not require any mechanism to expand the base and, as there were no sharp corners to the rifling, it did not suffer the problems with fouling as encountered with conventional rifling.

In 1854, Whitworth patented the first polygonal bore rifling system which overcame most of the problems and was extremely accurate as well. Unfortunately, Whitworth did not have the experience in the practical manufacture of weapons and was unable to produce guns with the consistency required. As a result, his invention was soon overtaken by others.

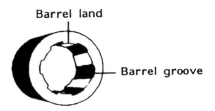

Figure 1.10 Rifling in the bore of a barrel.

The invention of the breech-loading weapon eliminated the problems of having to expand the bullet and fill the bore. The bullet could be made of the correct diameter and could simply be inserted into the rifling at the breech end of the barrel (Figure 1.10). In addition, instead of the deep grooving and a long soft bullet necessary for easy loading and expansion at the breech of a muzzle loader, shallow grooves and hard bullets could be used. This configuration resulted in more uniform bullets, higher velocities, better accuracy and improved trajectory.

1.1.12   Rifling twist rate calculation

One of the first persons to try to develop a formula for calculating the correct rate of twist for firearms was George Greenhill, a mathematics lecturer at Emmanual College in Cambridge, England.

His formula is based on the rule that the twist required in calibres equals 150 divided by the length of the bullet in calibres. This can be simplified to

$$\text{Twist} = 150 \times D^2/L$$

where D = bullet diameter in inches and L = bullet length in inches.

This formula had limitations, but worked well up to and in the vicinity of about 1800 fps. For higher velocities, most ballistic experts suggest substituting 180 for 150 in the formula.

The Greenhill formula is simple and easy to apply and gives a useful approximation to the desired twist. It was based on a bullet with a specific gravity of 10.9, which is approximately correct for a jacketed lead-cored bullet.

In this equation, bullet weight does not directly enter into the equation. For a given calibre, the heavier the bullet, the longer it will be. So bullet weight affects bullet length, which is used in the formula.

For bullets with a specific gravity other than 10.9, then the formula becomes

$$\text{Rifling Twist Rate Required} = CD^2/L \times \sqrt{SG/10.9}$$

If an insufficient twist rate is used, the bullet will begin to yaw and then tumble; this is usually seen as 'keyholing', where bullets leave elongated holes in the target as they strike at an angle.

Once the bullet starts to yaw, any hope of accuracy is lost, as the bullet will begin to veer off in random directions as it processes.

A too-high rate of twist can also cause problems. The excessive twist can cause accelerated barrel wear, and in high-velocity bullets, an excessive twist can cause bullets to literally tear themselves apart under the centrifugal force.

A higher twist than needed can also cause more subtle problems with accuracy. Any inconsistency in the bullet, such as a void that causes an unequal distribution of mass, may be magnified by the spin.

Undersized bullets also have problems, as they may not enter the rifling exactly concentric and coaxial to the bore, and excess twist will exacerbate the accuracy problems this causes.

The twist necessary to stabilize various calibres follows (Table 1.1):

Table 1.1 Rifling twist necessary to stabilize various calibres.

Calibre	Twist rate required
0.22 Short	1 in 24″
0.22 Long rifle	1 in 16″
0.223 Remington	1 in 12″
0.22–250 Remington	1 in 14″
0.243 Winchester	1 in 10″
6 mm Remington	1 in 9″
0.25–0.6 Remington	1 in 10″
0.257 Weatherby Magnum	1 in 10″
6.5 × 55 Swedish Mauser	1 in 7.5″
0.260 Remington	1 in 9″
0.270 Winchester	1 in 10″
7 mm–0.8 Remington	1 in 9.25″
7 mm Remington Magnum	1 in 9.25″
0.30 Carbine	1 in 16″
0.30–30 Winchester	1 in 12″
0.308 Winchester	1 in 12″
0.30–0.6 Springfield	1 in 10″
0.300 Winchester Magnum	1 in 10″
0.303 British	1 in 10″
0.357 Magnum	1 in 16″
0.357 Sig Saner	1 in 16″
0.380 Automatic Colt Pistol	1 in 10″
9 mm Parabellum	1 in 10″
0.40 Smith & Wesson	1 in 15″
0.45 Automatic Colt Pistol	1 in 16″
0.444 Marlin	1 in 38″
0.45–70 Government (US)	1 in 20″

Whilst it is of little circumstance, the question as to the revolutions made per minute by the bullet has been asked on several occasions. The formula for calculating this is as follows:

$$\frac{MV \times 720}{\text{Twist rate in inches}} = RPM$$

For example:

9 mm PB bullet at 1200 fps fired in a barrel with a 1 in 10 twist rate will have a rotational speed of $1200 \times 720/10 = 86\,400$ rpm

0.223″ bullet at 3000 fps fired in a barrel with a 1 in 12 twist rate will have a rotational speed of $3000 \times 720/12 = 180\,000$ rpm

Once again, whilst it has little relevance in everyday case examination, the question as to the rotational speed (revolutions per minute, rpm) and the number of times that a bullet will make a full rotation whilst passing through an object can be asked.

This question was posed in relation to a murder case where one of several bullets which had hit the deceased had cut a trough (often called a 'gutter wound') across the victim's arm. The bullet wound was black and the defence counsel were of the opinion that this was caused 'by the bullet rotating so fast that it had burnt the flesh to carbon'.

This was extremely easy to refute as the barrel of the weapon concerned had a 1 in 10″ rate of twist, which means that the bullet rotated once in every 10 in. of travel. As the wound on the arm was barely 2 in. in length, the bullet would not have made more than $\frac{1}{5}$ of a rotation during that distance.

The blackening, as can be seen from the following photograph, was simply old congealed blood (Figure 1.11).

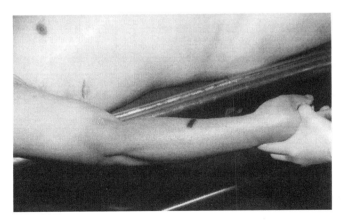

Figure 1.11 Gutter wound to forearm.

1.1.13 The revolver

A revolver is a weapon with a revolving cylinder containing a number of firing chambers (basically a revolving magazine) which may be successively lined up and discharged through a single barrel.

In the long history of revolvers, no name stands out more strongly than that of Samuel Colt. But as we have seen earlier, Colt did not, despite his claims to the contrary, invent the revolver.

The earliest forms of the revolver include a snaphaunce revolver made in the days of King Charles I, said to have been made before 1650 and an even earlier weapon made during the reign of Henry VIII some time before 1547.

Those early revolvers were, surprisingly enough, practically identical to the actions covered in Colt's early patents. The actions for those early patents are still in use today in the Colt Single Action Army or Frontier model.

Colt's original patent, dated 1835, dealt with the revolving of the cylinder by a ratchet and pawl arrangement. The original patents belonging to Colt were so tightly worded that no other manufacturer had any real impression on the market until the original patents ran out in 1850. After this the market was open with Dean–Adams in 1851, Beaumont in 1855, and Starr and Savage in 1865, all bringing out innovative designs. These were, however, still all muzzle-loading percussion systems.

It was not until the advent of the rimfire, which was introduced at the Great Exhibition in 1851, that breech-loading revolvers really started. Even then, it was not until 1857 that Smith and Wesson introduced the first hinged-frame 0.22″ rimfire revolver. The patent for bored-through chambers and the use of metallic cartridges gave Smith and Wesson the market until 1869.

With the passing of the Smith and Wesson patents, there was a flood of breech-loading arms in calibres from 0.22 to 0.50″. The day of the rimfire, except for 0.22″ target shooting, was, however, numbered by the introduction of the centre fire (Figure 1.12).

The first centre fire Colt revolver to be patented was the Colt Single Action Army Model 1873. In 1880, Enfield produced a 0.476″ hinged-frame revolver, but it was a design monstrosity and was soon superseded by the now familiar Webley top latching hinged-frame design in 1887. In 1894, it was slightly modified and became the standard Webley Mk 1 British Army service revolver. In 1889, the US government officially adopted a Colt 0.38″ revolver using the now familiar swing-out cylinder system.

A multitude of variations on the Smith and Wesson and Colt designs followed, but little has really changed in the basic design of the revolver mechanism since then, apart from improved sights, better metals allowing higher pressures and different grips. It would seem, however, that little can be done to improve on the efficiency of the basic Smith and Wesson and Colt designs.

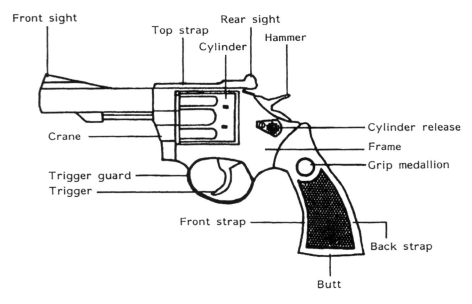

Figure 1.12 Revolver.

1.1.14 Self-loading pistols

The principle of the self-loading pistol was grasped long ago, but without the necessary combination of a self-contained cartridge, smokeless propellant and metallurgical advances, it was not possible to utilize the principles involved.

It is reported in Birche's History of the Royal Society for 1664 that a mechanic had made a claim of being able to make a pistol which could 'shoot as fast as presented and stopped at will'.

Whilst patent records from 1863 show numerous attempts to develop a self-loading pistol, it was not until 1892 that the first successful weapon appeared. This was a weapon patented by the Austrian Schonberger and made by the company Steyr. It was a blowback design and was made for the 8 mm Schonberger, a very powerful cartridge.

The first commercially successful design was by an American, Hugo Borchardt. Unable to finance his design, he took it to Germany to have it manufactured there. This weapon, although clumsy, was of radical design containing the first magazine to be held in the grip and the 'knee joint' toggle locking system. It was this design which was slightly modified by Luger to become Germany's first military self-loading pistol.

In 1893, Bergman produced a whole range of pistols, one of which, the 1897 8 mm 'Simplex', is of particular interest as the cartridge became the 0.32″ Automatic Colt Pistol (ACP) cartridge.

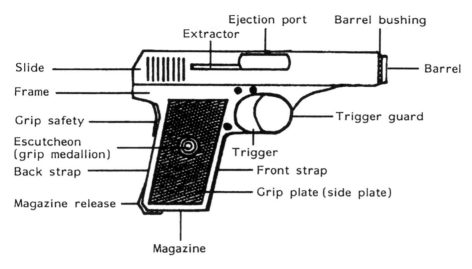

Figure 1.13 Self-loading pistol.

In 1896, the story of the truly successful self-loading pistol really began with the introduction of the 7.63 mm calibre Mauser, the 'broom handle' pistol. This was the pistol made famous by Winston Churchill who purchased one for use during the Sudan campaign of 1898. Winston Churchill credits the weapon with saving his life when he shot his way out of a native trap 'killing several Fuzzy Wuzzies'!

In 1898, the German factory of DWM (Deutsche Waffen- and Munitionsfabriken Atkien-Gesellschaft, German Weapons and Munitions Works) brought out the first model of the famous Luger pistol in 7.65 mm Parabellum calibre. In 1904, the weapon was made available in 9 mm Parabellum, which was the calibre adopted for the German service pistols.

In 1897, John Browning, the greatest of all American small arms designers, produced his first patent. This was finally introduced as the Model 1900 Colt 0.38″ automatic.

Webley made a few unsuccessful forays into the self-loading pistol market with the 0.455″ calibre 1904 model, the 0.45″ 1905 model, the 1910 0.38″ calibre and the 0.455″ navy model 1913. The Webley design was not, however, very successful and never became popular.

Probably the most successful pistol ever to be introduced was the Model 1911, Browning designed, Colt Government Model in 0.45″ calibre. With minor modifications, as the Model 1911 Al, the weapon was the standard issue military weapon for the United States until the late 1980s.

Since then, the main innovations have been in the use of lightweight aluminium and plastics for the weapons frame, the move towards smaller calibres and higher-velocity bullets, the development of magnum handgun ammunition and the use of gas-operated locking systems. These are, however, only variations on a theme and, as with revolvers, it would seem that there is little that can be done to improve on the basic design.

1.1.15   Brief glossary

Breech loader	Weapon in which the ammunition is inserted into the rear of the barrel.
Centre fire	Ammunition with the priming compound held in a cap in the centre of the base of the cartridge case.
Cock (v)	The spring-loaded hammer system which initiates the priming compound.
Cock (n)	The vice-like component of a flintlock mechanism which holds the flint.
Flash hole	Hole connecting the priming compound with the propellant charge; also called the vent or touch hole.
Flash pan	Shallow pan covering the touch hole into which the priming powder is placed.
Mercury fulminate	One of the earliest explosive priming compounds.
Muzzle loader	Weapon in which the propellant and ball are loaded from the muzzle.
Pinfire	Early self-contained cartridge which had a firing pin integral with the cartridge case.
Primer cap	Small cup containing the priming compound.
Priming powder	Finely divided black powder.
Propellant	Solid substance which, when ignited, produces a large quantity of gas to propel a missile down the bore of a weapon.
Revolver	A weapon with a revolving cylinder containing a number of firing chambers (basically a revolving magazine) which may be successively lined up and discharged through a single barrel.
Rifling	Spiral grooves in the barrel to impart spin to the projectile giving it stability in flight.
Rimfire	Self-contained cartridge with the priming compound held in the hollow base flange or rim.
Self-loading	A repeating firearm requiring a separate pull of the trigger for each shot fired. After manually loading the first round from the magazine, the weapon will use the energy of discharge to eject the fired cartridge and load a new cartridge from the magazine into the barrel ready for firing.

1.2 Weapon Types and Their Operation

Terrible confusion exists as to what is *a pistol, revolver, self-loading pistol* and *automatic*. This is very basic firearms nomenclature, but it is often wrongly applied. The use of the correct term is absolutely essential if any credibility is to be maintained.

This chapter attempts no more than to carefully explain the correct usage and, where they exist, alternatives which one might encounter.

1.2.1 Handguns

There are three basic types of handgun: *single shot, revolving* and *self-loading pistols*.

Such exotica as double-barrelled Howdah pistols, self-loading revolvers and self-loading pistols with revolving magazines can be ignored for the purposes of this chapter.

In English nomenclature, all handguns are pistols; some are single-shot pistols; others are revolving pistols, and the rest are self-loading pistols.

The Americans take a slightly more laid-back approach with the terminology using revolvers and pistols. Pistols are also referred to as semi-automatics.

The term automatic is often misused, and when applied to a pistol should be used with great care. Correctly used, the term signifies a weapon in which the action will continue to operate until the finger is removed from the trigger or the magazine is empty – hence 'automatic'.

A true self-loading pistol will, after firing, eject the spent cartridge case then reload a fresh round of ammunition into the chamber. To fire the fresh round, the pressure on the trigger has to be released and then re-applied.

A few true automatic pistols have been commercially manufactured. Examples are the Mauser Schnell-Feuer pistol and the Astra Mod 902. Fully automatic pistols have, however, never been a commercial success due to the near impossibility of controlling such a weapon under full automatic fire. Each shot causes the barrel to rise during recoil, and before the firer has time to reacquire the target within the sights, the next round has fired causing the barrel to rise even further. Even at close range, it is unusual for more than two shots to hit a man-sized target.

Single shot. The vast majority of single-shot pistols are 0.22″ LR (long rifle) calibre and are intended for target use. Generally, the barrel is hinged to the frame with some locking mechanism to keep it in place during firing. On unlocking, the barrel swings down allowing the empty cartridge case to be removed and a fresh one to be inserted. Other types exist in which the barrel is firmly fixed to the frame and some form of breech block which either swings out, pulls back or slides down to expose the breech end of the barrel for loading/unloading.

Revolving pistol.   In a revolving pistol, or revolver, the supply of ammunition is held in a cylinder at the rear of the barrel with each round having its own chamber. Cocking the hammer rotates the cylinder via a ratchet mechanism to bring a new round of ammunition in line with the barrel. Pulling the trigger then drops the hammer thus firing the round. This is the most simple type of revolving pistol mechanism and is called the *single-action* mode of operation. The earliest types of revolving pistol employed this type of mechanism. A prime example of a single-action revolver is the Colt Single Action Model of 1873.

The other type of revolving pistol mechanism is called *double action*. In this design, a long continuous pull on the trigger cocks the hammer, rotates the cylinder, then drops the hammer all in one operation. Most modern revolving pistols employ this type of mechanism with virtually all of them having the capability for single-action mode of operation as well.

In the past, very few self-cocking revolving pistols have also been manufactured. These have an action which, after firing a round, automatically rotates the cylinder and re-cocks the hammer. The most successful of this type was the Webley Fosberry. This type of weapon is, however, extremely rare and exists nowadays only as a collector's item.

Revolvers can be subgrouped into *solid frame*, where the frame is made from a single forging, and *hinged frame*, where the frame is hinged to tip either up or down for access to the cylinder. Access to the cylinder for loading or reloading in solid frame revolvers is generally accomplished by having the cylinder mounted on a *crane* which can be swung out from the frame (Figure 1.14). Some weapons also have the cylinder mounted on a removable axis pin which

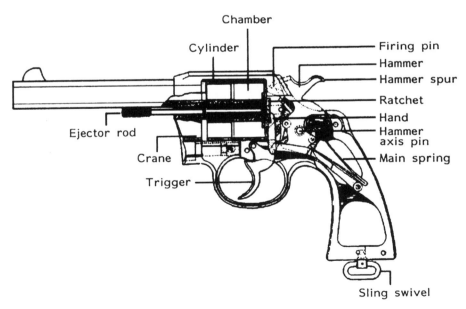

Figure 1.14 Modern revolver mechanism.

when removed allows the cylinder to be completely removed from the frame for loading and unloading. This type of frame is more commonly encountered in cheaper weapons, generally of 0.22″ calibre.

Of the two frame types, the solid frame is the most common, due to its inherent strength and ease of manufacture.

Self-loading pistol (slp).   In this type of weapon, the ammunition is contained in a removable spring-loaded magazine housed within the grip frame. The barrel of the weapon is surrounded by a slide with an integral breech block which is kept into battery (i.e. when the face of the breech block is up tight against the breech end of the barrel in a position ready for firing), with the rear of the barrel by a strong spring. Pulling back the slide allows the topmost round of ammunition in the magazine to present itself to the rear of the barrel. On allowing the slide to move forward under spring pressure, the round is pushed from the magazine into the chamber of the barrel by the breech block. This action also cocks the trigger mechanism.

On pulling the trigger, the hammer drops and the round is fired, the bullet being pushed down the barrel by the expanding gases. These gases also exert an equal and opposite force on the cartridge case which forces the slide and breech block to the rear. This ejects the spent cartridge case through a port in the side, or occasionally top, of the slide. At the end of its rearward motion, the spring-loaded slide moves forward stripping a fresh round off the top of the magazine and feeding it into the rear of the barrel ready for firing (Figure 1.15).

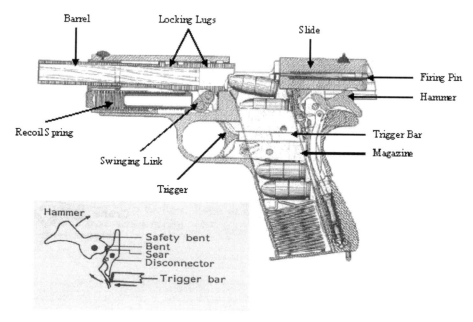

Figure 1.15 Self loading pistol (Colt 1911A1 model).

As the action is only self-loading, the pressure on the trigger has to be removed and then re-applied before another round can be fired. To prevent the weapon from firing continuously, a part of the action, called *a disconnecter*, removes the trigger from contact with the rest of the mechanism. Releasing the trigger disengages the disconnecter allowing the trigger to re-engage with the mechanism so that the fresh round can be fired.

An action such as that described, where the slide is kept into battery with the barrel by spring action alone, is the simplest type of self-loading pistol mechanism. It is generally referred to as *a blowback* action and is only of any real use *for* lower-powered cartridges. If a blowback action were used for any of the more powerful calibres, the unsupported cartridge would, on exiting from the barrel, explode due to the tremendous pressures produced during firing. For all practical purposes, the most powerful round which can safely be fired in a blowback action weapon is a 0.380″ ACP (9-mm Short) cartridge. Some blowback action weapons, such as the Astra Model 400 and the Dreys 1910 Military Model, have been designed to fire more powerful cartridges by having massive recoil springs. They are, however, either very difficult to cock due to the strength of the recoil spring and generally require some method of disconnecting the spring during the cocking operation.

Once more powerful ammunition is used, some other mechanism has to be employed to ensure that the pressures produced fall to a safe level before the fired cartridge case exits from the barrel. This is accomplished via a *locked breech* or *delayed blowback mechanism* in which the barrel is locked to the breech block by some mechanical means during the instant of firing.

With this type of action, the rearward thrust of the cartridge case against the breech block causes the barrel and attached breech block to move backwards together. At some point on its rearward travel, designed such that the bullet has exited the barrel and the barrel pressures have fallen to acceptable levels, the barrel is stopped and unlocked from the breech block. The breech block and slide can then continue to the rear and in so doing eject the empty cartridge case. On its return journey into battery with the barrel, a fresh cartridge is loaded into the chamber and the mechanism is cocked ready to fire again.

The variety of locked-breech mechanisms is vast and outside the scope of this book. They range from the very simple Browning 'swinging link' and Luger 'toggle joint' to the more modern systems using high-pressure gas tapped from the barrel either to keep the breech locked or to operate the unlocking mechanism.

1.2.2 Rifles

Rifle actions can be very roughly grouped into single shot, bolt action, self-loading and pump action.

Single shot. In single-shot weapons, the barrel can be hinged to the frame, allowing the barrel to be dropped down for loading and unloading, or can have some form of breech block which either swings out, pulls back or slides down to expose the breech end of the barrel.

Bolt action. In bolt-action weapons, a turning bolt slides in an extension to the barrel, which is basically the same system as in a turn bolt used to lock a door. Pushing the bolt forward brings the bolt face into battery with the breech end of the barrel and cocks the striker (or firing pin). Turning the bolt then locks it into place via bolt lugs engaging with slots in the barrel extension. Other bolt-action weapons cock the striker on the opening of the bolt (Figure 1.16).

Straight-pull bolt actions also exist in which the rotary motion required to turn the bolt locking lugs into their recesses is applied by studs on the bolt which slide in spiral grooves cut into the barrel extension.

Bolt-action weapons are generally magazine fed, either by a tubular magazine under the barrel, through the butt stock or via a box magazine under the bolt.

Self-loading rifles. Self-loading rifles are, with the exception of the lowest power weapons, of the locked-breech type. These are generally very similar to those used in locked-breech pistols, but of a much stronger design to cope with the higher pressures involved (Figure 1.17).

There are basically two types of self-loading rifle action:

- *Short recoil*, in which the bolt and breech block are only locked together for about 0.75″ of rearward travel before unlocking. It then operates as a normal self-loading pistol.

- *Long recoil*, in which the barrel and breech block are locked together for the full distance of the recoil stroke. After reaching the end of its travel, the barrel is then unlocked and pushed forward by spring action ejecting the spent cartridge during its forward motion. When the barrel is fully forward, the breech

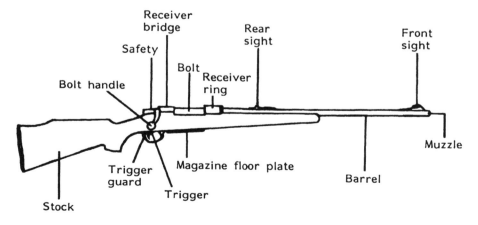

Figure 1.16 Bolt-action rifle.

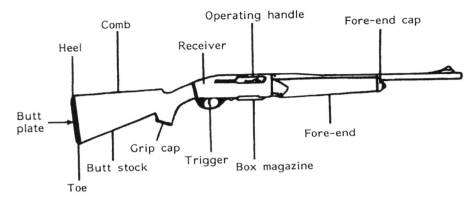

Figure 1.17 Self-loading rifle.

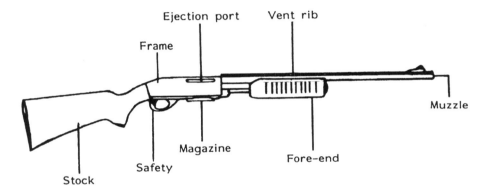

Figure 1.18 Pump-action rifle.

block begins its forward motion reloading a fresh cartridge into the chamber and cocking the action.

Pump action.   In pump-action weapons (sometimes also referred to as *slide action*), the breech block is attached, via operating rods, to a moveable fore-end. On pulling back the fore-end, the mechanism locking the breech block to the barrel is released. By pulling the fore-end to the rearmost extent of its travel then pushing it forward, the empty cartridge case is ejected, a fresh round is loaded into the chamber and the action is cocked (Figure 1.18).

1.2.3   Shotguns

Shotgun actions are basically the same as those found in rifles, with single/ double-shot weapons with barrels hinged to the frame for loading/unloading, bolt action, self-loading and pump-action. Barrels can be either positioned one on top of the other, over and under or 'superposed' or 'side by side'.

In the smaller calibres, that is, 0.22″, 9-mm and 0.410″, double-barrelled shot pistols are occasionally encountered.

Shotgun/rifle combinations are popular in Europe and can consist of one shotgun barrel and one rifle barrel (*vierling*), two shotgun barrels with one rifle barrel (*drilling*) or two rifle barrels and one shotgun barrel (also called *a drilling*).

1.2.4   Sub-machine guns (smg)

Sub-machine guns are really outside the scope of this book, but a brief description is relevant. These are fully automatic weapons generally chambered for pistol calibre ammunition. The simplest type of action encountered is a simple blowback. To overcome the problems of the cartridge exiting the chamber before the pressures have dropped to safe levels, a very heavy reciprocating bolt and a large spring are employed to delay the cartridge extraction. The classic example of this type of action is the Sten gun used by the British forces in World War II (WWII). Whilst this is an extremely simple, cheap to manufacture and reliable action, it does tend to be rather heavy. More modern weapons are equipped with some form of delayed blowback action of the type used in self-loading pistols and rifle actions, for example, the Uzi. Whilst this does produce a much lighter weapon, it is much more expensive to manufacture and, being more complicated, more prone to malfunction.

1.2.5   Machine guns and heavy machine guns

These are well outside of the scope of this book, but basically, a machine gun is a long-barrelled automatic weapon firing rifle calibre ammunition. A heavy machine gun is very similar to a machine gun, but it is much more sturdily built, often with a water jacket round the barrel to prevent overheating and a consequential rapid rate of wear. Being much heavier, it is generally mounted on a sturdy tripod and is designed for sustained high rates of fire.

1.2.6   Headspace

Headspace is not a subject that comes up in the everyday examination of firearms cases. It is, however, a subject that one should be aware of and be able to answer questions upon if asked.

In firearms terms, the headspace is the distance measured from the part of the chamber that stops forward motion of the cartridge (the datum line) to the face of the bolt.

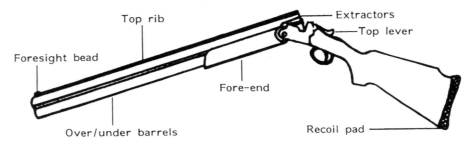

Figure 1.19 Over and under shotgun.

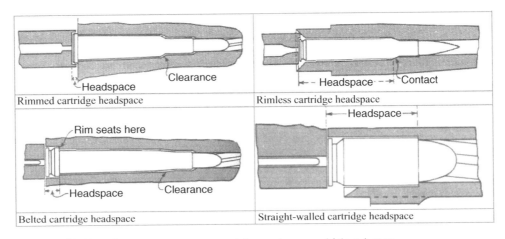

Figure 1.20 Headspace measurement for various cartridge types.

With cartridges having a rim, the headspace is measured from the back face of the barrel to the face of the breech.

With rimless cases, it is measured from either the mouth of the case (if a straight-walled case) or from a datum point on the shoulder of the case (Figure 1.20).

Headspace is measured using a precision gauge cut to the dimensions required.

Headspace gauges generally come in three sizes: a 'go' gauge on which the action will close and lock up, a 'no-go' gauge on which the action can only be partially closed or closed only with some effort and a 'field' gauge on which the action should not be able to be closed on (Figure 1.21).

Excessive headspace allows movement of the case during firing which can cause case stretching, case separation (ruptured case) and gas leakage.

When the powder is ignited, the base of the cartridge can move back whilst the sides of the case stick to the walls of the chamber. As a result, the case can

Figure 1.21 Rimless cartridge headspace gauge.

separate and rupture. If the bolt and receiver are not strong enough to contain and vent the blast, serious damage can be caused to both the firer and the firearm itself.

Some military firearms are designed to handle a problem like case rupture. The ported holes on the side of Mauser bolts are an example of a design to vent off gases that may be inadvertently sent through the bolt to the rear of the firearm.

Insufficient headspace prevents the closing of the bolt and possibly the complete chambering of the cartridge. If the bolt is forced closed, this can cause the bullet to be compressed further into the neck of the cartridge's case. This will lead to over-pressure conditions when the cartridge is fired and may cause very similar results to that caused by excessive headspace; the case may rupture sending very hot, high-pressure gases through the rear of the receiver.

1.2.7 Muzzle attachments

Rifles, pistols and revolvers can be found with six types of muzzle attachment. These are:

1. sound suppressors (often wrongly called silencers);
2. recoil reducers, also referred to as compensators;
3. flash hiders;
4. muzzle counter weights (mainly for target weapons);
5. grenade dischargers;
6. recoil boosters.

Shotguns can also be fitted with all of the above, although they are most likely to be found with either fixed or adjustable chokes or a recoil reducer.

1.2.8 Sound suppressors

There are four distinct components that together make up the noise we perceive as a gunshot. In order of loudness, these are:

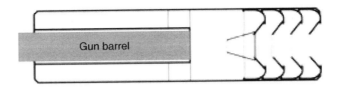

Figure 1.22 Typical silencer construction.

1. pressure wave from rapidly expanding propellant gases;
2. supersonic crack of bullet as it passes through the sound barrier;
3. mechanical action noise;
4. flight noise.

The pressure wave.   This is produced by the rapidly expanding propellant gases and is, generally, the only noise component that a suppressor can reduce.

Exceptions include those weapons where the silencer is integral to the barrel and is designed to bleed off gases before the bullet reaches supersonic speed. Examples would include the H&K MP5SD and High Standard Model HD.

As the expanding gases exit the barrel of an unsuppressed barrel, they rapidly expand causing a loud bang which is basically due to the gases exceeding the speed of sound (approximately 1100 ft/s). The suppressor reduces this noise by the slow release, through expansion and turbulence, of high-pressure propellant gases to the point where they no longer exceed this velocity.

The basic design of a sound suppressor consists of an expansion chamber (in Figure 1.22 this wraps back around the barrel to decrease the length of the suppressor) and a series of baffles to further reduce the speed of the emerging gases.

Suppressors can either be an integral part of the weapon or a muzzle attachment to be screwed on, attached via a bayonet type fitment or with grub screws.

Integral suppressors can be designed that the gases are bled off (ported) into the expansion chamber before the bullet reaches supersonic speeds. Example of weapons with an integral suppressor would include the High Standard HD 0.22″ slp and the H&K MP5SD 9 mm PB smg. In these weapons, bleeding the gases off early reduces the final velocity of the bullet to below that of sound thus allowing standard ammunition to be used rather than a reduced loading.

Most suppressors for supersonic cartridges can realistically be expected to reduce the noise of firing by 18–32 dB depending on the design.

Supersonic crack.   This can only be removed by either utilizing subsonic ammunition or via a ported barrel to bleed off propellant gas and thus reduce the velocity of the bullet.

Bullet flight noise.   Bullet flight noise is not loud enough to be sensed by the shooter, although they can be distinctly heard if they pass close by a person.

This noise resembles a distinctive high-pitched whirring sound as the bullet flies through the air. Flight noise is too quiet to be heard above the sonic crack.

Mechanical noise.   This is caused by the weapon's hammer, firing pin, locking mechanism and so on. This can, to a certain extent, be reduced by the use of single-shot weapons with a cushioned firing pin. The WWII Special Forces Welrod is an example of such a weapon. It was made in 9 mm PB, 0.380 ACP and 0.32 ACP calibres, and was virtually silent in operation.

Sound suppressors also function as flash suppressors and, to a certain extent, recoil reducers.

1.2.9   Recoil reducers

Muzzle brakes and recoil compensators are devices that are fitted to the muzzle of a firearm to redirect propellant gases with the effect of countering both recoil of the gun and unwanted rising of the barrel during rapid fire.

Generally speaking, a muzzle brake is external to the barrel of the firearm, whilst a recoil compensator is typically part of the structure of the barrel proper.

A properly designed muzzle brake can significantly reduce recoil. The actual effectiveness depends to an extent on the cartridge for which the rifle is chambered with claims of up to 60% being made.

Recoil compensators are generally less efficient than muzzle brakes.

Muzzle brakes/compensators are designed to reduce what is called the 'free recoil velocity' of the weapon. The free recoil velocity is how fast the gun comes back at the shooter. The faster a gun comes back, the more painful it is for the firer as the body has less time to absorb the recoil.

Weapons firing fast small-calibre bullets generally have a smaller recoil velocity than larger-calibre slow-moving bullets.

The following examples of recoil energy and velocity are all measured in 8 lb rifles (Table 1.2).

Table 1.2 Recoil energy and velocity for various rifle calibres.

Calibre	Bullet weight (g)	Muzzle velocity (ft/s)	Recoil energy (ft lbs)	Recoil velocity (ft/s)
6 mm Rem	100	3100	10.0	9.0
270 Win	140	3000	17.1	11.7
0.30–06	180	2700	20.3	12.8
0.35 Whelen	250	2400	26.1	14.5
0.450 Marlin	350	2100	35.7	17.0
0.458 Win Mag	500	2050	68.9	23.5

There are numerous types of recoil reducer from the simplest, a short length of tube attached at 90° to the end of the barrel to divert the gases sideways, to laser-cut slots in the muzzle end of the barrel (Magna Porting).

In conventional designs, combustion gases depart the brake at an angle to the bore and in a slightly rearwards direction. This counteracts the rearward movement of the barrel due to recoil as well as the upward rise of the muzzle. The effect can be compared to reverse thrust systems on aircraft jet engines. The mass and velocity of the gases can be significant enough to move the firearm in the opposite direction of recoil.

On the AKM assault rifle, the brake is angled slightly to the right to counteract the sideways movement of the gun under recoil.

A major disadvantage of recoil reducers is, however, the large increase in noise levels and the gas blast which directs back towards the firer.

One other problem with high-powered rifles such as the Barrett 0.50 Browning is the violent disruption of debris from the ground which can expose the firer's position. This is only a significant factor in military or law enforcement tactical situations.

1.2.10   Flash hiders

When a gun fires, only about 30% of the chemical energy released from the propellant is converted into the useful kinetic energy of actually moving the projectile down the barrel. Much of the remaining energy is primarily contained in the propellant gas–particle mixture which escapes from the muzzle of the gun in the few milliseconds before and after the bullet leaves the barrel.

This extremely hot mixture of incandescent gases and partially burnt propellant ignites on contact with the air causing an intense 'muzzle flash'. This can be disconcerting for the firer and a distinct disadvantage under night-time military or law enforcement tactical situations. Not only does it temporarily destroy the firer's night vision, but it also pinpoints his position for the enemy.

Flash hiders either physically hide the flash by way of a cone-shaped device on the end of the barrel (e.g. Lee Enfield No.5 Jungle Carbine) or by dispersing the flash upwards or sideways via a series of fingers or a tube containing longitudinal cuts (M16 rifle).

These attachments are often dual-purpose items designed to suppress the flash of firing and also to reduce recoil.

1.2.11   Muzzle counter weights

These are only used on highly specialized target weapons and are designed to add stability in sighting as well as to reduce the recoil-induced upward motion of the barrel.

1.2.12   Grenade discharger

In its simplest form, this is cup attached to the end of a rifle barrel into which a grenade can be launched via a blank cartridge. Utilizing this device, grenades can be propelled to much greater distances than by throwing alone.

More modern devices can be used with bulleted rounds and contain aluminium or mild steel baffles to capture the bullet.

1.2.13   Recoil booster

Very few of these have been manufactured, the most notable being the muzzle attachment to the German WWII MG 34 machine gun. This attachment was intended to increase the rate of fire in this short recoiling weapon.

Some recoil-operated semi-automatic pistols also have to be fitted with a recoil booster to compensate for the additional weight of the suppressor. Without a booster, short recoil pistols will not function in the self-loading mode of operation.

1.2.14   Brief glossary

Automatic or fully automatic	Correct terminology for a weapon which continues to fire until the trigger is released.
Blowback action	Simple form of self-loading pistol in which a spring retards the opening of the action after firing.
Bolt action	A method of closing the breech, generally involving a turning bolt.
Disconnecter	A mechanism in self-loading weapons which requires the trigger to be released and re-pulled between each shot, thus preventing the weapon from firing automatically.
Double action	Revolver mechanism where one long pull on the trigger rotates a fresh chamber in front of the firing pin, cocks then drops the hammer, all in one operation.
Drilling	German name for a three-barrelled long arm with a combination of smooth and rifled barrels.
Headspace	The distance measured from the part of the chamber that stops the forward movement of the cartridge and the face of the bolt.
Locked breech or delayed blowback	A weapon in which a mechanical delay is incorporated to ensure that the breech block cannot move back until the pressures in the barrel have subsided to a safe level.

Machine gun	Fully automatic weapon which will keep firing until the pressure is released from the trigger; normally designed to fire rifle calibre ammunition.
Pistol	In English terminology, all handguns are pistols; some are revolving, some single shot and some self-loading. In American terminology, refers to a self-loading handgun.
Revolver	Handgun in which the magazine is a revolving cylinder behind the barrel.
Rifle	Long-barrelled weapon with a rifled barrel.
Semi-automatic or self-loading	Weapon which uses a portion of the energy of discharge to eject the empty cartridge case, reload a fresh round into the chamber and cock the action ready for firing.
Shotgun	Smooth-bore shoulder firearm designed to fire cartridges containing numerous pellets or a single slug; can be of any calibre from 0.22″ upwards.
Single-action	Revolver mechanism where the hammer has to be manually cocked to rotate the cylinder.
Sub-machine gun	Automatic weapon, firing pistol ammunition, generally 9 mm PB, of a size in between a pistol and a rifle.
Vierling	German nomenclature for a long arm with two barrels, one of which is for shotgun ammunition and the other for rifle ammunition.

1.3   Proof Marks

Proof marks are stamps applied to various parts of a weapon during and after manufacture to show that the weapon is safe for use with the ammunition for which it was designed.

In England, the London and Birmingham proof houses were established (in 1637 and 1813, respectively) by Royal Charter to protect the public from the sale of unsafe weapons. A number of other countries have also established their own proof houses and by agreement at consular level, reciprocal arrangements have been made for their proof marks to be mutually accepted. At present, these include Austria, Belgium, Chile, Czechoslovakia, Finland, France, Germany, Hungary, Italy, Republic of Ireland, Spain and the United Kingdom.

A number of other countries have their own forms of proof, either in-house or centrally run. For various reasons, these have not been acceptable to the European commercial proof houses, and the weapons have to be fully proofed before they are legally saleable in those countries.

There are also a number of countries which have a separate military proofing system for service weapons. These, once again, are not accepted by the

European commercial proof houses. Weapons bearing military proof marks have thus to be commercially proofed before they can be legally sold in those countries.

There are basically three types of proof: *provisional proof, definitive proof* and *reproof.*

- *Provisional proof is* only for shotgun barrels in the early stages of manufacture. This type of proof is designed to prevent the manufacturer from continuing work on barrel blanks which may have hidden defects.
- *Definitive proof* applies to all weapons and shows that the weapon has been tested with an overcharge of propellant and missile. Generally, this calls for between 30 and 50% increase in pressure over the standard round of ammunition.
- *Reproof* is an additional test which may be applied after a weapon has been repaired or altered in some way.

1.3.1   Proof marks and the examiner

Proof marks can be a very valuable aid to the forensic firearms investigator as they can give information as to the age, history and country of origin of a weapon.

Many countries have specific exemption from their firearms legislation for weapons which are 'antique'. At one time, the situation was simple, with an antique being considered to be anything over 100 years old. This, however, no longer holds true as many weapons, for example, the Colt Single Action Army Model of 1873, are well over this age and can fire modern centre fire ammunition.

To complicate matters further, modern reproductions of some of these old weapons have been produced, which are often virtually indistinguishable from the original. In these cases, the proof mark could prove to be the only method of accurately dating a weapon.

This is, however, a very complex subject and requires much research and experience in the interpretation of the marks before accurate information can be obtained.

Many papers and books have been written on this subject, but probably the most authoritative is 'The Standard Directory of Proof Marks' by Wirnsberger, distributed by Blacksmith Co., Southport, Connecticut 06490 (Figures 1.23–1.36).

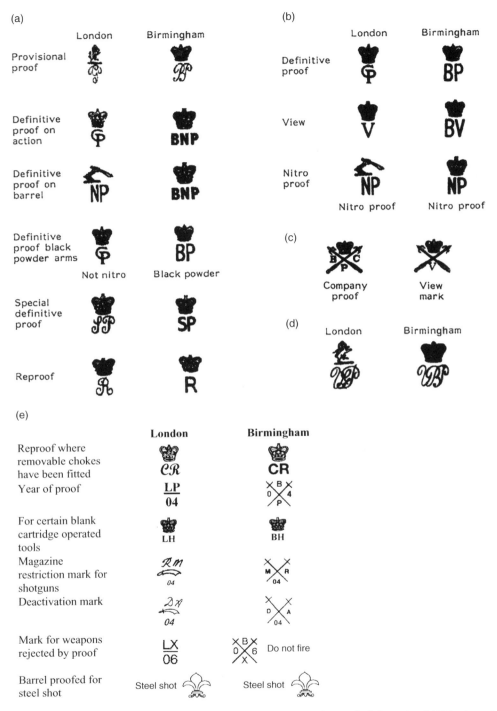

Figure 1.23 British proof marks. (a) Under 1954 rules of proof; (b) under 1925 rules of proof; (c) Birmingham proof marks – 1813–1904; (d) proof marks used between 1887 and 1925; (e) under 1988 rules of proof.

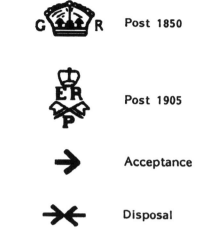

Post 1850

Post 1905

Acceptance

Disposal

Figure 1.24 British military proof marks.

Eibar house mark

Definitive black powder

Provisional black powder

Nitro proof

Definitive proof

Definitive proof
foreign weapons

Figure 1.25 Spanish proof marks.

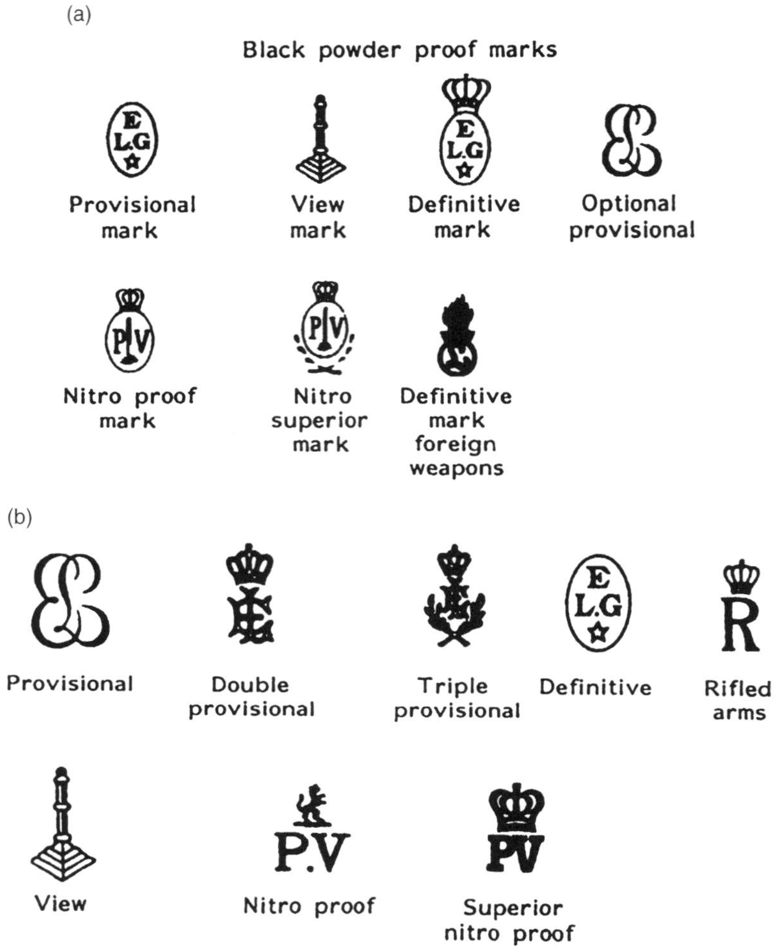

(a)

Black powder proof marks

Provisional
mark

View
mark

Definitive
mark

Optional
provisional

Nitro proof
mark

Nitro
superior
mark

Definitive
mark
foreign
weapons

(b)

Provisional

Double
provisional

Triple
provisional

Definitive

Rifled
arms

View

Nitro proof

Superior
nitro proof

Figure 1.26 (a) Belgian proof marks – since 1968; (b) Belgian proof marks – before 1968.

Provisional
shotguns

Definitive
shotguns

Definitive
rifles and
pistols

Figure 1.27 Czechoslovakian proof marks.

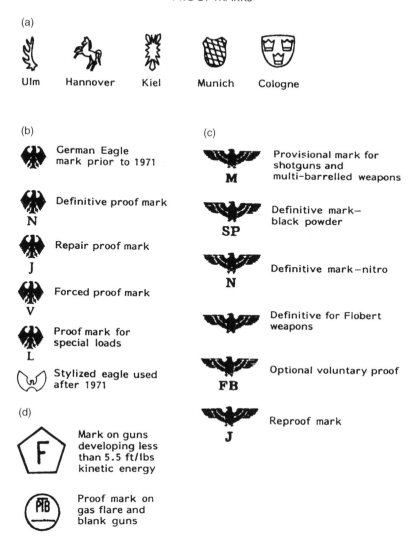

Figure 1.28 (a) German proof house marks since 1955; (b) West German proof marks after 1945; (c) German proof marks 1939–1945; (d) other German proof marks.

Figure 1.29 Republic of Ireland proof mark.

Figure 1.30 American military proof mark.

Voluntary proof: barrels in the finished state : ordinary proof

Voluntary proof: barrels in their finished state : double proof

Voluntary proof: barrels in their finished state triple proof

Compulsory proof: sample or model proof

Compulsory proof: guns in their finished state, ordinary black powder proof

Compulsory proof: proofed arm ready for sale (supplementary mark)

Compulsory proof: ordinary nitro proof of finished guns

Compulsory proof: superior nitro proof

Compulsory proof: long-barrelled firearms

Reproof of long barrelled firearms

Ordinary black powder reproof

Ordinary nitro reproof

Superior nitro reproof

Proof of short-barrelled firearms

Reproof of shot-barrelled firearms
Steel shot proof for smooth bored guns.
Note: This mark is now used on all EU proofed firearms

Figure 1.31 French proof marks post 1960.

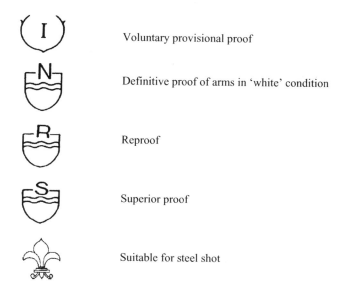

	Voluntary provisional proof
	Definitive proof of arms in 'white' condition
	Reproof
	Superior proof
	Suitable for steel shot

Figure 1.32 Hungarian proof marks.

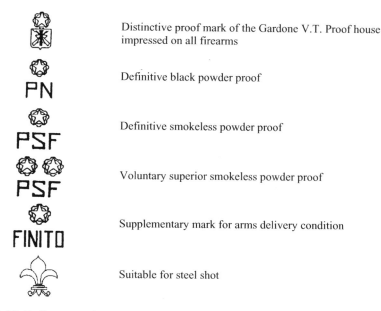

	Distinctive proof mark of the Gardone V.T. Proof house impressed on all firearms
	Definitive black powder proof
	Definitive smokeless powder proof
	Voluntary superior smokeless powder proof
	Supplementary mark for arms delivery condition
	Suitable for steel shot

Figure 1.33 Italian proof marks.

Symbol	Arsenal/subcontractor	Period of operation
	Koishikawa arsenal (Tokyo) on rifles	1870–1935
	Kokura arsenal on rifles	1935–1945
	Nagoya arsenal on rifles	1923–1945
	Jinsen arsenal (Korea) on rifles	1923–1945
	Mukden arsenal (Manchuria) on rifles	1931–1945
	Toyo Kogyo on rifles	1939–1945
	Tokyo Juki Kogyo on rifles	1940–1945
	Tokyo Juki Kogyo on rifles	1940–1945
	Howa Jyuko on rifles	1940–1945
	Izawa Jyuko on rifles	1940–1945
	Toyokawa arsenal on handguns	1940–1945
	Sasebo arsenal on handguns	1940–1945
	Yokosura arsenal on handguns	1940–1945
	Kure arsenal on handguns	1940–1945
	Maisuru arsenal on handguns	1940–45
	Current proof mark	

Figure 1.34 Japanese arsenal/proof marks.

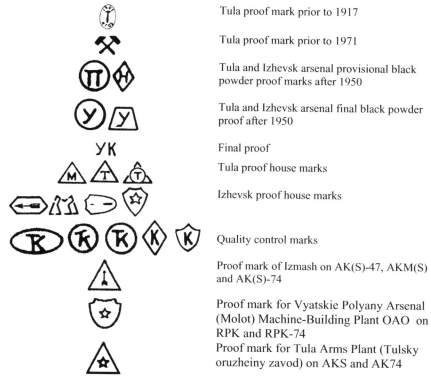

Tula proof mark prior to 1917

Tula proof mark prior to 1971

Tula and Izhevsk arsenal provisional black powder proof marks after 1950

Tula and Izhevsk arsenal final black powder proof after 1950

Final proof

Tula proof house marks

Izhevsk proof house marks

Quality control marks

Proof mark of Izmash on AK(S)-47, AKM(S) and AK(S)-74

Proof mark for Vyatskie Polyany Arsenal (Molot) Machine-Building Plant OAO on RPK and RPK-74

Proof mark for Tula Arms Plant (Tulsky oruzheiny zavod) on AKS and AK74

Figure 1.35 Russian proof marks.

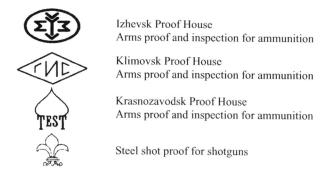

Izhevsk Proof House
Arms proof and inspection for ammunition

Klimovsk Proof House
Arms proof and inspection for ammunition

Krasnozavodsk Proof House
Arms proof and inspection for ammunition

Steel shot proof for shotguns

Figure 1.36 Russian federation proof marks.

Further Reading

Blackmore, H. (1965) *Guns of the World*, Batsford Press, London.

Blair, C. (1968) *Pistols of the World*, Batsford Press, London.

Hoyem, G.A. (1981) *History and Development of Small Arms Ammunition*, I–III, Armory Press, Missoula, MT, USA.

HMSO (1929) *Textbook of Small Arms*, His Majesty's Stationery Office, London.

Mathews, J.H. (1962) *Firearms Identification*, I, II & III, University of Wisconsin Press, Madison.

Smith, W.H.B. (1968) *Book of Pistols and Rifles*, Castle Books, New Jersey.

Smith, W.H.B. (1970) *Book of Rifles*, Castle Books, New Jersey.

2
Ammunition

2.1   A Brief History of Ammunition

2.1.1   Introduction

The first forms of ammunition consisted of loose powder, carried in a flask or horn, and various projectiles which were loaded into the barrel from the muzzle end. These early projectiles were often irregularly shaped stone balls or arrow-like objects.

By the fifteenth century, ammunition had become fairly standardized and consisted of 'black powder' propellant (a mixture of charcoal, sulfur and potassium nitrate), followed by some wadding, a spherical lead ball and further wadding to retain it all in place. Materials other than lead had been used for the projectile, and it was recognized from an early period that the lighter the material, the higher the velocity. However, due to its ballistics properties and the ease of casting it into spheres or bullet-shaped projectiles, lead remained the preferred material.

Elongated bullets with hollow bases (to move their centre of gravity towards the nose of the bullet) and pointed noses had been experimented with for some time, but they did not receive any real favour until the mid-1800s.

During the later part of the sixteenth century, as a result of the need for rapid reloading, pre-measured powder charges were introduced. These were contained in small paper bags which were torn open and the contents poured down the barrel. The paper bag followed this as did the wadding. The bullet, which was carried separately, was hammered into place last of all.

Handbook of Firearms and Ballistics: Second Edition   Brian J. Heard
© 2008 John Wiley & Sons, Ltd.

Towards the end of the 1600s, the bullet was tied into the top of the powder bag resulting in the first 'self-contained' cartridge.

These early 'self-contained' cartridges still required an external priming method to provide a flash to ignite the main propellant charge. It was not until the introduction of the breech-loader, where the ammunition was loaded from the rear of the barrel, that true self-contained ammunition appeared.

Early attempts at including the priming charge within the cartridge include the volcanic, lip, cup, teat, annular rim, needle, pinfire and rimfire systems. Most of these had a very short life span and, with the exception of the rimfire, only the pinfire attained any degree of popularity (Figure 2.1).

The pinfire was at its most popular between 1890 and 1910, and was still readily available on the continent until 1940. It had, however, fallen out of favour in the United Kingdom by 1914 and was virtually unobtainable by 1935.

Calibres available for use in pinfire revolvers were 5, 7, 9, 12 and 15 mm, whilst shotgun ammunition in 9 mm, 12 bore and various other calibres was also available.

Of the early ignition systems, only the rimfire has survived, and this only in 0.22″ calibre. In rimfire ammunition, the primer composition is spun into the

(a)   (b)

(c)   (d)

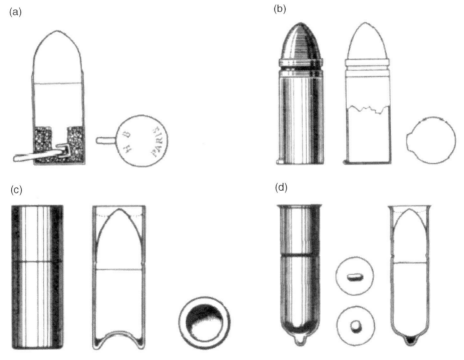

Figure 2.1 (a) Pinfire cartridge; (b) lip fire cartridge; (c) cup fire; (d) teat fire cartridge.

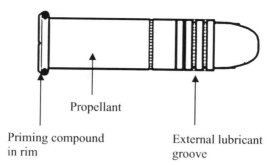

Figure 2.2 Rimfire cartridge.

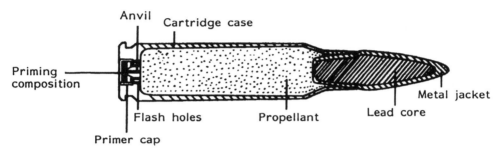

Figure 2.3 Centre fire cartridge.

hollow rim of the cartridge case. As a consequence, the propellant is in intimate contact with the priming composition. On firing, the weapon's firing pin crushes the thin rim of the cartridge case, compressing the priming composition and so initiating its detonation (Figure 2.2).

Calibres of rimfire ammunition up to 0.44″ rifle were available around the 1850s, but it was not possible, with the technology available at that time, to produce a cartridge case strong enough to withstand reliably the pressures produced.

The centre fire cartridge removed this limitation by providing a relatively soft cup containing the priming compound (the priming cap or 'primer') which was set into the centre of the base of a much stronger cartridge case. Although practical centre fire cartridges were available as early as 1852 in Britain, the final forms were not perfected until 1866 by Colonel Berdan (an American) and in 1867 by Colonel Boxer (an Englishman). These primer cap designs have never really been improved upon and are still in use today. Interestingly, Boxer-primed cartridge cases are normally used in American ammunition and Berdan in European ammunition (Figure 2.3).

A list of the dates of introduction for some of the more popular calibres of ammunition follows (Table 2.1).

Table 2.1 Dates for the introduction of various calibres.

Calibre	Date	Calibre	Date
0.17″ Remington	1971	0.30-06 Springfield	1906
0.17″ Rem Fireball	2007	0.30-30 Win	1895
0.204″ Ruger	2004	0.303″ British	1888
0.218″ Bee	1938	0.303″ Savage	1899
0.204″ Ruger	2004	0.30-40 Kraig	1892
0.22″ Short	1857[a]	0.307″ Win R	1982
0.22″ Long	1871	0.308″ Win	1954
0.22″ Daisy Caseless	1962	0.308″ Norma Mag	1960
0.22″ LR	1887	0.32″ ACP (7.65 mm)	1900
0.22″ WRF	1890	0.32″ Short Colt	1875
0.22″ Win Auto	1959	0.32″ Long Colt	1875
0.22″ Rem Jet	1960	0.32″ Win	1905
0.22″ Hornet	1930	0.32″ S&W Rev	1870
0.22″ PPC	1974	0.32″ S&W Long	1896
0.22–250 Rem	1965	0.32″ Win Spl	1895
0.220 Swift	1935	0.32″ H&R	1984
0.221″ Fireball	1963	0.32–20 Win	1882
0.222″ Rem	1950	0.325″ WSM	2005
0.222″ Rem Mag	1958	0.343″ WSSM	2003
0.223″ Rem (5.56 mm)	1955	0.338″ Win Mag	1958
0.223″ Win SSM	2003	0.338″ Lapua (8.6 × 70 mm)	1983
0.224″ BOZ (British)	2006	0.348 Win	1936
0.225″ Win	1964	0.35″ Rem	1906
0.299″ Cruz	2006	0.350″ Rem Mag	1965
0.243″ Win	1955	0.351″ Win SL	1907
0.243″ Win SSM	2003	0.357″ Mag	1935
0.25 Win SSM	2005	0.357″ Sig Auto	1994
0.25″ ACP (6.25 mm)	1906	0.358″ Win	1955
0.25–3000	1915	0.358″ Norma Mag	1959
0.25–06 Rem	1969	0.357″ H&H Mag	1912
0.25–20 Win	1894	0.357″ Sig	1994
0.25–35 Win	1895	0.375″ Win	1978
0.250″ Savage	1915	0.38″ Dardick	1958
0.256″ Win Mag	1961	0.38″ ACP	1900
0.257″ Roberts	1934	0.38″ Short Colt	1875
0.264″ Win Mag	1958	0.38″ Long Colt	1875
0.270″ WSM	2001	0.38″ S&W	1876
0.270″ Win	1925	0.38″ Spl	1902
0.280″ Rem	1957	0.38″ Super	1922
0.280″ British (EN1)	1948	0.38″ Super Auto	1929
0.284″ Win	1963	0.380″ ACP (9 mm Short)	1908
0.30″ Carbine	1940	0.38–40 Win	1878
0.30″ Luger	1900	0.38–55 Win	1884
0.30″ Rem	1906	0.40″ S&W	1990
0.30″ Herrett	1973	0.400″ Corbon	1997
0.300″ H&H Mag	1925	0.408″ Chey Tac	2001
0.300″ Savage	1920	0.41″ Action Express	1986
0.300″ Win Mag	1963	0.416″ Rem Mag	1988
0.300″ WSM	2001	0.416″ Barrett	2006

Table 2.1 Continued

Calibre	Date	Calibre	Date
0.44" S&W	1869	6.5 × 50mm Arisaka	1897
0.41" Rem Mag	1964	6.5 × 55mm Swedish	1895
0.41" Action Express	1986	6.5 × 68mm	1939
0.44" Spl	1907	6.8 × 43mm Rem SPC	2003
0.44" Rem Mag	1955	7 × 57mm Mauser	1892
0.44" AMP	1971	7mm Exp Rem	1979
0.444" Marlin	1964	7mm–08 Rem	1980
0.44–40 Win	1873	7mm Rem Mag	1962
0.450" Marlin	2000	7mm WSM	2002
0.450" Adams Revolver	1868	7.5 × 55mm Schmidt Rubin	1889
0.450" Mars	1902	7.62 × 39mm Russian	1943
0.450" Nitro Express	1895	7.62 × 51mm USA	1950
0.45" GAP Austrian	2003	7.62 × 51mm NATO	1953
0.45" ACP	1905	7.62 × 54mmR	1891[b]
0.45" Colt (0.45 Long Colt)	1873	7.65mm Browning (0.32acp)	1899
0.45" Win Mag	1978	7.6mm PB (7.65mm Luger)	1900
0.455 Webley	1889	7.7 × 58mm Arisaka	1939
0.45–70 US Govt.	1873	7.92 × 33mm Kurtz (German)	1938
0.454" Casull	1954	7.92 × 57mm Mauser	1888
0.458" Win Mag	1956	7.92 × 107mm DS	1934
0.460" Weatherby Mag.	1958	8 × 57mm	1905
0.470" Nitro Express	1907	8 × 68S	1939
0.476 Enfield	1880	8mm Rem Mag	1978
0.480" Ruger	2001	9mm PB (9mm Luger)	1902
0.50" Action Express	1988	9mm Browning Short	1812
0.500" S&W Magnum	2003	9mm Win Mag	1978
0.50" Remington Army	1867	9mm Federal Rev	1989
0.50" Browning M/G	1921	9 × 57mm Mauser	1894
0.50–90 Sharps	1872	10mm Auto	1983
0.600" Nitro Express	1903		

In the above table, the following abbreviations apply:[c]

Metric	Date		
4.6 × 30mm German	2000	ACP or acp	Automatic Colt Pistol
4.7 × 33mm H&K D11 Caseless	1989	Auto	Automatic, that is, for self-loading pistol
5mm Rem RF Mag	1968	Win	Winchester – cartridge designed by the company
5.45 × 39mm Russian M74	1974		
5.56 × 45mm NATO	1960	Rem	Remington – cartridge designed by the company
5.56 × 45mm Rem	1963		
5.56 × 45 S-109	1979	S&W	Smith & Wesson – cartridge designed by the company
5.6 × 45mm GP90 Swiss	1987		
5.7 × 28mm Belgium	1990	H&H	Holland and Holland – cartridge designed by the company
6mm Rem	1963		
6mm PPC	1975	Sig	Sig Sauer – cartridge designed by the company
6.5mm JDG	1978		
6.5 × 39 Grendel	2003	Mag	Magnum
6.5mm Rem Mag	1966	Rev	Revolver
		Exp	Express cartridge
		Spl	Special
		Win SSM	Winchester Super Short Magnum

[a] Oldest commercial cartridge being loaded today.
[b] Oldest cartridg e still in official military use.
[c] See Appendix for a full list of ammunition abbreviations.

2.1.2 Brief glossary

Black powder	A mechanical mixture of potassium nitrate, sulfur and charcoal
Calibre	A numerical value, included in the cartridge name, to indicate the approximate diameter of the missile.
Centre fire	A cartridge with the primer cap located in the centre of the cartridge head.
Propellant	A chemical or mixture of chemical which, when ignited, produces a large volume of gas which is harnessed to propel the missile from the weapon.
Rimfire	A flange-headed cartridge with the priming composition in the hollow rim.

2.2 Ammunition Components

2.2.1 Basic terminology

A round of ammunition. Generally refers to a single, live, unfired, cartridge comprising the missile, cartridge case, propellant and some form of primer. The term is also applied to live blank and tear-gas ammunition.

The *primer is* basically the means for igniting the propellant.

- In *rimfire* ammunition, the explosive priming compound is spun into the hollow rim of the cartridge case.
- In *centre fire* ammunition, there is a small cup, called *a primer cap*, containing the priming compound. This priming cap is inserted into a recess in the centre of the cartridge case.
- In *percussion weapons,* there is a small cup, very similar to the primer cap, which contains the priming compound and fits onto a hollow nipple screwed into the breech end of the barrel.

In all of the above, once the primer has been struck by the hammer, the priming compound explodes with great violence, sending a flame into the propellant thus igniting it.

The *propellant is* a chemical or mixture of chemicals which, when ignited, produces a very large quantity of gas. This gas, when confined within a barrel and behind a missile, provides the propulsion to drive the missile down the bore and out of the barrel.

A *cartridge case* refers to the ammunition case and primer and does not include the bullet. It can be either a 'fired cartridge case' or a 'live cartridge case'. A live cartridge case has a live, unfired, primer, but there is no propellant or bullet present.

A bullet refers to the missile alone. It can be either a 'fired bullet' or an 'unfired bullet'.

Pellets can be either the individual lead or steel balls found in shotgun ammunition, or the lead pellets for use in air weapons. 'Lead slug' is also sometimes used to describe air gun pellets, but this is not the correct term for this type of missile.

Shot is another term for the lead or steel balls in shotgun ammunition, that is, 'lead shot'. This is an acceptable alternative to 'pellet'.

2.2.2   Ammunition types

Small arms ammunition basically consists of a cartridge case, primer, propellant and some form of missile. There are really only three types of small arms ammunition in current production: 'rimfire', 'centre fire' and 'caseless'.

Rimfire ammunition consists of a short brass tube, generally 0.22 in. in diameter, closed at one end. The tube contains a charge of propellant and has a bullet at the open end. The closed end of the tube is formed into a flat head with a hollow rim which contains the priming compound. The round is fired when the firing pin strikes the rim, crushing and thus exploding the priming compound. The flame produced by this explosion ignites the propellant thus driving the bullet from the cartridge case.

Centre fire ammunition is also generally made from brass, but the head is thick and heavy with a central recess or pocket for the primer cap. A hole leading from the primer pocket into the cartridge allows the flash from the priming compound to reach the propellant thus igniting it.

Caseless ammunition consists of a bullet with the propellant formed around the bullet as a single solid piece, and there is no cartridge case. The primer is generally located at the rear of the propellant and is not enclosed in any metallic cup. This type of ammunition has not found any real favour due to problems with making the propellant strong enough to withstand rough treatment.

Blank ammunition is exactly the same as bulleted ammunition except for the omission of the missile. In blank ammunition, the case mouth is sealed by either crimping the metal or inserting a wax plug or paper disc. The wax or paper is usually coloured white or sometimes black. These cartridges are only used for military training, starting races or theatrical purposes, and are only intended to produce a sharp crack on firing. Blank ammunition is available in all calibres.

Tear-gas cartridges are the same as blank ammunition except they contain a small quantity of a lachrymatory/sternutatory substance which is either chloracetophenone (CN) gas or o-chlorobenzalmalonitrile (CS) gas. In tear-gas ammunition, the case mouth is never crimped, but is closed either with a card disc, wax plug or plastic cover which is invariably red or yellow in colour.

The most common calibre of tear-gas ammunition encountered is 8 mm. This is intended for use in small self-loading pistols specifically designed for the discharge of this type of ammunition. Tear-gas ammunition of 0.22″ calibre is also quite common, but this is generally intended for use in revolvers. Cartridges for use in 8 mm 'gas guns' have also been encountered which were loaded with talcum powder of various colours (for theatrical purposes), scent (for room freshening) and even fly killer!

Power tool, nail driving or *stud gun cartridges* are very similar to blank and tear-gas ammunition, and it is quite easy to mistake one for the other. In general, they are 0.22, 0.25, 0.32 or occasionally 0.38″ calibre. The mouth of the cartridge case is either rolled over onto a card disc or crimped. A colour-coding system, either coloured lacquer over the crimp or a coloured disc, is used to designate the strength of the cartridge. Care should be taken not to confuse a power tool cartridge using a red-coloured card disc with a tear-gas cartridge.

Grenade launcher cartridges are only encountered in military rifle calibres and, as the name indicates, are designed for the discharge of a grenade from a normal service rifle. The case mouth is invariably crimped, and some colour code, for example, the case painted black, distinguishes this type of cartridge from standard blank ammunition.

Dummy cartridges have neither primer nor powder and are only used for weapon functioning tests or for practising the safe loading and unloading of weapons. These cartridges are normally chromium-plated or painted a silver colour.

Snap caps are for the practice of firing a weapon without damaging the firing pin and lock mechanism by firing it without a cartridge case in place. This is generally called 'dry firing'. Snap caps usually have a piece of rubber or hard plastic in place of the primer, and the case is chromium- or nickel-plated for identification purposes. Although snap caps are available in all calibres, the most commonly encountered are in shotgun calibres.

2.2.3   Primer cap types

In rimfire ammunition, the firing pin crushes the soft hollow rim of the cartridge against the rear of the barrel to explode the priming compound.

In centre fire ammunition, the priming compound is held in a cup in the base of the cartridge case. Merely striking the base of the cup with a firing pin would do little more than dislodge the priming compound from the cup. An *anvil* has to be provided for the priming compound to be crushed against by the impact of the firing pin. In modern ammunition, there are basically three ways in which this is achieved. These are called the *Boxer*, *Berdan* or *battery cup* priming system.

The *Berdan primer* was designed in 1866 by Colonel Berdan of the US Army Ordnance Department. In this system, the anvil is actually part of the cartridge case in the form of a small peg in the primer pocket. Around the anvil are a number of small flash holes to permit the passage of the ignition flame from the primer to the propellant. Due to the ease and low cost of manufacture, Berdan primers are used mainly in military ammunition (Figure 2.4).

The *Boxer primer* was developed in 1866 by Colonel Boxer of the Laboratory at the Royal Woolwich Arsenal, England. In this type of primer, the anvil is a small bent disc of steel which fits into the cup making the primer completely self-contained. The flash hole in the cartridge case is centrally located and as it is of a relatively large diameter (approximately 1.5 mm in pistol ammunition), it is thus quite easy to push out the fired cup with a thin rod for reloading purposes. Boxer-primed ammunition is almost exclusively used in commercial ammunition (Figure 2.5).

The *battery cup* system consists of a plain cup with no anvil, which fits into a slightly larger inverted flanged cup containing its own anvil. The flanged cup

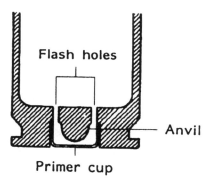

Figure 2.4 Berdan primer.

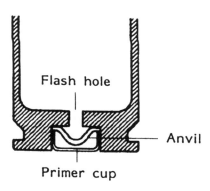

Figure 2.5 Boxer primer.

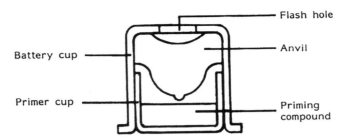

Figure 2.6 Battery cup primer.

provides a rigid support for the primer cup and anvil. This self-contained assembly fits into a recessed pocket in the base of the cartridge case. Battery cup primers are used exclusively in shotgun ammunition (Figure 2.6).

2.2.4 Cartridge cases

In the Western world, these are almost invariably made of brass with a 75:25 copper/zinc alloy. Other materials including steel and plastic have been used, but not on any commercial basis.

Aluminium-cased pistol ammunition has recently acquired some commercial success due to the cost saving of aluminium over brass. There are, however, a number of disadvantages. These include being non-reloadable and less robust than their brass counterparts. For large-scale users who do not wish to reload their empty cartridge cases or are firing for purely training purposes, the savings can, however, be very considerable and far outweigh the disadvantages.

In modern ammunition from Russia, Warsaw Pact countries and China, the cartridge cases are invariably made of steel. In China, the steel is coated with copper to prevent rusting whilst elsewhere, it has a heavy green/grey coat of lacquer for the same reason. In World War II, due to a shortage of raw materials, a number of countries, notably Germany and Russia, used lacquered steel cartridge cases as well. These are still encountered.

Shotgun cartridges generally have a brass base with a plastic, or sometimes paper, case. All-plastic shotgun cartridges have been produced, but they have not proved to be a commercial success.

The main purpose of the cartridge case, other than for holding the components together, is to expand and seal the chamber during firing. This is called 'obturation' and prevents the explosive escape of high-pressure gases through the breech. During manufacture, the brass is annealed to give the case the correct degree of hardness. If this is correct, the brass will regain its original shape after the pressure has subsided and the case will be easy to extract from the chamber.

If it is too hard, the case will crack, and if too soft, it will cling to the chamber walls and be extremely difficult to remove.

2.2.5 Cartridge case types

Cartridge cases generally come in one of three shapes:

1. *Straight cased,* where the case diameter is approximately the same along its length.
2. *Bottle-necked,* where a wide-bodied case is, just before the case mouth, reduced in diameter to that of the bullet. This permits a very much larger volume of propellant to be used, and consequently higher velocities to be obtained, than in straight-sided cases.
3. *Tapered case,* where a wide-based cartridge case is gradually reduced in diameter along its length. These tend to be in old European sporting rifle calibres and are seldom encountered.

The cartridge case can be subdivided further into five categories according to the configuration of its base (Figures 2.7 and 2.8).

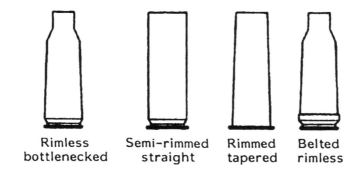

Rimless   Semi-rimmed   Rimmed   Belted
bottlenecked   straight   tapered   rimless

Figure 2.7 Various cartridge case forms.

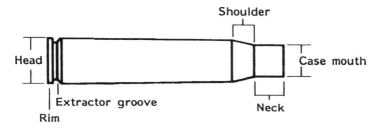

Figure 2.8 Parts of a cartridge case applicable to all forms.

(i) *Rimmed*. These have a flange at the base which is larger than the diameter of the body of the cartridge case. This flange is to enable the cartridge to be extracted from the weapon in which it is used. When describing rifle ammunition and the metric method of designating the ammunition is used, these are often identified by an 'R' after the case length measurement, that is, 7×57 mmR. The vast majority of revolvers are designed for use with rimmed ammunition.

(ii) *Semi-rimmed*. These have a flange which is slightly larger than the diameter of the cartridge case and a groove around the case body just in front of the flange. When describing rifle ammunition and the metric system is used, these are identified by 'SR' in the cartridge designation.

(iii) *Rimless*. In these, the flange diameter is the same as the case body and there is, for extraction purposes, a groove around the case body just in front of the flange. There is generally no letter system to designate this cartridge base type. Self-loading pistols are almost invariably designed for use with semi-rimmed or rimless ammunition.

(iv) *Rebated*. This has an extractor flange which is less than the diameter of the cartridge case. The designation used in the metric system is 'RB'. This type of cartridge case configuration tends to be reserved for high-powered cannon ammunition.

(v) *Belted case*. These have a pronounced raised belt encircling the base of the cartridge. This belt is for additional strength in high-pressure cartridges. The metric designation is 'B'. This type of cartridge case is generally only found in very high-powered rifle cartridges or military cannon ammunition.

2.2.6 Cartridge nomenclature

A basic understanding of this subject is essential as it is an area where the inexperienced can really show lack of knowledge. Knowing the difference between a 9×18 and 9×19 mm cartridge, for example, may seem a little insignificant, but it is an area where the unwary can easily be tripped up and made to look very foolish. Having said that, it is a vastly complicated subject, and there are very few set rules.

The first identifier is whether the cartridge in question is referred to in metric or imperial measurements. This generally indicates whether it is of European or British/American origin.

Where British/American cartridges are concerned, the designation is always in inches, and the nought in front of the decimal point is always omitted: for example, a cartridge with a bullet measuring 0.32 in. in diameter would be referred to as a .32″. Where European cartridges are concerned, the measurement is always quoted in millimetres, for example, 9 mm. Even this apparently simple identifier is confusing as a number of cartridges are identified by both systems, that is, 9 mm. Short is also 0.380″ Auto and 7.65 mm is also 0.32″ Automatic Colt Pistol (ACP).

Probably the most confusing part of cartridge nomenclature is the calibre. The calibre (United States – caliber) is basically a numerical approximation of the diameter of the bullet.

This very frequently bears little relationship to the actual bullet measurement, that is, the 0.455″ Webley revolver cartridge has a bullet measuring 0.450″ and a 0.38″ Special bullet measures 0.357″. This discrepancy is, however, much more of a problem with older English cartridge nomenclature than it is with modern metric designations: a 9 mm Parabellum bullet is 9 mm in diameter, and a 5.56 mm does have a bullet measuring 5.56 mm.

The nominal calibre is often further identified by a name which can identify it among groups of the same calibre, that is, 9 mm Parabellum, 9 mm Bayard, 9 mm Short, 9 mm Makarov, 9 mm Steyr, and so on. The addition of a name often identifies the weapon for which the cartridge was originally designed; thus, the 9 mm Mauser was designed for the 9 mm 'broom-handled' Mauser, 5.75 mm Velo-Dog for the 5.75 mm VeloDog revolver (designed, as its name implies, for early cyclists and motorcyclists to protect themselves against attack by dogs!) and a 0.32″ ACP for the Colt self-loading pistol.

In the European system, it is usual, especially in rifle calibres, to add the cartridge case length to further identify the cartridge, that is, 5.56×54 mm, 6.5×57 mm. Pistol ammunition can also take this form, although it is not always referred to, that is, 9×19 mm is 9 mm Parabellum; 9×18 mm is the 9 mm Makarov, and 7.62×25 mm is the Russian Tokarev pistol round.

As explained earlier, the case length can also be given a letter to indicate the type of case, that is, 6.5×57 R is a cartridge with a rimmed case; 7.92×61 RB is a cartridge with a rebated head. This can be even more confusing when a bullet type is appended to the suffix, that is, the 6.5×57 RS is a rimmed cartridge with a 'spitzer', or pointed, bullet.

Another suffix appended to the designation of self-loading pistol ammunition is 'ACP'. This merely indicates that it was originally designed for use in Colt self-loading pistols, that is, 0.32″ ACP and 0.380″ ACP. The letters ACP stand for Automatic Colt Pistol, which is somewhat confusing in itself. An automatic weapon is one in which the weapon will continue to fire 'automatically' until the finger is released from the trigger or the magazine is empty. The correct designation for the pistols for which the 0.380″ and 0.32″ ammunition were designed is a self-loading or semi-automatic pistol.

In American ammunition, there is often a set of figures which can indicate the year of introduction for that particular calibre of ammunition, that is, 0.30-06 is a 0.30″ calibre rifle round introduced in 1906, and a 0.30-03 is the same calibre but introduced in 1903. Where it really gets confusing is when the weight of 'black powder' for which the cartridge was originally designed is included, that is, a 0.30-30 is a 0.30″ calibre rifle bullet originally designed to be driven by 30 gr (grains) of black powder propellant. Even more confusing, if that is possible, is the system of including the bullet weight into the title, that is, 0.45–70–500, which is a 0.45″ calibre rifle bullet propelled by 70 gr of black powder with a 500 gr bullet. What makes this system particularly difficult to deal with is that the majority of these cartridges no longer use black powder, but instead use a much smaller charge of modern smokeless propellant.

In old British sporting and military cartridges, the term 'express cartridge' is often used. This originated with the introduction of a high-velocity rifle and cartridge by the gunmaker Purdy, who designated it the 'express train' model. The 'train' part was eventually dropped, and 'express' was reserved for any large-capacity cartridge with a high velocity. For cartridges with even higher velocities, the term 'super express' was also pressed into service. These cartridges were, however, all loaded with 'black powder', and when 'smokeless' propellants came into being, these 'express' cartridges were re-designated 'nitro express'. Realizing that even more power could be extracted from smokeless cartridges, the gunmakers increased the case length and called these new super rounds 'Magnum Nitro Express'.

In recent years, the term 'Magnum' has crept into the terminology for pistol ammunition and a 'Magnum' suffix, for example, 0.22″ Magnum, 0.32″ Magnum, 0.357″ Magnum, and so on, is now used to designate a round of much higher than standard velocity.

One other piece of information which can be included in the designation is the nominal velocity, that is, 0.25–3000, being a 0.25″ bullet at a velocity of 3000 ft/s. This is, however, unusual, and in the stated case was only used as an advertising gimmick.

2.2.7   Shotgun ammunition

Shotgun ammunition is once again a confusing subject with the smaller calibres being referred to by the approximate bore diameter, that is, 0.22″, 9 mm, 0.410″. Once past 0.410″, the calibre changes to a 'bore' (or if using the American nomenclature 'gauge') size where the bore is the number of lead balls of the same diameter as the inside of the barrel which weighs 1 lb. Thus, a 12-bore shotgun has a barrel diameter of 0.729″ and 12 round lead balls of 0.729″ diameter weigh exactly 1 lb.

It should be pointed out here that the 'bore' size when dealing with shotguns is different from the bore size of rifled weapons. In rifled weapons, the bore size is the diameter measured across the tops of the rifling lands (Table 2.2).

The term bore also relates to the measurement of the internal barrel size of black powder cannon. In these, however, the bore size refers to the weight of a single round iron ball which fits into the barrel. Thus, a 6 pounder would fire a 6 lb spherical cast iron ball. The actual bore diameter of this is about 3.6 in. (Figure 2.9).

To complicate matters further, by the sixteenth century, gunners had adopted the custom of describing the length of a cannon's bore in calibres, that is, in

Table 2.2 Bore size, diameter of bore and weight of lead ball.

Bore (gauge)	Diameter of bore		Weight of lead ball		
	(in)	(mm)	(oz)	(gr)	(g)
$1\frac{1}{2}$*	1.459	37.05	10.667	4667	302.39
2*	1.325	33.67	8.000	3500	226.80
3*	1.158	29.41	5.333	4667	151.20
8	0.835	21.21	2.000	875	56.70
10	0.775	19.69	1.600	700	45.36
12	0.729	18.53	1.333	583	37.80
13	0.710	18.04	1.231	538	34.89
14	0.693	17.60	1.143	500	32.40
16	0.663	16.83	1.000	438	28.35
20	0.615	15.63	0.800	350	22.68
24	0.579	14.70	0.667	292	18.90
28	0.550	13.97	0.571	250	16.20
32	0.526	13.36	0.500	219	14.17
$67\frac{1}{2}$	0.410	10.41	0.237	104	6.71

NB. The bores marked * are found only in punt guns and other rare weapons.
The 410 shotgun is never referred to as a $67\frac{1}{2}$ bore only as 0.410″.
Similarly, 9 mm and 0.22″ calibre shotguns are only referred to as 9 mm and 0.22″.
The bore diameter for these two calibres is 9 mm and 0.22″, respectively.

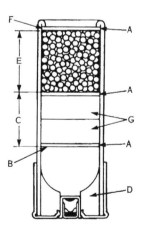

A. Over/undershot card
B. Overcharge card
C. Wad column
D. Base wad
E. Shot column
F. Rollover crimp
G. Felt cushion wads

Figure 2.9 Shotgun cartridge.

multiples of the bore diameter. Thus, a barrel with a 5 in. diameter barrel described as a 50 calibre weapon would have a barrel length 50 times the bore diameter, or 250 in. long.

This has, however, been superseded by more modern methods of measurement which are outwith the scope of this book.

2.2.8   Size of pellets in shotgun ammunition

The missiles used in shotgun cartridges can vary from a single ball or cylinder of lead of the same diameter as the bore down to pellets so small they are referred to as 'dust shot'. As each country has its own method of nomenclature for these shot sizes, the matter can be quite confusing. Table 2.3, giving the shot sizes, weights and equivalent sizes for a number of countries, follows.

The pellets used in shotgun cartridges have traditionally been made of lead with a small amount of antimony to increase their hardness. Lead accumulation in wildfowl has prompted the use of other materials, the most common being:

- soft steel, usually with a copper coating;
- bismuth, a heavy metal often alloyed with iron;
- tungsten, a very heavy metal often alloyed with iron.

Table 2.3 Shot sizes, weights and equivalent sizes (various countries).

Shotgun pellet size								
Number (shot/oz)	Diameter (in.)	Diameter (mm)	English	American	French	Belgian	Italian	Spanish
6	0.36	9.1	LG					
8	0.33	8.4	SG	00 Buck		9G	11/0	
11	0.30	7.6	Special SG	1 Buck	C2	12G	9/0	
15	0.27	6.8	SSG	3 Buck	C3			
35	0.20	5.2	AAA	4 Buck	0			
70	0.16	4.1	BB	Air Rifle	1	00	00	1
100	0.14	3.6	1	2	3		1 or 2	3
140	0.13	3.3	3	4	4		3	4
170	0.12	3.1	4	5	5		4	5
220	0.11	2.8	5	6	6	5	5	6
270	0.10	2.6	6			6	6	
340	0.095	2.4	7	$7\frac{1}{2}$	7	7	$7\frac{1}{2}$	7
400	0.09	2.3	$7\frac{1}{2}$	8	$7\frac{1}{2}$	$7\frac{1}{2}$	8	$7\frac{1}{2}$
450	0.085	2.2	8		8	8		8
580	0.08	2.0	9	9	9	9	$9\frac{1}{2}$	9

The abbreviations used in the table are as follows: LG, Large Goose; SG, Small Goose; Special SG, Special Small Goose; SSG, Small Small Goose; BB, bulleted breech.

It should also be noted that cartridges for clay pigeon shooting are often loaded with lead shot which has been copper coated to increase its hardness. This could be confused for the copper-coated steel shot.

2.2.9   Shotgun slugs

A shotgun slug is a single projectile primarily designed to be fired from a smooth-bored shotgun. Shotgun slug ammunition is available in most of the common shotgun calibres.

The simplest form of slug is a round ball (sometimes referred to in the United States as a pumpkin ball or pumpkin shot). Since it is a symmetrical projectile, it will not significantly deviate from its intended path if it begins to spin due to air pressure. However, a smooth-bored shotgun firing a round ball is essentially a musket with its inherent short range and accuracy problems.

To enhance a slug's performance, both externally and terminally, it requires to be elongated and to have its centre of mass moved forwards. Being elongated, it is also preferable for the missile to be spin stabilized to prevent it from tumbling.

The original *Brenneke slug* (see Figure 2.10) overcame these problems via the use of a solid lead, pre-rifled projectile with an attached plastic, felt or cellulose fibre wad. The wad provides drag stabilization by moving the centre of mass forwards. The cast rifling has little or no effect in spinning the projectile as it passes through the air.

Another early design was the *Foster slug* (see Figure 2.11). This was basically a short round-nosed bullet with a deep cup in the base. Foster slugs are also made with rifling-type grooves cast into the outside of the missile. The cupped base also expands on firing producing a seal with the bore.

Whilst it is generally accepted that shotgun slugs do not have to be fired through a cylinder barrel, it is not recommended that full choke barrels be used. This is due to the fact that the pressure required to compress the slug through the choke will eventually flare the end of the barrel thus reducing the degree of choke.

Figure 2.10 Brenneke slug.

Figure 2.11 Foster slug.

Figure 2.12 Sabot slug.

Saboted slugs (Figure 2.12) are sub-calibre missiles which have a discarding plastic collar surrounding the missile to bring it up to standard calibre. They are generally designed to be fired from a special rifled shotgun barrel to spin stabilize the missile. Originally, these were called Paradox weapons and had a short length of rifling at the muzzle end of the barrel. More modern weapons can have rifling at the end of the barrel or along its full length.

Due to the reduced drag and high initial velocity, saboted slugs have significant advantages in external ballistics over a normal shotgun slug. Some saboted slugs use fins or a lightweight plastic portion at the rear of the missile to provide stability from smooth-bores.

The brenneke slug. The Brenneke slug was developed by the German gun and ammunition designer Wilhelm Brenneke (1865–1951) in 1898.

The original Brenneke slug was a solid lead projectile with fins cast onto the outside, much like a modern rifled Foster slug (see Figure 2.10). There was a plastic, felt or cellulose fibre wad screwed to the base that remains attached after firing. This wad serves both as a gas seal and as a form of drag stabilization, much like the mass-forward design of the Foster slug.

The fins or rifling is easily deformed to pass through choked shotgun barrels and do not impart any significant stabilizing spin on the projectile.

Since the Brenneke slug is solid, rather than hollow like the Foster slug, the Brenneke will generally deform less on impact and provide deeper penetration. The sharp shoulder and flat front of the Brenneke mean that its external ballistics restrict it to short-range use as it does not retain its velocity well.

The Brenneke slug is available in a number of normal shotgun calibres, but 12 bore and 0.410″ calibre are probably the most popular.

The foster slug. The Foster slug was developed by Karl Foster in 1931. The defining characteristic of a Foster slug is the deep depression in the base, which places the centre of mass very near the tip of the slug, much like a shuttlecock. If the slug begins to tumble in flight, drag will tend to push the slug back into straight flight. This gives the Foster slug stability and allows for accurate shooting out to ranges of about 50–70 yd.

Foster slugs may also have rifling, which consists of 11 or 12 fins either cast or swaged on the outside of the slug. Contrary to popular belief, these fins impart little or no spin to the slug as it travels through the air.

The actual purpose of the fins is to allow the slug to be safely swaged down when fired through a choked shotgun barrel, although accuracy will suffer when such a slug is fired through chokes tighter than improved cylinder. Cylinder choke is the one recommended for best use.

As with all shotgun slugs, it is possible to fire Foster slugs through a Shotgun Slug,[1] that is rifled, Barrel. It should be noted, however, that as the slug is not lubricated, leading of the rifled portion of the barrel becomes a great problem necessitating regular cleaning to maintain any degree of accuracy.

The sabot slug. The main characteristic of a sabot slug is the plastic carrier or sabot, which is of bore size or sometimes a little larger to enable the sabot to engage the rifling found in modern slug barrels.

The slugs contained in sabots can be anything up to 0.50″ calibre and are usually hollow pointed. Those for police use are usually of a solid hard metal alloy material for barricade penetration or door lock and hinge removal.

Although the sabot slug is used primarily in rifled barrels, some designs of sabot slugs can be fired in smooth-bore shotguns most notably the Brenneke Rubin Sabot, a sub-calibre slug utilizing the familiar Brenneke attached wad system.

The smaller projectile held within sabots will have a much flatter trajectory, and will travel at much higher velocities than the more traditional foster or rifled slug. Saboted slugs will, when fired from a rifled barrel, produce near rifle-type accuracy.

Another advantage of the sabot type of shotgun slug is that no lead comes into contact with the barrel, thus preventing lead fouling.

Penetration of foster and sabot slugs. The following table gives an indication of the penetration potential of shotgun slugs. Penetration figures for normal shot are for comparison purposes (Table 2.4).

It is generally accepted by those involved in the wound ballistics field that a minimum penetration of 12 in. of 10% ordnance gelatin is one of the criteria needed to provide reliable incapacitation of a human assailant.

---

[1] A shotgun with rifling at the muzzle end of the barrel.

Table 2.4 A comparison of shotgun pellet and solid slug penetration in 10% ordinance gelatine.

12-Gauge penetration tests in 10% gelatin		
Load	Number of pellets	Penetration at 7 yd
000 Buck	8	14″–16″
00 Buck	9	13″–15″
1 Buck	16	12″–14″
#4 Buck	27	9″–11″
#6 Shot (copper-plated hard shot)	280	4″–6″
1 oz Foster slug	—	18″
450 g sabot slug	—	21″

When used in a police or military situation, shotgun slugs are often used against hard targets.

To illustrate the penetration potential of shotgun slugs, the test was carried out using standard NATO 0.138″ steel test plates. Buckshot loads are shown for comparison purposes.

Results are shown in Table 2.5.

The common misconception is that the shotgun slug has an extremely short range as well as a very poor trajectory. This is not quite true, although past 125 yd, the velocity and hence kinetic energy does drop off quite considerably (Table 2.6).

Other types of specialized, single missile, shotgun ammunition include the breaching or **Hatton** cartridge and tear-gas rounds.

The **Hatton round** is made specifically for police or military use and is designed for the breaching of doorways (Figure 2.13).

It is typically fired at a range of 4–6 in., aimed between the doorknob and door jamb, destroying the locking mechanism. It can also be used to remove the hinges in a similar way.

The missile is a single 12-bore, frangible slug weighing 770 gr (1.6 oz). The round is made of compressed zinc or lead powder bonded with hard wax. When fired, the full force of the round is delivered to the target, minimizing the risk

Table 2.5 A comparison of shotgun pellet and solid slug penetration against 0.138″ NATO steel plate.

12-Bore penetration tests against SAE 1010 0.138″ NATO steel plate		
Load	7 yd	25 yd
000 Buck	N	N
00 Buck	N	N
1 Buck	N	N
4 Buck	N	N
1 oz Foster slug	P	D
450 g sabot slug	P	P

P, penetrated; D, dented; N, no effect.

Table 2.6 External ballistics for Foster-Type 12B slug.

Range (yds)	Velocity (ft/sec)	Deviation (ins) from Point of Aim when zero = 75 yards	Deviation (ins) from Point of Aim when zero = 100 yards
0	1440	−1.0	−1.0
25	1320	0.7	1.4
50	1200	1.1	2.5
75	1120	0	2.1
100	1050	−2.8	0
125	1000	−7.5	−4.0
150	960	−14.4	−10.2

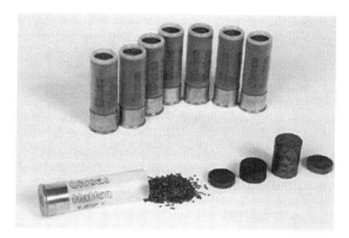

Figure 2.13 Hatton round.

of injury to persons behind the door being opened. On impact, the missile breaks up into powder, thus removing any chance of ricochet.

These rounds will penetrate vehicle tyres, fire doors clad on both sides with metal plate, cell-type doors, 12 mm thick Makralon and bullet-proof glass from a range of 1.5 m. Hatton ammunition can only be used in Magnum shotguns with 3 in. chambers and unchoked barrels.

Tear-gas ammunition – the ferret round – usually contains a finned, plastic bomblet-type missile filled with CS gas. The plastic comes in various grades depending upon the material being penetrated. These are only for police and military use.

The **Dragon's Breath** is another highly specialized shotgun round. This contains a zirconium-based pyrotechnic material. When the round is fired, a huge flame erupts from the gun's barrel that can extend up to 300 ft. The Dragon's Breath is only for extremely specialized military use as the effect it produces is similar to that of a short-ranged flame-thrower.

The **bean bag ammunition** is basically a nylon or Kevlar bag containing lead shot. For extremely short-range, non-lethal, anti-personnel use.

The **baton round** is a plastic or rubber missile designed to be ricocheted from the ground for crowd control.

2.2.10   Headstamps

This is a potentially a very important subject as it enables the determination of country of origin, whether it is of commercial or military manufacture, and if military, the date of manufacture. Whilst this may seem to be of minor importance, in cases involving terrorism, such information can be vital.

This subject alone could fill several volumes, and many books have been written on the identification of 'headstamps'. The subject is dealt with more comprehensively in Section 2.6, but a few words are required at this stage.

Basically, the headstamp is a series of marks, letters and/or numbers impressed upon the base of the cartridge by the manufacturer to indicate the calibre and by whom it was manufactured.

Commercial ammunition usually contains little more information in the headstamp other than to show the maker and calibre. The date of manufacture is rarely, if ever, included in commercial ammunition headstamps. Often, the only way in which this information can be obtained is from the packaging material (i.e. box) in which the ammunition was supplied.

The advertising value of a cartridge headstamp has been recognized for a long time. As a result, many firearms dealers will have ammunition marked with their own name or trademark. Under these circumstances, it is very difficult to ascertain the actual manufacturer.

Military ammunition is, however, much more informative and, if one can understand the system of letters and numbers, details such as the calibre, year and month of manufacture, batch number, cartridge case material, bullet type, that is, tracer, incendiary, armour piercing, and so on, can be ascertained.

Military ammunition usually has its headstamp applied to a rigid set of rules with each country rarely deviating from the official pattern. It is thus often possible to identify the source of the ammunition without being able to decipher the headstamp itself. Another identifier of ammunition with a military origin is that, almost without exception, the year of manufacture will be included in the code system.

2.2.11   Colour coding of ammunition

In addition to the headstamp, military ammunition often has some form of colour coding in the form of bands of coloured lacquer round the bullet, a stripe across the bullet-case joint or round the joint between the primer and cartridge case (primer annulus). Caution should be exercised when attempting to identify the stripe of colour round the case-bullet joint or primer annulus as this is often no more than a waterproofing varnish. As a general rule, if there is no coloured varnish on the bullet, then it is a standard ball (military nomenclature for standard bullet) round.

Examples of coloured lacquer used and their significance follow.

China. Originally, China used the Russian system of colour coding as their ammunition was originally supplied from this source. In 1967, however, China adopted her own system as follows.

Bullet tip code

Green	Tracer
Black and red	Armour piercing/incendiary – pre-1967
Black	Armour piercing/incendiary – post-1967
Violet and red	Armour piercing/incendiary/tracer – pre-1967
Violet	Armour piercing/incendiary/tracer – post-1967
Red	Incendiary
White	Mild steel bullet core – pre-1967

Israel

Bullet tip	Primer annulus	Bullet type
None	Purple	Ball
Red	Green	Tracer
Black	Green	Armour piercing
Black	Red	Armour piercing/incendiary
Blue	Green	Incendiary

NATO countries. All NATO countries use the same bullet tip colour-coding system.

Red	Tracer
Black	Armour piercing
Silver	Armour piercing/incendiary
Blue	Incendiary
Yellow	Observation (a bright flash and smoke on impact)
Yellow/red	Observation/tracer
Orange	Dark ignition tracer

United Kingdom prior to formation of NATO in 1955

Primer annulus

Purple   Ball or practice
Green   Armour piercing
Red   Tracer
Blue   Incendiary
Yellow   Proof (a special high-pressure cartridge)
Black   Observation

Bullet tip

Blue   Incendiary
Black   Observation
Green   Armour piercing
White   Short-range tracer
Grey   Dark ignition tracer
Red   Long-range tracer

United States

7.62×51 mm ammunition uses NATO code
0.30″ Carbine and 0.45′ ACP – red tip for tracer
0.50″ Browning machine gun – NATO Code plus

Red tip silver band   Armour piercing/incendiary/tracer
Yellow tip red band   Observation/tracer
Brown Tip   Tracer
Light blue tip   Incendiary

USSR. In the 1930s, the colour coding was very poor, but during and after World War II, it was regularized and expanded. The following bullet tip colour-code system is now standard for all Warsaw Pact Countries:

Yellow   Heavy ball
Silver   Light ball
Green   Tracer
Black   Armour piercing
Black/red   Armour piercing/incendiary (now obsolete)

Black/yellow	Armour piercing/incendiary (current)
Purple/red	Armour piercing/incendiary/tracer
Red	Incendiary/tracer
Black/green	Reduced velocity for silenced weapons

2.2.12   Bullet types

Originally, a bullet was a simple lead sphere which worked well with the smooth-bored muzzle loading early firearms. The sphere, however, has a very poor ballistic shape, and it rapidly loses velocity. With the introduction of rifling came the ogival-shaped bullet (basically the profile of a pointed arch) which had a length in excess of twice its diameter. This provided an easily stabilized bullet with excellent accuracy and a good shape for penetrating the air (i.e. good ballistic profile).

2.2.13   Bullet materials

Modern ammunition comes with a bewildering variety of bullet profiles, materials and construction to cater for every conceivable circumstance. To attempt to cover all the available varieties is beyond the scope of this book. The following, however, covers the basic types of bullet which may be encountered.

In small arms ammunition, bullets are either jacketed or unjacketed. Whilst unjacketed bullets can be made from all manner of materials, the most common by far is lead. The lead will be alloyed with varying quantities of antimony to give it hardness and tin (if it is a cast bullet) to assist in the moulding process. Plain lead bullets can be manufactured either by casting from molten metal or swaged from lead wire. In swaging, lead wire is cut into the appropriate length then cold forged with hydraulic pressure into a die with the correct dimensions and shape of the finished bullet. Nowadays, virtually all commercially manufactured lead bullets are swaged.

Jacketed bullets have a plain lead core covered with a thin layer of a much harder material. This can be a copper/zinc alloy (gilding metal), a copper/nickel alloy (cupronickel) or plain steel coated with either a copper wash or a thick coat of lacquer to prevent corrosion. Jacketed bullets are used for a variety of reasons, that is, to grip the rifling more in high-velocity bullets, to prevent bullet damage and feeding jams in weapons with a self-loading mechanism and to prevent bullet break up in hunting ammunition when used on heavy or thick-skinned game.

A variation on the jacketed bullet theme is to coat plain lead bullets with a thick layer of black nylon. This ammunition, called 'Nyclad', prevents lead fouling in the bore of the weapon, reduces lead contamination in ranges and is said to reduce friction with the bore, thus enhancing velocity.

Ammunition with a wash of copper over the lead, known as 'Luballoy' or 'Golden Bullets', is also available. This coating is intended to reduce the deposition of lead on the inside surface of the barrel. Lead deposition in the weapon's bore effectively reduces the internal diameter, giving rise to an increase in the internal pressures and a loss of accuracy due to a drop in the efficiency of the rifling.

At one time, copper washed bullets were quite popular, but nowadays, this construction is unlikely to be found in calibres other than 0.22″ rimfire. This is probably due to the fact that the copper coating was found to be no more effective than the much cheaper standard bullet lubricant.

To reduce lead contamination in ranges, ammunition is also manufactured with a thick coating of copper, electro-deposited over a plain lead core. As the surface coating is electro-deposited, the jacket material extends over the whole surface of the bullet. This ammunition is very popular for training purposes as there is no exposed lead surface on the bullet from which volatilization can take place. As lead volatilized from the bullet's base is the major source of lead contamination in ranges, this type of bullet construction can significantly reduce the health hazard due to lead contamination in heavily used ranges.

Almost every imaginable material has been used at one time or another to replace lead, for example, wood or compressed paper for bulleted blanks, phosphor bronze or aluminium for lightweight extremely high velocity, Teflon-coated tungsten for metal penetrating, compressed lead or iron dust for fairground gallery ranges, plastic for short-range training and magnesium for use as a signalling flare.

2.2.14 Other bullet types

Exploding bullets are available in most small arms calibres. These have a very large cavity in the nose into which is placed a small amount of explosive material. A primer cup, with a small ball bearing to act as an anvil, inserted backwards, is used as a detonator. The 1982 assassination attempt on the American President Ronald Reagan was made using 0.22″ calibre explosive bullets.

Although they are more commonly encountered in military ammunition, tracer bullets are also available commercially. The bullets in these rounds have a very brightly burning chemical compound in the base which permits observation of the bullet during its flight. Virtually all calibres are available including 12-bore shotgun.

A case to illustrate the dangers of tracer ammunition involved a husband venting his frustration with his wife by shooting his bedroom wardrobe (!) with a 12-bore shotgun. Unfortunately, the round he fired contained a tracer pellet which set light to the wardrobe and then the house. His only comment when

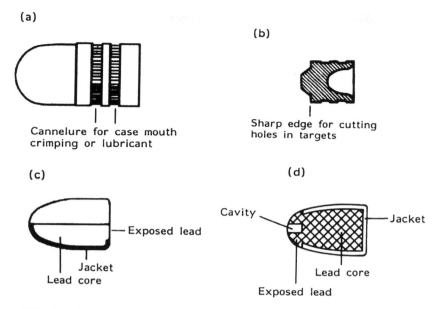

(a)

Cannelure for case mouth
crimping or lubricant

(b)

Sharp edge for cutting
holes in targets

(c)

Exposed lead

Jacket
Lead core

(d)

Cavity

Jacket

Lead core

Exposed lead

Figure 2.14 (a) Round-nosed bullet; (b) wadcutter bullet; (c) jacketed bullet; (d) semi-jacketed hollow-point bullet.

being questioned by the police in front of the wreckage of his home was 'but I only shot the door once'!

Apart from the normal *round-nosed* configuration, properly called 'ogival', the list of bullet shapes is almost endless (Figure 2.14). Some of the more common shapes include:

- *Wadcutter* – flat-nosed bullet with a sharp shoulder. Generally used by target shooters and designed to produce a clear-cut punched-out hole in the paper target.

- *Spitzer* – a German term applied to an elongated ogival bullet with a sharp point.

- *Soft point* or *semi-jacketed* – a jacketed bullet with the jacket cut back at the nose to reveal the lead core.

- *Hollow point* – generally a semi-jacketed bullet the nose of which has a cavity. This is designed to expand on impact with soft targets, thus increasing the wounding effect of the bullet.

- *Dum-dum* – a 0.303″ rifle bullet design developed in the Indian arsenal of Dum-dum in 1894. This initially consisted of a standard 0.303″ rifle bullet which had the front of the metal jacket trimmed back to expose the lead core. It was designed to expand rapidly on impact causing a massive wound and was first used against the 'savage tribesmen' at the battle of Omdurman in 1898. Whilst it was very effective, it did have one major drawback. As the modified bullet was a standard 0.303″ bullet with the lead core exposed at the base, there was a tendency for the lead core to be blown out of the jacket, making it all but impossible to load the next round. This was rectified by the Mk III bullet which had a jacket completely covering the base of the bullet. A hole was bored in the nose of the bullet and a short metal tube was inserted into this to increase expansion. In 1899, the Hague Convention outlawed this type of bullet in military service. It should be noted here that the Hague Convention is not applicable to civilian applications and police forces are not restricted by any military conventions in the type of bullets they can use. The term Dum-dum is often misused to denote hollow-point bullets.

- *Rifled slug* – generally plain lead (but can also be steel and lead or plain steel) projectile for use in smooth-bored shotguns. To impart spin, and therefore stability, to the projectile, wing-like helical ribs are formed on the outside surface. These fins, however, have been found to impart little or no spin to the projectile. It is generally intended for use against large soft-skinned game, such as deer, but is also used by police and security forces against cars and taking the locks from doors.

- *Saboted bullet* – a sub-calibre (i.e. smaller than the bore of the weapon) bullet surrounded by a lightweight sheath, generally of plastic, which is discarded as soon as the missile leaves the barrel. By using a smaller, much lighter bullet in a larger barrel, exceedingly high velocities can be obtained. Whilst most calibres have been manufactured, only the larger rifle calibres have ever become popular, and these are generally referred to by the trade name 'Accelerator'. Solid steel saboted missiles are available in 12-bore shotgun calibre for penetrating cars, but this type of ammunition is generally restricted to police and security forces.

- *Flechette* – a thin nail-like missile, stabilized by fins. Originally designed as extremely high velocity, single projectile saboted loadings for rifles developed by the US military in the 1950s, they proved to be rather inaccurate and unreliable. Multiple missile loadings in 12-bore shotgun cartridges proved to be much more satisfactory, and this version is in general use with the US Army as the 12-bore Close Assault Weapon.

2.2.15   Non-toxic and frangible bullets

Lead contamination of firing ranges, both indoor and outdoor, has been a continuing and serious problem. The (US) National Bureau of Standards claims that 80% of airborne lead on firing ranges comes from the projectile, whilst the remaining 20% comes from the combustion of the lead styphnate primer mixture.

In the early 1980s, a concerted move was made towards eliminating this health hazard, especially at training facilities and indoor ranges.

The first step in this process was to eliminate the lead in the priming mixture and as a result, most ammunition manufacturers now retail a line of ammunition with a non-lead-based priming compound.

The problem over lead being torn off a plain lead bullet as it passed down the bore and lead being volatilized from the base in normally jacketed bullets still existed with the concomitant toxic levels of lead in the air.

To counter this, manufacturers produced a totally jacketed bullet (TMJ, Total Metal Jacket; FMJ, Full Metal Jacket) which had a thick coating of gilding metal electroplated over the lead core. However, as the bullet core was still made from lead, it would, on impacting with the butts, disintegrate leading to the release of large quantities of lead dust. As a non-toxic training round, TMJ bullets were not entirely successful.

The obvious answer was to follow the lead of non-toxic shotgun ammunition and utilize a frangible and/or totally non-toxic bullet using materials other than lead in the production of the bullet.

As a result, virtually every major ammunition manufacturer now has a line of frangible and/or non-toxic small arms ammunition.

There appears, however, to be some confusion between frangible ammunition and non-toxic ammunition. To delineate between these two rounds, it must be understood that whilst frangible ammunition may be loaded with non-toxic materials, frangible projectiles completely turn to powder upon impact with any surface that is harder than the bullet itself. However, non-toxic projectiles can ricochet or splash back akin to a conventional bullet.

Many alternative substances are presently being used in the manufacture of frangible or non-toxic ammunition, for example, iron powder; zinc; tungsten; combinations of nylon, zinc and/or tin coupled with tungsten; bismuth; copper and bullets containing steel cores.

Whilst copper and steel both have the desired weight factor, these bullets are much harder than lead, causing a serious ricochet factor or bullets which may return back down the line of flight to the firing line.

In soft tissue, a frangible bullet performs in exactly the same way as a full metal-jacketed bullet, which clearly makes it a lethal round. Frangible ammunition is, however, an ideal round to use on indoor ranges due to the elimination of ricochets and splash back.

Frangible bullets have been in production since 1845 in the form of compressed iron or lead dust. These were designed for use in the Flobert indoor target ranges and fired from rimfire weapons known as 'saloon' or 'parlour' pistols and rifles. The rounds were designated conical ball (CB) cap and bulleted breech (BB) cap.

In 1975, Glazer Co. introduced the Glazer safety slug. This was simply a gilding metal jacket filled with no. 12 birdshot (0.05"). The voids between the shot were filled with Teflon, and a flat polymer cap sealed the front end of the casing. To improve ballistic performance, a polymer-tipped ball round was introduced in 1987. The current compressed core form was first sold in 1988.

The formation of the polymer was also changed in 1994 to improve fragmentation reliability.

On hitting the target, the jacket broke open distributing the shot inside the target. It was thus a non-ricocheting round which completely removed any chance of over-penetration. However, being filled with lead shot, it was hardly non-toxic.

Current situation. As with non-toxic lead shot, frangible and non-toxic bullets are areas of intense research, and the development of new combinations of binding agents and metals is ongoing with new combinations being released on a virtually weekly basis

Some of the currently available non-toxic and frangible bullets follow:

Blount/speer ZNT. These rounds are made with lead-free primers and feature a newly designed projectile.

The projectile has a fluted copper jacket combined with a cast zinc alloy core and is designed to break into small pieces upon impact with steel targets, backstops or other similar objects.

Delta Frangible Ammunition, LLC. Delta Frangible Ammunition (DFA) produces a line of frangible cartridges utilizing a nylon composite bullet. The nylon projectile will break apart into small pieces upon impact with hard surfaces, resulting in the reduced penetration of objects which are not intended to be penetrated.

DFA also has a reduced ricochet potential, reduced maximum range capability, and eliminates airborne lead contamination and lead-contaminated environments.

Currently, DFA provides these bullets which are then loaded and distributed by Winchester for law enforcement use only.

Longbow, Inc. Longbow's frangible bullet made of a polymer–copper compound. This is claimed to completely eliminate ricochet and splash back and to be non-toxic.

Remington Arms Co., Inc. Remington manufactures a lead-free frangible bullet called the Disintegrator.

The Disintegrator's lead-free bullet design provides instant and complete break-up upon impact, with no ricochet or lead accumulation. Furthermore, the totally lead-free primer eliminates the hazards of airborne lead residue in enclosed ranges. Point of impact and recoil performance reportedly duplicates that of equivalent standard duty ammunition.

Blount Clean-Fire Ammunition. Whilst Blount's Clean-Fire ammunition is not totally non-toxic or lead-free, it does eliminate airborne lead with a totally metal-jacketed bullet. It also has a priming mixture that contains no lead, barium, antimony or other toxic metals.

Federal cartridge company BallistiClean. This ammunition uses a copper-jacketed zinc core bullet, a non-toxic copper-coloured primer and is loaded in brass cases headstamped 'NT'. The primer mix is of particular interest as it contains no heavy metals or toxic metals; instead, the primer mix contains diazodinitrophenol (DDNP) as the primary explosive instead of lead styphnate. Furthermore, the oxidizer is calcium silicate instead of barium and strontium compounds. This round is reportedly the first completely toxic metal-free line of ammunition to be developed.

Winchester Ammunition Super Clean NT. Winchester has introduced a new line of training ammunition called 'Super Clean NT' – using tin instead of zinc, which is used in frangible ammunition. The bullets are a jacketed soft point type, non-toxic and lead-free, and specifically designed to eliminate pollution from lead dust. Additionally, they are loaded with a primer that is lead-free and does not contain heavy metals.

Winchester has also introduced a new clean centre fire pistol ammunition primarily designed for indoor ranges called 'WinClean'. WinClean incorporates Winchester's latest generation primer which is lead-free and heavy metal-free. The cartridge features a TMJ bullet.

Remington UMC leadless. Remington now offers UMC (Union Metallic Cartridge) leadless pistol and revolver ammunition. The bullet with a flat nose enclosed base (FNEB) bullet design prevents the hot expanding propellant gases from vaporizing lead from the bullet's base.

FrangibleBullets.com. FrangibleBullets.Com projectiles are manufactured using a compressed copper/tin powdered metal. The bullets are then heat treated in a nitrogen furnace and then tumble polished. This results in a non-lead bullet with no jacket or core.

AccuTec USA. AccuTec USA produces RRLP Ultra-Frangible bullets which are composed of a tungsten–polymer mix and R2X2 Ultra-Frangible made from a copper–polymer mix.

SinterFire ammunition. SinterFire produces a range of copper/tin based frangible non-toxic bullets containing a 'dry lubricant'. The Cu/Sn sintered powder is compressed then heated in an inert atmosphere.

Other non-toxic bullets

Très Haute Vitesse (THV). The French THV bullet is made from phosphor bronze. Intended as an ultra-high-velocity metal-penetrating round, it is, however,

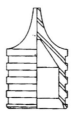

Figure 2.15 French THV (Très Haute Vitesse) phosphor bronze bullet.

essentially a non-toxic bullet. The primer was of the normal lead styphnate type (Figure 2.15).

Chinese 7.62×25 mm pistol round. Up until about 1985, the standard 7.62×25 mm round of ammunition consisted of a very heavily copper-coated steel jacket surrounding a lead core. After that date, the military changed its specification to a sold steel bullet with a copper wash. There was not a copper or gilding metal gas check to take up the rifling, merely two raised band of steel about 1 mm high and 1 mm across. After 50 rounds, the rifling of the Type 54 pistol, for which this round was intended for use in, completely disappears.

Whilst this bullet is 'non-toxic', it was introduced simply to save on manufacturing costs. The primer, however, was definitely not and often contained mercury.

KTW. In the mid-1970s, KTW (from the last names of the inventors, Dr Paul J. Kopsch, Dan Turcus and DonWard) brought out a range of metal penetrating rounds including 0.357 Magnum, 0.30 Carbine, 9 mm PB and 0.380 ACP. Originally, the bullets were made from sintered tungsten and were coated in bright green Teflon to enhance the penetration. To prevent barrel wear and to take up the rifling, there was a gas check on the base of the bullet. In the late 1980s, the tungsten was replaced with a hardened phosphor bronze. Once again, the bullet was coated in green Teflon. Whilst this round was intended for metal penetrating, it was, essentially, non-toxic. The primer, however, was not, as it contained lead styphnate.

2.2.16 Bullet base configuration

Whilst most small arms bullets have a base which is the same diameter as the body, long-range rifle bullets have the rear section of the bullet tapered. This is to reduce base drag and is referred to either as a *boat-tailed bullet* (US nomenclature) or a *streamlined bullet* (British nomenclature). These bullets are generally military, but can also be encountered in commercial ammunition.

A *heeled bullet* is one in which the rear portion of the bullet, which fits into the cartridge case, is reduced so that the case diameter is the same as the driving

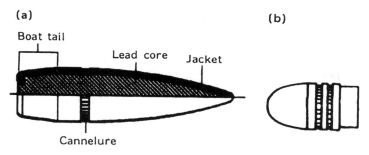

(a)   **(b)**

Boat tail

Lead core   Jacket

Cannelure

Figure 2.16 (a) Boat-tailed bullet   (b) Heeled bullet.

surface of the bullet. Whilst this type of bullet is now only encountered in 0.22″ rimfire ammunition, in the past, virtually all revolver ammunition was of this type (Figure 2.16).

2.2.17   Bullet lubrication

Plain lead bullets must have some type of lubrication on their outside surface to reduce friction with the bore. Jacketed bullets do not generally require any form of lubrication.

Lead bullet lubricant generally contains a mixture of vaseline, beeswax and graphite, although modern silicone based waxes are being used to a certain extent. In modern ammunition, this lubricant is held in a groove round the bullet, called a cannelure, which is generally located on the portion of the bullet inside the cartridge case. This is called an *inside lubricated bullet*. This obviously makes the round cleaner to handle and prevents the grease picking up pieces of grit and other material which might damage the bore of the weapon.

In older ammunition, the grease is either in a cannelure outside the case or is applied to the whole exposed area of the bullet. This is called an *outside lubricated bullet*. Apart from 0.22″ rimfire ammunition, this type of lubrication system is hardly ever encountered.

An example of how important bullet lubrication is involved the purchase of 10 000 000 rounds of revolver ammunition by a police force. The brand chosen was not one of the most well known, but they did advertise their bullets as having 'a state-of-the-art lubricant'.

Unfortunately, it was found that after the first 10 or so rounds through a weapon, it became increasingly difficult to hit the target and after 50 rounds, the bullets were not even coming out of the barrel at all. The so-called 'state-of-the-art lubricant' was an exceedingly thin smear of varnish which had little or no lubrication value. With each round fired, lead was being stripped from the bullet and was welding itself to the inside of the bore. After 50 rounds, there was so little of the bore open that the bullets stuck in the barrel.

2.2.18   Brief glossary

Bore size	In shotgun terminology, the number of lead balls of the same diameter as the inside of the barrel which weighs 1 lb. Thus, a 12-bore shotgun has a barrel diameter of 0.729″, and 12-round lead balls of 0.729 in. diameter weigh exactly 1 lb.
	In terminology applicable to weapons with a rifled bore it is the inside diameter of the barrel measured across the tops of the lands, that is, the raised part of the rifling.
Bullet	Refers to the missile alone. It can be either a 'fired bullet' or an 'unfired bullet'.
Cartridge case	Refers to the ammunition case and primer and does not include the bullet; can be either a 'fired cartridge case' or a 'live cartridge case'. A 'live cartridge case' has a live, unfired, primer, but there is no propellant or bullet present.
Centre fire cartridge	Cartridge with a cup containing the priming composition located in a cavity in the centre of the cartridge head.
Headstamp	Basically, the headstamp is a series of marks, letters and/or numbers impressed upon the base of the cartridge by the manufacturer to indicate the calibre and by whom it was manufactured.
Pellets	Can be either the individual lead or steel balls found in shotgun ammunition, or the lead pellets for use in air weapons. 'Lead slug' is also sometimes used to describe air gunpellets, but this is not the correct term for this type of missile.
Primer	Basically the means for igniting the propellant.
Propellant	A chemical or mixture of chemicals which, when ignited, produce a very large quantity of gas. This gas, when confined within a barrel and behind a missile, provides the propulsion to drive the missile down the bore and out of the barrel.
Rimfire cartridge	Cartridge with a thin-walled base flange containing the priming compound.
Round of ammunition	Generally refers to a single, live, unfired cartridge comprising of missile, cartridge case, propellant and some form of primer. It also, however, includes live blank and tear-gas ammunition.

Shot	Another term for the lead or steel balls in shotgun ammunition that is 'lead shot'. This is an acceptable alternative to 'pellet'.

2.3   Non-toxic Shot

In the United States, lead shot has been recognized as posing a threat to water-fowl since 1874. Efforts to phase out lead shot began in the 1970s, but a nationwide ban on lead shot for all waterfowl hunting was not implemented until 1991.

Canada and the United Kingdom instituted a complete ban on the use of lead shot in 1999 with France following in 2006.

The first, and probably still the most common, alternative non-toxic substitute for lead was soft steel shot.

Whilst soft steel shot is relatively cheap to produce, it is only about 70% as dense as lead and as a result, pellets of the same size differ considerably in the amount of energy they deliver at the target. Another problem is the number of pellets that can be fitted into a cartridge of a given size. This problem is, however, largely offset due to the fact that steel shot is considerably harder than lead and does not require such thick cushion wads to reduce deformation on firing.

Table 2.7 shows the number of pellets per ounce for various sizes of steel and lead.

Lead shot, which is easily deformed upon firing, develops a relatively long, large-diameter shot string. However, as steel shot is three times harder than lead, it deforms less on firing and develops a shot string that is 50–60% shorter and 60–70% narrower than lead.

Table 2.7 A comparison between the number of steel and lead shot pellets per ounce of shot.

Size Diameter	Pellets per oz – lead	Pellets per oz – steel
BBB 0.190″ (4.83 mm)	No equivalent lead pellet	62
BB 0.180″ (4.57 mm)	50	72
1 0.160″ (4.06 mm)	81	103
2 0.150″ (3.81 mm)	87	125
3 0.140″ (3.56 mm)	108	158
4 0.130″ (3.30 mm)	135	192
5 0.120″ (3.05 mm)	170	243
6 0.110″ (2.79 mm)	225	315

2.3.1   Other alternatives to lead

The list of other materials used or under review is exhaustive, and many more
will almost definitely follow in the future. At present, the following are just
some of those either used or currently being considered:

 1. soft steel (often copper coated to reduce corrosion);
 2. iron-scrap tungsten (Hevi-Steel);
 3. bismuth–tin;
 4. bismuth–tin–copper;
 5. tungsten–iron;
 6. tungsten–iron–bronze (Remington HD Shot);
 7. tungsten–polymer;
 8. sintered tungsten–nylon;
 9. tungsten matrix;
10. tungsten–bronze;
11. tungsten–nickel–iron;
12. tungsten–tin–bismuth;
13. tungsten–tin–iron–nickel (Hevi-Shot);
14. nitro-steel (zinc galvanized steel) – Remington.

A comparison of the various densities for some of the non-toxic shot compositions with that of lead follows (Table 2.8).

An impression of the relative shot sizes that must be used to generate the
same ballistics with various non-toxic alternatives to lead can be appreciated
from Table 2.9.

A relative comparison of the energy and penetration in standard ballistic
gelatin of the various pellet materials for no. 4 size shot can be seen in
Table 2.10.

Table 2.8 The relative densities of some non-toxic
pellet compositions (g/cc).

Steel	7.86
Hevi-Steel	9.06
Bismuth	9.60
Tungsten/iron	10.30
Tungsten matrix	10.60
Lead	11.10
Hevi-Shot	12.0
Tungsten/iron/bronze (HD Shot)	12.0

Table 2.9 Equivalent shot sizes for lead and non-toxic pellets.

Material	Shot no.	Density (g/cc)	Load (oz)	Velocity at 3 ft
Steel	BB	7.86	$1\frac{1}{4}$	1375
Bismuth	2	9.6	$1\frac{5}{8}$	1250
Tungsten/iron	3	10.3	$1\frac{1}{8}$	1400
Tungsten matrix	4	10.8	$1\frac{5}{8}$	1330
Tungsten-poly	4	10.7	$1\frac{3}{8}$	1330
Lead	3	11.34	$1\frac{5}{8}$	1350
Hevi-Shot	5	12.0	$1\frac{1}{4}$	1375

BB, bulleted breech

Table 2.10 Performance of lead and non-toxic No. 4 pellets in ballistic gelatin.

Shot type	Yards	Velocity (fps)	Energy (ft/lb)	Penetration in ballistics gelatin
Hevi-Shot	20	1023	8.13	3.63
	40	799	4.95	2.64
	60	647	3.25	1.95
Tungsten matrix	20	986	6.56	3.02
	40	749	3.80	2.12
	60	594	2.39	1.53
Tungsten–iron	20	981	6.45	2.97
	40	745	3.72	2.08
	60	590	2.33	1.49
Bismuth	20	962	5.79	2.71
	40	721	3.25	1.86
	60	563	1.99	1.30
Lead	20	1001	7.16	3.26
	40	770	4.25	2.33
	60	616	2.72	1.70
Steel	20	906	4.17	2.04
	40	647	2.13	1.30
	60	485	1.19	0.83

For comparison purposes, the velocity has been adjusted to 1350 fps.

The much higher velocity attained by steel pellets is readily demonstrated by this comparison of various commercial bismuth, tungsten and lead loads (see Table 2.11).

It has been noted that many of the non-toxic alternatives to lead possess pellets with a less than uniform shape. Whilst this would be expected to result in extensive 'flyers', this does not appear to be the case, the patterns being dense, uniform and often equivalent or better to those produced by lead shot fired from a barrel with a choke size one quarter greater.

Table 2.11 The velocities of various lead and non-toxic loadings.

Manufacturer	Velocity (ft/s)	Number of pellets
Winchester		
Bismuth BBs 1 5/8 oz.	1267	81
Bismuth no. 2 shot 1 5/8 oz.	1246	138
Federal		
Tungsten BBs 1 1/8 oz.	1358	59
Tungsten No. 2 shot 1 1/8 oz.	1388	106
Federal		
Steel BBs 1 1/8 oz.	1402	81
Steel no. 2 shot	1428	141
Federal		
Lead BBs 2 oz.	1087	94
Lead no. 2 shot 2 oz.	1123	174

It should be noted that lead shot is sometimes copper coated to increase its hardness. This can be mistaken for copper-coated steel shot. It is, however, readily identified by use of a magnet.

2.4   A Brief History of Propellants

2.4.1   Introduction

Gunpowder, whether it is 'black powder', 'nitrocellulose' or a 'double-based powder', is a solid substance that, on combustion, is converted into a very large volume of gas within a very short period of time. Whilst nitrocellulose-based powders can be detonated, in small arms ammunition, they are merely propellants which on ignition produce a very large volume of gaseous material which propels the missile down the bore.

During combustion, the rate of reaction is exponentially proportional to the pressure. Thus, unconfined gunpowder or a nitrocellulose powder will gently burn at a fairly steady rate. However, if the powder is confined within the chamber of a weapon with a bullet in the bore, the rate of burning will increase dramatically as the pressure builds up. This will continue until the bullet begins to move down the barrel. If the type and quantity of propellant have been correctly chosen for the bore size, bullet weight and barrel length, the rate of burning will proceed at a level where the pressure will be maintained until the bullet leaves the barrel. At the point at which the bullet leaves the barrel, all the propellant should have burned to its gaseous components. Should the bullet for some reason be unable to move down the barrel, the pressure would rise to such an extent that a gaseous explosion would occur. In this instance, the weakest part of the gun would rupture with catastrophic consequences. Conditions under which this could occur are many, but the basic causes of such an incidence are a barrel obstruction, a propellant with a burning rate too high for the bullet weight/bore size combination or too great a charge of propellant.

Propellants can be loosely divided into two classes: (i) black powder and (ii) nitro-based powders. Whilst both types of propellants are commercially available, the use of black powder tends to be restricted to enthusiasts firing muzzle-loading weapons. Virtually all modern cartridges are loaded with some form of nitrocellulose powder.

A brief history follows.

2.4.2 Black powder

Black powder was undoubtedly the earliest form of gunpowder or propellant used in firearms. It is, however, impossible to determine with any degree of authority who invented it.

The use of 'Greek Fire' to capture the city of Delium by the Boetans in 424 BC is well recorded, although it was probably used as no more than an incendiary device.

The Chinese are known to have fired incendiary and explosive devices from a bow or catapult as early as 1000 AD, and their name for gunpowder (Huo Yao – fire chemical) was standardized by 1040 AD. This Chinese gunpowder probably spread to Europe via the Mongols under Genghis Khan.

The earliest European reference to gunpowder is found in the writings of Friar Roger Bacon who lived in England (1214–1294) and prepared his manuscript on the subject around 1250. He was familiar with its explosive properties, but does not appear to have had any idea as to its use as a propellant. His formula of seven parts of potassium nitrate, five parts of sulfur and five parts of charcoal remained standard until improved upon by the French in 1338.

Another document written by an obscure monk Marcus Graecus also deals with gunpowder. The original portion of the document is dated 846 AD and is written in Greek. That portion dealing with gunpowder was added to Graecus' document at a later date, and in Latin and is dated 1240. Roger Bacon spent some time in Spain and his knowledge is thought to have originated from the Marcus Graecus document.

Berthold Schwartz, a famous monk of Freiberg, Germany, studied the writings of Bacon and carried out considerable experimentation. It was following his announcement of his researches, in 1320, that gunpowder really started to spread through central Europe. Mr Oliver of Boklerberry appears to have been one of the first English dealers in gunpowder and its manufacture, as an industry, dates back to Elizabeth I (1533–1603) when gunpowder mills were first established in Kent.

From time to time, various changes have been made to the composition of gunpowder to make it burn faster or slower. In 1781, it was found that by *corning* gunpowder, that is, wetting it then compressing it, then, after allowing it to dry, grinding it up again into the desired grain size, a much more efficient powder could be produced. It was also found that with each successive 'corning', the powder improved in performance.

Between 1890 and 1900, a type of powder called 'cocoa' or 'brown powder' appeared. This was made by substituting semi-burned charcoal for the regular charcoal. This probably represents the highest development of black powder.

Black powder has, due to its ability to absorb water from the atmosphere, a high propensity for ignition by static electricity and low-impact ignition tolerances, a difficult powder to store and keep. It is also, due to the aforementioned properties, a difficult material to have transported, and in many countries, a special explosives licence is required before it can be purchased.

To overcome these problems, a propellant called *Pyrodex* was introduced in the early 1970s by the Hodgdon's Powder Company of America. Pyrodex has the same burning characteristics as black powder and has the same bulk characteristics (That is, a given volume of Pyrodex will give the same performance as the same volume of black powder). It does not, however, have the same drawbacks as black powder and is much easier to transport, being regarded as a very low-grade explosive. Also, its flameless temperature of ignition is 400 °C whilst that of black powder is only 260 °C. The exact composition of Pyrodex is a tightly held trade secret.

2.4.3 Nitro powders

The development of smokeless powder was closely associated with the discovery of gun cotton and nitroglycerine, both of which are high explosives.

When first discovered, attempts were made to use these nitro explosives as propellants. However, the detonation occurred with such instantaneous violence that the weapons were blown apart before the bullet even started to move down the barrel.

Some way had to be found to tame the violent detonation of the explosive into a controlled and progressive burning which would produce large volumes of gas in a predictable manner.

The first form of 'smokeless powder' was probably made by Vieille, a French chemist, in 1884. By dissolving nitrocellulose, or gun cotton as it is also known, in a mixture of ether and alcohol, a gelatinous colloid is formed. This can be rolled into sheets or extruded into rod or tube form. When dried, it forms a hard, stable material which can easily be handled. This type of smokeless propellant is called *single-base powder*.

Another form of propellant was developed by Alfred Nobel in 1887. In this form, the nitrocellulose was dissolved in nitroglycerine. Vaseline was added as a lubricant and stabilizer, and the material so formed could then be extruded or rolled and cut into the shape or size required. This type of propellant is called *double-based powder*. Probably the most familiar form of a double-based powder is the British military propellant *cordite*. This propellant was, until quite recently, used in all British military rifle and pistol ammunition. Cordite contains 37% nitrocellulose, 58% nitroglycerine and 5% vaseline.

2.4.4 Moderation of nitrocellulose-based propellants

When a propellant is ignited within the confines of a cartridge case enclosed in the breech of a weapon, large quantities of gas are produced. The pressure so formed pushes the bullet down the barrel and so discharges it from the weapon. The problem is that once the bullet starts to move down the barrel, the space occupied by the gases increases and the pressure starts to fall. Some method of modifying the burning rate of the propellant is thus necessary to ensure that the pressure exerted on the base of the bullet is fairly consistent during its progress down the length of the barrel.

Small thin flakes of powder will obviously have a larger surface area than solid lumps, and these are obviously preferable for short-barrelled, small-calibre weapons. The problems come, however, when longer barrels and larger calibres are used. Under these circumstances, other methods to moderate or alter the rate of burning are required. The simplest of these is to perforate the grains of powder. On ignition, both the inside surface of the perforation and the outside surface of the grain burn together. As the grain burns, the outside surface diminishes as does the production of gases. This is, however, countered by the inside surface becoming larger as it burns. By altering the number of perforations and the ratio of the inside diameter to the outside diameter, the burning rate can be closely controlled.

Other methods of modifying the burning rate include the addition of chemical 'moderators' during manufacture and the coating of the grains with graphite and other surfactants to reduce the rate at which the grains ignite.

The range of additives and moderators is enormous and many are very tightly controlled trade secrets. The identification of these components can, however, be extremely important in the identification of propellants and their origins.

An example of how important this can be involved the use of propellants in a terrorist device which was used to kill a police officer. The device was a very simple pipe bomb using a simple twist of thin wire connected to a battery and switch for ignition. Fragments of unburnt firearms propellant found at the scene were, at a later date, successfully matched to similar fragments found in a suspect's pockets. The propellant particles were quite unusual in that they were of an American variety not often seen in the United Kingdom. As it was a single-based propellant, it was necessary to analyze the moderators before a successful identification could be made.

A list of the more commonly known additives and moderators follows.

Additive	Purpose
Resorcinol	Plasticizer
Triacetin	Plasticizer
Dimethyl sebacetate	Plasticizer
Dimethyl phthalate	Plasticizer
2:Dinitro diphenylamine	Plasticizer
Calcium carbonate	Adsorb free nitrogen dioxide for long-term propellant stability
Diphenylamine	Adsorb free nitrogen dioxide for long-term propellant stability
Dinitro toluene	Gelatinizer to slow rate of burning
Dibutylphthalate	Gelatinizer to slow rate of burning
Carbamate	Gelatinizer to slow rate of burning
Barium nitrate	To increase rate of burning
Potassium nitrate	To increase rate of burning
Graphite	Surface moderator
Woodmeal	A fuel – only in shotgun ammunition

Other additives include:

Cresol	Nitroglycerine
Carbazole	N-nitrosodiphenylamine
Carbanilide	Trinitrotoluene
Nitrophenylamine	N,N-dimethylcarbanilide
Dinitrocresol	2,4-Dinitrodiphenylamine
Triacetin	Dibutylphthalate
Nitrotoluene	Pentaerythritol tetranitrate
Cyclonite or RDX (Royal Demolition eXplosive)	N,N-dibutycarbanilide
Diethylphthalate	Methycentralite

In an attempt to combat metal fouling (from jacket material stripped off the bullet and welded to the bore during firing) in rifles, Du Pont, the American powder manufacturer, added powdered metallic tin to the propellant. The patent for this was taken out in 1918, and to identify those powders containing tin, a 'half' was added to the powder designation; for example, powder $17\frac{1}{2}$ contained tin; powder 17 did not. These powders originally contained approximately 4%

of metallic tin. It was found, however, that whilst the old copper/zinc fouling from the bullet jacket was eliminated, metallic tin volatilized by the heat of combustion was condensing inside the bore near the muzzle. The percentage of tin was slowly decreased to 1% and was then eliminated altogether.

One peculiar propellant introduced around 1910 was called *Lesmok*. Primarily used in 0.22″ calibre ammunition, it was a mixture of 85% black powder and 15% pure gun cotton. Whilst this was a distinctive improvement over plain black powder, it still left a considerable quantity of corrosive residues in the bore. Consequently, it had a very short life. As far as can be ascertained, the last batch of 0.22″ calibre Lesmok ammunition was made by Winchester in February 1947.

The advantages of nitro-based propellants over black powder are many and include:

- a very small quantity of a nitro-based propellant is required in comparison to black powder;
- the ease with which it can be modified to fit almost any circumstance;
- a negligible quantity of combustion residues left in the bore;
- the low corrosive nature of the combustion residues.

The flameless temperature of ignition for nitrocellulose propellants is rather low at approximately 350 °C. However, if ammunition is subjected to a fire, it is the primer which will almost invariably ignite first as the ignition temperature of this is around 250 °C.

How fast a propellant burns gives an indication as to its intended use. Very fast burning powders are best suited for use with lightweight bullets and short barrels, whilst the slower burning ones are for heavy magnum calibre weapons with long barrels. Propellants for use in shotgun ammunition also tend to be fast burning as most of the acceleration imparted to the shot has to occur in the relatively heavy breech end of the barrel. Rifle calibre propellants are slow burning and become progressively more so as the power increases to magnum calibres.

It is possible, in some instances, to approximately date commercial ammunition by the type of propellant it contains.

Some examples follow:

- Lesmok   1910–1947
- ball powder   1941–to date
- cordite   1885–1956
- Schultzite   1867–1935
- Smokeless Diamond   1920–1939

Target shooters tend to use very small quantities of a very fast burning powder (often a shotgun propellant) in their hand-loaded ammunition to ensure accuracy.

Whilst this is perfectly safe as long as only small amounts of propellant are used, to do the same with a slow-burning powder can cause catastrophic consequences.

Whilst the actual mechanism involved is unclear, it would appear that a pressure wave is set up within the cartridge case which reflects back off the base of the bullet. This is reinforced by the still-burning propellant giving rise to sufficient internal pressure to detonate the remaining powder. Such an instantaneous release of energy is too great for the weapon to handle, and the chamber of the weapon explodes. There are numerous instances of this effect including high-power rifles being totally destroyed by a charge of propellant so small the bullet would normally only just reach the end of a 50 yd range.

One other instance of propellant detonating has been experienced by the author, but this was for a different reason altogether. This involved a packet of World War I 0.455″ revolver ammunition which, although very old, appeared to be in perfectly good condition. After firing several rounds, the weapon completely exploded depositing the barrel, top strap and cylinder into the walls and ceiling of the range. On carefully opening some of the rounds, it was discovered that the cordite had started to deteriorate and the nitroglycerine was leeching out of the propellant. The amount of free nitroglycerine was sufficient to cause detonation within the rest of the charge, destroying the weapon.

2.4.5 Brief glossary

Black powder	Mechanical mixture of potassium nitrate, sulfur and charcoal.
Gun cotton	Nitrated cotton, a form of nitrocellulose.
Lesmok	Trade name for obsolete propellant containing 85% black powder and 15% gun cotton.
Nitrocellulose	Nitrated cellulose which forms the basis of all modern propellants.
Propellant moderator	A method by which the burning rate of a nitrocellulose-based propellant can be controlled by physically altering the grain shape or addition of a surfactant or chemical.
Pyrodex	Modern alternative for black powder.

2.5 Priming Compounds and Primers

2.5.1 Introduction

A *priming compound* is a highly sensitive explosive chemical which, when struck by the firing pin or hammer of a weapon, will explode with great violence, causing a flame to ignite the propellant.

This explosive chemical is often mixed with other chemicals which provide oxygen to assist in the production of the flame, a fuel to increase the length and temperature of the flame and ground glass as an abrasive to assist in the initial ignition of the explosive.

In the realms of forensic science, the detection of primer discharge residue on the hands can provide crucial evidence as to whether a person has recently fired a weapon. To fully utilize the evidential value of gunshot residue (GSR) analysis, a basic understanding of the history, composition and manufacture of primers is essential.

Short history of priming compounds. The earliest priming compound was almost certainly mercury fulminate as used in the *Forsythe scent bottle* priming system which was introduced around 1806. This compound is highly sensitive and liable to spontaneously explode for no apparent reason. As a result, the Forsythe scent bottle, which required a considerable quantity of this compound to be carried in a container on the side of the pistol, did not achieve a great deal of popularity.

In 1807, Forsythe introduced a priming compound with a formula consisting of 70.6 parts potassium chlorate, 17.6 parts sulfur and 11.8 parts of charcoal. Whilst this was somewhat more stable than mercury fulminate, it was terribly corrosive.

The first real percussion cap (a small metal cup containing the priming composition which was placed on a nipple at the rear of the barrel) was introduced by Joshua Shaw in 1814 and contained mercury fulminate. As a result of the unpredictability of plain mercury fulminate, it was superseded in 1818 by a mixture of mercury fulminate, potassium chlorate, sulfur and charcoal. The residues produced by this mixture were, however, still terribly corrosive, requiring the weapon to be cleaned immediately after firing.

In 1828, Dreyse patented the 'needle gun', which had a paper cartridge case with the primer cup inside the case with the propellant. The firing pin on this weapon was a very long thin needle which penetrated the paper case striking the primer within. This primer cup contained a mixture of potassium chlorate and antimony sulfide.

It was found that purification of the mercury fulminate would lead to a more stable compound, and in 1873, a mixture of mercury fulminate, potassium chlorate, glass dust and gum arabic became the standard US military priming compound. This mixture suffered from two major drawbacks: (i) the mercury tended to make the brass cartridge cases brittle, which led to case failure on firing and dangerous leakage of high-pressure gas from the breech of the weapon; and (ii) the potassium chlorate left terribly corrosive residues in the bore of the weapon after firing.

As a result of these problems, the search began for a non-mercuric, non-corrosive primer composition. Early attempts revolved around the use of potassium chlorate as the main ingredient. Potassium chlorate is, however, a fairly unstable material and is very deliquescent, that is, it absorbs water from the atmosphere.

It also forms potassium chloride on decomposition, which is also deliquescent and is very corrosive to the weapon's bore.

Just prior to World War I, it was discovered that thiocyanate/chlorate mixtures were sensitive to impact. These, however, had the same drawbacks as straight chlorate primers, that is, they produced corrosive residues on firing.

The German company RWS was the first to substitute the potassium chlorate with barium nitrate. Lead styphnate was used as the main explosive component giving the first 'rust free' primer. This was patented in 1928 under the name Sinoxid.

The first true non-corrosive, non-mercuric (NCNM) primers were commercially produced in America between 1935 and 1938. These, however, did not meet the stringent US government specifications as to storage, misfires, and so on, and military ammunition continued to use the old corrosive chlorate mixtures right through World War II.

In the United Kingdom, the change to non-corrosive military primers was even slower, and it was not until the early 1960s that all calibres in military and commercial primers used NCNM priming compounds.

Up to early 2000, the most common primer composition encountered was still the lead styphenate, barium nitrate, antimony sulfide and tetrazine type. In this priming compound, lead styphenate and tetrazine are the sensitive explosive ingredients; barium nitrate provides additional oxygen to increase the temperature of the flame, and antimony sulfide acts as a fuel to prolong the burning time. Aluminium, and occasionally magnesium, can also be encountered, but mainly in the higher-powered magnum pistol or rifle calibres.

Powdered glass was also often added to the mixture to increase the friction and to assist detonation when the mixture is crushed by the firing pin.

Modern 0.22″ calibre rimfire ammunition is slightly different in that the composition almost invariably consists of lead styphenate, barium nitrate, tetrazine and powdered glass.

Lead-free and non-toxic primers.   It began to become apparent in the early 1970s that in heavily used training facilities, the range personnel were suffering from the symptoms of lead poisoning. Whilst a large proportion of this lead was being volatilized from the base of the bullets, a portion was obviously coming from the lead styphenate primer.

The US National Bureau of Standards claims that when lead-based primers are used, 80% of airborne lead on firing ranges comes from the projectile and 20% comes from the priming composition. These percentages obviously depend on whether the bullet is plain lead or jacketed. In the case of a non-jacketed bullet, the rifling will strip lead from the bullet's surface, thus dramatically increasing the percentage of non-primer-based airborne lead.

The change to a bullet with a copper/zinc jacket extending over the base was a fairly simple matter of reducing the bullet sourced airborne lead, but finding a non-mercuric non-corrosive non-lead-based primer was another.

The problem was first solved in the early 1980s by Geco, who released a zinc- and titanium-based primer which they called 'Sintox'. Since then, there have been a number of other lead-free primers produced by, for example, CCI Blazer, Speer, Federal and Winchester (Haag, 1995). The exact composition of the priming compounds used is not available, although SEM/EDX (scanning electron microscope/energy dispersive X-ray) analysis generally shows the presence of strontium in the Speer and Blazer cartridges, potassium in the Winchester cartridges and calcium and silicon in the Federal cartridges.

Most of the more recent primer formulations contain an initiator explosive compound called 'dinol', the chemical name of which is DDNP (diazodinitrophenol).

Other initiator explosives include:

- dinitrodihydroxydiazobenzene salt (diazinate);
- dinitrobenzofuroxan salts;
- potassium dinitrobenzofuroxan;
- various diazo, triazole, and tetrazaole compounds;
- perchlorate or nitrate salts of metal complexes of ammonium, amine or hydrazine an example of which is 2-(5-cyanotetrazolato)pentaaminecobalt III perchlorate (CP).

Oxidizers include:

- zinc oxide;
- potassium nitrate;
- strontium nitrate;
- zinc peroxide.

Fuel components include:

- amorphous boron;
- metal powders, such as aluminium, zirconium, titanium, nickel and zinc;
- carbon;
- silicon;
- metal sulfides such as:
  - antimony sulphide;
  - bismuth sulphide;
  - iron sulphide;
  - zinc sulphide;

Table 2.12 A brief history of primer development.

Date	Primer type	Primer composition
1898	US Krag cartridge	Potassium chlorate Antimony sulfide Glass powder
1901	German RWS	Mercury fulminate Barium nitrate Antimony sulfide Picric acid
1910	US Frankford Arsenal primer	Potassium chlorate Antimony sulfide Sulfur
1910	German RWS	Mercury fulminate Antimony sulfide Barium peroxide TNT (trinitrotoluene)
1911	Swiss military primer	Mercury fulminate Barium nitrate Antimony sulfide Barium carbonate
1917	US Winchester primer	Potassium chlorate Antimony sulfide Lead thiocyanate TNT (trinitrotoluene)
1927	US commercial primers	Mercury fulminate Barium nitrate Lead thiocyanate
1928	German RWS sinoxid primer	Lead styphenate Barium nitrate Antimony sulfide Calcium cilicide Tetrazine
1930	Herz/Rathburg non-mercuric primer	Nitro-amino-guanyl-tetrazine Lead styphenate Barium nitrate Antimony sulfide/calcium suicide
1940	American P-4 primer	Red phosphorous Barium nitrate Aluminium hydroxide
1943	British 0.455 military revolver	Mercury fulminate Sulfur Potassium chlorate Antimony sulfide Mealed black powder
1938 (approx)	American commercial primers	Lead styphenate Antimony sulfide Barium nitrate Tetrazine

Table 2.12 Continued

Date	Primer type	Primer composition
1962	Stabenate primer	Lead nitroaminotetrazole Lead styphenate Barium nitrate Antimony sulfide Aluminium dust Tetrazine
1983	Geco sintox primer	Zinc and titanium-based priming compound containing no lead compounds
1994/5	CCI Blazer, Speer	Strontium-based priming compound containing no lead compounds

- metal silicides, such as:
  - calcium silicide and
  - copper silicide.

The **explosive sensitizer** is generally tetrazine.
'Fast Fuels' may also be included such as:

- potassium styphnate;
- nitrate esters such as nitrocellulose-based propellants;
- PETN (pentaerythritol tetranitrate).

Additional ingredients include:

- PVA (polyvinyl acetate);
- karaya;
- tragacanth;
- guar;
- gum arabic;
- powdered glass.

A typical non-toxic, non-lead priming composition would be:

- DDNP (diazodinitrophenol);
- potassium nitrate;
- nitrocellulose;

- boron metal;
- nitro-glycerine;
- tetrazine;
- nickel.

2.5.2 Manufacture

The loading of the highly explosive and exceedingly sensitive mixture into the primer cup or cartridge rim of rimfire ammunition is a very delicate and dangerous undertaking. With most commercial primers, this is done with the compound slightly wetted, but in military primers, it is carried out as a dry powder to give a more consistent result.

In the 'Eleyprime' process, a mixture of dry, relatively safe chemicals is placed into the primer cup. On the addition of a small quantity of water, the chemicals react to form an explosive composition. Basically, the mixture consists of tetrazine, lead monoxide, lead dioxide, antimony sulfide, styphenic acid, barium nitrate and calcium silicide.

2.5.3 Other considerations

The sensitivity of primers is a difficult subject due to the varying standards not only from country to country, but also between the commercial and military sectors. In the United Kingdom, the commercial standard for 9 mm Parabellum primers states that the primer should discharge when a 57 g steel ball falls from a height of 330 mm onto a firing pin. The lower limit for this must not be less than 203 mm.

Military standards vary enormously, but the NATO standard for 9 mm Parabellum ammunition is that all primers should fire when a 1.94 oz steel ball is dropped onto a firing pin from a height of 12 in., and none shall fire from a height of 3 in. The NATO standard 7.62 × 54 mm rifle ammunition uses a 3.94 oz steel ball with all firing from 16 in. and none from 3 in.

It should be noted that the sensitivity for military primers will always be less than that for the equivalent commercial primers. This is to take into account the harsher conditions and treatment accorded to military weapons and ammunition.

2.5.4 Accidental discharge of primers

Following on from the subject of primer sensitivity is the frequently mentioned possibility of cartridge cases exploding in the pocket through coming into contact with keys or change, and of cartridges exploding when dropped onto the ground. Experience and an extensive series of tests has shown this to be exceedingly unlikely.

Both rimfire and centre fire cartridges have been repeatedly thrown with great force onto their base without the slightest effect. Cartridges have been dropped down lubricated tubes in excess of 30 ft in length onto small pebbles and even firing pins, with hardly a dent on the primer.

An unusual case of accidental discharge did, however, occur where a cartridge discharged due to a very light impact on its primer. This involved a batch of ammunition which was known to have primers which were slightly softer than would normally be expected. Firing pin impressions were noticed to be particularly deep on fired ammunition and even when fresh out of the box, small dents were observed on some of the primers. These dents probably resulted from a manufacturing process whereby the finished rounds were tumbled in corn husks, or some other slightly abrasive material, to polish them.

The accidental discharge in this case happened during a range course which was being held in the midday sun with measured temperatures of over 35 °C in the shade and over 50 °C in the sun.

During the range course, the live ammunition was held base uppermost in boxes at the firer's feet and had, at the time of the incident, been baking for nearly an hour in the direct sun.

After one cylinder had been fired, the empty cartridges were tipped on to the ground straight over the unfired cartridges. Presumably, the rim of one of the fired cartridges struck the extremely hot primer of a live round and it exploded, slightly injuring the firer.

It is known that the sensitivity of the priming compound rises exponentially with temperature, and it is assumed that this, together with the softer than normal primer, caused the discharge. Whilst such a discharge should, in theory, be impossible, there is no other logical explanation for this event.

Another case of accidental discharge occurred when a fully loaded 9 mm Browning HP (high power) magazine was dropped into a large tub of live ammunition. The lip on the base plate struck a primer causing it to discharge. Not being contained, the cartridge case merely split open, causing virtually no damage to the rest of the ammunition.

2.5.5 Ignition of primers in a fire

As far as spontaneous combustion of the priming compound is concerned, the flameless ignition temperature of small arms priming compounds is generally in the region of 190–260 °C. This is considerably lower than the ignition temperature for most small arms propellants, which is in the region of 350 °C. It can be assumed, therefore, that during a fire, the first thing to spontaneously ignite will be the primer which will, in turn, ignite the propellant.

Such ignitions are virtually harmless as the soft brass case of the round and the lightly held bullet in the case mouth do not allow the pressures to build up sufficiently for the case to explode. At most, the case wall will rupture, with no more than the odd piece of brass being projected a few feet and the primer being pushed out of its pocket.

2.5.6 Brief glossary

Aluminium/magnesium	Metal in a finely divided form to act as a fuel in a priming compound.
Antimony sulfide	Chemical which acts as a fuel to prolong the flame produced in the detonation of a priming compound.
Barium nitrate	Chemical used to supply oxygen to the detonation of the priming compound.
Lead styphenate	Highly sensitive explosive component used in most modern priming compounds.
Mercury fulminate	Old explosive component, now only found in Warsaw Pact and Chinese ammunition.
NCNM	Non-corrosive, non-mercuric priming composition.
Percussion cap	A small metal cup containing the priming composition which is placed on a nipple at the rear of the barrel.
Primer cap	A small metal cup containing a priming composition which fits into a recess in the base of centre fire ammunition.
Primer cup	A small metal cup containing a priming compound for use with muzzle-loading percussion weapons.
Priming compound	A highly sensitive explosive chemical which, when struck by the firing pin or hammer of a weapon, will explode with great violence causing the flame to ignite the propellant.
Tetrazine	Highly sensitive explosive component used in modern priming compounds.

2.6 Headstamp Markings on Ammunition

2.6.1 Introduction

A *cartridge headstamp* is a mark, or series of marks impressed, or sometimes embossed, on the head of the cartridge case during its manufacture. The mark can consist of numbers, letters, trademarks, figures or any combination of these.

Systems of headstamp markings are used worldwide. They can be in any language, numbering system or can relate to any calendar.

From these impressions, one can, depending on the type of ammunition and its origin, determine the manufacturer, calibre, type, date of manufacture, batch number, case material, and so on.

This information only relates, however, to the cartridge case and does not necessarily indicate that the other components, that is, primer, bullet and propellant, were of the same origin as the case. Many cartridge case manufacturers sell their cases to small companies who load them to their own specifications, and it is not unusual to find that the bullet, cartridge case, propellant and primer all have different sources.

Occasionally, the base of the bullet may be marked to indicate its origin, and in some cases, the primer itself can be marked to show its origin as well. This will aid the identification of the separate components, but it is not nowadays a common practice.

The headstamp is also sometimes used as a medium for advertising, and a gun manufacturer, such as Holland and Holland, can have ammunition supplied with its own brand name impressed on the base. In such cases, it can be extremely difficult to find the original manufacturer of the cartridge case.

In general, however, the headstamp found on commercial ammunition will only show the manufacturer and calibre. Occasionally, other information such as bullet type, case material and priming compound, that is, 'Staynless' is also impressed on the base. It is rare for commercial ammunition to include the date of manufacture and/or batch number.

In many cases, it is possible to assign an approximate date of manufacture to commercial ammunition and sometimes its exact factory of manufacture by the design of the headstamp.

Three examples of this are:

1. Remington 0.22" long rifle ammunition, the company logo, a 'U', gives an indication of the date and country of manufacture as follows (Figure 2.17).

2. Browning ammunition was made by Amron up until January 1973, and had the word 'Browning' stamped at the 12 o'clock position. From November 1972, when the ammunition company Winchester Western started to manufacture the ammunition, 'Browning' was stamped at the 6 o'clock position.

3. From 1867 until 1911, the American company Union Metallic Cartridge Company used 'UMC' on its ammunition. After 1911, it was changed to 'Rem UMC'.

Military ammunition, on the other hand, will, with very few exceptions, always include the year of manufacture as well as the month or batch number. Other information can include case material, propellant type, bullet type, that is, tracer, armour-piercing, and so on (Figure 2.18).

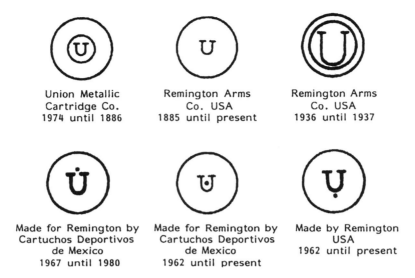

Union Metallic
Cartridge Co.
1974 until 1886

Remington Arms
Co. USA
1885 until present

Remington Arms
Co. USA
1936 until 1937

Made for Remington by
Cartuchos Deportivos
de Mexico
1967 until 1980

Made for Remington by
Cartuchos Deportivos
de Mexico
1962 until present

Made by Remington
USA
1962 until present

Figure 2.17 Codes used by Remington.

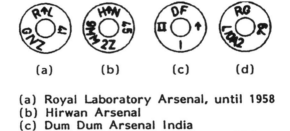

(a)   (b)   (c)   (d)

(a) **Royal Laboratory Arsenal, until 1958**
(b) **Hirwan Arsenal**
(c) **Dum Dum Arsenal India**
(d) **Radway Green Arsenal, post 1944**

Figure 2.18 Examples of British military headstamps.

Headstamps on military ammunition are usually applied in a strict pattern, rarely deviating from the official pattern. Thus, from the position of the various numbers and characters around the rim, it is often possible to source the ammunition without actually deciphering the headstamp itself.

One anomaly with respect to military headstamps is Japan. Up until 1945, all Japanese Army ammunition was bereft of markings. Only the Japanese Navy used headstamps on its ammunition. These headstamps consisted of a mixture of a Japanese ideogram and Western numerals. When deciphering these headstamps, it should be remembered that the Japanese calendar was used for the year markings; thus, the Japanese year 2600 relates to the Western year 1940. Taiwan also has its own calendar system based on 1912, the year which signalled the end of dynastic China and the formation of the Republic of China. Mexico also uses 1912 as the starting date for its headstamps, this being the year of its revolution.

One problematical area in the sourcing of ammunition arises with ammunition produced for clandestine purposes. In cases of insurgency or irregular warfare, friendly nations will often attempt to hide their part in the supply of arms and ammunition. Obviously, cartridge cases picked up after an incident are a potentially valuable source of information as to the other side's supporters (Figure 2.19).

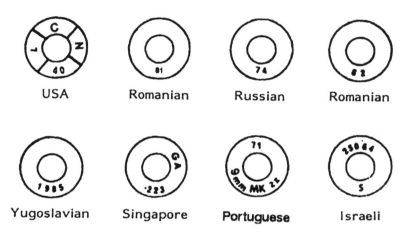

Figure 2.19 Examples of headstamp markings on clandestine ammunition.

Broadly, three methods have been used in attempts to disguise the origins of the ammunition. The most obvious is by the complete omission of the headstamp. This can, however, lead to problems in identifying the date of manufacture should a problem arise with the ammunition. It can also prove problematical for the end user in sequentially using the ammunition.

The next method is to omit all but the date, or a code identifying the date. Finally, the use of a completely false manufacturer's code can be used. It is possible, however, to penetrate the disguise by identification of the components, primer and neck lacquer or even by the style of the letters used.

Early examples include ammunition smuggled into Ireland in 1914, ammunition supplied to General Franco in the Spanish Civil War and British manufactured ammunition supplied to the Norwegian underground during World War II. More recently, the United States has supplied clandestine ammunition for use in the Bay of Pigs operation in Cuba and to the underground in Cambodia.

Probably the most prolific supply of clandestine ammunition has been the Warsaw Pact countries. Where once this was openly distributed with standard

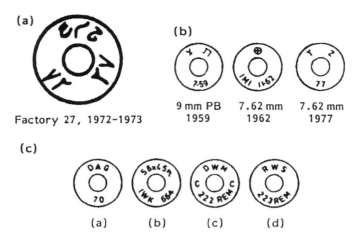

(a) Factory 27, 1972–1973

(b)
9 mm PB 1959   7.62 mm 1962   7.62 mm 1977

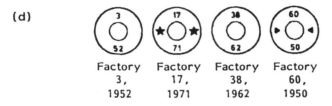

(c)

(a)   (b)   (c)   (d)

(a) Dynamit A/C 5.56 mm 1970 Military
(b) Industrie Werke Karlsruher 5.56 mm 1966 Military
(c) Deutsche Waffenu Mutionsfabriken .222 REM Commerci
(d) Rheinisch Westfalische Sprengstoff .223 Commercial

(d)

Factory 3, 1952   Factory 17, 1971   Factory 38, 1962   Factory 60, 1950

Factories 10, 30, 46, 60, 529, 541, 543, 545, 710 now all closed
Headstamps can be found on 7.62 x 25 mm, 7.62 x 39 mm and 9 mm MAK

(e)

Factory 61, 1974   Factory 81, 1964   Factory 661, 1968   Factory 71, 1965

Headstamps found on both 7.62 x 25 mm and 7.62 x 39 mm

Figure 2.20 Examples of headstamps: (a) Egypt; (b) Israel; (c) Germany; (d) USSR; (e) China.

markings, more recently, it has been turning up with either the manufacturer's mark omitted or with no markings at all.

Some general examples of headstamps from different countries follow (Figure 2.20).

Reference

Haag, L. (1995) American Lead Free 9 mm-P Cartridges. *AFTE Journal*, 27, 2.

Further Reading

Erlmeier, H.A. and Brandt, J.H. (1967) *Manual of Pistol and Revolver Cartridges*, J. Erlmeier Verlag, Wiesbaden, Germany.

Guns & Ammo Magazine *Hevi Hitter by Ralph Lermayer*

Heavi-Shot Brochure

Hogg, I.V. (1982) *The Cartridge Guide*, Arms and Armour Press, London and Melbourne.

Labbett, P. (1980) *Military Small Arms Ammunition of the World*, Arms and Armour Press, London.

Mummery, J. (1979) *The Identification of Small Arms Ammunition*, Royal Military College of Science, Shrivenham, England.

Remington Arms Catalogue

White, H.P. and Munhall, B.D. (1963) *Cartridge Headstamp Guide*, H.P. White Laboratory, Bel Air, Maryland, USA.

Wincheser Arms Catalogue

3
Ballistics

3.1 Internal, External and Terminal Ballistics

There are basically three types of ballistics, *internal, external* and *terminal*.

Internal ballistics is the study of what happens within the barrel of a weapon from the moment the firing pin hits the primer to the time the bullets exits from the barrel. It is mainly concerned with propellant pressures, acceleration of the missile whilst it is in the bore, muzzle velocity and recoil.

Esoteric considerations such as primer ignition time, primer pressure/time curves and temperature also come within the general subject matter of interior ballistics. These considerations are, however, far too specialized to be dealt with in this book.

External ballistics deals with the flight of the bullet from the muzzle of the weapon to the target. This is truly a terribly complicated subject involving parameters such as bullet shape, sectional density, atmospheric pressure and even, in larger-calibre weapons, the rotation of the earth. With the advent of powerful personal computers, this subject has, however, now come within the realms of the average person. What took hours of complex calculations and reference to books of flight time tables can now be achieved in a few moments.

Terminal ballistics deals with the behaviour of the missile once it reaches the target. This is obviously not concerned with simply piercing a paper target, but what the missile does once it encounters a material considerably denser than air. Whilst this will usually be concerned with the missile's performance and wounding capabilities in animal tissue, this could also include its performance in water, soil, brick, concrete, wood or bullet-resistant materials.

Handbook of Firearms and Ballistics: Second Edition   Brian J. Heard
© 2008 John Wiley & Sons, Ltd.

3.2 Internal Ballistics

3.2.1 Introduction

Internal ballistics is an enormous subject and one on which many books have been produced. The mathematics involved can be highly complex and once again outside of this book. It is, however, possible to give an insight to the subject by use of a few simplified equations.

When the firing pin strikes the primer, the priming compound explodes with great violence causing an extremely high temperature jet of flame to pass through the flash hole and into the propellant charge. This jet of flame, which is about 2000 °C, ignites the propellant which burns at high speed to form a large volume of gas. This high-pressure gas accelerates the bullet down the barrel and out of the muzzle.

Nitrocellulose propellant will, if ignited in an unconfined space, gently burn. If it is in a confined space, the heat and pressure built up will accelerate the rate of combustion exponentially.

In a weapon, the propellant is confined within the cartridge case, the mouth of which is closed with a bullet. The round of ammunition is then supported by the chamber walls and standing breech of the weapon. Under these conditions, the pressure build-up will continue until it is sufficient to overcome the inertia of the bullet and start its acceleration down the bore. The heavier the bullet, the greater the resistance and the higher the pressure. The higher the pressure, the greater the rate of combustion.

Cartridge case capacity.   Another factor affecting the rate of combustion is the density of the propellant load, that is, the ratio of case volume to propellant volume. The greater this ratio, that is, the larger the unfilled space in the cartridge case, the slower the initial rate of combustion.

Internal pressure.   When the propellant burns, the majority of it turns into gas, mainly comprising carbon dioxide and water vapour. At first, the gases are contained completely within the cartridge case and the pressure is exerted equally on the base of the cartridge, its walls and the base of the bullet. Once the bullet starts to move, the volume filled by the gases increases and the pressure starts to fall.

In modern propellants, this fall in pressure can be compensated to a certain extent by *moderating* the propellant grains. This moderation involves the addition of various chemicals and the surface coating of the powder grains. In some propellants, the grains are also pierced with holes. This moderation has the effect of increasing the rate of burning as the propellant is consumed. As a result of this, the internal pressure does not drop so drastically once the bullet begins to move.

The moderation of the propellant grains has to be carefully regulated to ensure that they are totally consumed just before the bullet reaches the end of the barrel. Any propellant not consumed before the bullet exits the barrel will not only result in a low efficiency rate for the cartridge but will also produce a large muzzle flash. This muzzle flash can be extremely disconcerting when firing at night as it has the effect of destroying the firer's night vision.

Recoil. This considers the forces acting on a fired weapon which cause a handgun to either gently rotate in the hand or violently bite into the palm, or a rifle to gently push against one's shoulder or produce a bone-bruising kick.

Recoil is probably one of the most misquoted subjects in the field of firearms, and a basic knowledge of the forces involved and how the vectors are calculated is a distinct asset for anyone in the field of forensic firearms examination.

During the firing of a weapon, the pressure on the inside of the cartridge case acts not only on the base of the bullet, but also on the standing breech of the weapon. It is this mechanism which causes the pistol, rifle or shotgun to recoil.

By knowing the pressure produced (from manufacturers' published figures) and the weight of the bullet, the recoil energy can be calculated. For example, the pressure in the chamber of a 0.45″ calibre self-loading pistol is 14 000 lb per sq. in. The base of a 0.45″ bullet being 0.159 sq. in., the total pressure on the base of the bullet is 2225 lb, that is, $14\,000 \times 0.159$. This means that when the pistol is fired, there is a pressure of over 1 ton pushing the bullet forwards and the gun backwards. With a rearward pressure of over 1 ton, the only thing which prevents the gun from being unfireable is that the pressure is only exerted over a fraction of a second. The duration of this pressure is dependent on the period over which the bullet is still in the barrel. Once the bullet leaves the barrel, there is no longer any pressure being exerted on its base and therefore no pressure on the base of the cartridge case.

Time of bullet in barrel. It is possible with some fairly simple mathematics to approximate the length of time the bullet will be in the barrel.

If we, once again, take the case of a 0.45″ calibre self-loading pistol with a 5 in. barrel, with a bullet velocity of 810 ft per second. If the velocity were constant it would travel 1 in. in $\frac{1}{12} \times \frac{1}{810}$ s. As the length of the barrel is 5 in., it would travel this distance in $\frac{5}{12} \times \frac{1}{810}$ s, that is, $\frac{1}{1944}$ s. The bullet does, however, start from rest and accelerate to 810 ft/s by the time it reaches the muzzle. This would give an average speed of 405 ft/s which by the same token gives a time of $\frac{1}{972}$ s or 0.00102 s. Although this figure is still only partially correct, it does give an indication as to how long the recoil pressure will be experienced.

3.2.2 Velocity

Using the example of the 0.45″ self-loading pistol once again, with a chamber pressure of 14 000 lb per square inch, the actual pressure on the base of the bullet equates to 2225 lb as the base is only 0.45″ in diameter. According to Newton's laws of motion, velocity is equal to the force, in pounds, divided by the mass. Mass is the weight of the object divided by the acceleration acting upon it due to gravity, that is, 32.17 ft/s or in round numbers 32. This is given by

$$V = \frac{FT}{M}$$

where
V is the velocity;
F is the force in pounds;
T is the time during which the force acts, and
M is the mass of the object.

Also, if the force is allowed to act through a distance rather than a given length of time, the velocity will be

$$V = \sqrt{\frac{2FS}{M}} \text{ or } V^2 = \frac{2FS}{M}$$

where
S is the length of barrel;
F is the force in pounds;
M is the mass of the missile, and
V is the velocity.

For the sake of simplicity, these calculations use the English/American measuring system for ammunition components which is 'grains'. In this system, 7000 gr are equal to 1 lb.

Thus, if we have a force of 2225 lb acting on the base of a 0.45″ bullet which weighs 230 gr along a barrel of 5″ in length. As there are 7000 gr to a pound, to bring the bullet weight to pounds, the weight must be divided by 7000 and multiplied by 32. Thus, the velocity is

$$V = \sqrt{\frac{2 \times 2225 \times 7000 \times 32 \times 5}{230 \times 12}} = \sqrt{1815390} = 1347 \text{ ft/sec}.$$

However, we know from manufacturers' published figures that the velocity of the 0.45″ calibre self-loading pistol bullet in this case is only 810 ft/s. The difference can be accounted for by the fact that the pressure is not constant for the whole length of the barrel. By the time the bullet has moved to the end of the barrel, the original case volume would have expanded to $12\frac{1}{12}$ times its original size as it now includes the internal volume of the barrel.

If the formula is transposed to calculate the pressure knowing the velocity, we arrive at an average pressure of 5100 lb per square inch. This figure is very close to that recorded using piezoelectric barrel pressure measuring equipment.

3.2.3   Recoil and muzzle lift

As mentioned earlier, the force which acts on the rear of the bullet to propel it forwards is also exerted on the base of the cartridge case to move the gun backwards. The formula for this is as mentioned before:

$$V = \frac{FT}{M}.$$

It is this force which causes the weapon to recoil. This force not only drives the gun to the rear, but because the barrel is situated above the hand, and therefore above the rotational axis of the wrist, it also rotates the gun in an upwards direction. As the bullet is travelling down the bore during the period in which the barrel is lifting, it will strike the target above the point at which the barrel was pointed when the trigger was pulled.

As was seen earlier, the actual time the bullet is in the barrel is very short, and for the worked example of a 0.45″ calibre self-loading pistol, it is only 0.00102 s. During this very short period of time, the muzzle lifts above its point of aim only a fraction of an inch. This does, however, have a pronounced effect on the striking point of the bullet as only a minute ($\frac{1}{60}$ of a degree) of barrel lift will change the impact point by 1.047 in. at 100 yd. To compensate for this, the sights of a weapon are set, or regulated, at the factory. The sights are regulated for a certain weight bullet travelling at a certain velocity. If a heavier bullet is used, the bullet will remain in the bore longer. The longer the bullet is in the bore, the more time the recoil has an effect on the hand and the greater the degree of barrel rotation. Thus, a heavier bullet will strike above the point of aim and a lighter one below. This is exactly the opposite of what common sense would indicate.

To give an example of the magnitude of barrel lift: when a standard military P14 0.303 rifle is fired with standard military ammunition, weapon recoil will cause the barrel to rise by 0.1″ between the time the trigger is pulled and the bullet leaves the barrel.

3.2.4   Theory of recoil

As seen earlier, the velocity of the bullet leaving the weapon or the velocity of the recoil of the weapon is calculated by the following formulae:

$$V = \frac{FT}{M} \text{ or } FT = VM$$

where
M is the mass of the gun or bullet;
F is the force in pounds, and
T is the time during which it acts.

During the period which this force is acting on the bullet, it is, therefore, also acting with an equal degree of force on the gun.

If the velocity of the bullet is v, the mass of the bullet m, the rearwards velocity of the gun V, the mass of the gun M and the time during which the force acts T, it therefore follows that the forward motion of the bullet will be $FT = vm$, and the backward motion of the gun will be $FT = VM$.

This also tells us that $vm = VM$, or by rearranging the equation, we have

$$V = \frac{vm}{M}.$$

In other words, the recoil velocity of the gun equals the bullet velocity times the bullet weight divided by the weight of the gun.

If, for example, we have a gun weighing 2 lb firing a 158 gr bullet at 860 ft/s and as there are 7000 gr in a pound, we have the following formula:

$$\frac{860}{2} \times \frac{158}{7000} = 9.7 \, \text{ft/sec}$$

This is the *velocity of recoil* of the weapon.

When working out the recoil velocity of the weapon, one thing is often neglected and that is the weight of propellant. This should be included in the bullet weight, as it leaves the barrel of the weapon with the bullet and does form part of the total mass of the bullet for these equations. The mass of gas does in fact have an effect greater than its weight would indicate due to the sudden expansion of the gases as they leave the confines of the weapon's bore. An approximation found to compensate for this is to multiply the weight of the propellant by one and a half.

In cartridges loaded with nitrocellulose propellants, the weight is very small and adds little to the overall figure. For cartridges loaded with black powder, however, the weight is considerably greater and the effect is quite pronounced. This illustrates why a cartridge loaded with black powder propellant will give much greater recoil energy than one with the same bullet weight and bullet velocity but loaded with nitrocellulose propellant.

3.2.5 Recoil energy

All the above is concerned with the *velocity of the gun's recoil*, which tells us very little about the actual force, or more correctly, the *energy of the recoil*.

The energy of the recoil is calculated by use of the formula

$$KE = \frac{1}{2}MV^2.$$

The kinetic energy (KE) of the recoil, or the *recoil energy*, gives us a much clearer picture of the actual forces involved.

The recoil energy of a weapon and, for that matter, the kinetic energy of a bullet are calculated in exactly the same way and are measured in foot pound (or joule in the metric system). This force can be expressed in two ways: (i) 1 ft/lb is the energy necessary to lift a 1 lb weight 1 ft off the ground or (ii) the force of 1 lb being dropped from a height of 1 ft.

If we consider the same weapon as used in the calculation for recoil velocity, that is, a 2 lb 0.38" Special calibre revolver firing a 158 gr bullet at 860 ft/s with a calculated recoil velocity of 9.7 ft/s, then we have

$$\frac{1}{2} \times \frac{2}{32.2} \times 9.7^2 = 2.9\,\text{ft/lb}.$$

As mentioned earlier, the weight of the propellant charge, multiplied by one and a half, should be added to the total weight of the bullet. The propellant charge for a 158 gr 0.38" Special calibre cartridge would be 3.6 gr, which would be $5\frac{1}{2}$ for the above equation. Substituting this into the above equation would give a final figure for the recoil energy of 3.15 ft/lb.

From the above, it can be seen that the weight of the weapon has a very great influence on the recoil energy. If the weight of the weapon is reduced to 1 lb, then the recoil velocity is 20.0 ft/s and the recoil energy is 6.3 ft/lb.

In simple terms, the recoil velocity is the factor which makes a gun unpleasant to shoot. The higher the recoil velocity, the greater the discomfort. In *1929 Textbook of Small Arms* (HMSO, 1929), the figure of 15 ft/s was given as the highest recommended recoil velocity of a rifle. Above this figure, 'gun headache' would be experienced.

The recoil energy is what gives the push to the shoulder and the muzzle lift to a handgun; it is expressed in foot pound and has the same magnitude as the kinetic energy of the bullet.

3.2.6   Methods of measuring barrel pressure

Assuming that the weapon is in good condition and that the correct type of ammunition is being used, it is the pressure produced in the barrel which ultimately decides whether the bullet will either reach the muzzle, exit from the barrel at an acceptable velocity or destroy the weapon completely.

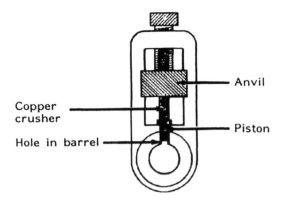

Figure 3.1 Pressure barrel.

Often weapons are received with reloaded or home-made ammunition and for safety sake, it is often necessary to determine whether the ammunition is in fact safe to fire. At other times, it is necessary to evaluate the suitability of an ammunition/weapon configuration and once again knowing the barrel pressure produced could be advantageous.

A knowledge of the basic facts concerning how the pressure is measured and what the figures mean is therefore a useful adjunct in this field.

The measurement of maximum chamber pressure is carried out with a 'pressure gun'. This is a very strongly built action and barrel with a hole drilled into the top of the chamber. Clamped over this hole is a closed tube with a free-moving piston (Figure 3.1).

Between this piston and the closed end of the tube is inserted a small disc of metal of a known and uniform hardness. On firing the cartridge, the pressure produced forces the piston up against the metal disc which is crushed against the closed end of the tube. Crushing the metal disc in this way reduces its thickness by a measurable amount. By subjecting similar discs to known pressures, it is possible to calculate the pressure of any cartridge by measuring the compression of the disc.

As no single metal will give consistent results over a wide range of pressures, discs made of lead and copper are used. The lead discs are for lower-pressure cartridges and the copper discs for cartridges producing higher pressures.

As the discs only give accurate pressure figures over the mid part of their range, they cannot be accurately related to actual pressures in pounds per square inch or kilograms per square centimetre. As a result of this, the results are referred to as 'lead or copper units of pressure'.

In more modern pressure guns, the metal disc is replaced by a small quartz crystal. This crystal will, when subjected to pressure, produce a tiny quantity of electricity which can be directly related, with great accuracy, to the pressure exerted upon it. These are called 'piezoelectric' pressure guns. The pressures

Table 3.1 Some illustrative chamber pressure figures for modern ammunition.

Cartridge	Velocity (ft/s)	Bullet weight (gr)	Pressure (psi)
0.22″ LR	1200	40	15 300
0.32″ ACP	960	71	21 700
0.38″ Special	650	148	21 700
9 mm PB	1200	125	35 500
0.45″ ACP	855	234	14 000
5.56 mm M16	3250	56	52 000
12B Shotgun			
2.5″ Cartridge	1200	490	10 000

measured with these guns are referred to in pounds per square inch or kilograms per square centimetre and are absolute figures (Table 3.1).

3.3 External Ballistics

3.3.1 Introduction

External ballistics is the study of the missile's flight from when it leaves the muzzle until it strikes the target. It is an extremely complicated subject and before the advent of powerful desktop computers, the calculations were laborious and time consuming, requiring the use of many mathematical tables. With modern computers and ballistic programmes, it is now possible to calculate the most complex trajectory equations with just a few key strokes.

The two main factors which affect the performance of a bullet on leaving the barrel are air resistance on its nose and the effect of the gravitational pull of the earth. As a result of these forces, the bullet will, on leaving the barrel, describe a downward curved path or trajectory.

The exact shape of this trajectory can be predetermined by knowing:

- the gravitational effect;
- the muzzle velocity;
- the angle of elevation of the barrel;
- the sectional density of the bullet;
- the bullet shape.

The rate of fall can easily determined by using the formula

$$h = \frac{1}{2}gt^2$$

where

h = drop of missile;
g = gravity which is 32.1725 ft per second per second;
t = time in seconds.

Thus, a bullet would have dropped 1 ft below the line of flight in 0.25 s of flight (i.e. $h = \frac{1}{2} \times 32.17 \times 0.25 \times 0.25$) and 4 ft in half a second and 16 ft in 1 s.

The drop is, of course, totally independent of the velocity and weight of the bullet. All bullets, no matter whether they are travelling at 200 or 4000 ft/s will drop 4 ft in one half a second of flight. The only difference being that the 4000 ft/s bullet travels much further in half a second than the bullet which is only going at a speed of 200 ft/s.

It is obvious, however, that the bullet does not continue at the same velocity throughout its flight. Air pressure on the nose of the bullet causes resistance which gradually reduces its velocity.

The difference in air resistance is referred to in ballistics as the *form factor* and is given the symbol i. Some examples of form factor are given in Table 3.2.

Another important factor is the proportion of the missile's diameter to its weight. The weight is what gives the bullet its 'carrying power', whilst the cross-sectional area is what causes the air resistance. This is called the sectional density of the bullet and is the weight divided by the retarding area which is the square of the diameter.

Thus, the sectional density of a bullet is

$$\frac{\text{weight}}{\text{diameter}^2}$$

If we take as an example a 0.38″ Special 158 gr bullet which has a diameter of 0.357″ (see section on ammunition nomenclature), the sectional density is

$$\frac{158\,\text{gr}}{0.357\,\text{in.} \times 0.357\,\text{in.}} = 1239\,\text{gr}/\text{in.}^2$$

Table 3.2 Examples of various form factors.

Missile profile	Form factor
Very sharp profile	0.60
Moderately sharp profile	0.70
Moderately sharp profile with a small flat on nose	0.85
Moderately blunt profile	1.00
Very blunt profile	1.20
Wadcutter type profile	1.3

For more accuracy: subtract 0.06 for a boat tail bullet; add 0.20 for large flat on nose.

A much lighter, 125 gr bullet of the same calibre will give a sectional density of

$$\frac{125\,gr}{0.357\,in. \times 0.357\,in.} = 980\,gr/in.^2$$

As can be seen, the sectional density of the lighter bullet is much lower, indicating a lower carrying power.

3.3.2 Ballistic coefficient

The sectional density is not the only factor affecting the retardation (the degree of velocity loss due to the air) of a bullet, as the shape also plays a very large part.

If the form factor i is inserted into the formula, the resulting figure is called the 'ballistic coefficient' of the missile and is the proportion of the bullet's diameter to its weight.

The ballistic coefficient C is calculated by using the formula

$$C = \frac{w}{id^2}$$

where
C = ballistic coefficient;
w = weight of bullet;
i = form factor;
d = diameter of the bullet.

Table 3.3 The ballistic coefficients of various types of ammunition.

Calibre	Brand	Bullet weight (grains)	Bullet type	Ballistic coefficient
.17 Rem	R	25	P–HP	0.151
.223 Rem	R	55	P–SP	0.201
.30 Carbine	R	110	R–SP	0.166
.308 Win	W	180	S–SP	0.248
.308 Win	W	150	P–SP	0.314
.30-06	F	165	P–BT	0.47
.38 Spl	W	158	R–LD	0.149
.38 Spl	R	158	SWC	0.146
.357 Mag	W	110	F–HP	0.099
.357 Mag	F	158	F–SP	0.145
.44 Mag	R	240	SWC	0.143
.44 Mag	F	240	F–HP	0.172
.45 ACP	F	185	F–HP	0.148
.45 ACP	R	230	R–FJ	0.158

Brand: R Remington, W Winchester, F Federal
Type: P Pointed, S Semi-pointed, R Round nosed, F Flat nosed, SWC Semi-wadcutter, HP Hollow point, SP Soft point, FJ Full jacket, BT Boat tail, LD Lead

The form factor is basically a measure of how streamlined a bullet is. For example, a wadcutter bullet will have a form factor of about 2.0, and a sleek, highly streamlined, pointed bullet will have a form factor of 0.55. These figures are published by the various ammunition manufacturers.

Thus, the larger the ballistic coefficient, the better the bullet will retain its velocity and the lower the bullet drop for any given distance.

3.3.3   Maximum range of missiles

The instant the missile leaves the barrel of a weapon, gravity starts to act and it will accelerate towards the ground at a speed of 32.17 ft/sec/sec. The maximum range which a missile will obtain when fired is dependent upon the elevation of the barrel, the bullet shape and the initial velocity.

The computations to accurately determine the external ballistics of a missile are exceedingly complicated and outside the scope of this book. There are, however, a few approximations and rough calculations which will give figures of sufficient accuracy for use in normal crime scene examinations.

3.3.4   Angle of elevation of the barrel

With small arms bullets, it is found that the maximum range is attained at an elevation of about 29°. From 29° to 35°, there is little increase in range. The angle of elevation at which maximum range is obtained is called the *critical angle*.

At elevations in excess of 35°, the maximum range attained begins to decrease.

This is clearly illustrated in the following study which utilized a Swiss boat tailed bullet of 0.30 calibre, weighing 174 gr with a ballistic coefficient of 0.284 and a muzzle velocity of 2600 fps (Table 3.4).

Table 3.4 Range table for Swiss .30″ calibre boat tailed bullet.

Elevation (degree)	Range (yd)	Flight time (s)	Final velocity (fps)	Angle of fall (degree)
5	2464	7.56	588	11.25
10	3273	12.65	447	24.1
20	4097	20.95	390	47.68
30	4413	27.91	405	62.40
34	4455	30.2	416	66.15
35	4456	31.06	417	67.4
40	4413	34.01	429	71.35

The table shows that the bullet attains its maximum range of 4457 yd at an angle of departure of a little over 34°. At angles greater than this, the range decreases. A full study of this subject can be found in the *British Textbook of Small Arms* (HMSO, 1929).

Formula for calculating the maximum range of bullets. There is no simple and accurate way of determining the maximum range of a bullet.

The use of ballistics tables or ballistics software based on the Siacci/Mayevski G1 drag model, introduced in 1881, is usually considered the most appropriate method for general use.

A more modern alternative is probably that presented in 1980 by Prof. Arthur J. Peisa (Peisa, 1991).

These are, however, far too specialized to delve into within this book.

A short table showing the maximum ranges of various rounds follows (Table 3.5).

Table 3.5 Maximum range for various rounds.

Cartridge	Bullet weight (gr)	Muzzle velocity (ft/s)	Maximum range (yd)
0.22″ LR	40	1145	1500
0.22″ HV LR	40	1335	1565
0.380 ACP	95	970	1089
0.38″ Spl	148	770	1700
0.38″ Spl + P	158	890	2150
0.357″ Magnum	158	1235	2350
9 mm PB	125	1120	1900
0.40 S&W	180	1000	1800
0.44″ Magnum	240	1390	2500
0.45 ACP	234	820	1640
0.223″ Remington	55 Boat-tailed bullet	3240	3875
0.30 M1 Carbine	110	1900	2200
0.30-30	170	2220	2490
0.30-06 Rifle	180 Flat-base bullet	2700	4100
0.30-06 Rifle	180 Boat-tailed bullet	2700	5700
0.300 Win Mag	200	2700	5390
0.30-40 Krag	220	2000	4050
0.308 Win (7.62 NATO)	175 (BT)	2600	4800
0.375 H&H	270	2695	3370
0.50 Browning AP	718	2840	775
12-Bore shotgun ball	583	1200	1420
16-Bore shotgun ball	437	1200	1340
20-Bore shotgun ball	350	1200	1200
0.410″ Shotgun ball	104	1200	850
00 Buck	54	1200	726
1 Buck	40	1200	660
No. 2 shot	4.86	1200	330

Table 3.5 Continued

Cartridge	Bullet weight (gr)	Muzzle velocity (ft/s)	Maximum range (yd)
No. 3 shot	4.00	1200	308
No. 4 shot	3.24	1200	286
No. 5 shot	2.58	1200	264
No. 6 shot	1.95	1200	242
No. $7\frac{1}{2}$ shot	1.25	1200	209
No. 8 shot	1.07	1200	198
No. 9 shot	0.75	1200	176

3.3.5 What is the maximum altitude that a bullet will attain?

As with many other subjects that one comes across in forensic firearms examinations, this has little real relevance in everyday case examinations. There was an occasion, however, when a commercial airliner which had been flying in the air space above Northern Ireland was found, on landing, to have a 7.62 mm calibre hole in one side of the tailfin. Unfortunately, the airline concerned was unwilling to have the tailfin dismantled and taken apart due to the costs involved, and it was not possible to determine the exact calibre of weapon used.

The question was, therefore, what weapon could have fired a bullet with sufficient velocity to reach the altitude of 9000 ft at which the airliner was flying.

In 1909, Major Hardcastle fired a number of rounds vertically into the air and shortly after World War I, Julian S. Hatcher carried out a similar set of experiments using the 30-06 rifle round.

A very simple rule of thumb to calculate the maximum altitude that a bullet will reach is that it will be approximately $\frac{2}{3}$ the maximum horizontal range.

The results of some actual test firings are tabulated as follows (Table 3.6):

The above table indicates, from the limited data available, that only the 30-06 or 0.303 rounds would have sufficient initial velocity to reach an airliner flying at 9000 feet. There are, however, a vast number of hunting cartridges which would be equally capable of reaching this altitude.

Terminal velocity. The terminal velocity of a missile is obviously much more relevant to the investigator as any bullet fired vertically into the air will come down with potential wounding capability. The ability to calculate the actual terminal velocity of a missile could, therefore, be critical to the investigation.

When any object falls through the atmosphere, eventually, the retarding force of drag will balance with gravity, and the object's terminal velocity will be reached. It is easy to calculate this terminal velocity if the drag coefficient is known.

When the forces are balanced,

$$Mm_2 v_2 = Mg$$

Table 3.6 Maximum altitude attained by various rounds.

Calibre	Bullet weight (gr)	Velocity (fps)	Maximum height (ft)
0.22 LR	40	1257	3868
0.25 ACP	50	751	2287
0.44 Mag	240	1280	4518
5.56 mm. SS109	50	3200	2650
7.62 NATO	150	2756	7874
30-06 M2	150	2851	9331
0.303	175	2785	9420
30-06	180	2400	10 105
12B	No. 2 shot (US)	1312	330
12B	No. 4 (US)	1312	286
12B	No. 6 (US)	1312	242
12B	No. $7\frac{1}{2}$ (US)	1312	209
12B	No. 8 (US)	1312	198

where
M = mass of object;
m_2 = ballistic coeficient;
g = gravity;
v = velocity.

The mass of the bullet (M) drops out of the equation, which at first may seem strange, since mass clearly should have an effect on terminal velocity. Actually, the ballistic coeficient itself depends on mass (among several other things, e.g. bullet shape, air density and cross-sectional area), so M dropping out of the above equation is merely illusionary.

Because air resistance depends largely on surface area whilst weight depends on volume, larger bullets will drop faster than smaller bullets.

Small bullets will start to tumble, and come down relatively slowly, whereas larger bullets can maintain their stabilizing rotation and come down much faster.

Some examples of the terminal velocity of everyday articles follow:

$$\text{Raindrop} = 15\,\text{miles/h} = 22\,\text{fps}$$

$$\text{Baseball} = 95\,\text{miles/h} = 139\,\text{fps}$$

$$\text{Golf ball} = 90\,\text{miles/h} = 131\,\text{fps}$$

These figures are well within the penetration limit for skin showing that a falling bullet does have the potential to wound (Table 3.7).

Table 3.7 The terminal velocity of various rounds.

Calibre	Bullet Weight (gr)	Initial velocity (ft/s)	Terminal velocity (ft/s)
0.22 LR	40	1257	197
0.44 Magnum	240	1280	250
30-06	150	2756	325

Other factors affecting maximum range.   Bullet shape also has a pronounced effect; with sharply pointed bullets and those with a streamlined base (boat-tailed) having a far greater range than a round ball. As can be reasonably expected, the higher the velocity, the greater the range.

Journee's formula and the ballistics of shotgun pellets and round balls.   The formula most often quoted for maximum range of shot is known as Journee's Formula, which states simply that the maximum range in yards is equal to 2200 times the diameter of the shot in inches. Thus, a no. 7 shot, which is 0.10″ in diameter, should fly 2200 × 0.10″ or 220 yd. This formula is so simple that it is sometimes dismissed as too crude to be useful.

It should be noted that this only relates to shotgun ammunition and round balls and has no relevance at all to conventional bullets.

The work of Gen. Journee, a French officer, was actually much more sophisticated than his simple formula for maximum range would seem to imply. In experiments that he began in 1888, Journee actually measured the times of flight of shot, fired from shotguns, at various ranges from about 3–65 yd. From these observations, he deduced the aerodynamic properties of small shot with surprising accuracy and used these aerodynamic data to calculate trajectories.

Considering the relatively primitive instrumentation then available, Journee's work was quite remarkable. His omission of the muzzle velocity in his formula for maximum range was not a matter of ignorance of its effect, but recognition that it makes no important difference, within the practicable levels of shot shell velocities, as can be seen in Table 3.8.

The ballistic properties of large spherical projectiles were also studied intensively in the years before the twentieth century, because cannon in those days were mostly smooth-bores, firing round shot and shell.

Table 3.8 Maximum range of shot vs muzzle velocity for various shot sizes.

	Maximum range (yd)		
Shot size	MV = 1200 ft/s	MV = 1500 ft/s	MV = 2400 ft/s
$7\frac{1}{2}$	210	219	236
2	303	317	343
00 Buck	561	591	650

Accurate artillery fire is an important factor in winning wars, and a knowledge of exterior ballistics is essential to the science of gunnery. The aerodynamics of cannon balls was, therefore, a matter of national importance, and it received the attention of such distinguished scientists and engineers as Benjamin Robins, Sir Isaac Newton and Professor Bashforth in England, Mayevski in Russia, Didion in France, Col. Ingalls in the United States, and many others.

Later investigators in the US Army Ballistics Research Laboratories and elsewhere have extended the base of information by measuring the aerodynamic drag characteristics of smaller spheres, using more modern methods and equipment. A technical report prepared in 1979 by Donald G. Miller in the Lawrence Livermore Laboratory of the University of California brought together much of the information from previous experiments on the drag of spheres.

Miller's report contains information from which the trajectories of small spherical projectiles can be computed accurately by the methods commonly used for other types of small arms projectiles.

Unfortunately, the modern experimental data on spheres does not include those as small as birdshot. The Livermore Laboratory report deals specifically with spheres from 1.0″ down to 0.3″ in diameter, the smallest being the size of no. 1 buckshot.

It is known that cannon balls from 2 to 8″ in diameter, fired in earlier experiments, do not have quite the same aerodynamic properties as small spheres, especially at velocities below the speed of sound. No great difference is found, however, in the aerodynamics of spheres between 1.0 and 0.3″ in diameter, and it is probably not greatly in error to apply the same characteristics to smaller shot.

Table 3.9 includes the maximum ranges for various lead shot sizes, computed by Journee's Formula.

A muzzle velocity of 1200 fps was assumed for all shot sizes to afford a direct comparison with shots of different sizes. As can be seen in Table 3.8, the exact muzzle velocity makes little difference in the maximum range.

Table 3.9 Maximum range and striking velocity for various sizes of lead shot.

Shot size (lead shot)	Diameter (in.)	Maximum range	Striking velocity (ft/s)
12	0.050	110	63
9	0.080	176	79
8	0.090	198	82
$7\frac{1}{2}$	0.095	209	85
6	0.110	242	89
5	0.120	264	94
4	0.130	286	96
2	0.150	330	99
BB	0.180	396	107
4 Buck	0.240	528	125
1 Buck	0.300	660	135
00 Buck	0.330	726	139

Table 3.10 Terminal velocity of various sizes of shot
fired at an elevation of 22°.

Shot size	Return velocity (ft/s)
12	63
9	79
8	83
$7\frac{1}{2}$	85
6	91
5	95
4	98
2	105
BB	115
No. 4 buckshot	132
No. 1 buckshot	147
No. 00 buckshot	154

Table 3.8 illustrates that no great error is introduced by neglecting the effect of muzzle velocity on the maximum range of small shot. This results from the poor ballistic shape of spheres which causes the aerodynamic drag to be very high at supersonic velocities. However, small shots soon drop to the velocity of sound, irrespective of the velocity at which they are launched.

For example, a no. $7\frac{1}{2}$ shot fired at a muzzle velocity of 2400 fps, twice that of a normal target load, would have its velocity reduced to 1120 fps, the speed of sound, within about the first 26 yd of flight. Doubling the velocity would increase the maximum range by only about 26 yd.

Table 3.10 shows the remaining velocity for no. 6 shot at its maximum range of 237 yd, achieved at a firing elevation of 22°.

For all shots from No. 12 up to 00 buckshot, the maximum range is achieved at firing elevations of about 20°–25°. It is important to note, however, that a firing elevation of only 10° produces nearly 90% of maximum range.

Whilst the striking velocity of about 80 fps for these small shots would not be fatal in itself, a pellet in the eye could cause serious injury from which death could result. In the case of no. 2 or BB shot, the maximum range exceeds 300 yd and the striking velocity is about 100 fps. This would produce a much more serious injury.

Many shooters want to know the velocity of shot returning to earth after it has been fired upward at very steep angles. The answer is that the returning velocities are not much different from those shown in Table 3.9 for shot fired at its maximum horizontal range.

This is illustrated by Table 3.11, which shows the returning velocity of shot fired vertically upward.

There is, for any body falling through the atmosphere, some velocity at which the force of aerodynamic drag equals the weight of the body. When that velocity is reached, the body ceases to accelerate under the influence of gravity and falls

Table 3.11 Returning velocity of various sizes of shot fired vertically upwards.

Firing elevation (degrees)	Distance to impact (ft)	Angle of fall (degrees)	Time of flight (s)	Impact velocity (ft/s)
0	0	0	0	1200
1	119	2.6	0.75	224
5	187	18.8	2.28	100
10	212	37.8	3.53	83
15	231	51.1	4.48	82
20	236	59.5	5.23	89
25	236	64.8	5.82	92
30	231	69.0	0.27	95
35	222	71.2	6.63	97
40	209	73.0	6.78	97
45	193	74.0	6.84	96

All figures are for no. 6 shot fired at a velocity of 1200 ft/s.

at constant velocity, sometimes called the 'terminal velocity of return', regardless of how far the body falls.

It should also be mentioned that other factors not considered in the calculations can affect the maximum range of shot.

A strong wind could, since the time of flight is several seconds, materially affect the maximum horizontal range.

Deformation of the individual pellets will generally shorten the maximum range.

It is also possible for several pellets to be fused together if hot propellant gases leak past the obturating wad into the shot charge. This is far less likely now, due to efficient plastic obturating wads, than it was with felt and card wads. However, when this does happen, the clusters of shot can travel considerably farther than individual pellets in the charge.

Maximum effective range. As can be seen from the chapter on Bullet Performance and 'Wounding Capabilities', the amount of energy needed to be 'effective' on a given target is an extremely difficult thing to quantify.

The 'maximum effective range' is probably even more difficult to quantify due to the number of variables which come into play, that is, bullet weight, bullet design, velocity, bullet diameter, bullet placement, weapon accuracy, and so on. Each and every situation must, therefore, be taken on its own merit.

It has been stated that the 'maximum effective range is the greatest distance that a weapon may be expected to fire accurately and inflict casualties or damage'.

Another source, somewhat nebulously, states it is 'the range at which a competent and trained individual has the ability to hit the target sixty to 80% of the time'.

The US Military states 'the maximum effective range is the maximum range within which a weapon is effective against its intended target,' and calls for 'a delivery of between 35 and 270 ft/lbs to be effective'. A somewhat rather large spread of values.

To complicate matters further, the US Army defines the maximum effective range of a 0.308 as 800 m. The US Marine Corps defines the effective range as 1000 m. The US Army also states that bullets are no longer effective once they become subsonic, which happens at around 1000 m with a 0.308. Why this velocity is chosen is not stated.

According to tests undertaken by Browning at the beginning of the century and recently by L.C. Haag, 'the bullet velocity required for skin penetration is between 147 and 196 ft/sec which is within the velocity range of falling bullets.'

This wide range of opinions is indicative of the difference in specifications and ideas on the subject.

It could be considered, and in fact English law takes this opinion, that any missile with sufficient velocity to penetrate skin is capable of inflicting a potentially lethal wound. Thus, virtually any missile at its extreme range could be considered as 'effective against the target'.

Of course, skin penetration is not required in order to cause serious or fatal injury; a serious bruise on an elderly person could cause death by shock alone.

Everyone has his or her own opinion as to the maximum effective range of a cartridge and, for illustrative purposes only, a list of published figures from various sources follows (Table 3.12).

Use of sight to compensate for bullet drop. To compensate for the bullet drop due to gravity, the sights are raised to give the barrel sufficient elevation that the bullet will strike the target at a set distance. For handguns, this is generally 10 yd; for a 0.22″ rifle, 25 yd and for full-bore rifles, generally 200 yd (Figure 3.2).

Table 3.12 Published figures giving 'maximum effective range' for various cartridges.

Cartridge	Maximum effective range
9 mm. PB	<230 ft
0.45 ACP	<164 ft
5.56 × 45 mm	<1800 ft
7.62 × 51 mm (Rifle)	<2700 f
7.6 × 51 mm (M60 GPMG)	<3600 ft
7.62 × 54 mm. R	<3300
0.300 Winchester Magnum	<3950 ft
0.338 Lapua Magnum	<5248 ft
0.50 BMG/12.7 × 107 mm	<6550 ft
14.5 × 114 mm	<6232 ft

GPMG, General purpose machine gun, PB, Parabellum, ACP, Automatic colt pistol.

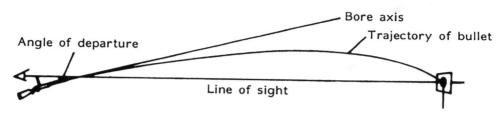

Figure 3.2 Diagram showing flight of bullet.

With the rear sight so elevated, the sight line would be parallel to the ground and the sight line along the barrel axis considerably elevated above the target. Thus, the bullet leaves the barrel below the sight line but along the barrel axis. At some point from the barrel, it passes through the sight axis line, describes a trajectory between the barrel axis and sight line eventually striking the target at the point of aim.

Other influencing factors. In addition to air resistance and gravity, there are other forces which influence the flight of the bullet.

Wind will cause the bullet to drift with it in proportion to the wind direction and velocity.

Thus, a wind blowing from the right of the bullet will cause it to drift to the left. Rear winds will have an increasing effect on the velocity and nose winds a decreasing effect. The amount of wind drift, when striking the bullet at 90°, can be calculated by the following:

$$D = \left(T - \frac{R}{V}\right)W$$

where
D = deflection of bullet by wind;
R = range;
V = muzzle velocity;
T = time of flight;
W = cross wind speed.

Drift is caused by the rifling of the bullet. This is a result of the gyrostatic properties of the rifling-induced spin of a bullet. This effect gives bullets with a right-hand spin a drift to the right and left-hand spinning bullets a drift to the left. It is hardly of any significance in rifles and virtually none at all in handguns.

With a 0.303″ rifle, the drift will be approximately 13 in. to the right at a range of 1000 yd.

Yaw is something which only has real relevance to rifle ammunition. This is due to a slight destabilization of the bullet as it leaves the barrel and is probably the result of excessive spin on the bullet. This causes the bullet to describe an air spiral whilst at the same time having a spin round its own tail axis. At close ranges, this results in a larger target group than would be expected. As the range becomes greater, the effect disappears and the target groups return to their expected dimensions. The effect is very similar to that of a spinning top which wobbles slightly before settling down into a stable spinning condition.

3.3.6   Muzzle energy

Muzzle energy is probably the most important property when dealing with ballistics. This figure gives an indication of the overall power of the bullet as it leaves the barrel and, as a result, an indication as to its wounding potential. Naturally, many other factors have to be taken into consideration when dealing with wound ballistics, but these will be dealt with at a later stage.

Muzzle energy is the potential work energy possessed by the missile as it exits the muzzle. It is quoted in terms of kinetic energy, which is the ability to do work. The formula for calculating the muzzle energy of a missile is

$$KE = \frac{1}{2} MV^2,$$

where
KE = kinetic energy;
M = mass of the projectile;
V = velocity of the projectile.

If using imperial measurements. it is usually quoted in foot pound (ft/lb) with the weight of the projectile being measured in grains (7000 gr = 1 lb) and the velocity in feet per second.

When the appropriate figure for gravity (32.174) is placed into the formula, it becomes

$$KE\,(ft\,lb) = \frac{MV^2}{2 \times 32.174 \times 7,000}.$$

If working in the SI (Système International d'Unités) system, the kinetic energy is quoted in joule with the mass of the bullet in kilograms and the velocity in metres per second. The equation then becomes

$$KE\,(J) = \frac{MV^2}{2}.$$

The elimination of g in the SI system occurs simply because the two systems have different size relationships between their physical units.

3.3.7 Momentum

The most important property of momentum, as far as ballistics is concerned, is that it is conserved in collisions, that is, if two or more objects collide, the total of their momenta is the same after collision as it was before. The importance of this will be seen in the next section on *terminal ballistics*.

Momentum is the quantity of motion of a missile and is calculated by the formula

$$\text{Momentum} = M \times V,$$

where Momentum is expressed in pounds feet per second (lb ft/s) or, in the SI system, kilogram metres per second (kg m/s)
M = mass of projectile;
V = Velocity

3.3.8 Brief glossary

Angle of elevation	Angle between the axis of the barrel and the baseline.
Baseline	Straight line connecting the muzzle of the weapon to the target.
Drift – rifling	Result of the gyrostatic properties of the rifling-induced spin of a bullet, which gives bullets with a right-hand spin a drift to the right and left-hand spinning bullets a drift to the left.
Drift – wind	Bullet drift due to effect of wind direction and velocity.
	A wind blowing from the right of the bullet will cause it to drift to the left. Rear winds will have an increasing effect on the velocity and nose winds a decreasing effect.
Extreme range	Distance obtained by the bullet when a weapon is fired with the barrel elevated to its optimum angle. This angle is usually between 29° and 35°.
Line of aim	Straight line connecting the rear sight, the front sight and the point of aim on the target.
Mid-range trajectory height	Vertical distance from the baseline to the trajectory curve at mid-range.
Momentum kinetic energy	Is the quantity of motion of a moving body. Generally expressed in joule or foot pound.

Muzzle energy	The kinetic energy of the missile as it leaves the muzzle.
Point-blank range	Range over which the trajectory of a bullet is so flat that no allowance, for practical purposes, is necessary to allow for bullet drop.
Range	Distance measured along the line of aim.
Trajectory	Curved path of the bullet from the muzzle to the strike point on the target.
Yaw	Over-stabilization of the bullet as it leaves the muzzle resulting in the bullet describing an air spiral whilst at the same time having a spin round its own tail axis.
Zero of a weapon	Range at which the sight setting will cause the bullet to strike the aimed point.

3.4   Terminal Ballistics

3.4.1   Introduction

Terminal ballistics is the study of missile penetration in solids and liquids. It can be subdivided into *penetration potential,* which is the capability of a missile to penetrate various materials and *wound ballistics,* which is the effect the missile has on living tissue.

The misinformation surrounding these two subjects is staggering. It is therefore extremely important to have an overview of the main concepts surrounding these topics and a basic understanding of the mechanisms involved.

3.4.2   Penetration potential

The penetration of various materials can be of great assistance in the investigation of shooting incidents. It is also of considerable general interest if for no other reason than to show how often the movie makers and novel writers make appalling blunders.

In the past, one of the standard tests performed to assess bullet and cartridge performance was the penetration of pine boards of various thicknesses. This, as with any other type of penetration test, is plagued with inaccuracies.

Many factors, including the moisture content, knot content, tree age and even the separation of the boards, can give rise to highly variable results. Other than for general interest, this type of test is of little use in the scientific examination of firearms-related situations.

For the sake of interest, some indicators of the penetrative powers of various types of ammunition follow:

- 0.22″ Lead air gun pellet requires a minimum of 250 ft/s velocity to penetrate fresh human skin.

- 0.177″ Lead air gun pellet requires a minimum of 300 ft/s velocity to penetrate fresh human skin.

- 0.22″ Lead air gun pellet at 450 ft/s will make a hole in, but not penetrate $\frac{1}{4}$″ plate glass.

- 0.22″ Lead air gun pellet at 600 ft/s will penetrate $\frac{1}{4}$″ plate glass.

- Steel BB (0.170″ ball bearing) at 200 ft/s will make a hole, but will not penetrate $\frac{1}{4}$″ plate glass.

- Steel BB or 0.177″ lead pellet at 200 ft/s will detach part of the coloured portion (iris) of a human eye leaving what appears to be a second pupil.

- Steel BB or 0.177″ lead pellet at 450 ft/s will burst a human eye.

- 0.177″ Steel air gun dart will penetrate to shank, in skin, at 120 ft/s.

- 158 gr 0.38″ Special plain lead bullet will generally not penetrate the outside skin of a car body.

- 158 gr 0.357″ Magnum semi-jacketed bullet will penetrate outside skin of car door and sometimes just penetrate the inside skin.

- 125 gr 9 mm PB fully jacketed bullet will generally penetrate both skins of a car door.

- 158 gr 0.38″ Special plain lead bullet will only penetrate one side of a human skull.

- 158 gr 0.38″ Special plain lead bullet will generally not exit from a human body.

- 158 gr 0.38″ Special + P and 0.357″ Magnum semi-jacketed bullets will penetrate both sides of a human skull.

- 0.38″ Special + P, 158 gr non-expanding bullet will, unless it strikes a bone, pass straight through a human body.

Virtually all calibres (excepting air weapons) will penetrate the tread or side wall of a motor vehicle tyre.

Penetration of $\frac{7}{8}$″ pine boards for various pistol calibres:

0.22″ LR	five boards
0.32″ ACP	five boards
0.38″ S&W revolver	five boards
0.38″ Special	seven boards
9 mm PB pistol	nine boards
0.45″ ACP	seven boards

Illustrative penetration capabilities of a 30-06 full-jacketed rifle bullet at a velocity of 2700 ft/s and at a range of 200 yd:

$\frac{1}{4}''$ of armour plate

7″ of gravel

4.5″ of brick

4″ of concrete

32″ of oak wood

6.5″ of dry sand

7″ of moist sand

26″ of loam

24″ of clay

19″ of loose earth

60″ of 1″ pine boards

3.4.3   General wound ballistic concepts

There are three concepts generally held by most as to the effect of a bullet striking a human being. The first is that the bullet 'drills' its way through leaving a small entry and an equally small exit hole. The second is that the bullet leaves a small entry hole and an enormous exit hole. The third is that when someone is shot by anything other than an air rifle, the impact is enough to lift the person off his feet and send him flying through the air. Basically, all three concepts are incorrect in one way or another.

Firstly, as a bullet passes through human tissue, it imparts some or all of its kinetic energy to the surrounding tissue (Figure 3.3). The energy so supplied

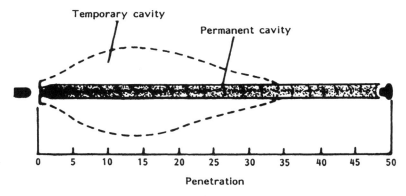

Figure 3.3 Diagram showing temporary and permanent cavities.

throws the tissue away from the bullet's path in a radial manner leaving a temporary wound cavity much larger than the diameter of the bullet. The temporary nature of this cavity results from the natural elasticity of animal tissue (French, 1962), which allows it to regain its original structure after the bullet has passed. There is also a permanent cavity which results from the destruction of tissue caused by the bullet itself. This permanent cavity is dependent on the cross-sectional area of the bullet and any secondary missiles which may be produced from the break up of the bullet during its passage.

The temporary cavity has a very short life span and is followed by a number of aftershocks decreasing in severity. The final, permanent cavity may be many times greater than the diameter of the missile, but it is also many times smaller than the temporary cavity. Unlike the temporary cavity, where the tissue is merely being thrown away from the wound track and no permanent damage is being caused to the tissue, the permanent cavity is caused by the actual destruction of the tissue by the passage of the bullet.

The dimensions of this temporary cavity are dependent upon the shape, weight, size and velocity of the missile and the elasticity of surrounding structures.

With extremely high-velocity missiles, in excess of 3000 ft/s, there is an explosive movement of the tissue away from the wound track. This results in enormous temporary cavities as well as extensive fracturing to bones and damage to veins and arteries in the immediate vicinity. In addition, there is often a back splash of tissue out of the entry hole giving the impression of an exit wound.

The second misconception, that the entry hole is always small and the exit hole large, is a major factor when interpretation of close range or suicide wounds is called for.

When dealing with high-power handgun ammunition firing hollow-point ammunition, it is often the case that the entry hole is smaller than the exit hole. Tissue entering the hollow-point cavity causes the bullet to expand; in some cases, this can increase the surface contact area of the bullet by up to 200%. Not only does this increased surface area enable the missile to transmit more of its energy to the target, but it also increases the possibility of the bullet damaging a vital organ or blood vessel due to the much larger permanent cavity of the wound track. This expansion of the hollow-point bullet within the tissue will, if the bullet does exit from the body, give rise to an exit hole considerably larger than the entry hole.

Expansion of a hollow-point bullet in soft tissue does not appear to be dependent upon its calibre. It does, however, generally require a velocity in excess of 900 ft/s for this to happen. At velocities below this, the bullet will not, unless it hits bone, expand at all.

Another factor influencing the expansion of hollow-point bullets is bullet yaw. A yawing bullet will not strike the target at 90° and as a result of this, bullet expansion will not occur (Knudsen and Soensen, 1994).

There is, however, some controversy over the necessity for a hollow-point bullet to strike at 90° for expansion to take place. Poole *et al.* (1994) are of the opinion that up to striking angles of 45°, this is not the case.

Plugging of the hollow point by fabric from the bullet's passage through clothing or any other intermediate material will also inhibit the expansion of hollow-point bullets.

If, on the other hand, even a moderately powered handgun is held with the muzzle in tight contact with the skin, the entry hole can be massive. In this case, the high-pressure gases which follow the bullet out of the barrel have nowhere to go other than into the wound behind the bullet. These gases expand at a rate greater than the speed at which the bullet is passing through the tissue and, as they have nowhere else to go, burst back out through the bullet entry hole.

The resultant hole can be enormous and to the inexperienced can give every indication of an exit wound. The presence of partially burnt propellant in the wound and blood and tissue in and on the barrel of the weapon will correctly identify the wound as an entry rather than an exit wound. Another identifier is the deep cruciform tearing around the wound called 'stellate tearing'(Figure 3.4).

Other indicators of a contact wound can be the flare from the side of a revolver's cylinder and sometimes the presence of a mark made by the front sight of the weapon.

In double-barrelled shotguns, the second unfired barrel can often leave a large impact type mark. This mark results from the high-pressure gases which, before bursting back out, balloon out the tissues crushing the skin into the other muzzle (Figure 3.6).

The third concept, that when someone is shot by anything other than an air rifle the impact is enough to lift the person off his feet and send him flying

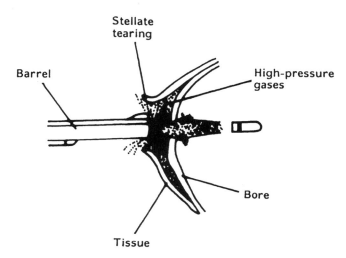

Figure 3.4 Diagram showing effects of contact wound to the head.

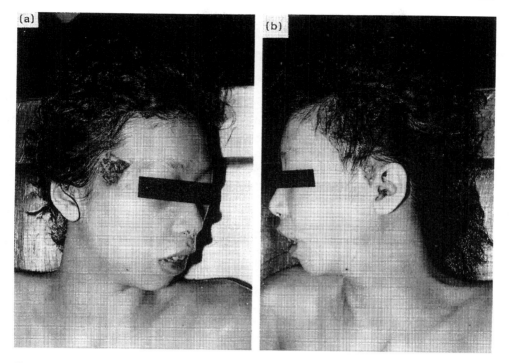

Figure 3.5 (a) Stellate tearing, 0.38″ Special, entry hole right side of head; (b) stellate, tearing, 0.38″ Special, exit hole left side of head.

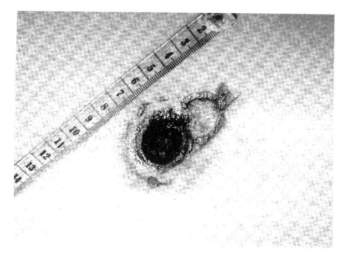

Figure 3.6 Contact wound from over and under 12-bore shotgun, showing imprint from unfired barrel, foresight and foresight protector wings.

through the air, is completely untrue. This once again enters the realms of mathematical ballistics, but it is a very important concept to be aware of especially when dealing with multiple-shot suicides (Eisele, Reay and Cook, 1981; Stone, 1986).

The common misconception is that after the first shot, the body will be thrown away with such force that a second shot would not be possible. This is, of course, completely false as a brief examination of the mathematics will show.

There are two factors to consider when dealing with the effect of a bullet on the human body; one is *momentum* and the other is *kinetic energy*.

Momentum is mass × velocity, and possibly its most important property is that it is conserved during collisions, that is, if two or more objects collide, the total of their momenta is the same after collision as it was before.

If we consider a rifle bullet of 0.02 lb (140 gr) being fired at 3000 ft/s into a 200 lb stationary log, the momentum of the bullet, M_1, before collision, is thus

$$M_1 = 0.02 \times 3000 = 60 \, \text{lb ft/s}$$

If M_2 is the momentum of the log plus bullet after being struck by the bullet, then $M_1 = M_2$.

The log will, after being struck, have a mass of 200 + 0.02 = 200.02. Thus, 200.02 × velocity of the log must equal the momentum of the bullet before striking the log, that is, 60 lb ft/s. By rearranging the equation and substituting the known figures, we have:

$$\text{Velocity of log after being struck} = 60/200.02 = 0.2999 \, \text{ft/s}$$

With such a minimal velocity, it can be easily appreciated that if the log were a person, then the body would not fly very fast or far through the air.

The next question is how far would the body be lifted off the ground by such an impact? If the mass is 200.02 and the velocity 0.2999 ft/s,

$$KE = \frac{1}{2} M V^2$$

where
KE = kinetic energy;
M = mass of the projectile;
V = velocity of the projectile;

$$KE \, (\text{ft lb}) = \frac{200.02 \times 0.299^2}{2 \times 32.174} = 0.27 \, \text{ft lb}$$

A kinetic energy of 0.27 ft lb is enough to lift 1 lb by 0.27 ft or 200 lb by 0.00135 ft or 0.016 in. A distance of 0.016 in. is hardly on a par with the com-

Table 3.13 A comparison of the velocity, monentum and kinetic energy of various common objects.

Object	Mass (lb)	Velocity (ft/s)	Momentum (lb ft/s)	KE (ft lb)
0.22" LR, (40 gr)	0.0057	1200	6.85	120
0.38" Special, (158 gr)	0.0226	850	19.2	253
Cricket ball (60 mph)	0.328	88	30	40
0.303" Rifle	0.025	2440	61	2313
12B Shotgun	0.078	1300	101	2051
600 Nitro Express rifle, (900 gr)	0.129	1950	251	7 600
150 lb Runner (15 mph)	150	22	3 300	1 128
Elephant (5 t, 20 mph)	11 200	29.33	328 500	149 700
1 t car (1 mph)	2 240	1.467	328	74.89

KE, kinetic energy.

monly perceived notion of a body being lifted off the floor and flung against a wall or through a window.

Table 3.13 comparing the velocity, momentum and kinetic energy for various common objects will place these figures into perspective.

It should be remembered, when using this table for comparison purposes, that *momentum* is the ability to move the target or to stop it from moving in the opposite direction, and the KE is the ability to lift a weight off the floor.

It is an interesting comparison that the most powerful elephant rifle ever commercially produced would have little or no stopping effect on a charging elephant running at 20 mph.

When talking about the wounding capabilities of a bullet, many people wrongly refer to kinetic energy as 'power'. Power is the rate of doing work and is generally measured in 'horse power'. If the power of a bullet is required, one has to know how long the bullet takes to stop in inches. The kinetic energy of the bullet is then divided by this distance, and then this figure is divided again by 550 to convert the answer into horse power. Thus, the power of the bullet is dependent upon the material into which it is fired. As a result, this is a fairly meaningless figure.

Generally speaking, the only way a body is likely to leave the floor after being shot is because of involuntary muscle spasm caused by a shot to the brain.

3.4.4 Other factors influencing the wounding capabilities of a missile

Immediately after leaving the barrel, the bullet is in a slightly unstable condition which is due, in the main, to three factors: 'yaw', 'precession' and 'nutation'.

Yaw.   Yaw can be described as the angle between the longitudinal axis of a projectile and its line of flight as exists before the bullet achieves full gyroscopic stability (Figure 3.7).

Precession.   This is the rotational effect of the bullet about its mid axis (Figure 3.8).

Nutation.   This is the progressive corkscrew motion of the bullet. This action is very similar to the wobble observed immediately after a top or gyroscope is initially set spinning and is a function of the spin rate being too great (Figure 3.9).

As in a top, these factors eventually settle down to a stable flight pattern which in rifles can be anything up to 200 yd. It is this initial instability that often accounts for the far greater close range wounding effects of hard-jacketed rifle bullets when compared to those at greater distances.

There is a fourth condition which imparts a sideways drift to the bullet's path called either 'spin drift' or 'gyroscopic drift'. This is to the right for right-handed rifling and to the left for left-handed. It is caused by air pressure under the slightly nose up attitude of the bullet as it descends its trajectory. This effect is really only noticeable on extreme range rifle bullets or artillery shells.

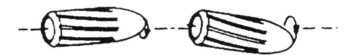

Figure 3.7 Bullet yaw.

Figure 3.8 Precession of a bullet.

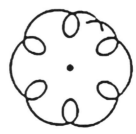

Figure 3.9 Nutation of a bullet.

Angles of yaw have only received detailed examination in military weapons, for example, the measured angle of yaw for a 0.303″ rifle bullet is 1.5° and for a 5.56 mm M16 rifle bullet 6°.

This yaw does have a pronounced effect on the wounding capabilities of the missile. The greater the degree of yaw, the greater the wounding effect of the bullet. This yaw effect also explains the commonly observed effect of a rifle bullet having greater penetrative powers at 200 yd than at the muzzle.

Case example. For a long time, I had been aware of the instability of rifle bullets at short ranges and their apparent inaccuracy due to a changing point of impact resulting from nutation and precession. However, it was not until I was asked to explain some external and terminal ballistics effects to camera that the extent of this instability was fully realized.

The programme was designed to explain the capabilities of various historical and current military weapons and the wounding effects they would have on a human body. To visualize the temporary cavitational effect of the bullets, the weapons were fired at large blocks of modelling clay. This was carried out at a range of 25 m.

As a result of the close range instability factor of the 0.303″ Enfield bullet, I extended the range of firing for this weapon to 250 yd.

As expected, the bullet made a small hole straight through the modelling clay with little in the way of any temporary cavitational effect.

The director was of the opinion that firing at such a range was not good TV footage and insisted that the block be shot again at 25 m. This time, the effect of the bullet on the 2 × 2 × 4 ft block of modelling clay was catastrophic with it literally exploding into small pieces. On gathering up the pieces, all that could be found of the bullet was a very small piece of jacket and two equally small pieces of lead core.

It was obvious that the instability due to the nutation and precession of the bullet had been greatly increased when the bullet entered the clay. The resulting G forces on the bullet had literally torn it apart releasing its kinetic energy in a very short period of time. The dumping of such a huge amount of energy in a very short period of time had caused an almost explosive effect on the clay.

Despite it not being representative of the battle range wounding capabilities of the 0.303″ round, the footage was included as part of the series.

The rate of spin imparted to a bullet by the barrel's rifling is calculated to ensure that the bullet is stable in air. Once it enters a denser medium, however, the spin is insufficient to stabilize the bullet and it begins to wobble. As this exposes a greater cross-sectional area of the bullet to the tissue, the wobble becomes greater until eventually, the bullet begins to tumble end over end.

As the tumbling bullet exposes a much greater area of the bullet, the wound track and the kinetic energy loss will be tremendously increased.

In lightly jacketed bullets, this tumbling can also cause the bullet to break up causing a massive increase in the kinetic energy loss and a consequential increase in the temporary and permanent wound cavities. This effect is much greater in short projectiles, such as the 0.223″ (5.56 mm) Ml6 bullet, than with longer bullets such as the 0.303″ British military round.

The wounding effect of a missile is also dependent on the shape of the bullet nose. A round-nosed bullet will be retarded more than a sharp-pointed bullet. An expanding, hollow-point bullet will be retarded even more.

The amount a bullet will deform during passage through soft tissue will depend very much on the construction of the bullet. A fully jacketed bullet will hardly deform at all, whilst a soft-lead hollow-point bullet will deform very easily.

For a hollow-point soft-nosed bullet to expand, a velocity of at least 900 ft/s is required. A round-nosed plain lead bullet will require at least 1200 ft/s.

Numerous reports exist to the effect that the 5.56 mm (0.223″) M16 bullet 'blows up' on striking soft tissue. This is nonsense. What does happen, however, is that the thinly jacketed bullet, which is only just stable in air, becomes very unstable in tissue and starts to tumble. This tumbling action presents a much larger surface area of the bullet to the retarding tissue. This increased surface area causes tremendous strain on the bullet's structure which results in the jacket rupturing and the lead core fragmenting.

With an initial bullet velocity of over 3000 ft/s, the kinetic energy loss is already tremendous, but as the bullet breaks up, it becomes even greater. Massive permanent cavities, huge temporary cavities and tremendous damage to organs, blood vessels and bone remote from the wound track give rise to an appearance which many associate with the result of the bullet exploding.

3.4.5   Bullet performance and 'wounding capabilities'

This is another of those subjects surrounded by myth and misinformation. In many ways, this is understandable as the number of factors influencing how a bullet reacts on entering a human body is so diverse as to make a scientific study of the subject virtually impossible.

If the body were made uniformly from a material of constant density, it would be extremely simple to simulate the effects of a bullet. The body is, however, full of voids with a hard bone skeleton and is associated cartilaginous materials. The effects of a bullet hitting the thigh bone and muscle will be completely different to one striking the chest area which has little muscle or hard bony material.

In an attempt to obtain some meaningful results for the wounding capabilities for handgun ammunition, the US War Department constituted a board, in 1904, consisting of Col. T. Thompson (the inventor of the Thompson sub-machine gun) and Col. Louis A. La Garde. This board was to conduct a series of tests to determine the stopping power and shock effect necessary for a service pistol. The results of the board's experiments were fully described in Col. La Garde's book, *Gunshot Injuries*.

This is one of the most important investigations undertaken into the wounding effects of handgun bullets, as it consisted of controlled shots into human cadavers.

Many of the calibres used in the tests are no longer popular, but the basic findings, that it is the bullet's cross-sectional area and nose shape rather than the speed, which are the all-important considerations in the wounding capabilities of a bullet, still hold today.

In the tests, the cadavers were suspended by the neck whilst being shot. The quantity of shock to the cadaver by being struck by the bullet was estimated by the disturbance to the body. The bodies were also dissected to determine the degree of tissue damage.

The ammunition used during these tests was as follows:

- 7.65 mm Parabellum, full jacket;
- 9 mm Parabellum, full jacket;
- 0.38″ long Colt revolver, plain lead;
- 0.38″ super ACP, full jacket and soft point;
- 0.45″ long Colt revolver, plain lead and hollow point;
- 0.455″ revolver, 'man stopper' (a flat-nosed bullet with a very large cup-shaped hollow point);
- 0.476″ revolver, plain lead.

The results were quite interesting in that the higher-velocity small-calibre bullets, even when they had a soft or hollow point, caused almost no shocking power at all. The shocking power was, in fact, found to be proportional to the cross-sectional area of the bullet with velocity being only of secondary importance.

These tests were of course on cadavers which could not give any indication of the propensity for a round to incapacitate the subject. To investigate this aspect, a series of rapid firing tests were carried out on live steers in an abattoir. A series of up to 10 shots were fired into the lung or intestinal area of the animal after which it was humanely dispatched.

Once again, the smaller-calibre bullets had virtually no effect on the animals at all. The 0.38″ calibre bullets had little effect until the sixth or seventh shot had been fired. Only the 0.45″ and above calibre bullets were found to have any appreciable effect, on the first shot.

This type of testing is the only way in which meaningful results, as to the actual wounding effect of bullets, can be obtained. Firing into human cadavers and live animals are both, however, extremely sensitive subjects and are open to much adverse comment.

In an attempt to set some standard by which a bullet's performance may be measured without shooting cadavers or live animals, many different materials have been used to simulate body tissue. Among these are wet telephone books, bars of industrial soap, Plasticine, Dukseal, water and 'ballistic gelatine'. Whilst most of these can be used for strictly comparative purposes, they do not give a realistic picture as to how the missile will perform in human tissue.

The only medium which gives a close approximation as to the effects of a bullet on human tissue is *ballistic gelatine*.

Water also gives an approximation as to the expansion capabilities of various bullet constructions, but it does not, of course, give any indication as to the temporary and permanent cavity produced.

Ballistic gelatine (from Gelatin Manufacturers Institute of America Inc., www.gelatin-gmia.com) is made by dissolving type 250 A ordnance gelatine in water to make a 10% solution. During the preparation, the temperature of the gelatine solution should never be allowed to rise above 40 °C as higher temperatures result in hardening of the gelatine. The solution should be set in a refrigerator at 4 °C for at least 36 h and the blocks should be used within 30 min of removal.

After use, the blocks may be reconstituted by re-melting at a temperature not exceeding 40 °C and set in a refrigerator as before.

Theoretically, the wounding effect of a bullet would depend upon its striking energy, that is, kinetic energy. But here, theory and practice decidedly part company. Other factors have a very profound effect on the bullet's effect in animal tissue or other simulant, including the bullet shape, cross-sectional density, weight, speed and bullet construction.

Major Julian Hatcher was one of the first to seriously attempt to assign a numerical figure to the wounding capabilities of a particular bullet/cartridge combination (Hatcher, 1935). He called the numerical value the 'relative stopping power' (RSP).

The original formula he used to calculate the RSP was as follows:

$$RSP = \text{bullet cross sectional area} \times \text{muzzle energy} \times \text{shape factor}$$

Hatcher came to realize, however, that this formula was flawed, as the factor which permits the transfer of velocity to the surrounding tissue is not the muzzle energy of the bullet but rather its momentum.

He therefore modified his formula for RSP using momentum as follows: RSP = bullet cross sectional area × momentum × shape factor.

The shape factor was an empirical figure assigned by Hatcher. The factors he gave for various bullets are as follows:

- round-nosed jacketed bullet = 900;
- round-nosed but with a flat top = 1000;
- round-nosed plain lead = 1000;
- plain lead with blunt nose = 1050;
- plain lead with a large flat on nose = 1100;
- wadcutter bullet = 1250.

Table 3.14 Relative stopping power (RSP) of various bullets.

Cartridge	Momentum	Cross-sectional area	Shape factor	RSP
0.22″ Long rifle	0.097	0.039	1000	3.8
0.25″ ACP	0.083	0.049	900	3.7
7.65mm Parabellum	0.246	0.075	900	16.6
0.32″ ACP	0.147	0.076	900	10.0
0.38″ Super Auto	0.347	0.102	900	31.8
9mm Parabellum	0.288	0.102	1000	29.4
0.38″ Special	0.302	0.102	1000	30.8
0.44″ Special	0.416	0.146	1000	60.6
0.45″ ACP	0.420	0.159	900	60.0

Using Hatcher's figures, we can construct Table 3.14.

The momentum is measured in pounds feet per second and the cross-sectional area in square inches.

A major contribution of this formula was the recognition that the bullet's cross-sectional area has a very significant effect on its effectiveness in animal tissue. This gave a useful set of figures for direct comparison purposes between various bullet configurations, but it was not in total agreement with actual case incidents.

In 1973, the American National Institute of Law Enforcement and Criminal Justice sponsored research into determining the effectiveness of handgun cartridges as definitively as technology, at that time, would permit.

The effectiveness of a bullet configuration was given a numerical value called the *Relative Incapacitation Index (RII)*. This was calculated on the basis of three factors, *target vulnerability, hit distribution* and *bullet terminal ballistics*.

Target vulnerability was calculated by determining the relative sensitivity of the various areas of the body. This was done by dividing an anatomical model of the human body into 1 in. thick slices. Each of these horizontal slices was then divided into rectangular solids by vertically imposing a 0.2″ square grid onto the slice. Doctors then assigned a numerical value to each of these rectangular solids representing the vulnerability of that solid. This formed the basis of the 'computer man' which was used as a vulnerability model for the study.

Hit distribution was obtained by live firing using soldiers firing 0.45″ Colt self-loading pistols at 'pop-up' targets. The hit distribution data was weighted against the penetration data in the anatomical model with respect to incapacitation potential.

The *bullet terminal ballistics* data was obtained by an examination of the bullet's behaviour in 20% gelatine (this is counter to the normal use of 10% gelatine), a standard set by the US Army Surgeon General. The factor used in determining the potential wounding capability of the bullet was to measure, via high-speed motion picture, the temporary cavity formed in the gelatine.

Table 3.15 Relative Incapacitation Index (RII).

Calibre	Weight (grains)	Bullet type	Velocity (ft/s)	RII
0.44″ Mag	200	JHP	1277	54.9
0.38″ Spl+P+	125	JHP	1108	25.5
0.45″ ACP	185	JHP	895	21.1
0.357″ Mag	158	JSP	1030	17.5
0.357″ Mag	158	WC	821	14.7
0.357″ Mag	158	JHP	982	11.1
9 mm PB	125	JSP	1058	9.9
0.38″ Spl	125	JHP	911	7.0
0.45″ ACP	230	FJ	740	6.5
0.38″ Spl	158	LRN	795	5.0
0.22″ LR	37	LHP	872	2.3

JSP, jacketed soft point; FJ, full jacket; JHP, jacketed hollow point; WC, wadcutter; LRN, lead round nose; LHP, lead hollow point; +P+, a very high-pressure cartridge available only to police departments.

It is interesting that a dramatic 'ballooning' effect was noted in the temporary cavity when the projectiles' velocity exceeded 1100 ft/s, which is approximately the speed of sound in air.

In calculating the RII figures, the analysis was run using the centre of vulnerability of the computer man which is located in the chest area at armpit level. These results give the RII figures seen in Table 3.15.

This is a very abbreviated table as there were 142 different cartridges evaluated in the original paper. It does, however, give some interesting data. For example, the 0.45″ ACP, which has always been considered to be a very effective round, is rated only marginally better than the 0.38″ Spl lead round nose (LRN) which has long been recognized as totally inadequate in a combat situation.

Using these figures, it was considered that any round with an RII below a factor of 9.0 was not suitable for a military or police round.

In 1991, a privately funded group was formed to study the physiological effects of bullet impact on medium-sized animals. These are now known as the *Strasbourg tests*. These tests were politically very sensitive in nature as the animals were shot whilst in a conscious condition.

The animals selected were French Alpine goats as they were very similar in weight, lung capacity and thoracic cage dimensions to those of man. To measure the effects of being shot, transducers were implanted in the carotid artery and electroencephalograph needles inserted into the scalp.

The animals were shot in the lung area as this was considered the most likely place a human being would be struck by a bullet. In all, there were a total of 611 goats shot during these tests.

The results for these tests are in the form of 'average incapacitation time' (AIT), which is deemed to be the average time (usually over tests on five individual goats) it took the animal to collapse and be unable to rise again. A selection of the results follow (Table 3.16). When reviewing these results it should be noted that there is some speculation as to whether these tests ever took place with such comments as 'Strasbourg was either done in the Goat Lab at Bragg [US Military Base in Texas, USA], or a replication of that lab, or someone who is familiar with that lab did a helluva thorough job constructing an elaborate hoax.' (Retired US Army Special Forces officer) being common.

Evan Marshall, an ex-patrol officer with the Detroit Police Force, spent 15 years collecting data on actual shooting incidents. Any incident where one shot was sufficient to incapacitate the assailant so that he was incapable of further fight was classified as a *one-shot stop*. Some of his figures are given in Table 3.17.

Table 3.16 A selection of results from the Strasbourg Tests showing the average incapacitation time (AIT) for various rounds.

Calibre	Weight (gr)	Bullet type	Velocity (ft/s)	AIT
9 mm PB	115	JHP	1175	9.3
9 mm PB	115	FJ	1163	14.4
9 mm PB	147	JHP	962	9.68
0.45″ ACP	185	JHP	939	10.66
0.45″ ACP	230	FJ	839	13.84
0.45″ ACP+P	185	JHP	1124	7.98
0.38″ Spl	158	RNL	708	33.68
0.38″ Spl	125	JHP	986	14.28
0.38″ Spl+P	125	JHP	998	10.92
0.38″ Spl+P	158	LHP	924	10.86

Table 3.17 Abbreviated list of Marshall's 'one-shot stops'.

Calibre	Weight (gr)	Bullet type	Velocity (ft/s)	Total shootings	One-shot stops	Percentage
0.38″ Spl	158	RNL	704	306	160	52.28
0.38″ Spl+P	158	LHP	926	114	79	69.29
0.38″ Spl+P	158	JHP	991	183	126	68.85
0.38″ Sp1+P	110	JHP	1126	16	11	68.75
9 mm PB	115	FMJ	1149	159	99	62.26
9 mm PB	115	JHP	1126	32	20	62.50
9 mm PB	147	JHP	985	25	19	76.00
9 min PB+P+	115	JHP	1304	76	68	89.47
0.357″ Magnum	158	JHP	1233	23	22	81.48
0.357″ Magnum	125	JHP	1391	83	73	87.95
0.357″ Magnum	125	JHP	1453	426	448	96.96

LHP, lead hollow point; JHP, jacketed hollow point; RNL, round nosed lead.

Of all the various tests and simulations dealing with handgun ammunition effectiveness, probably the most important is the Marshall list of 'one-shot stops'.

From all the above, it is clear, however, that even La Garde in 1904 had it correct in that it is not the velocity which really matters; it is the necessity of getting a large-calibre missile deep into the body. Back in 1904, this was done with large, 0.455″ and 0.476″, calibre, slow-moving missiles which punched their way through the tissue. Today, the move is towards smaller missiles but with a hollow point which, when travelling in excess of 900 ft/s, will expand to give the effect of a large-calibre missile.

3.4.6 Penetration of bullet-resistant jackets and vests

One of the tasks the forensic firearms examiner is often called upon to perform is the testing and evaluation of bullet-resistant vests and jackets, generally called *soft body armour*.

As this aspect comes within the realms of terminal ballistics, it would be a good point to review the subject.

History.   Body armour, in the form of metal plates, was widely used during the time of hand-to-hand combat with swords, knives and various bludgeoning instruments. With the advent of the crossbow and firearm, the plain steel suits were found inadequate to defeat the missiles and they rapidly became obsolete.

During World War II (WWII), *ballistic nylon* (a copolymer of the basic polyamide) was used against shrapnel from munitions. This was, however, of little use against bullets other than low-velocity soft-lead projectiles.

The major advance in soft body armour came with a generation of what are loosely referred to as 'super fibres' which were introduced by Du Pont. The best known of these was a para-aramid fibre called *Kevlar* which was originally used in fabric-braced radial tyres. It did not take long, however, for it to be realized that it could be woven into a fabric which was so strong that it could be used in bullet-resistant, soft body armour.

The Kevlar fibres were simply woven into sheets, with varying thicknesses of yarn and density of weave (called *denier*), to provide the particular properties required. The sheets were then assembled into 'ballistics panels' which were permanently sewn into a carrier in the form of a vest.

It is undeniable that Kevlar does produce a very effective, lightweight and flexible jacket which can be tailored to stop virtually any handgun missile. It does, however, suffer from a number of problems. Firstly, it is not stable to UV light and has to be kept inside a light-proof pouch. It is also very susceptible to attack by many household chemicals, and thirdly, if wet, it loses most of its ability to stop bullets.

A recent development in the field of soft body armour is the use of an ultra-high molecular weight polyethylene fibre called *Spectra* which is produced by Allied Signal Inc. This consists of exceedingly fine-spun fibres of polyethylene. These fibres are laid, in dense mats, at 90° to each other then covered top and bottom with a thin sheet of polyethylene. This is then heat treated to semi-melt the fibres together or bonded with a plastic resin to form a sheet. With the thousands of bonded fibres which must be pulled from the matrix to allow the passage of a bullet, the sheets are even more efficient than Kevlar.

This material is not affected by water, nor is it affected by UV light or any chemical, and it is considerably lighter than Kevlar. If it has a disadvantage, it is that its melting point is much lower than Kevlar.

Mechanism of bullet-resistant materials. To effectively stop a bullet, the material must first deform the missile. If the surface area of the bullet is large enough and the material has sufficient resistance to the passage of the bullet, then the energy transfer to surrounding fibres can occur. A non-deformed bullet will merely push apart the weave and penetrate.

If the bullet is sufficiently soft, that is, plain lead, semi-jacketed or a thinly jacketed bullet, then the material alone will often be sufficient to cause the deformation. If, however, the bullet is heavily jacketed or of the metal-penetrating type, then some intermediate, much more rigid material will be required to deform the bullet. This generally takes the form of a hard plate which fits in front of the soft body armour.

Ballistic inserts. This is the name generally given to rigid plates which are placed in front of the soft body armour. Their purpose is to break up high-velocity, hard-jacketed and metal-penetrating missiles. Once the bullet's velocity has been reduced and its shape deformed, it will be easily stopped by the underlying Kevlar or Spectra material. These inserts are generally made from either a fused ceramic material, heat-treated aluminium, hardened steel or, more recently, titanium. These can be either solid plates or small overlapping tiles.

Case examples. Soft body armour is not infallible as the following two cases illustrate. The first involved a police officer wearing a very substantial bullet-resistant vest capable of defeating 0.357″ Magnum and 9 mm PB calibre bullets. He was shot at close range with a 0.45-70 rifle which has a large soft bullet weighing 400 gr at a velocity of 1500 ft/s. Whilst the jacket was successful at defeating the bullet, it was driven into the officer's chest, killing him.

The second involved a live demonstration of a ballistic insert plate made of metal. The plate was designed to defeat an armour-piercing round, but the demonstration was merely to show how effective it was against a full magazine from a sub-machine-gun. The soldier wearing the jacket was not killed, but the fragments generated by the bullet breaking up on the plate neatly severed the lower part of his jaw.

3.4.7   Brief glossary

Ballistic gelatine	Tissue simulant made by dissolving type 250 A ordinance gelatine in water to make a 10% solution.
Ballistic insert	Name generally given to rigid plates which are placed in front of the bullet-resistant vest; can be made of ceramic, hardened steel, aluminium or titanium.
Ballistic nylon	A copolymer of polyamide; used in 'flak jackets' during WWII against shrapnel from munitions.
Ceramic plates	Fused ceramic material used in rigid plates which are placed in front of the bullet-resistant vest.
Dynema	Trade name for soft body armour
Kevlar	Trade name for aramid soft body armour fibre.
Kinetic energy	Potential for doing work – measured in foot pound or joule.
Momentum	Quantity of motion of a moving body – measured in pound feet per second.
Nutation	This is the progressive corkscrew motion of the bullet. This action is very similar to the wobble observed immediately after a top or gyroscope is initially set spinning and is a function of the spin rate being too great.
Penetration potential	The capability of a missile to penetrate various materials.
Permanent cavity	Cavity left by the bullet due to the actual destruction of tissue.
Precession	This is the rotational effect of the bullet about its mid axis.
Soft body armour	Bullet-resistant vest or jacket usually made from Kevlar, Spectra or Dynema.
Spectra	Trade name for ultra-high molecular weight polyethylene fibre used in soft body armour.
Stellate tearing	Deep cruciform tearing round the entry hole of contact gunshot wounds.
Temporary cavity	Cavity left by a bullet immediately after it passes through tissue. It is caused by the transfer of energy from the missile to the tissue causing the tissue to rapidly move away from the bullet's path. As the tissue is elastic it will, after a few minor aftershocks, regain its original form.
Wound ballistics	The effect the missile has on living tissue.

Yaw   Yaw can be described as the angle between the longitu-
                       dinal axis of a projectile and its line of flight as exists
                       before the bullet achieves full gyroscopic stability.

References

Eisele, J.W., Reay, D.T., Cook, A. *et al.* (1981) Sites of suicidal gunshot wounds. *Journal of the Forensic Science Society*, 26, 480–485.

French, G.R. (1962) *Wound Ballistics*, US Government Printing Office.

Gelatin Manufacturers Institute of America Inc.

Hatcher, J.H. (1935) *Textbook of Pistols and Revolvers*, Small Arms Publishing Co., Plantersville, SC, USA.

HMSO, (1929) *1929 Textbook of Small Arms*, His Majesty's Stationery Office, UK.

Knudsen, P.J.T. and Soensen, O.H. (1994) The initial yaw of some commonly encountered bullets. *International Journal of Legal Medicine*, 107, 141–6.

Peisa, A.J. (1991) *Modern Practical Ballistics 2nd edn*, Kenword Publishing, Minneapdis, MN, USA.

Poole, R.A., Cooper, R.E., Emanuel, L.G. *et al.* (1994) Angle: effect on hollow point bullets fired into gelatine. *AFTE Journal*, 26 (3), 193–198.

Stone, J. (1986) Observations and statistics relating to weapons. *Journal of the Forensic Science Society*, 32, 711–716.

Further Reading

Rinkler, R.A. (1991) *Understanding Firearms Ballistics*, Mulberry House Publishing Company, Corydon, IN, USA.

Whelen, T. (1945) *Small Arms Design and Ballistics*, Small Arms Technical Publishing Co., Georgetown, SC, USA.

4

Forensic Firearms Examination

4.1   A Brief History of Forensic Firearms Identification

4.1.1   Introduction

As with any evolving science, the exact origins of forensic firearms identification are shrouded in obscurity.

Exactly when it was first noted that fired bullets from a given weapon possessed a certain number of equally spaced impressed grooves, all inclined in the same direction and at the same angle, and which were the same on every other bullet fired through that weapon, will probably never be known.

Likewise, it will never be known when the next logical step was taken to compare the width, number and degree of inclination of the grooves with those from weapons of a different make.

The next step, however, required a quantum leap in lateral thinking to show that all bullets fired through the same weapon bore microscopic *stria* (parallel impressed lines) which were unique to the weapon in which they were fired.

Early cases of bullet identification.   In June 1900, an article appeared in the *Buffalo Medical Journal*, by Dr A.L. Hall, to the effect that bullets fired through different makes and types of weapon, of the same calibre, were impressed with rifling marks of varying type. Unfortunately, Dr Hall never expanded on his original article.

In 1907, as a result of riots in Brownsville, Texas, where members of the US infantry opened fire, staff at the Frankfort Arsenal were tasked with identifying

Handbook of Firearms and Ballistics: Second Edition   Brian J. Heard
© 2008 John Wiley & Sons, Ltd.

which of the weapons were fired. As a method of identification, magnified photographs of the firing pin impressions on the cartridge cases were used. By this means, they were able to positively identify that of the 39 cartridge cases examined; 11 were from one weapon, 8 from a second, 11 from a third and 3 from a fourth. The six remaining cartridge cases were not identified. As to the recovered bullets, the examiners concluded that the bullets bore no distinctive markings as to the particular weapon from which they were fired. The only conclusions reached were that they had, by the rifling characteristics, been fired from either a Krag or a Springfield rifle.

Use of photomicrographs.   This epochal work by the staff at Frankfort Arsenal was not recognized for a number of years and it was not until 1912 when Victor Balthazard made the next profound advancement to this science. Balthazard took photomicrographs of bullet lands and grooves in an attempt to identify the weapon from which the bullet was fired. From these examinations, he came to the conclusion that the cutter used in rifling a barrel never leaves exactly the same markings in its successive excursions through a barrel. These markings, which by inference must be unique to that barrel, are then imprinted as a series of striations on any bullet passing through that barrel. He thus reasoned that it is possible to identify, beyond reasonable doubt, that a fired bullet originated from the barrel of a certain weapon and none other. The significance of Balthazard's work cannot be overestimated, for it is upon this premise that the whole of modern science of bullet identification rests.

Balthazard's work, however, extended beyond that of matching striations on bullets and included the markings imprinted on fired cartridge cases in self-loading pistols. The markings he identified as being those bearing identifiable stria and markings unique to a certain weapon were those caused by the firing pin, breech face, cartridge extractor and ejector. He reasoned that the final pass made by a cutting or finishing tool in, for example, the cartridge extractor, left a series of striations which were unique to that extractor. Likewise, the finishing strokes made by a hand-held file, for example, in rounding off the firing pin tip, once again left marks which were unique to that piece of work.

Balthazard's work was, however, exceedingly labour intensive, requiring the production of numerous photomicrographs under exactly the same lighting and magnification. These photomicrographs then had to be painstakingly enlarged under identical conditions to produce the photographs which could be compared to the unaided eye.

In 1923, a paper was published in the *Annales de Medicine Legale* by De Rechter and Mage which discussed the merits of using firing pin impressions for the identification of the weapon used. Whilst some reference was made in this paper to the work carried out by Balthazard, it did not fully credit him for his work with self-loading pistols.

At about the same time, Pierre Medlinger also mentioned the reproduction of minute irregularities in the breech face on the soft brass of American primers.

The matter was, however, taken no further than that, with no mention of the possibility of identification of the weapon in which it was fired.

Identification of weapon from breech face markings.   Whilst it was accepted at this time that it was possible to match a fired bullet and cartridge case with a given weapon, there was no information available to indicate, from fired bullet or cartridge case alone, which make and model of weapon it was fired in. In 1932, Heess, Mezger and Hasslacher rectified this via the publication of an immense amount of data in volume 89 of the *Archiv fur Kriminologie* entitled 'Determination of the Type of Pistol Employed, from an Examination of Fired Bullets and Shells'. This article was translated and reprinted in the 1932 edition of the *American Journal of Police Science*. Appended to the paper was an 'atlas' containing photographs of 232 different self-loading pistols each containing an illustration of the breech face and the markings produced on fired cartridge cases. Measurements of width, number, direction and angle of rifling twist were also included. This atlas was produced commercially as a series of cards which were added to on a regular basis. Unfortunately, this has been unavailable for several decades with copies being much sought after as collector's items.

Early use of comparison microscope.   It was not, however, until 1925 that mention was first made of a comparison microscope which enabled the simultaneous viewing of magnified images of two bullets or cartridge cases for forensic comparison purposes. Calvin Goddard in a paper published in the 1936 edition of the *Chicago Police Journal* attributes the development of the comparison microscope to a Philip Gravelle in 1925. This, he states, was a development of the comparison microscope used by Albert Osborn for document examination. The microscope so formed consisted of a Zeiss optical bridge, Spencer microscope bodies, Leitz eyepieces, Bausch and Lomb objectives and bullet mounts constructed by Remington Arms Company.

The optical bridge referred to is a 'Y'-shaped tube, the two arms of which fit over the vertical tubes of two microscopes. By a series of prisms inside the 'Y' tube, the images are directed into a single eyepiece. The resultant image is a circular field of view composed of the image from the left microscope in the left side of the field and that from the right in the right side of the field. The images are separated by a fine line in the centre of the field.

Emile Chamot of Cornell University also describes the use of a comparison microscope, using an optical bridge designed by Bausch and Lomb, for examining small arms primers in 1922. The optical bridge, however, dates back to a Russian mineralogist, A.V. Inostrszeff, who, in 1885, designed an optical bridge for comparing the colour of minerals.

It does not matter who actually invented the comparison microscope, for it was Philip Gravelle who first realized its use in the forensic comparison of stria on bullets and cartridge cases.

Shortly after the 1925 publication of the paper in the *Army Ordnance Journal*, the Spencer Lens Company manufactured the first commercial comparison microscope. This was very soon followed by Bausch and Lomb, and Leitz.

In 1927, Mr Robert Churchill, the famous English gunmaker, became interested in the comparison microscope. After seeing illustrations of a comparison microscope in an American periodical, he had a similar instrument manufactured for himself.

There is some dispute as to when Churchill first used his comparison microscope, with Mathews (1962) indicating it was in solving the famous Constable Gutteridge murder case. Major Burrard (1934) is convinced, however, that the Gutteridge case was solved by the War Office experts using a simple monocular microscope and photomicrographs.

The brief facts concerning the murder of Constable Gutteridge are as follows. In a motor car, used by the murderers of Constable Gutteridge, was found a fired revolver cartridge case. After many months' work, the police were convinced that two men, Brown and Kennedy, were the murderers. Two revolvers were found in the possession of Brown, and the whole case hinged on whether one of these was the murder weapon. Eventually, it was established that one of the revolvers did in fact fire the cartridge case and, after trial at court, Brown and Kennedy were hanged for the murder.

Whilst the fact that a microscopic comparison had been made was not particularly significant, this was the first time that such evidence had been presented to a court of law in the United Kingdom.

These early commercial comparison microscopes still consisted of the bottom half of two normal microscopes joined by an optical bridge. In the 1930s, the first real purpose-built microscope appeared in which the objective lenses were attached directly to the optical bridge. This made for a very compact instrument which could be mounted on a single base stand.

Introduction of the binocular comparison microscope. The next major improvement was the introduction of binocular eyepieces. It should be noted here that this did not give stereoscopic images as each stage still only had a single objective lens. It merely made operational use of the instrument much more comfortable.

It is often claimed that two-dimensional (2D) photographic reproductions of striation comparisons do not represent the three-dimensional (3D) views obtained on the microscope. Whilst there is some truth in the statement that photographic representation of striation matches is of little evidential use, this is not due to photographs being only 2D. In fact, the view obtained through the eyepieces is 2D, as the single objective lens system used in comparison microscopes is incapable of representing three dimensions.

Improvements in illumination. Apart from considerable improvements in optical quality, the only other real improvement in comparison microscope design has been the introduction of optical fibre and coaxial illumination.

Obtaining the correct lighting balance to enhance the micro stria under observation is one of the most difficult aspects of comparison microscopy. To achieve this using a conventional focused tungsten bulb system for each stage so that the light intensity, colour temperature and angle of illumination is identical for both is exceedingly difficult. Modern instruments are, however, now supplied with a single source halogen bulb serving two focused, fibre optical arms. Each stage is thus supplied with a light source of exactly the same intensity and exactly the same colour temperature. Being highly manoeuvrable, the fibre optic light sources can be positioned with an accuracy previously unobtainable.

More modern instruments use a form of lighting once called the 'Ultrapak' or coaxial lighting system. Originally, this lighting system was used on Leitz microscopes which were specifically designed for the examination of paint flakes and fibres. In this type of examination, which was usually concerned with colour determination, a shadowless but incident lighting of the object was required. Shadowless lighting required that the light source be vertically over the object being examined, which presents some problems where a microscope is concerned. The problem was solved by introducing the light into the lens barrel around the outside of the lens system. The light was directed down the lens barrel and, via a lens surrounding the objective lens, was focused on the object being examined. As the light source was now coming from around the objective lens, it gave a 360° shadowless illumination of the object. The system has now been updated and appears on modern Leitz comparison microscopes giving a brilliantly clear, shadowless light. The stria appear, not as peaks and furrows as with normal incident lighting, but more as a series of 'bar codes'. Its real use is, however, in the examination of deeply indented firing pin impressions where normal incident lighting would be almost impossible due to the shadows produced. This considerably simplifies the examination and reduces the eye strain of the examiner.

Photography of stria.   Whilst most comparison microscopes have some form of photographic system for recording the striation matches, this is only of any real use in toolmark examination. In toolmark examination, the stria are generally on a flat surface and are easily photographed.

With striations on bullets, the stria are on the circumference of a curved surface, and only a small portion of this can be adequately represented in focus on a single photograph. Modern instruments can now be fitted with a closed circuit television (CCTV) and monitor connected to a video recording device. With this, it is possible to record the striation match around the whole of the circumference of a bullet.

In general, the use of comparison photomicrographs in a court of law to illustrate stria comparisons should be discouraged. At best, they are illustrative of a stria match and at worse, they can be totally misleading to a layman jury. A video recording of the whole circumference of a bullet comparison or the various parts of a match on a cartridge case, however, is far more informative for the court and will remove most of the perceived 'mysticism' behind striation comparisons.

4.1.2   Modern technology for stria comparison

In 1989, the drug-related crime in Washington DC, USA, reached a stage where the law enforcement agencies were forced to implement a 'war on drugs' campaign. As a result, the forensic laboratories became overwhelmed with the quantity of fired ammunition submitted. In an attempt to assist the forensic laboratories as much as possible, 'target' cases were selected by the Federal Bureau of Investigation (FBI) for special attention.

Comparing each bullet and cartridge case in this list with those from a submitted case was, however, still, very manpower intensive. To simplify matters, large photographs of the bullets and cartridge cases from the targeted cases were pinned onto the wall behind the comparison microscopes. The examiner could use these photographs as a rough screen to determine whether there were any similarities between the exhibits on the comparison microscope and those on the wall. If there were, then the relevant exhibit would be taken from the Outstanding Crime Index (OCI) and compared directly on the microscope.

Realizing that this could be carried out more effectively with the use of modern technology, the FBI sponsored research into digitalizing the photographs. These were displayed on a high-resolution computer screen in a tiled pattern surrounding the exhibit under examination. The system was called 'Drugfire'.

Drugfire went through a series of developments until eventually, it utilized computer-based comparison algorithms for the matching of stria on digitized images of the fired cartridge cases and bullets. In its eventual form, it was a highly effective system.

Around the same time as the FBI contract was issued, the Bureau of Alcohol, Tobacco and Firearms (ATF) established its own automated ballistics identification system. However, instead of developing a custom-made system like the FBI, the ATF opted to build its network on an existing platform which had already been developed by Forensic Technology Inc. (FTI) for general industrial comparison purposes.

From the very start, the FTI system utilized computer-based comparison algorithms and did not have to go through the same developmental process as Drugfire.

Initially, the system was only capable of comparing bullets and was called Bulletproof. Later, it was upgraded to handle cartridge cases and was then renamed the Integrated Ballistic Identification System (IBIS).

As a result, from 1993 to 1998, the United States had two, non-capable, automated ballistics identification systems in place: Drugfire, which was under the FBI, and IBIS, under the ATF. Although there were attempts to interconnect the two systems under the National Integrated Ballistic Identification Network (NIBIN), it was not successful.

In 1999, the FBI and ATF finally decided to phase out Drugfire and to standardize NIBIN on the IBIS platform. This decision was arrived at after a thorough joint FBI–ATF evaluation revealed the superiority of IBIS over the other system.

The adoption of IBIS as the NIBIN standard made FTI the world's biggest manufacturer of automated ballistic identification systems.

In 2005, FTI released its 'Bullet TRAX' and in 2006, the 'Brass TRAX' systems which enabled both 2D and 3D imaging of bullet and cartridge case stria. This not only enabled users to take qualitative measurements of the surface topography of a bullet and cartridge case, but also considerably enhanced the capability of the IBIS system.

Examples of 3D imaging follow (Figures 4.1 and 4.2).

A number of other ballistic identification systems are also in the market, including:

- ARSENAL by Papillon Systems of Russia;
- CONDOR by SBC Co. Ltd;
- EVOFINDER by SCANBII Technology;
- CIBLE, a French system;
- TAIS, another Russian system;

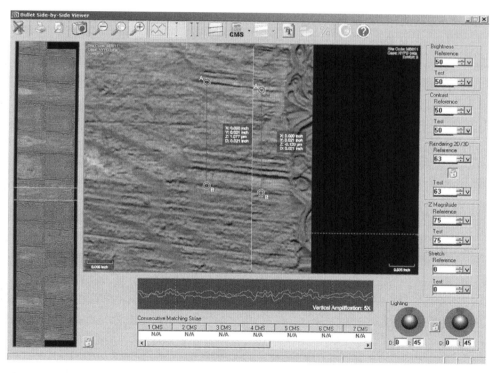

Figure 4.1 Three-dimensional imaging of rifling stria. Image reproduced by permission of Forensic Technology Inc.

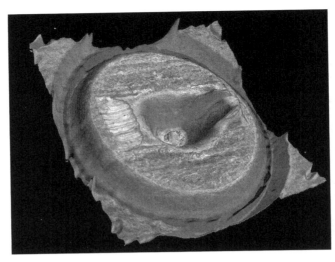

Figure 4.2 Three-dimensional imaging of firing pin indentation on a primer. Image reproduced by permission of Forensic Technology Inc.

- BALİSTİKA from Turkey;
- FIREBALL from Australia.

There are also a large number of issued patents covering this technology, so more systems can be expected in the future.

It should be strongly emphasized that these systems cannot, at present, replace the comparison microscopist. All they do is generate a list of 10 or 20 top candidates as possible matches. The firearms examiner uses this list to select the actual bullets/cartridge cases from the OCI for visual examination on a comparison microscope.

It is the examiner who makes the final decision as to whether there is a match, and it is he or she who testifies to this in court.

4.1.3   Other instruments used in forensic firearms examination

Apart from the everyday instruments commonly found in any forensic laboratory, for example, microscopes, micrometers, and so on, there are a number of others which, although probably no longer in common use, one should be aware of.

Rifling meter.   In this instrument, the barrel of the weapon under examination is clamped to the bed of a lathe. Into the tailstock of the lathe is fixed a long steel rod, one end of which has a lead plug of the same diameter as the bore of the weapon. The other end of the rod has a graduated disc which rotates with the rod. As the rod is pushed down the bore of the weapon, the rifling bites into the plug on the end and causes the rod to turn. The degree of rotation of the disc is measured against the distance the rod travels down the bore.

There being very little necessity, in forensic firearms examination, to measure the actual rifling twist of a barrel, this instrument is hardly, if ever, encountered.

Comparison camera.   Basically, a comparison camera is a plate camera with an exceedingly long body and two lenses. In front of the lenses are two bullet stages with operating rods stretching back to behind the plate holder. The operator sits behind the ground glass screen operating the bullet holders by remote control until a match is obtained. A plate is inserted and exposed in the normal way. This instrument is exceedingly difficult to operate and, as it has not been commonly used for over 35 years, it will probably only be encountered in a museum.

Tallysurf.   In this instrument, a fine diamond-tipped stylus is drawn across the toolmark. The small variations in height caused by the striations are magnified and plotted on graph paper. These can then be compared without the aid of a comparison microscope. As toolmarks are never consistent along their total length, several passes have to be made before a representative sample can be obtained.

This instrument is possibly of some use in the comparison of toolmarks, but the stylus does permanently damage the toolmark. It also requires a great deal of experience to interpret the graphs produced and, even when a possible match is encountered, they nearly always have to be verified with a comparison microscope.

Tallyron.   The tallyron has the same basic principle as a tallysurf, but it is designed for the examination of bullets. In this instrument, the stylus is stationary and the bullet rotates, giving a circular graph. It is of very little use other than as a rough screen for possible matches (Figure 4.3).

As with the tallysurf, the bullet is permanently damaged by the stylus. It also has the disadvantage that it is all but useless with even slightly damaged or distorted bullets.

It was, however, used to great effect in Northern Ireland to screen the vast number of bullets received for possible matches. These were then examined manually on a conventional comparison microscope. It is probably not used any more.

Peripheral camera.   With this camera, a magnified image of the circumference of the bullet is obtained on a strip of film. As the bullet is rotated, the film passes by the bullet being exposed at the same time. Thus, all the grooves and lands are recorded on one continuous strip of film.

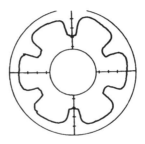

Figure 4.3 Print of tallyron (six-groove bullet).

Assuming that the lighting is correct, the bullet is not damaged and the magnification is sufficient to record the finest of stria, this instrument can be of some use.

It is, without prior knowledge of how the grooves match, necessary to photograph the entire surface of the bullet twice on one strip of film that all the lands and grooves may be compared on one continuous strip.

4.2   Rifling Types and Their Identification

4.2.1   Introduction

Rifles, revolvers, self-loading pistols and most single-shot pistols have rifled barrels. Shotguns are generally smooth bored, although some older weapons were provided with a short length of rifling at the muzzle for use when firing solid slugs. This system of rifling was called *paradox rifling*. Some of the more modern shotguns specifically designed for firing shotgun slugs are also found with rifling. This can either be a short section of rifling at the muzzle end, similar to the old paradox rifling, or rifled down the whole length of the barrel. These are sometimes referred as 'slug barrels'.

Rifling consists of a series of spiral grooves cut into the inside surface of the bore of the barrel and are there to impart a spin to the bullet through its longitudinal axis. This gyroscopic effect stabilizes the bullet during its flight, preventing it from tumbling end over end and losing its accuracy.

Rifling in a barrel consists of *lands* and *grooves*. The *grooves* are the depressions cut away by the rifling cutter. The *lands* are the portions of the barrel not touched by the rifling cutter and are therefore left standing proud.

The number of inches of the barrel required for the rifling to prescribe one complete spiral is called the twist. For most modern weapons, this is consistent throughout the barrel's length. The actual degree of twist cut into a barrel will be carefully calculated in relation to the bore of the weapon, the velocity, the length of the intended projectile, its density and its weight. This is, however, an extremely complex subject and beyond the scope of this book.

The actual degree of twist is critical. Too high a degree of twist and the bullet will be unstable, as a top is when first spun, with a consequential loss of accuracy. Too little spin and the bullet will lose stability and will start to tumble end over end.

Older weapons often had *a gain twist* in which the rate of twist increased from breech to muzzle. This was to assist in the soft-lead bullet gripping the rifling with the high rate of acceleration given by black powder propellants.

Rifling can be right- or left-hand twist, with neither appearing to have any advantage over the other.

The number of grooves cut into a barrel can range from 1 to 24 or even more in what are called *micro-grooved* barrels. Once again, the difference in 5- and 24-groove rifling seems to be more academic than practical.

The main interest of rifling as far as the forensic firearms examiner is concerned is the *micro stria* (microscopic scratch marks) it contains. These micro stria are produced as part of the manufacturing process and are totally random in their distribution, shape and size. As such, they are individual to a particular weapon and form an identification system which is, statistically speaking, approaching that of fingerprints.

A general overview of the characteristics of rifling, its form and manufacturing processes follows.

4.2.2 Class characteristics

When dealing with rifling, each weapon will possess a series of family resemblances which will be present in all weapons of the same make and model. Correctly called *class characteristics*, they relate to the number of lands and grooves, their direction of twist, inclination of twist and their width.

Class characteristics have been measured and technical information obtained for literally thousands of different firearms. These measurements have been compiled into vast databases and are commercially available for use either in table form or on a PC (Crime Laboratory Information System (1998); Mathews, 1962).

By simply measuring the number, width and degree of rotation of the rifling grooves on a bullet, it is possible, with a fairly high degree of accuracy, to determine which make and model of weapon it was fired from.

The spiral grooves which constitute the rifling in a barrel are there to impart a rapid spin on the bullet's longitudinal axis. The gyroscopic effect of this spin stabilizes the bullet, preventing it from tumbling or yawing during its flight, improving its accuracy.

In the past, barrels were often rifled with a *gain twist* where the rate of twist increases from breach to muzzle. This is also referred to as *progressive rifling*. The purpose of gain rifling was to allow lead bullets to build up the rate of spin gradually along the length of the barrel. The sudden acceleration of the bullet at the breech end of the barrel could cause the soft lead to strip through the rifling and thus not acquire the correct degree of stabilization on leaving the barrel. This effect is called *skidding*.

With modern lead alloys, jacketed bullets and progressive burning propellants, this is not such a problem, and gain twist rifling is hardly ever encountered.

One class of weapon in which the phenomenon of skidding is very prominent, however, is in revolvers. In a revolver, the chambers of the cylinder are smooth bored and possess no rifling. During the bullet's progress from the chamber to the beginning of the rifling in the barrel, considerable linear velocity is built up. At this point, however, the bullet has no rotational velocity at all. As the bullet enters the rifling, there is a very short period during which the bullet is attempting to catch up with the rifling, for example, travelling along the rifling but with little or no rotational velocity. This results in an observed short length of rifling engraved on the bullet which appears to be parallel with its longitudinal axis. As these marks are more pronounced at the nose end of the bullet, they have the appearance of a widening of the land impression at this point. The marks so produced are called *skid marks* and are a very useful and simple identifier for bullets which have been fired in a revolver (Figure 4.4).

This skidding is really a by-product of a problem with revolvers concerning the gap between the barrel and cylinder. This gap not only causes skidding of the bullet, but also allows the escape of high-pressure gases, thus losing some of the potential energy of the propellant.

Attempts have been made to overcome both problems, the most notable of which was the Russian 7.62 mm Nagant revolver used during World War II. This weapon fired a round of ammunition which had a bullet seated entirely

Figure 4.4 Bullet fired from a revolver showing skidding.

inside the cartridge case with the case mouth tapering to a smaller diameter than the bullet. When the hammer was cocked, the mechanism moved the whole of the cylinder forward so that the breech end of the barrel actually entered the chamber to be fired. In so doing, the case mouth of the cartridge entered the rear of the barrel, presenting the bullet to the start of the rifling. This was neither particularly good at preventing the skidding nor the leakage of gases. It was also a very complex and expensive mechanism to place in what was a service issue revolver.

In self-loading pistols, this skidding is not exhibited to any significant degree as the chamber is the same length as the cartridge case. As a result, the bullet virtually touches the rifling and has very little, if any, opportunity of building up longitudinal velocity without rotational velocity.

4.2.3 General introduction to rifling

There are a number of different methods by which the rifling may be cut into the barrel of a weapon. A competent forensic firearms examiner should not only be aware of the various methods, but should also be able to identify which method has been used in a particular weapon.

The ability to correctly identify the type of rifling is, in fact, of little or no use to the examiner when carrying out a micro-stria comparison. It is, however, one of those frequently, albeit nonsensical, questions encountered during the qualification of an expert in court.

Rifling process. The actual rifling of a weapon is carried out in a number of stages. Firstly, the weapon is rough bored using a simple drill. It is then reamed to smooth out the roughest of the spiral scratches produced during the drilling.

The barrel is then rifled using one of the methods as listed under Rifling Methods. After rifling, the barrel is then given a final smoothing. The most frequently used methods for this are *lead lapping* and *ball burnishing*.

In lead lapping, a lead plug of the same diameter as the bore is repeatedly pulled through the rifling whilst being washed through with a fine abrasive. As the barrel becomes progressively smoother, the fineness of the abrasive is increased. This is the most commonly used method and gives a finish satisfactory for most uses.

Ball burnishing is generally only carried out on high-quality rifles and consists of repeatedly pushing a steel ball bearing of the same size as the barrel lands through the bore. This flattens out any irregularities in the bore, leaving a mirror-like finish.

Very high-quality weapons and military rifles, in which the bore is subjected to extremely high temperatures, can also have the bore of the barrel chromium-plated. This results in an extremely hard, mirror-like surface which is very resistant to corrosion, metal fouling and bore wear.

4.2.4   Rifling methods

Hook Cutter rifling.   The most simple method of cutting the grooves is by use of a 'single hook cutter'. In this, a hardened steel cutter, in the shape of a crochet hook, is set into a recess in a steel rod of slightly smaller diameter than the bore of the barrel being rifled. As the cutter is dragged through the bore, the barrel is rotated at a fixed rate to impart the spiral of the rifling. Each pass of the tool only cuts one groove, and the barrel must be repositioned and the process repeated for the number of grooves required. As each pass of the cutter only removes a few thousandths of an inch of metal, the height of the 'hook' must be raised and the grooves all cut again, with up to 80 passes being made for each groove. This is a very time-consuming and, as the hooks rapidly wear out, an expensive method of rifling (Figure 4.5).

Hook rifling can be identified by (i) the presence of longitudinal striations in the cut grooves and (ii) the similarity, as the same tool is used for every groove, between the micro stria in the grooves.

Scrape cutter rifling.   The 'scrape cutter' method of rifling uses a bar with curved and hardened steel scrapers set into it. The number of these scrapers corresponds to the number of grooves required. As a result, all grooves are cut with one pass after which the height of the scrapers is increased and further

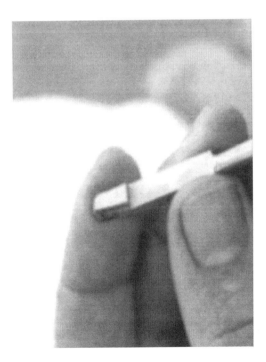

Figure 4.5 Hook cutter.

passes are made. This method produces extremely fine rifling and is used on some of the best weapons.

Scrape cutter rifling is very similar to hook cutter except that as a different scraper is used for each groove, there will be no underlying similarity between the grooves.

Broach rifling. The most commonly used rifling method is called 'broach rifling'. This, in a very simplified form, can be thought of as a series of 20 or 30 steel discs on a rod, with each disc being slightly larger than the one preceding it. Into each disc is cut the profile and number of grooves required with the last disc possessing the final calibre and dimension required. A broach cutter can thus cut all the grooves and lands to the final dimensions in a single pass.

Broach cutter rifling can be recognized by the longitudinal striations on the lands as well as the grooves on the weapon's bore (Figure 4.6).

Button rifling. 'Button rifling' is a very commonly used method but is generally only used on the cheaper weapons, particularly those of 0.22″ calibre.

In this type of rifling, the barrel is bored slightly smaller that the final required diameter. A 'button' on the end of a long rod, containing an exact negative of the rifling required, is then pushed or pulled through the bore forcing the metal to expand into the final shape required (Figure 4.7). This is a single operation and is a very cheap way of rifling a weapon.

Button rifling is, especially in the cheaper weapons, very easy to identify as the circular marks produced during the reaming of the bore are not eliminated during the rifling. These marks are simply pressed into the metal and are visible on both the lands and grooves (Figure 4.8).

Figure 4.6 Broach rifling cutter.

Figure 4.7 Button rifling tool.

Figure 4.8 Section through button-rifled barrel.

Swage or hammer rifling. Another method which is similar to button rifling but produces a very much higher quality is called 'swaging or hammer rifling'. In this method, the bore is reamed slightly larger than the required final diameter. A mandril (an extremely hard steel plug tapered at both ends) containing an exact negative of the rifling profile required is then passed through the bore whilst the outside of the barrel is either hammered or hydraulically squeezed on to it. This method causes the metal not only to work-harden, but also to increase in density. Assuming the mandril is of a good quality, rifled barrels of an exceptional quality are produced.

This type of rifling can, if the outside of the barrel has not been turned down, be recognized by the peculiar spiral indentations on the outside surface due to the hammering or squeezing process. Other than that, the only other identifying characteristic is the mirror-like finish and lack of striations in the rifling.

Other methods of rifling. Other methods of rifling, such as electrolytic and gas cutting, do exist and are used but only to a very limited extent.

A report on the use of *electrochemical machining* for the production of rifling in barrels appeared in the journal of the *Association of Firearms and Toolmark Examiners* in 1988 (Pike, 1988). The barrels reviewed in the report were being made by Cation Co., a small company in Rochester, New York, USA, for an arms manufacturing company called Coonan Arms.

Since 1993, Smith & Wesson (S&W) has also been using an electrochemical machining technique to rifle most of their revolver barrels. The only revolver barrels that S&W still broach rifle are their 0.22 calibre barrels and ported barrels.

Electrochemical machining is not exactly a new method of rifling barrels as it was reportedly used by Krupp, the famous German arms-making company, to manufacture their cannon barrels as early as 1920.

In the modern process, a mandril is made slightly smaller than the bore size of the drilled barrel blank. Strips of plastic are glued to the mandril in a spiral pattern corresponding to the desired shape of the rifling. The mandril is then inserted into the barrel blank and an electrolytic fluid is circulated down the gaps left between the plastic strips and the bore.

A direct current is then applied between the barrel blank and the mandril, with the mandril being made the cathode. The current strips away metal from the exposed areas of the barrel between the plastic strips forming the grooves.

4.2.5 Rifling forms

When black powder was used as a propellant, the extremely heavy fouling produced was a major problem. After a few rounds, the bore became so heavily fouled that subsequent rounds would hardly touch the rifling, leading to a subsequent fall-off in the weapon's accuracy.

In an attempt to counter this problem, a whole variety of rifling profiles were designed with each claiming to have distinct advantages over the rest. Every shape imaginable was tried at one time including square, round, triangular, ratchet, comma and polygroove rifling, which looked like the petals on a flower (Figures 4.9–4.16). Whitworth and Lancaster, both very prolific arms inventors, were both very successful with oval (Whitworth), bored and square bored (Lancaster) rifling.

With the advent of smokeless propellants, the necessity for these complicated rifling profiles and their expensive production costs virtually disappeared.

Figure 4.9 Polygroove rifling.

Figure 4.10 Conventional eight-groove rifling.

Figure 4.11 Polygonal rifling.

Figure 4.12 Lancaster oval-bore rifling.

Figure 4.13 Ratchet rifling.

Figure 4.14 Whitworth rifling.

Figure 4.15 Conventional rifling.

Figure 4.16 Polygonal rifling.

Figure 4.17 Reaming marks on lands of electrochemically etched barrel.

Modern rifling tends to be either square or *polygonal*. Polygonal rifling has no sharp edges and consists of a rounded profile which can be difficult to discern when looking down the barrel. This type of rifling is almost exclusively manufactured using the hammer or swage process.

The advantages of polygonal rifling include:

- no sharp edges to wear;
- no corners for fouling to build up;
- less metal fouling on driving surfaces of the rifling and
- lower friction between bullet and rifling resulting in higher velocity.

It is interesting to compare the profile of the Lancaster oval rifling and polygonal and see how little the science of rifling has advanced since the early 1850s.

Electrochemical rifling is more similar in shape to the button- and broach-rifled barrels, but the shoulders between lands and grooves are not as sharp as commonly seen. This is also apparent upon examination of test-fired bullets.

Whilst it would appear that striation matching on fired bullets could be problematical due to the non-machine tool method of manufacturing the rifling, this has not been found to be the case. This results from two distinct factors: (i) as the barrel lands are not etched during the rifling process, the reaming marks are still present, and (ii) the stripping away of metal during the etching process leaves a totally random stippled effect on the barrel grooves. Hence, both lands and grooves bear individual matchable characteristics (Figure 4.17).

4.2.6   Brief glossary

Ball burnishing	A steel ball bearing of the same size as the barrel lands is repeatedly pushed through the bore. This

flattens out any irregularities in the bore, leaving a mirror-like finish.

Broach rifling	A tool with a series of discs each with a profile of the required rifling. Each disc is slightly larger than the previous one so that the whole depth of the rifling may be cut with one pass of the tool.
Button rifling	A hardened steel 'button' or 'plug' on the end of a long rod, containing an exact negative of the rifling required, which is pushed or pulled through an undersized bore forcing the metal to expand into the final shape required.
Class characteristics	Relate to the number of lands and grooves, their direction of twist, inclination of twist and their width.
Hook cutter	A cutting tool which is hook shaped, like a crochet hook, which cuts one groove at a time.
Lead lapping	A lead plug of the same diameter as the bore is repeatedly pulled through the rifling whilst being washed through with a fine abrasive, giving a highly polished finish.
Polygonal rifling	Land and groove rifling which has a rounded profile instead of the traditional rectangular profile.
Rifling	A series of spiral grooves cut into the inside surface of the bore of the barrel to impart a spin to the bullet through its longitudinal axis.
Rifling grooves	The depressions cut away by the rifling cutter.
Rifling lands	The part of the barrel left standing proud after the rifling cutter has made the rifling grooves.
Skid marks	Rifling engraving produced on the bullet parallel to its axis as a result of the bullet entering the rifling with little or no rotational velocity. This results in a short length of rifling engraved on the bullet which appears to be parallel with its longitudinal axis.
Swage or hammer rifling	A mandril, being an exact negative of the rifling required, is pulled through the bore whilst the barrel is hammered or squeezed on to it.
Twist	The number of inches required for the rifling to prescribe one complete spiral.

4.3   Fluted, Annular Ringed, Helical, Perforated and Oversized Chambers

Fluted, annular ringed, helical and perforated chambers exist in a number of modern weapons and can assist in identifying both class and individual firearm characteristics.

Cutting grooves in a weapon chamber to improve the weapon's functioning was first proposed as early as 1914. This was via a patent issued to Giovanni Angelli for various chamber modifications designed to retard and accelerate the extraction of a fired cartridge case. However, it was not until 1920 that the German Mann 0.25 acp pistol was commercially produced with an annular ringed chamber. The technique was then virtually abandoned until the early 1950s.

Kcrma (1966) lists some 150 current and obsolete weapons with fluted and annular ringed chambers. Most of these are self-loading pistols and sub-machine guns (many of which are made by Heckler and Koch), but there are also several rifles together with one 12 B Bernadelli shotgun, the Automatico V.B.

The main types of chamber markings encountered are as follows:

4.3.1   Fluted chamber

Fluted chambers are longitudinal flutes which are deeper at the forward end of the chamber and taper off towards the rear. These allow the gases produced on firing to flow back over the outside of the cartridge case during firing. This counters the internal pressure and 'lubricates' the case, thus facilitating the extraction process. This is utilized in blowback and delayed blowback weapons where pressures are relatively high, thus making extraction difficult (Figure 4.18).

Figure 4.18 Longitudinal fluted chamber.

4.3.2 Scoop flutes

These are generally wider than those in a normal fluted chamber and are deep in the middle tapering off to nothing at each end. The pressure produced on firing flow forms the case into these depressions, thus retarding the extraction process. Mainly utilized in low-pressure blowback self-loading pistols.

4.3.3 Helical flutes

These are similar to longitudinal flutes in their manner of operation and are designed to assist extraction. Only seen in low-pressure blowback self-loading pistols.

4.3.4 Annular rings

These can be anywhere along the length of the chamber and are quite shallow. Once again, these are designed to retard the extraction process via flow forming of the cartridge case into the depression.

4.3.5 Perforations

These are mainly seen in 0.22″ calibre self-loading pistols where the depressions/perforations are designed to slow down extraction of the cartridge.

4.3.6 Oversized chambers

The German FG42 (Paratroop rifle 42) and some issues of the MP44 make use of the same principle as a fluted chamber in that they have chambers that permit escape of gases around the cartridge case. These chambers, however, are not conventionally fluted, but are of larger diameter for approximately the rear half of the chamber. This allows the gases to escape into this area, thus equalizing the pressure and easing extraction.

A list of some of the more current weapons using these chamber markings appears in Table 4.1.

The depth of the impression left of the fired cases varies enormously with longitudinal flutes leaving the most significant markings, and the helical almost none at all other than the slight blackening from the discharge residues.

The variation in depth of marking produced on the cartridge cases can be seen in Figures 4.19–4.23.

Table 4.1 Some of the move recent weapons utilising chamber markings.

Chamber marking	Weapon	Reason for marking
Longitudinal flutes	H&K P7 9 mm PB	Ease extraction
Longitudinal flutes	H&K MP5 9 mm PB	Ease extraction
Longitudinal flutes	H&K21 m/g 223 Remington/ 5.56 mm NATO or 7.62 × 39 mm	Ease extraction
Longitudinal flutes	H&K33 m/g 223 Remington/ 5.56 mm NATO	Ease extraction
Longitudinal flutes	H&K 91 7.62 × 51 NATO	Ease extraction
Longitudinal flutes	H&K 300 0.22 WMR	Ease extraction
Longitudinal flutes	12B Bernadelli shotgun, the Automatico V.B.	Ease extraction
Longitudinal flutes	Russian Tokarev M1940 7.62	Ease extraction
Scoop flute	H&K4 0.380 acp	Retard extraction
Scoop flute	Seecamp 0.32 acp	Retard extraction
Helical flute	PRC Type 64, 7.62 × 17 mm slp	Ease extraction
Single annular groove	PRC Type 77, 7.62 × 17 slp	Retard extraction
Multiple annular grooves	Kimball 0.30 M1 Carbine	Retard extraction
Multiple annular grooves	Colt National Match Mk III 0.38 Spl	Retard extraction
Perforations	AMT Automag II	Retard extraction
Increased chamber size	German FG42 and some issues of the MP44	Ease extraction

H&K, Heckler & Koch; PRC, Peoples Republic of Clina; AMT, Arcadia Machine and Tool.

4.3.7 Matchability of stria on fluted chamber impressions

The quality and quantity of stria produced varies greatly and depends upon the pressure produced by the cartridge, the malleability of the cartridge case, the material the case has been manufactured from, whether the cartridge case has been plated, the depth of the depressions in the chamber and most important of all, the type of chamber depression.

Longitudinal fluted, scoop fluted and perforated chambers generally produce the best markings on the cartridge case, whilst helical and annular fluted chambers produce very little. With the PRC helically fluted chambers, the 7.62 × 17 mm ammunition is of very low pressure, and the lack of markings is probably more due to this than the depth of the helical flute itself.

Aluminium cases are better than brass at taking up any transfer of stria, and steel cases generally take none at all.

Any type of plating applied to the cartridge case will generally prevent any matchable stria being transferred, although with longitudinal fluting, the general outline of the markings will often be clearly visible.

Figure 4.19 Longitudinal fluted chamber marks on fired cartridge case.

Figure 4.20 Scoop chamber marks on fired cartridge case.

Figure 4.21 Helical chamber marks on fired cartridge case.

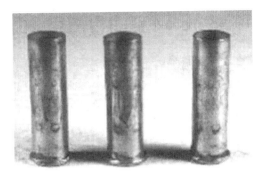

Figure 4.22 Perforated chamber marks on fired cartridge case.

Figure 4.23 Annular ring chamber marks on fired cartridge case.

Having said that, the longitudinal flutings found in most H&K weapons produce extremely clear stria on brass cartridge cases. These are normally readily matchable and can provide a valuable adjunct in the investigation of armed crime incidents.

4.4   Basic Concepts of Striation Matching

4.4.1   Class characteristics

As explained in Section 4.2, the rifling of each weapon will possess a series of family resemblances which will be present in all weapons of the same make and model. Correctly called 'class characteristics', they relate to the number of lands and grooves, their direction of twist, inclination of twist, width and profile. Whilst these dimensions can be extremely useful in identifying the calibre, make and model of the weapon which fired a particular bullet, they cannot be used to individualize the weapon.

4.4.2 Individual characteristics

Whilst all weapons of the same make and model will have the same class characteristics, statistically and empirically, it can be shown that no two weapons will have exactly the same individual rifling characteristics. These individual characteristics are caused by small defects in the rifling which are produced during the manufacturing process. They are totally random and, as such, are as individual to a particular weapon as fingerprints are to a person. These marks are called *individual characteristics*.

It is thought by many that the individual characteristics in a weapon's rifling result from the actual cutter which makes the rifling. Whilst the actual cutter does wear very slightly with each pass it makes, and factors such as inclusions in the metal of the barrel and swarf build-up, do produce individual characteristics, this is not the primary source of the marks used when individualizing a weapon.

The marks inside a barrel which characterize that weapon are not longitudinal, as produced by rifling cutters, but are rotational or spiral. These rotational marks are produced during the initial drilling and reaming of the weapon's bore and, as such, are totally random. They result from wear of the drilling tool, build-up of swarf on the cutting edge and hard inclusions in the metal's crystalline structure. Being rotational, they leave far more characteristic marks on a bullet passing over them than longitudinal striations.

Despite any actions subsequent to the rifling, for example, lead lapping and ball burnishing (Section 4.2), it is exceedingly difficult to eradicate totally these rotational marks.

It is the rotational or spiral marks on the barrel's lands which translate into longitudinal striations on the grooves of a bullet as it passes down the bore, and it is these striations which enable a fired bullet to be connected, *beyond reasonable doubt*, to a particular weapon.

Whilst the majority of these individual characteristics will remain with the weapon for its working life, the bore of a weapon will also acquire additional individual characteristics as it ages. These additional marks can include, for example, small corrosion pits, damage caused by improper use of a cleaning rod and accidental damage to the muzzle.

Overzealous cleaning with abrasives and steel wire brushes to remove metal fouling can also damage or alter the appearance of a weapon's individual characteristics. In some instances, the excessive use of force can actually erase some of the individual characteristics. It can thus be seen that the individual characteristics in the bore of a weapon are constantly evolving.

4.4.3   Purposeful eradication of individual characteristics

It is often assumed that the last part of the rifling to touch the bullet before it leaves the barrel produces the only stria of any significance. In part, this is true as the last part of the bore does have the ability of erasing any stria which came earlier. It is also true that if the marks made nearer to the breech were deeper than those at the muzzle, then they will not be erased.

There have been many instances where the last few inches of a barrel have been sawn off in an attempt to prevent a weapon from being linked with previous cases. In one case, the felon used a saw to remove the last 2 in. of a barrel between the first and second bank robberies. In between subsequent armed robbery cases, he placed the barrel in a lathe and removed the top two thousandths of an inch of the rifling lands. By the time of the last robbery, no rifling was visible in the bore at all. Matching the bullets from the first and second robberies was straightforward as the individual characteristics had only been slightly altered. Matching the rest was somewhat problematical as the tops of the lands had changed so much between subsequent cases they could no longer be used. It was possible, however, to find an area of accidental damage to one of the grooves, probably caused by a steel cleaning rod, which enabled all the bullets to be matched.

4.4.4   Life expectancy of individual stria

If a weapon's bore is well maintained, kept clear of metal fouling, regularly cleaned and kept free of rust, it is probable that the individual striations in the bore will not change significantly during a weapon's life. Practically speaking though, the constant evolution of its individual characteristics will, over time, cause a significant change in these marks.

This evolution of individual characteristics can be so significant that whilst it is possible to match bullets fired one after the other, bullets fired months apart or even numbers of rounds apart may not be matchable.

In this respect, rusting of the bore is the method by which the individual characteristics are most likely to be permanently altered. Such pitting and corrosion of the bore can be so serious that it is impossible to match the micro stria from consecutively fired bullets.

4.4.5   Identification of weapon type

When a revolver is fired, the fired cartridge cases remain in the weapon until the weapon is manually opened and the cartridge cases are ejected. Unless all the rounds have been fired and the weapon has been reloaded, it is unusual to find fired cartridge cases from a revolver at the scene of a shooting incident.

With fully automatic weapons and self-loading pistols, rifles and shotguns, the empty cartridge case is automatically ejected from the weapon after firing. Unless there is a mechanical fault, a fired cartridge case will always be found at a crime scene where one of these weapons has been fired.

In pump, bolt action and other repeating weapons, it is also possible that after firing, the action will be manually cycled to load a fresh cartridge into the chamber. During this process, the fired cartridge case will be ejected from the weapon. As a result, a fired cartridge case will often be recovered from a crime scene where a repeating weapon has been used. The absence of a cartridge cannot, however, rule out the use of a repeating weapon.

As in the case of fired bullets, these fired cartridge cases will also possess 'class' and 'individual characteristics'. These class characteristics will include the position and shape of the extractor claw (the hook at the end of the extractor which clips over the cartridge rim to enable extraction) and ejector pin, marks made by the lips of the magazine and feed ramp into the barrel, cut-outs on the standing breech face, marks made by the edge of the ejector port on the slide and, in certain weapons, the actual shape of the tip of the firing pin (Figure 4.24).

These will, once again, enable the calibre, type, make and model of the weapon to be ascertained with a high degree of accuracy.

An example illustrating how easy it can be to make a wrong identification involved the case of a very wealthy woman who was shot five times in the back with a 0.22″ Magnum calibre weapon. Matching the cartridge cases and bullets proved an extremely difficult task due to the very fine stria present. Eventually, it was concluded that as the cartridge cases and bullets could be grouped into one batch containing three and the other two, then two 0.22″ Magnum calibre self-loading pistols had been used. Several months after the shooting, a man surrendered to the police and confessed to the murder. It turned out that he had

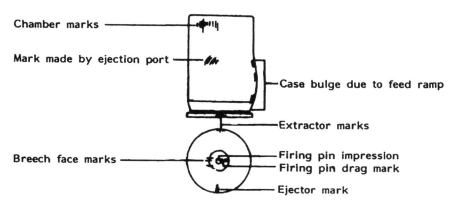

Figure 4.24 Diagram showing extractor, ejector, breech face and other marks on a fired cartridge case.

been the woman's butler and had been terribly badly treated by her. Finally, he had snapped and shot her in the back with a 0.22" Magnum calibre double-barrelled Derringer. He had reloaded twice during the shooting, ejecting the fired cartridge cases, leaving one live unfired round which he took away with him.

4.4.6 Individual characteristics on cartridge cases

The parts of a weapon which imprint class characteristics on the fired cartridge case have, of course, been individually manufactured. The manufacturing process involves cutting, drilling, grinding, hand filing and, very occasionally, hand polishing. Each of these processes will leave individual characteristics in much the same way as the boring process, which is the initial step in making a barrel.

An example which conveniently illustrates the production of individual characteristics would be the final step in the production of a firing pin. After the automated manufacturing processes have produced the rough pin, the final step would be the rounding off of the tip with a smooth file. Each pass of the file across the firing pin tip will involve removal of metal, some of which will be deposited on the cutting edges of the file. This deposited metal will alter the cutting characteristics of part of the file, which will continue to be altered further as the metal build-up continues.

During this whole process, the surface of the file is constantly changing, giving an endless variety of striation marks on the tip of the firing pin. Other variables which will also radically affect the stria left on the pin's surface are the force applied, the gradual wearing and blunting of the tool's cutting surface, and the direction and angle at which the file is used. Such are the variables involved, that the chance of two firing pins having exactly the same manufacturing stria is so low as to be negligible.

It is the combination of these randomly produced patterns of individual stria which enable, with a degree of certainty beyond reasonable doubt, to match a weapon to fired ammunition.

4.4.7 Formation of stria

During the firing of a weapon, the individual stria are transferred from the hard surface of the weapon on to the softer surface of the bullet or cartridge case during the firing.

As the tremendous pressures build up during the first few moments of firing, the base of the bullet swells to fill and so obturate the weapon's bore. As it passes down the barrel, the minute irregularities in the bore form longitudinal scores or striations down the length of the bullet. Some of these are obviously rubbed off or modified by subsequent barrel imperfections and others remain during the bullet's flight through the weapon's bore (Figures 4.25–4.28).

Likewise, the tremendous pressures on the base of the bullet are also exerted in an equal and opposite direction on the cartridge case. The case is thus slammed into the standing breech face replicating, in reverse, the toolmarks thereon. As the cartridge is extracted from the chamber, the extractor claw imparts its own class and individual toolmarks on to the rim of the cartridge. The ejector striking the base of the cartridge to tip it away from the gun will also leave its own class and individual characteristics.

Other marks such as the lips from the magazine, the ramp, which directs the round of ammunition into the chamber (feed ramp), and the indicator pin, which shows whether the chamber is loaded, will also leave individual characteristics.

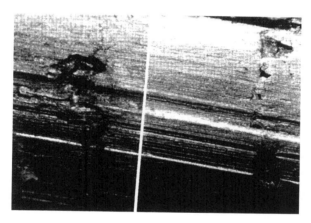

Figure 4.25 Striation match on a bullet.

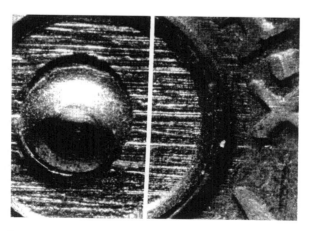

Figure 4.26 Striation match on a cartridge case.

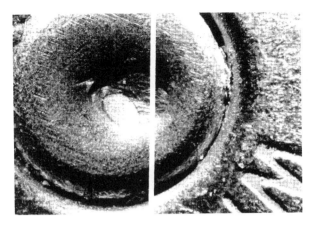

Figure 4.27 Striation match in firing pin impression.

A good example of class and individual characteristics can be found on many of the 7.62×25 mm calibre type 54 Chinese military pistols. In these, the end milling striations from the standing breech are clearly visible on the fired cartridge case. These are often mistaken for individual characteristics, and it is very easy to make an incorrect identification on this basis. As the class characteristics run in an arc across the standing breech (the gross milling marks) and the individual characteristics (the fine finishing marks) run from top to bottom, if the cartridge is turned through 90°, the individual characteristics reveal themselves (Figure 4.28).

4.4.8 Problematical areas

Damaged bullets, bullets fired through rusty barrels, bullet fragments and barrels with little or no rifling, all produce their own problems. Polygonal rifling, however, produces problems of a completely different type.

The main difficulties with trying to match two bullets from a polygonal rifling are:

- There are no sharp-edged rifling grooves; it is extremely difficult to locate land and groove marks.
- The barrel is hammered on to a mandril; there will be no reaming marks to replicate themselves on the bullet.
- A mandril will often be used to make hundreds of barrels. In addition, as there will be little or no wear on the mandril, each barrel should be virtually identical.
- To improve manufacturing efficiency, the barrel blank is of sufficient length that three or even four barrels can be made with one pass of the mandril.

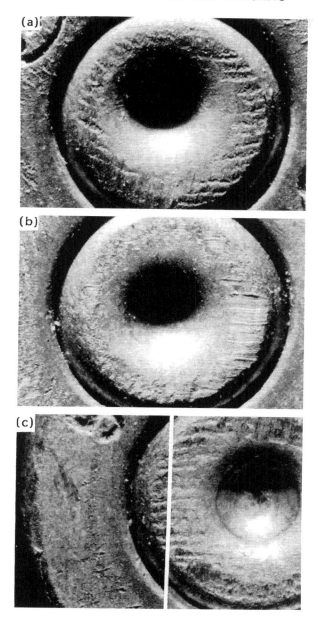

Figure 4.28 Photomicrographs showing (a) class; (b) individual characteristics on a cartridge case fired in a type 54 pistol (from the same weapon); (c) false match of class characteristics (from two different weapons).

Generally speaking, it is possible, although extremely difficult, to match bullets from polygonal rifled barrels. The individual characteristics which are generally of most use are not from the rifling, but from other barrel finishing processes. These include the production of the *leade* (also spelt leed and lead) from the chamber or from the *crowning* of the muzzle.

The *leade* is the area forward of the chamber where the rifling is slightly cut back. This is to allow the bullet to gradually engage the rifling. Also called *chamber throat*, it is generally cut with a reaming tool. The marks left by the reaming tool will leave individual marks on the bullet.

In crowning, the rifling at the muzzle end of the barrel is very slightly counter-bored (cut back) to reduce the chance of accidental damage to this vulnerable area of the rifling. Whatever process is used, the cutting implement will leave its own individual characteristics which will be reproduced on the bullet as it leaves the muzzle.

Problems with striation visualization and matching of non-lead and non-toxic bullets.   Most of the non-lead and non-toxic bullet types pose little problem with respect to the visualization of stria and the subsequent matching on a comparison microscope. Some do, however, have to be treated somewhat differently in order to visualize what stria might be present. The various bullet types available are numerous and new ones are being added virtually by the day. Some of the currently available ones follow:

- Winchester Lubalox. Introduced in 1991. Some confusion exists over this coating with Winchester calling it an 'oxide coating similar to blueing' (could be a form of Parkerizing) and others refering to it as a molybdenum disulphiode coating.
- Federal Nyclad – bullet coated with a shiny black nylon-type material;
- molybdenum disulphide and Nylon 11 (possibly Nyclad);
- totally metal jacketed (TMJ);
- nickel-plated copper jacket – sometimes with copper disc over exposed lead at base of bullet;
- copper-plated steel jacket – sometimes with copper disc over exposed lead at base of bullet;
- solid brass Tres Haute Vitesse (THV);
- sintered tungsten – early KTW;
- hardened solid brass – KTW;
- sintered iron;
- sintered zinc;
- nylon/zinc composite;

- combinations of zinc, tin, tungsten, bismuth and copper with nylon or some type of polymer;
- steel jacket – copper coated (Chinese 7.62 × 25 mm pre-1985, also current 7.62 × 39 mm);
- solid steel (Chinese 7.62 × 25 mm post-1985).

As most of the above composites have some softer, usually organic, material blended in with the sintered metal, they pose little or no problem in respect of barrel wear or the transfer of stria from the barrel to the bullet and the subsequent examination on a comparison microscope.

Please note, however, the problems listed in Table 4.2.

Methodology for magnesium smoking. Magnesium smoking can be used:

- to render translucent and highly reflective materials such as polyvinylchlonde (PVC) and nylon opaque that they can be examined under a comparison microscope
- for the examination bullets fired through lightly rusted barrels. In this instance, the smoking eliminates the very fine stria which results from the corrosion. This leaves the stria due to the weapon's individual signature clearly visible;
- to eliminate differences in colour of the areas under examination.

The smoking itself is quite an art (Burd, 1965). It is, however, non-permanent and non-destructive, and if the layer of deposited magnesium oxide is too thick, it can simply be blown off or brushed clean with a very soft bristled brush. If the covering is insufficient, it can be thickened up by re-smoking.

Care must be taken, however, when dealing with low melting point materials such as polyethylene, PVC or nylon as the heat from the burning magnesium can melt the material under examination.

To carry out the smoking, a short length of magnesium ribbon, about 4 in. long, is held in a pair of pliers and ignited. The material being smoked is then wafted in the plume of smoke until an even deposit over the entire surface is achieved. Metallic materials are best held at a distance of about 3 in. above the burning magnesium and low melting point materials at a greater distance.

A light coating over transparent or translucent materials will enable any stria present to be easily seen under a comparison microscope.

Case example. This case involved a murder committed with a heavily used 0.22″ RF target rifle.

A bore scope examination of the suspect weapon showed the rifling to be heavily fouled and to contain significant quantities of deposited lead.

Table 4.2 Some of the problems associated with stria visualization on nonlead missiles.

Bullet Type	Problem	Solution
Nyclad	A black shiny coating completely covering the bullet. Stria are not visible under normal lighting due to the reflection of light.	Lightly smoking the bullet with burning magnesium will eliminate light reflection and visualize any stria present.
Sintered iron	This is quite a hard material and stria are not easily transferred. Care should be taken not to fire too many rounds as the bullet can remove the finer stria.	No solution; limit the number of rounds fired.
Sintered tungsten	Early KTW ammunition was provided with a gas check to take up the rifling. This does tend to fall off on hitting the target.	Ensure that the gas check is not overlooked as the bullet itself does not contact the rifling
Solid steel	This type of ammunition simply tears out the bore of a weapon. Each round produces a huge ball of sparks as a result of the rifling being removed from the barrel!	Rounds 1–3 will probably be matchable, but 1 and 4 will probably not. After 50 rounds, the bore will be all but bereft of rifling.
Steel jacket	Once again extremely hard on the barrel's rifling.	Not as bad as solid steel, but care must still be taken with the number of rounds fired.
Totally metal jacketed	Lead core completely covered by a very thick electroplated copper/zinc (Cu/Zn) jacket.	Coating tends to be very much harder than a normal Cu/Zn jacket. Problems have been noted with certain weapons which have fairly shallow rifling (older Colt revolvers). It has been found that the rifling is too shallow to gain sufficient purchase on the bullet and slippage occurs. Not only are the rounds very difficult to match but as a result of insufficient spin stabilization, the weapons become very inaccurate.
Saboted bullets	The sabot is lost once the bullet leaves the muzzle, leaving a completely unmarked bullet. Also, the sabot is manufactured from a somewhat reflective and translucent polyethylene or plastic-type material. This renders a normal microscopic comparison virtually impossible.	As with Nyclad bullets, lightly smoking the sabot with burning magnesium strip will eliminate light reflection and visualize any stria present.
Plastic shotgun wads	Once again, these are manufactured from a shiny translucent polyethylene-type material which renders a normal microscopic comparison virtually impossible.	Stria from the front sight bead staking, adjustable chokes, etc. can be transferred to the plastic wad. These can likewise be visualized by smoking with burning magnesium.

As was normal practice at that time, a clean, tight patch of '4 × 2' cotton was pushed through the bore to determine whether the fouling was fresh or otherwise. Subsequent to this, two rounds were fired and the bullets recovered. These bullets were compared as a reference prior to carrying out a comparison with the bullet recovered from the victim. These two bullets matched perfectly. There was, however, virtually no similarity between these and the bullet recovered from the body.

There was no question as to whether any other weapon was involved as it was known for certain that the case exhibit rifle was the murder weapon.

In an attempt to determine why the bullet from the body could not be matched with the controls from the suspect weapon, I took 20 heavily used 0.22″ RF target weapons of the same make and model and collected the first and second bullet from each. In each case, these two bullets matched perfectly. I then fired 50 more bullets from each rifle and collected the next two from each gun. Once again, the fifty-third and fifty-fourth bullets from each rifle matched each other perfectly. As expected, these two also matched the first and second bullets fired from each gun.

I then pushed a tight 4″ × 2″ patch through the barrel of each rifle bore and then fired two more bullets through each.

Of the 20 rifles, the bullets fired from eleven (which were the ones which started out with the heaviest fouling) could not be matched with the bullets fired prior to the cleaning. Of the rest, four were marginal matches and the rest were satisfactorily matched (B.J. Heard, unpublished paper).

It was obvious that the bullets from the eleven rifles were unmatchable due to the removal of the lead from the rifling by the patch of 4 × 2″. Once this lead had been removed, the fine stria underneath was exposed. Bullets fired through this clean barrel took up the fine stria, whilst those fired through the barrel before it was cleaned had no fine stria present. The only stria present of the bullets before the barrel was cleaned was the gross stria on the leading and trailing edges of the rifling.

The absence of fine stria on the bullets fired prior to cleaning the barrel rendered a positive match with bullets fired after cleaning, a far from positive undertaking.

In an attempt to reproduce the effect the heavy barrel leading had on bullets fired through it, the bullets fired after cleaning were smoked with burning magnesium. This effectively covered up the fine stria leading to matchable bullets in every case. It was noted that the bullets fired through the barrel before cleaning also required a light smoking to ensure that there was no colour difference between the two bullets being compared.

The bullet recovered from the deceased and the bullets fired from case rifle after the barrel had been cleaned were smoked in exactly the same way, and a positive match was found.

As a result of the above findings, it is strongly suggested that if it is deemed necessary to examine the barrel of 0.22″ RF weapons for signs of fouling from firing, it should be done with great caution and then only using a very loosely fitting patch.

4.4.9 Brief glossary

Class characteristics	A series of family resemblances which will be present in all weapons of the same make and model.
Crowning	Chamfering or cutting back the rifling at the muzzle end of the barrel to reduce the chance of accidental damage to this vulnerable area of the rifling.
Individual characteristics	Random imperfections produced during manufacture or caused by accidental damage, rusting, and so on, which are unique to that object and distinguish it from all the others.
Leade, leed or lead (also called chamber throat)	The area forward of the chamber where the rifling is slightly cut back to allow the bullet to gradually engage the rifling.

4.5 Basic Methodology Used in Comparison Microscopy

4.5.1 Introduction

It has been quoted (Walls, 1968) that up to 25% of the stria in a non-match and in excess of 75% of the stria in a match will show concordance. Such a degree of accidentally matching lines is exceedingly high and has not been supported by personal experience. There is no dispute, however, that out of the thousands of lines present in any one comparison, a number must, by pure chance alone, show agreement.

When carrying out a microscopic comparison, the accidental agreement in a non-match must be recognized by the examiner and mentally discounted as being non-relevant. It is this ability to reject non-matching stria whilst accepting those of relevance which is the identifying feature of an experienced comparison microscopist.

The actual process of assessing which stria are of relevance is quite simple. Firstly, each of the available fired ammunition components (for this example, fired bullets) is compared to all the other test-fired bullets until one, which is representative of a 'match', is found. This is then used as a reference for comparison with the fired bullets in the actual case.

During this search for a representative 'match', one is attempting to find a pattern of easily recognizable stria which can be mentally retained and used in subsequent comparisons with the case bullets. This identification of a stria pattern can only be obtained through extensive experience in the matching of stria and cannot be taught in a book.

Should there be a suspected match with the case bullet, then each of the other test bullets must also be compared with the case exhibit to determine whether the agreement was accidental or a match exists which is beyond reasonable doubt.

4.5.2 Obtaining control samples

When a weapon has been located, it will be necessary to recover 'control' examples of bullets, and cartridge cases for comparison with those recovered from the crime scene.

Before firing the weapon, it is necessary to carefully wipe any excess grease, oil or debris from the barrel which might cause additional accidental stria on the fired bullets. It is also necessary, if it is a self-loading pistol, to clean any grease or debris from the standing breech face. Such grease could act as a cushion preventing the transfer of stria on to the cartridge case. In addition, the first round fired could impress the debris into the standing breech face with sufficient force as to leave marks which would be reproduced during subsequent firings.

Before removing any grease or debris, it is always worth examining the breech face under a microscope as it is often possible to see an imprint in the dirt or oil of the headstamp of the last cartridge to be fired.

After carefully cleaning the weapon, a minimum of four, preferably more, rounds of ammunition of exactly the same make and type should be fired and the components collected for examination. These rounds should be collected in sequence as there could be a progressive change in the barrel, due to rusting or some other factor, which could effect the striation comparison.

It is extremely important that exactly the same type and make of ammunition to be used as minor variations in the hardness of components or pressures produced could seriously affect the appearance of the impressed stria.

The bullets should then be cross compared until a mental picture is obtained as to what are the salient features and what marks can be disregarded.

4.5.3 Manufacturing marks on ammunition

Mention has already been made of weapons class characteristics, for example, end milling on the standing breech face of Chinese type 54 pistols (Section 4.4). However, one should also be aware that manufacturing marks also exist on unfired ammunition as well.

An example of how confusing ammunition manufacturing marks can be came to light in a laboratory accreditation examination. A number of cartridge cases were submitted and the examiners were asked to determine how many weapons had been used. The problem appeared to be very simple and everyone returned the same results, four cartridges in one gun and two in another. The examiners had, however, been rather unfair and obtained two batches of the same make of ammunition, one of which had very pronounced manufacturing marks and the other none. Four cartridges had been fired from one batch and two from the other, and, as the breech face marks were extremely faint and the firing pin featureless, the mistake was easy to make. The test was eventually withdrawn as every participating laboratory returned the same results.

4.5.4   Recovery methods for fired bullets

If a weapon has been recovered, it will be necessary to compare fired ammunition from this weapon with fired ammunition recovered from the scene.

Obtaining a series of test cartridge cases from a self-loading pistol presents little difficulty as they merely have to be picked up. Obtaining fired bullets in a near pristine condition is, however, a little more difficult.

In the past, *cotton waste* or *wadding* has been used, but this material can be quite abrasive to soft-lead bullets especially those of 0.22″ rimfire calibre.

High grade, long-fibre cotton wool is extremely good at preserving the finest stria on the softest of lead bullets. It is, however, very expensive and has to be frequently replaced.

Vertical and *horizontal water tanks* for bullet recovery are currently very popular, but these also have their own problems.

One of the major problems faced with all water recovery tanks is that of algae formation. The nitrates in gunshot residues form an ideal breeding ground for algae and the tank soon becomes a thick green soup. Whilst this does not effect the bullet recovery, it is not a pleasant medium to work with. Bleach or a bactericide can be used to remove this algae, but great care must be taken to ensure that the bullet surface is not corroded by whatever is added to the water.

Horizontal bullet recovery tanks, where the bullet is fired at an angle from one end into the top of the tank, suffer from bullet recovery problems. Once the bullet loses its velocity, it drops to the bottom of the tank and the only practical way of recovering it is with a piece of Plasticine or Blue-tak on the end of a long stick. Locating the bullet is another problem as the formation of algae can make it very difficult to find the bullet in the first place.

In addition, the firer has to be extremely careful that the bullet does not ricochet from the water's surface. Too steep an angle and the bullet will penetrate the bottom of the tank, too shallow, and it will ricochet.

The tanks, when full of water, are also extremely heavy, often requiring floor reinforcement and, as they are generally made from sheet stainless steel, very expensive.

Vertical bullet recovery tanks do not suffer with ricochet problems, but they do have to be a minimum of 6 ft deep to ensure that the bullet loses all its velocity before reaching the bottom of the tank. With a minimum depth of 6 ft, the tank is often sited on one floor of a building with the base resting on the floor below.

One problem which all water recovery tanks suffer from is the propensity for the bullet to spiral down the tank, eventually hitting the sides and becoming damaged. This problem is, for some unknown reason, particularly acute with vertical tanks.

This problem is commonly referred to as *bullet progression* and appears to be a function of bullet yaw in which the bullet prescribes a spiral round the axis of its flight. This is due to over-stabilization of the bullet by the rifling, much as in the wobbling motion of a top when it is first spun.

This spiral round its flight axis is accentuated by the increased density of water over air which sends the bullet into an ever-increasing spiral as it progresses down the tank. If the tank is not of sufficient diameter, the bullet will contact the sides of the tank and become badly damaged. A vertical tank diameter of 3 ft (1 m) is considered the absolute minimum.

Another problem with vertical recovery tanks is the hydraulic shock produced when a bullet is fired into water. As water is non-compressible, a shock wave is produced when it is struck by a bullet. This shock wave travels down the tank, bulging the walls quite alarmingly. When the tank regains its original shape, it rebounds, lifting it off its base and sending large quantities of water out of the top of the tank. The continual hammering action of the tank jumping off its base (even though this might be just a fraction of an inch) and the bulging of its sides can have quite serious consequences for the building in which it is sited.

In one instance, a very large tank was sited in the corner of a forensic laboratory building. After several hundred rounds of ammunition had been fired into it, the bulging sides and hammering action on its base had pushed out the walls of the building to such an extent that there was a 6 in. gap straight through the brickwork on either side.

Probably one of the most convenient and cheap materials for bullet recovery goes under the trade name of 'Crocell (Crocell Hot Dip)'. This is a high molecular weight petroleum jelly which is used as a protective coat on high-quality engineering tools. The material, which comes in granulated form, is simply melted then cast into 1 in. (25 mm) thick slabs which are placed into a long wooden or steel box. Bullets fired into this material stop in a surprisingly short space (12 in. for a 0.38″ Special and 20 in. for a 9 mm PB) and can be recovered quite easily by pulling out the sheets.

The material is exceedingly good at preserving fine stria even for the softest of lead bullets. In addition, after 30 or so shots, the damaged sheets are merely recast.

Care should be taken to ensure that during firing, a piece of card is placed in front of the first sheet of Crocell. If this is not done, unburnt propellant particles which issue from the muzzle of the weapon will accumulate in and on the front sheet of Crocell. After a few recastings, the quantity of propellant in the Crocell can reach levels where a distinct fire hazard will exist.

Probably one of the most unusual cases involving bullet recovery resulted from the strafing of a fishing boat by a military aircraft. The boat was not sunk but was badly damaged. Upon examination of the boat, two 30 mm cannon bullets were found lodged in the smashed engine block and mountings. A microscopic examination of the copper driving bands on the bullets showed that they had been fired through different barrels. Eventually, a number of aircraft were located which could have carried out the shooting, each of which was armed with four 30 mm cannons.

Obviously, Crocell and cotton wool were not going to be the first choice of recovery materials for this type of missile. In the end, a 200 ft trench was dug, which was 6 ft wide and 6 ft deep. Into a pit at one end of the trench was mounted an action from a 30 mm cannon onto which the barrels from the suspect aircraft could be attached one at a time. The pit was filled up with sawdust, which was then soaked in oil. A soldier was positioned every 10 ft along the pit and as the disturbance from the cannon bullet passing through the sawdust was seen, he raised his arm. The last soldier to raise his arm was then given a shovel and told to dig! After much noise and hours of digging, sufficient bullets were located, which were used to determine whose guns were used to strafe the ship.

4.6   Mathematical Proof of Striation Matches

4.6.1   Introduction

This is a difficult subject to comprehend due to the statistics involved. As such, it is often, when dealing with questions on the subject in court, glossed over with such comments as 'statistically it can be shown, but as I am not a statistician' or 'empirical studies have shown' or even 'a match is one which exceeds the best known non-match'.

But, how large does an empirical study have to be before it can be determined that a match between two bullets is beyond reasonable doubt? Does an empirical study with one weapon type necessarily have any bearing on other weapon types? And, even more difficult to quantify, what is a best known non-match and how many require observation before one can be recognized?

All are crucial questions and, if not correctly answered, or for that matter correctly handled by the prosecution or defence, they could lead to misrepresentation of evidence or even the witness being unnecessarily discredited.

These matters do involve quite difficult statistics, and such mathematical concepts can become very complex. This chapter will attempt to show why no match, no matter how good, will ever be 100% perfect. It will also attempt to handle the statistical side as simply as possible, allowing even the non-mathematically minded to grasp the basics of the subject.

4.6.2 Stria individuality

Many papers have been written with a view to analyzing statistically, using idealized computer modelling or digitally enhanced striations marks, the probabilities affecting positive striation comparisons. Among these, Tsuneo Uchiyama (Uchiyama, 1988, 1993), Biasotti (1980, 1984, 1991) and Brackett (1965) are notable.

Most of the papers examined have, however, been of a very esoteric nature and only of any real use to theoretical statisticians.

It is possible, however, to use a very simplified approach and to obtain an idea of the probabilities of grooves on bullets from different sources having corresponding stria.

If, to simplify the matter as far as possible, we take an analogy of randomly filling a number of boxes, so that the analogy can be translated into matching striations in a rifling groove, there will be three conditions:

(1) There are 20 boxes, 10 of which will be randomly filled.
(2) Each of the filled boxes can be heavily shaded or lightly shaded.
(3) Each of the filled boxes can have either an 'X' or a 'Y'.

Taking condition 1 alone:
In this condition, there are 20 boxes, 10 of which will be randomly filled.

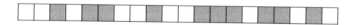

The chance that in a similar 20 boxes, exactly the same combination, will be filled is given by the standard statistical formula:

$$_mC_n = \frac{m!}{n!(m-n)!}$$

where C = chance of stria accidentally matching;
  $_mC_n$ = chance of accidentally matching stria within the parameters 'm' and 'n';
  m = number of boxes;
  n = number of filled boxes;
  ! = factorial, that is, $5! = 5 \times 4 \times 3 \times 2 \times 1$

For this example, if m = 20
    n = 10

$$\text{Chance} = {}_{20}C_{10} = \frac{20!}{10!(20-10)!} = \frac{20!}{10! \times 10!} = 184,756.$$

Thus, the chance of having two sets of 20 boxes each having 10 randomly filled boxes in the same combination is a chance of *1 in 184,756*.

If we now take into consideration condition 2 in addition to condition 1:
Condition 2 states that each of the *filled boxes* can be lightly shaded or heavily shaded.

As each box has one of two possible shadings, the chance that the first box will be the same in both sets is 1:2. The chance that the second box is the same will also be 1:2. But as this is dependent upon the first box, the chance that the first two boxes will be shaded exactly the same is $1:2 \times 1:2$, for example, 2×2.

Thus, the chance of all 10 filled boxes in both sets having the same shade of filling is $2 \times 2 \times 2 \times 2 \times 2 \times 2 \times 2 \times 2 \times 2 \times 2 = 2^{10} = 1024$.

The chance of 10 randomly filled boxes out of 20 each with a randomly chosen dark or light shading is therefore $184,756 \times 1024 = 189,190,144$.

The chance of the two sets of 20 boxes each with randomly matching 10 filled boxes which are either light or dark shading is a chance of 1 in 189,190,144.

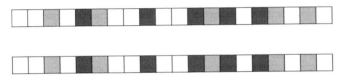

If we now take into consideration condition 3 in addition to conditions 1 and 2:
Condition 3:
If each of these shaded boxes can then have either an 'X' or a 'Y'.
The same probability factor as above is relevant that is, 2^{10}.
Thus, the figure becomes $189,190,144 \times 1024 = 193,730,707,456$.
The chance of two sets of 20 boxes with 10 boxes randomly filled with either light or dark shading and either an 'X' or a 'Y' is *a* chance of 1 in 193,730,707,456.

If now we place this into the context of a bullet, we have a single groove on a bullet which we divide into 20 longitudinal sections, and in 10 of these longitudinal sections are randomly placed 10 striations. The chance of two grooves on bullets from different weapons accidentally matching is thus:

A chance of *1 in 184,756*.

If each of these striations can have one of two profiles, for example, a pointed shape or a square shape, then the chance of two grooves from different weapons accidentally matching under these criteria is $184,756 \times 1024 = 189,190,144$, that is,

A chance of *1 in 189,190,144*.

If each of these striations can now be one of two widths, say thick or thin, then the chance of two grooves from two different weapons accidentally matching under all three criteria is $189,190,144 \times 1024 = 193,730,707,456$, that is,

A chance of *1 in 193,730,707,456*.

This is, of course, taking a very simple case. In reality, there will be not just 20 possible positions for striations in a groove but hundreds. There will not just be 10 striations but, once again, hundreds, the number only being limited by the resolving power of the microscope. There will not be just two profiles but tens of possibilities, and the width once again will be tens of possibilities.

Just taking one groove alone, the number becomes so vast that it must approach infinity. If this is extended to the possibility of finding two bullets where all the grooves match, then the number must be infinitely large and reach a stage where it is beyond the realms of possibility.

It can thus be seen that the chance of finding a complete set of accidentally matching stria in bullets from different sources is so infinitesimally small as to be negligible.

This statement is just as viable for other impressed striation marks as it is for the striations found within the rifling of bullets.

It thus follows that the pattern of surface contours comprised of peaks, ridges and furrows found within an impressed toolmark can be considered unique to that tool. It is immaterial whether the tool be the standing breech face of a weapon, a firing pin, the tip of a pry bar or the faces of a bolt cutter, for the marks produced will be individual to that tool.

4.6.3 Philosophy

Factors such as the hardness of the materials, pressures produced, build-up of fouling and general debris mean that the striations found on fired bullets and cartridge cases will inevitably exhibit variations from shot to shot. It is thus an impossibility for two bullets or cartridge cases fired from the same weapon to have absolute concordance in their stria.

Conversely, in bullets and cartridge cases fired from different weapons, there will always, due to the sheer numbers of stria present, be some degree of accidental agreement.

It has been quoted (Walls, 1968) (Section 4.5) that up to 25% of the stria in a non-match and in excess of 75% of the stria in a match will show concordance. This exceedingly high degree of accidentally matching lines has not, however, been supported by personal observation. There is no dispute that out of the thousands of lines present in any one comparison, a number must, by pure chance alone, show agreement.

It is by experience alone that the examiner is able to mentally exclude those striations which are not of significance and to award the necessary degree of credibility to those which form the basis of a positive match.

It is also by experience alone that the examiner is able to ascribe an opinion of common origin based upon significant agreement between two sets of unique stria. This significant agreement relates to the duplication of a unique pattern of surface contours comprised of peaks, ridges and furrows.

It should be re-emphasized here that it is not the individual stria which form the basis of a match but the duplication of a series of groups and patterns of stria. It is this duplication which enables an expert examiner to determine that a degree of concordance exists which by chance alone could not happen.

Due to the subjective nature of the processes involved in the elimination of insignificant detail, the criteria used by the expert to ascertain the degree of accordance of stria cannot be mathematically quantified. The following principle can, however, be used to quantify the basic concepts used in the assignment of a positive match:

> *A positive match between two sets of stria is one in which the extent of agreement exceeds that of the best accepted non-match.*

This is an oft quoted reference, the exact origin of which is unsure. Biasotti (1959) quotes this phrase in several of his papers on the subject and could well be the originator.

When positive agreement is said to exceed the best known non-match, it is implying that it must exceed, to some considerable degree, the agreement witnessed in non-matches. What can numerically be ascribed to the statement 'exceed to a considerable degree' is not precisely quantifiable and once again comes down to the experience and competence of the examiner.

That the process of assigning a positive match to a stria comparison is an evaluative and thus subjective procedure has been accepted by many. Kind *et al.* (1979) states 'much of the knowledge accumulated in the procedure, and used in subsequent comparisons, is of a subjective type, which at present defies numerical classification'; Biasotti (1959) says 'Firearms and toolmark identification is still more art (subjective) than science (objective)', and Kingston (1970) says 'Objective estimates of probability are based upon quantitative experimental data. Subjective estimates are based upon personal knowledge, experience and reasoning. When we know exactly what to quantitate, objective estimates are superior to subjective ones. When we do not know exactly what to quantitate, subjective may be far more realistic than forced objective ones.'

An informative and very interesting paper by Charles R. Meyers (1987), 'The Objective vs. the Subjective Boondoggle' reviews some of the references dealing with objective and subjective criteria in respect to stria comparisons.

Another interesting paper by Evett (1996) explores the mistaken phrase 'exact science' in relation to the 16 points of comparison used in fingerprint examination and whether forensic science is in fact a 'science'.

The days of the mystical all-knowing 'expert' have, however, long gone. Nowadays, the courts of law demand, very justifiably, a much more scientific approach and will not be bulldozed by the 'you must trust me' expert. The competent examiner should always strive to reduce subjectivity to a minimum whilst accentuating the objectivity, for example, scientific aspects, of his examination as much as possible.

The basic difference between an 'expert' and a layman is that due to his experience and training, the expert can observe and understand the significance of features and phenomena which the layman would overlook. It is the expert's job to be able to demonstrate to the layman, for example, the court, the significance of his observations. Hiding behind a mask of 'I am the expert, you will have to trust me' no longer holds sway in modern judicial systems. In this, as in all aspects of forensic science 'objectivity is everything'; subjectivity alone accounts for nothing.

4.7 Accidental Discharge

With the safety mechanisms employed in modern weapons, incidents labelled as 'accidental discharge' have to be treated with some scepticism.

Basically, cases of accidental discharge have to be placed into one of five categories:

1. faulty lock mechanism;
2. discharge due to inappropriately low trigger pressure;
3. failure of the safety mechanism;
4. inadvertently pulling the trigger;
5. inadvertently pulling the trigger by contact with some object other than the trigger finger.

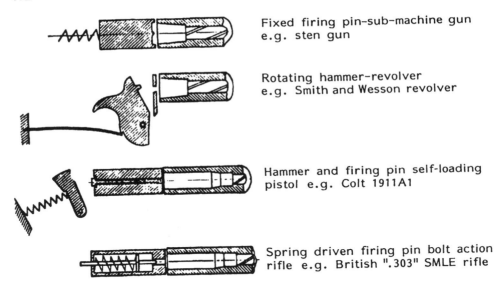

Fixed firing pin–sub-machine gun
e.g. sten gun

Rotating hammer–revolver
e.g. Smith and Wesson revolver

Hammer and firing pin self-loading
pistol e.g. Colt 1911A1

Spring driven firing pin bolt action
rifle e.g. British ".303" SMLE rifle

Figure 4.29 Basic lock mechanisms. SMLE, Short Magazine Lee Enfield.

4.7.1 Faulty lock mechanism

Basically, all locks work on the same principle: a spring-loaded rotating (as in a weapon with a hammer) or sliding (as in a bolt action weapon) hammer with a small notch cut in it called a 'bent'. Into this bent fits one end of a pivoting lever which is called the 'sear'. The other end of this lever either forms or is actuated by the trigger. When the lock mechanism is cocked, the sear contacts the bent and holds the hammer or striker in the cocked position until the trigger is pulled.

The contact between the bent and sear must be minimal; otherwise, the pressure required to disengage the two would be excessive. Likewise, the contact surfaces must be parallel to ensure a smooth disconnection. A hooked bent would be all but impossible to disengage, whilst a rounded surface could slip out of contact under the spring tension of the lock.

Most accidental discharges caused by faulty lock mechanisms can be attributed to a bent/sear fault. Illustrative cases would be appropriate to exemplify this aspect of accidental discharge.

Case example: Faulty lock mechanism.   An alleged case of accidental discharge involved a husband/wife dispute where it was claimed the gun went off accidentally whilst unloading the weapon in the front room. The wife was shot in the head, killing her instantly.

The weapon involved was an extremely expensive Italian side-by-side double-barrelled 12-bore shotgun which had only been used twice before. Trigger pull testing showed that the right and left trigger required a pressure of 4 and $4\frac{1}{2}$ lb, respectively, which is considered acceptable for a weapon of this type.

Tests for accidental discharge consisted of blows with a soft mallet to the heel of the butt, the top and bottom of the lock mechanism, and the muzzle end of the barrel. These tests showed that there was no tendency to accidentally discharge, though jarring was found.

During test firing, it was noted that with each successive pull of the trigger, the pressure required decreased significantly.

Further tests to determine what actual pressure was required on the trigger to fire the weapon showed that it had, after just a few test firings, fallen to less than 2 lb. It was also found to be very prone to accidental discharge by jarring. After just two additional trigger pull tests and two accidental discharge tests, the trigger pull had dropped to less than 1 lb and then to the point of not being able to cock the mechanism at all.

On disassembling the lock mechanism, it was found that the steel bents of the lock mechanism had not been case hardened during manufacture. On each pull of the trigger, the much harder sear had stripped metal away from the bent until it no longer existed.

Although the weapon was in good working order and not at all prone to accidental discharge when received, there were doubts as to the changing characteristics of the weapon's lock mechanism, and the case was dismissed.

Case example: Gun damage through poor exhibit handling. Another case involved the shooting of a man by a gypsy armed with a 0.410″ shotgun. As usual, it was claimed that the gun had gone off accidentally whilst trying to fend off the allegedly aggressive man and that there was no intention to kill him.

The weapon concerned was a cheap quality, single-shot, bolt action weapon of continental manufacture. It had an excessively high trigger pressure of 12 lb, and there was absolutely no tendency for it to accidentally discharge.

During the trial, the prosecution requested a demonstration as to the method used to test for accidental discharge. The weapon was cocked and as the gun was turned round to strike the heel of the weapon on the floor, it lightly brushed the top of the witness box. There was a very audible click as the firing pin fell which at that point sounded like thunder. At that stage, prosecution asked for a recess.

On disassembling the weapon, it was found that the action had been driven back into the woodwork of the stock to such an extent that the sear was being pushed out of contact with the bent. In addition, the heel of the stock was found to be battered and cracked where it had been repeatedly hammered on to the floor.

Obviously, nobody was going to accept responsibility for this damage, but it was suspected that everybody involved in the case had to convince themselves that the weapon was not prone to accidental discharge.

After the recession, I informed the jury that when I received the weapon, it was in good working order and not at all prone to accidental discharge. I also explained that at some point after the weapon left my control, it had been dropped on its butt, probably many times, and damaged to the point where it was not at all in the condition as first received. The prosecution counsel did not object to this explanation and the case was allowed to continue on the evidence as to what the condition of the weapon was in when originally received by me.

4.7.2   Discharge due to inappropriately low trigger pressure

For target use, trigger mechanisms are often 'tuned' to give a smoother, lighter trigger pull. It is not unusual to find target pistols and rifles with trigger pulls in the region of 1 lb.

Accepted commercial and military trigger pulls vary tremendously, but generally, the following could be considered as acceptable:

- 0.22″ Rimfire rifles   3–5 lb
- military rifles   4–7 lb
- revolvers – single action   4–6 lb
- revolvers – double action   10–15 lb
- self-loading pistols   4–8 lb
- shotgun   4–5 lb

Whilst a 'tuned' trigger pressure as low as 1 lb may be totally acceptable in the very specialized arena of a target shooting competition, in other circumstances, it can be extremely dangerous.

Basically, tuning a trigger mechanism involves the polishing of the sear/bent mating surfaces and reducing the contact area between the two. This is an extremely difficult procedure and practically beyond the scope of anyone other than a highly trained armourer.

Decreasing the strength of the sear spring (which keeps the sear in contact with the bent) and the trigger return spring is also often carried out to improve the trigger pull.

One other modification is to reduce the 'trigger backlash'. 'Trigger backlash' is the continuing rearward movement of the trigger after the sear has become disengaged from the bent. Excessive trigger backlash can, at the moment of firing, cause the target shooter to inadvertently pull the weapon to one side, thus decreasing accuracy.

Such modifications, even when competently carried out, can, to even an experienced shooter in times of crisis, lead to the weapon being inadvertently fired.

4.7.3 Failure of the safety mechanism

One very common fault in shotgun lock mechanisms of the old external hammer type involves a faulty 'rebound safety'. In this type of weapon, there is an additional bent in the form of a hook rather than a notch called the 'half cock' or 'rebound bent'. As the bent is hook shaped, the sear is firmly locked into place and it should not be able to manually push it forward or to pull the sear out of contact with the bent via the trigger. When in this half-cock or rebound position, the only way of releasing the sear is by pulling the hammer back to the full-cock position. The internal springing of the lock mechanism is so arranged that when the hammer is in the down or uncocked position, a spring will pull the hammer slightly to the rear into this half-cock notch. In this position, the hammer will be unable to reach the striker.

In cheaper weapons where the manufacturing tolerances are larger and the materials are not always of the best quality, it is not unusual for there to be sufficient 'play' in the mechanism for the hammer to be pushed forward. This 'play' is often sufficient for the firing pin to touch the primer. Dropping the weapon or inadvertently striking the hammer will often accidentally discharge such a weapon when it is in this half-cock safety position.

Many self-loading pistols and revolvers have a 'half-cock' safety so that the gun may safely be carried with a live round in the chamber. Unless the weapon is of very low quality, it is very unusual to find a faulty half-cock safety mechanism in a modern pistol.

Case example: Weapon accidentally fired killing a burglar. Being awakened by the sound of breaking glass, the house owner armed himself with an old double-barrelled shotgun. On confronting the burglar, a fight ensued during which the house owner was violently thrown back against a door frame. At that stage, the weapon discharged, removing most of the burglar's head. The house owner claimed that the weapon was in the safety or rebound position and that the gun had discharged accidentally on the weapon hitting the door frame.

On examining the scene, a deep impression of one of the weapon's hammers was found in the woodwork of the door frame. This and the fact that the half-cock bent was worn to the extent that the firing pins actually rested on the cartridge primer was enough to show that there was no intent on the part of the house owner.

4.7.4 Inadvertently pulling the trigger

In general, this is very difficult if not impossible to prove one way or the other. Numerous cases are on record of a violent fight during which the person holding the weapon has been violently thrown back against a wall with a claimed inadvertent discharge of the weapon.

Hundreds of tests have be carried out (B.J. Heard, unpublished work) using volunteers under controlled conditions to test the probability of this happening. In the majority of these tests, unless the trigger pressure is exceptionally low, it has been found that for self-loading pistols and revolvers in the single-action mode, there is little tendency for the trigger to be pulled. If anything, the person holding the weapon generally releases the trigger. For revolvers in the double-action mode, it has been found that there is no tendency at all for the trigger to be pulled.

These are controlled tests and what happens when there is a violent confrontation or when one person fears for his life is another matter completely.

One area where one can be a little more definitive in respect to the accidental pulling of the trigger is when the weapon is violently pulled away from the person holding it. It is easy to simulate the unexpected snatching of a weapon, and persons both experienced and unexperienced in weapon handling can easily be tested as to their likely response. These tests have shown that there is a far greater likelihood of the trigger being released when the weapon is snatched away. In fact, trained shooters invariably react in this way. Figures show (B.J. Heard, unpublished work) that there is approximately a 75% chance that an experienced shooter will inadvertently release the trigger if an attempt is made to pull the gun away from him. With inexperienced shooters, the probability drops to about 65%, which is still quite significant.

Once again, these are controlled tests and what happens when there is a violent confrontation or when one person fears for his life is completely another matter.

Accidental discharge whilst placing the gun in or taking the gun out of a holster. Two cases illustrate this type of 'accidental discharge' quite well.

Case Example 1: Accidental Discharge whilst Holstering a Weapon.　This case involved a police officer who was trying to insert a 2″ barrelled Colt revolver, held in his right hand, into a holster which was in his left hand. The weapon discharged taking a large portion of the holster and the bullet through the palm of his left hand. A careful examination of the internal surface of the holster and a gun-handling test (see Chapter 7, 'Gun-Handling Tests') on his right hand showed that the index finger had been on the trigger at the time of firing and that the weapon was almost fully holstered. For some reason, he had his finger in the trigger guard whilst holstering the weapon. The act of trying to force the weapon into the holster whilst his finger was snagged on the top of the holster fired the weapon.

Case Example 2: 'Quick-Draw Accidental Discharge'.　The second involved another police officer who was found in a men's toilet with a hole in his right foot. His statement said that he had taken his gun out of the holster to disentangle his lanyard, and when he re-holstered the weapon, it went off shooting him in the foot. His explanation was that the lanyard had caught on the trigger and fired the weapon. A number of test firings made with exactly the same type of holster showed that the weapon must have been almost completely out of the holster at the time the firing occurred. In that position, it was impossible for the lanyard to have pulled the trigger. It was plainly obvious that he had been practising 'quick draws' in front of the mirror and had inadvertently pulled the trigger.

4.7.5   Inadvertently pulling the trigger by contact with some object other than the trigger finger

This is probably the cause of more hunting accidents than all the other causes added together. There are numerous recorded cases of twigs snagging on the trigger of loaded shotguns and rifles, and I am sure that many of them are genuine accidents. Less likely are those incidents allegedly involving inquisitive dogs, rabbits twitching in game pockets and even shot pheasants landing on the trigger guard!

Case example: Fingerprint expert inadvertently discharging a shotgun. It would be highly unlikely for the soft touch of a fingerprint dusting brush to have sufficient force to discharge a weapon whilst the trigger was being searched for prints. There was, however, an incident where the fingerprint officer, having found nothing on the trigger, proceeded to use the trigger to steady the weapon whilst dusting the butt stock. Sufficient force was applied to the trigger to discharge one barrel of the shot gun. The shot went straight through the ceiling and into the room above, much to the consternation of the police officers who were searching there for evidence.

Case example: Tractor driver shot by own gun. This involved a farmer who kept his shotgun behind the back seat of his tractor, just in case he saw the odd rabbit. Whilst backing the tractor up to a hedge prior to starting a ploughing run, the gun became entangled in some brambles. On starting forward, one barrel discharged completely removing the back of his head.

4.8   Identification of Calibre from the Bullet Entry Hole

4.8.1   Introduction

In skin and fabrics, it is, unless a wadcutter-type bullet is used, all but impossible to determine the calibre of a missile from its entry or exit hole.

Wadcutter bullets, as discussed earlier, are intended for target practice. As such, they are designed to cut a clean hole through the target to facilitate the determination of the shooter's accuracy.

When round-nosed or even hollow-point bullets are used, the hole produced by the bullet is very much smaller than its calibre. In skin, this is caused by its natural elasticity, which allows the bullet to force apart the cell structure. After passage of the bullet, the skin regains its original shape exhibiting only a very small entry hole surrounded by a bullet wipe mark much smaller than the original calibre of the bullet.

In fabrics, it is the weave which separates, allowing the bullet to pass. Often, torn fibres will be visible, but these indicate little other than the direction in which the bullet was travelling.

With wood, the bullet entry hole is, once again, much smaller than the diameter of the bullet. The wood fibres stretch and eventually tear as the bullet passes through. The majority spring back, making it extremely difficult to determine the calibre.

When dealing with wood, there is, however, a little-known method of determining the calibre with a reasonable degree of accuracy (Beta TAM Chi-Kung, unpublished work). If a piece of fairly strong white paper is placed over the wood surrounding the hole and a soft-lead pencil is carefully rubbed over the surface, as in brass rubbing, a circle, very closely approximating the diameter of the bullet, will appear.

Vehicle tyres are almost self-sealing, and it is often impossible to determine even the point of entry without immersing the tyre in water.

The determination of calibre from a bullet hole in a vehicle body can also be extremely difficult.

For example, semi-jacketed hollow-point bullets can expand on impact, giving the impression of a much larger calibre. At other times, the jacket material can be stripped off leaving the lead core to penetrate, giving the impression of a much smaller calibre.

Conversely, extremely high-velocity bullets, such as the 0.223″ (5.56 mm) AR15 bullet can leave an extremely large entry hole. Often, there will also be a 'splash back' effect where metal flows back out of the hole, giving the impression it is an exit, not an entry hole. Identification of just the entry/exit holes in these circumstances can require considerable experience.

When high-pressure handgun cartridges loaded with plain lead bullets are fired through short-barrelled weapons, there is an additional problem. The problem here is that as the bullet emerges from the barrel, the gases which follow are still at an extremely high pressure. Once the bullet is freed from the constraints of the barrel, the pressure of the gases on its base is so great that it will expand. Sometimes, this base expansion can increase the diameter of the bullet by 50% or more, giving rise to a much larger entry hole than one would normally expect. In addition, the bullet can become unstable as the base expansion is not always constant. This can, in extreme cases, cause the bullet to tumble in flight.

In handguns, this phenomenon is only of any consequence with plain lead bullets fired in 0.357″ and 0.44″ Magnum weapons with a barrel length of less than 3″ (Figure 4.30).

Figure 4.30 Magnum bullets fired through 6″ and 2″ barrels.

Rifles which have had their barrels shortened can exhibit this bullet base expansion with fully jacketed bullets as well.

4.8.2 Determination of bullet type

As the bullet passes down the barrel, the rifling will tear off small fragments of the bullet. Some of these fragments will remain in the bore and others will be blown out of the bore by the gases following the bullet. Some of these fragments do, however, remain attached to the bullet in the form of sub-microscopic pieces of swarf. As the bullet passes through any material, whether it is human flesh, fabric or wood, these fragments are often transferred to the medium through which it is passing.

These fragments are exceedingly small, but if an adhesive taping is taken from the periphery of the bullet entrance hole, they can be recovered. Examination under the electron microscope will enable these fragments to be qualitatively analyzed and the bullet type and/or country of origin identified.

It is important in the interpretation of these results to distinguish between volatilized lead from the bullet base and lead fragments from the bullet driving surface. Volatilized lead will be spheroidal or have smooth contours, whilst lead from the bullet's surface will be more rough and swarf-like. The importance here is that as the metallic components of the lead alloy will volatilize at different rates, the results from the volatilized lead will be different from those torn off the driving surface.

Likewise, it is important to distinguish between copper zinc alloys from contamination and those particles torn from the bullet's jacket by the rifling. Size and morphology is one identifier; the other is from the quantitative analysis, if this is possible.

Examples would include the identification of lead and copper/zinc alloy as coming from a semi-jacketed bullet. Another would be the identification of copper-coated steel from 7.62 × 25 mm ammunition of Chinese manufacture.

With larger fragments, accurate quantitative analysis will often enable the make of ammunition to be determined. The fragments recovered from the periphery of bullet entry holes are, however, invariably too small for this type of analysis. The problem here is that for accurate energy-dispersive X-ray (EDX) analysis via the scanning electron microscope (SEM), a mirror-like surface is required.

With larger fragments, 0.25 mm or greater, which can be seen under an optical microscope, it is possible to crush them between microscope slides to give the mirror-like surface required. The rough irregular swarf-like shape of the particles torn from the bullet's driving surface is normally too small for manipulation and is therefore unsuitable for this type of analysis.

Case example: Police exchange of fire.   During a particularly bad shoot-out with a gang of armed robbers, five innocent bystanders were injured and two were killed by gunfire. The police were using semi-jacketed 0.38″ Special+P calibre revolver ammunition and the robbers 7.62 × 25 mm Chinese ammunition. In the wound of one of the victims, there was a bullet fragment, and this proved to be a very small piece of copper/zinc jacket from a police round. From its appearance, this had obviously ricocheted before striking the bystander. The rest of the victims all had fully penetrating wounds.

It was obviously of some importance to show whether any of the other bystanders had been accidentally shot by the police. Tapings were taken from the entry holes, and an analysis of these revealed the presence of copper-coated steel fragments in all instances. This proved beyond reasonable doubt that they had all been shot by the robbers and not the police.

4.9   Ricochet Analysis

4.9.1   Introduction

When a bullet strikes any surface, there is a critical angle at which the bullet will bounce off or *ricochet* from the surface rather than penetrate. After ricocheting from the surface, the missile will lose a considerable amount of its velocity (anything up to 35% in test firings) and, invariably, lose its stability. This is contrary to the popular belief that a ricocheting bullet will carry further than one fired at the elevation for maximum range.

The actual degree at which a bullet will ricochet from a surface is called the *critical angle*. Predicting this critical angle for any bullet/surface configuration is, however, extremely difficult. Factors such as bullet shape, construction, velocity and ricocheting surface all have a pronounced effect on the outcome (Figure 4.31).

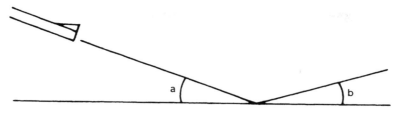

Figure 4.31 Ricochet nomenclature: a = incident angle; b = ricochet angle.

A case illustrating how variable this can be involved the shooting at a taxi in central London by a terrorist group. The weapon involved was a 0.357″ Magnum revolver which was loaded with semi-jacketed bullets, some of which had a hollow point and others which had a solid round nose.

The front windscreen of a British taxi is only angled back by approximately 15° and under normal circumstances, such a low angle would not be expected to support a bullet ricochet.

The first round fired at the front windscreen had a hollow-point bullet which cleanly ricocheted from the screen leaving a stripe of lead up the glass. This bullet was located at a later stage and was found to have a mirror-like flat surface on the lead portion of the nose. The second bullet fired was a round-nosed fully jacketed bullet which cleanly penetrated the glass narrowly missing the driver.

In this instance, the angle of the screen was clearly insufficient to support a ricochet with a round-nosed bullet. The hollow-point nose did, however, collapse on impact, effectively increasing the angle and allowing the bullet to ricochet from the glass.

Considering the number of times in the investigation of armed crime that incidents of ricocheting bullets are encountered, it is surprising how little literature there is on the subject. Probably the most authoritative work was by Lucien Haag (1975). Several other papers (Jauhari and Mohan, 1969; McConnell, Triplett and Rowe, 1981; Hartline, Abraham and Rowe, 1982; Rathman, 1987) have also investigated the effects of shotgun pellets ricocheting from steel and concrete.

The parameters affecting the potential to ricochet are so diverse, however, that it is difficult to lay down any firm and fast rules as to ricochet potential. Empirical studies should, therefore, be carried out for each individual case.

There are, however, a few generalizations which can be applied.

1. In most cases of bullets ricocheting from a hard surface, the angle of ricochet is considerably less than the angle of incidence (Tables 4.3 and 4.4).

   As can be seen from the following tables, with hard-jacketed, high-velocity missiles striking a frangible material such as stone or concrete, it is not always the case that the angle of ricochet is less than the angle of incidence.

Table 4.3 Ricochet angles vs. incident angle for various bullets on smooth concrete.

Calibre	Bullet type	Velocity (ft/s)	Ricochet angle at incident angle of	
			10°	30°
0.22″ LR	RN	1100	1.33	1.88
0.22″ LR	HP	1100	1.3	1.19
0.38″ Spl	RN	650	1.02	1.5
0.357″ Mag	SJHP	850	1.3	1.7
7.62 × 25 mm	FMJ	1300	2.0*	12–35*
7.62 × 39 mm	FMJ	2700	3.5*	2–25*

*Indicates severe cratering leading to variable results and, in some cases, disintegration of bullet.

Table 4.4 Ricochet angle for 0.45 ACP FMJ bullet from various surfaces at various incident angles.

Material	Calibre	Ricochet angle at incident angle of	
		15°	25°
Glass	0.45 ACP	Broke glass	Broke glass
Concrete	0.45 ACP	2″	3°
Steel plate	0.45 ACP	2.5°	4°
Wood	0.45 ACP	17°	17″
Sand	0.45 ACP	Penetrate	Penetrate

It would appear that if sufficient cratering of the surface occurs on bullet impact, the exit plane of the crater will be of greater angle than the incidence angle. This equates to the bullet striking the surface at a greater incidence angle and therefore a greater ricochet angle.

2. The critical angle for a soft or hollow-point bullet is lower than that for an equivalent fully jacketed bullet. In this instance, it would appear that the collapsing hollow-point bullet nose increases the incidence angle, thus increasing the propensity for ricochet.

3. The critical angle for a given bullet type/target medium is not velocity dependent. This effect is illustrated by Table 4.5.

4. Bullets will invariably lose their gyroscopic stability and tumble after ricocheting. This tumbling gives rise to a distinctive whine or whirring noise as the tumbling bullet passes through the air.

5. Bullets which have ricocheted from glass, steel, concrete or wood have a very distinctive flat spot which is characteristic of the material where the contact has been made. This contact point will often have paint, wood fibres or

Table 4.5 Critical angle vs. velocity for various calibres fired at water.

Calibre	Velocity (RN bullet) (ft/s)	Critical angle (degree)
0.22"	850	8
0.22"	1000	8
0.22"	1250	7.50
0.38" Spl	650	6°
0.38" Spl	800	7°
0.357" Mag	900	6°
0.357 Mag	1050	7°

NB. Some of the bullets used in this test were hollow-point. The nose was, however, filled with epoxy resin and shaped to give the desired round-nosed profile.

concrete adhering to it for easy identification. If the material was glass or polished steel, the mirror-like surface is quite distinctive.

This is not, however, the case with a bullet which has ricocheted from water. Even with hollow-point bullets, it is unlikely that it will be possible to differentiate between a bullet which has ricocheted from water and one which has not.

6. Wounds produced by bullets ricocheting from hard surfaces will generally be easy to identify due to the bullet's tumbling action. If the bullet does happen to strike point first, the misshapen bullet will leave a distinctive entry hole generally with ragged edges. Once it enters the body, the bullet will, due to its inherent unstable condition, tumble end over end, leaving a large irregular wound channel. Jacketed bullets tend to break up on ricocheting, peppering the skin with jacket and lead core fragments.

7. High-velocity bullets with a thin jacket, for example, 0.223" or 0.220" Swift, will invariably break up before ricocheting. This applies even to water.

It is interesting to note that when round shot was used by naval vessels, ricocheting missiles from the water were a recognized form of tactics in sea warfare. By skipping a missile across the water at hull height, it was much easier to hit an enemy ship than to try and calculate the correct elevation for the missile to strike the ship during its trajectory.

This method worked well with round shot where the angle of incidence and the angle of ricochet were approximately the same. However, modern projectiles which are spin stabilized and have an aerodynamic shape do tend to rise at a greater angle after ricocheting from water, and the technique was found to be of little use.

4.9.2 Brief glossary

Angle of incidence   The angle at which a missile strikes a surface before ricocheting.

Angle of ricochet   The angle at which a missile leaves a surface after ricocheting.

Critical angle   The actual degree at which a bullet will ricochet from a surface is called the critical angle.

Ricochet   The deflection of a missile after impact.

4.10   Bullet Penetration and Trajectory through Glass

4.10.1   Introduction

It is generally thought that a bullet will, after penetrating glass, experience a large deviation from its normal flight path. There is some confusion over this with published papers reporting extremes.

A paper by Harper (1993) reported a relatively small deviation as does Rathman (1993), whilst Thornton (Thornton and Cashman, 1986) reports a much larger deviation.

Papers by Haag (1987) describe the measurement of deflection; Garrison (1995), the penetration of auto body parts in general and Bell (1993), the effect of bullets fired through tempered glass. Mostly, however, they add little to the understanding of the mechanics involved with respect to the bullet's trajectory after penetration. The author's experience has shown that after penetrating glass, there is, generally speaking, little deviation of the bullet from its normal flight path.

4.10.2   Penetration of normal window glass

Very low velocity steel balls (BB) will generally cause a very small hole, often no more than 0.1″ (2 mm) in diameter, through the glass ejecting a large cone of glass (*spalling*) from the side opposite the impact print. If the cone is not uniform it can give an indication of the direction from which the shot was fired. For $\frac{1}{4}$″ (5 mm) plate glass, this can happen at velocities as low as 200 ft/s.

For lead air-gun pellets which are soft and readily deformable, a velocity of over 400 ft/s is required to effect the same damage. To penetrate the same glass, the velocity must be increased to at least 550 ft/s. With these readily deformable and relatively slow missiles, it is difficult to estimate from the damage to the glass their calibre.

With larger higher-velocity missiles, the diameter of the hole through the glass will only give a very rough approximation of the missile calibre and little else.

4.10.3   Penetration of laminated glass

When struck by a bullet, laminated glass (which consists of two sheets of glass bonded together with a plastic film) will first bulge away from the site of impact.

This causes a series of radial cracks. As the glass continues to bulge, concentric cracks are produced, the quantity of which are determined by the energy given up by the bullet to the glass (Salferstein, 1982). The quantity of crushed glass round the periphery of the entrance hole is also a function of the energy given up.

Easily deformed, low-velocity bullets, such as 0.32 S&W and 0.38" S&W, will generally have insufficient velocity to penetrate laminated windscreen or bank teller glass, giving up all their energy on impact. As a result of the transfer of energy, the glass round the impact site, both on the contact and remote glass laminates, will be crushed. Glass will be thrown off the rear face (spalled) from the remote side of the glass with considerable force. Crushed glass will also be projected some distance back from the contact side towards the firer. Often the laminate will have been stretched beyond its elastic limit and will have torn in the process. The torn plastic laminate and the quantity of glass on the remote side will often give the distinct impression of penetration.

4.10.4   Penetration of tempered or toughened glass

The mechanism of penetration for tempered glass is somewhat different as once the surface is punctured, the glass shatters into tiny pieces. Radial crack lines spread out from the point of impact to the very edges of the glass, cross-linking as they go. There is a degree of bulging away from the impact site which results in the production of peripheral crushing rather than concentric crack rings.

Determination of the impact site, calibre of weapon and type is often rendered impossible due to the disintegration of the glass round the bullet entry site. If the hole or part of it is still intact, the site must be preserved with clear adhesive sheets so that a later examination can be performed.

Even if the impact site has disintegrated, an approximation of its position can still be obtained by following the major radial cracks back to their origin.

It should be noted that tempered glass can take heavy impacts if spread over a large area. A low-velocity steel ball will, however, have a sufficiently high point of impact energy to completely craze a pane of tempered glass. Here, the mechanism is one of a non-deforming steel sphere transferring all its energy over an exceedingly small impact area. The resulting energy transfer per unit area is sufficiently high to defeat the integrity of the tempered glass causing it to craze.

4.10.5   Determination of bullet type from entry hole

Determination of the calibre of bullet from the resulting hole and degree of concentric cracking can be made, although the variables make this a difficult task.

In *laminated glass*, the degree of concentric cracking is directly proportional to the amount of energy given up to the glass as the bullet passes through.

The amount of energy given up by the bullet will depend upon the bullet calibre, its construction and velocity. The softer the bullet, the greater the deformation. The greater the deformation, the larger the transmission of energy. As the deformation increases, so does the size of the resultant penetration site. The resultant bullet hole thus represents the actual size of the bullet after deformation by impact with the glass.

For example, a lightweight, hollow-point 0.22″ bullet will easily deform on penetrating glass, giving up a large percentage of its energy, forming a large entry hole with considerable concentric cracking. On the other hand, a fully jacketed 9 mm PB bullet will impart a similar quantity of energy to the glass but will not deform as it penetrates. Thus, the entry holes and concentric cracking will be similar for both rounds of ammunition.

In *tempered glass*, the situation is somewhat different, as any penetrating missile will cause radial and concentric cross-linked cracking over the whole of the glass. The degree of crushing round the periphery of the entrance hole can give an indication of the calibre, but this is exceedingly difficult in practical situations due to the disintegration of the glass.

4.10.6   Determination of angle of entry

Due to the disintegration of tempered glass, it is unusual to find enough of the entry hole left intact to determine the angle of entry.

Laminated glass does stay together and it is possible to make some approximation of the bullet entry angle. As the angle of impact increases, so does the length of the bullet hole. It should be noted that the length of the bullet entry site will only give a very rough approximation of the angle of entry especially as the energy transfer to the bullet entry site increases. The greater the deformation of the bullet, the greater the perceived angle of entry from the length of the bullet hole. It has been found, however, that a much better approximation of the angle of entry can be obtained from the actual deformation of the bullet itself. At angles of entry of up to 45°, the damage to the bullet has been found to duplicate the angle of impact with the glass to a reasonable degree of accuracy.

4.10.7   Deflection of bullet by glass

A series of tests (B.J. Heard, unpublished work) with various calibres of weapon fired at laminated windscreen glass held at varying angles has indicated that there is very little deviation of the bullet from its intended path. These can be conveniently illustrated by the following table (Table 4.6):

Table 4.6 Deflection of bullet from intended path at three different impact angles.

Calibre	0°	25°	45°
0.22″ LR	0°	20°	50°
0.25″ ACP		0°	5°
0.38″ Spl		2°	2°
9 mm PB	0°	0°	0°

A very limited number of tests have also been conducted on tempered glass with a very similar set of results.

Crime scenes do not, however, always follow the observations made under carefully controlled conditions. A case of note in this respect involved a police officer firing through the rear windscreen of a car which was dragging his colleague down the street. The shot was aimed at the driver, but on passing through the tempered glass, it split into two pieces. The larger piece passed through the headrest and into the head of the driver. The other clipped the top of the passenger's seat, lodging in the passenger's shoulder. There was no intervening object which could have caused this break-up, only the glass.

Another case involved an armed robbery in a bank which had recently been fitted with 'bandit-proof glass'. After being given the money, the robber, who was armed with a sawn-off shotgun, calmly walked up to one of the tellers and shot her through the security glass. Whilst the shotgun pellets did not actually penetrate the glass, the spalling from the rear face of the glass (the teller's side) was so severe that some of the larger particles completely penetrated her body, killing her (Figure 4.32).

The glass used in this case was one laminated with three sheets of glass and two sheets of plastic. To reduce scratching, the outside layers were both glass. In more modern bullet-resistant glass (as it should correctly be called), the non-impact side always consists of a sheet of clear acrylic plastic which is heavily bonded to the last layer of glass. This will limit the degree of spalling very considerably.

Another case involved a more modern type of bullet-resistant glass which did have a sheet of clear acrylic plastic bonded to the non-strike face. In this case, the teller was an avid shooter and he 'just happened' to have his 0.22″ calibre target pistol loaded and under the counter. The would-be robber was armed with a 0.38″ Special calibre revolver. When the teller pulled out his gun, the robber immediately opened fire as did the teller. When the smoke had cleared, there were eight 0.22″ bullets from the teller's pistol imbedded in the anti-spalling sheet and six completely smashed 0.38″ special bullets lying on the floor by the robber's feet. His hands and face had been cut to shreds by the shards of glass thrown back from the glass and he had to be taken to hospital with one eye missing.

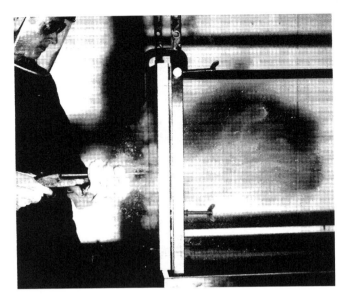

Figure 4.32 Glass fragments thrown from rear of a sheet of laminated glass which does not have an anti-spalling face.

4.10.8 Brief glossary

Acrylic glass	Clear plastic used in bullet-resistant 'glass' either as a laminate or by itself in thick sheets.
Laminated glass	A number of layers of glass bonded together with sheets of clear plastic to improve its bullet-resistant properties and to prevent spalling.
Spalling	Material dislodged from the face opposite the strike face by the impact of a missile.
Toughened/tempered glass	Glass which has been heat treated to improve its surface hardness.

References

Bell, P. (1993) Characteristics of bullets fired through tempered automobile window glass. Paper presented at The California Association of Criminalists Seminar 1993.

Biasotti, A.A. (1955) A Study of Fired Bullets Statistically Analyzed, *M. Crim Thesis*, University of California, Berkeley, CA, USA.

Biasotti, A.A. (1959) A statistical study of the individual characteristics of fired bullets. *Journal of Forensic Sciences*, **4** (1), 34–50.

Biasotti, A.A. (1964) The principles of evidence evaluation as applied to firearms and toolmark identification. *Journal of Forensic Sciences*, **9** (4), 428–33.

Brackett, J.W. (1965) A study of idealised striated marks and their comparison using models. Paper presented to 26th Semi-annual Seminar of California Association of Criminalists, October. U.S. Department of Justice. Federal Bureau of Investigation. NCIC. Criminalistics Laboratory Information System (CLIS) Operating Manual. 2001–2002.

Burd, D.Q. (1965) Smoking bullets. A technique useful in some bullet comparisons. *Journal of Criminal Law, Criminology, and Police Science*, **56** (4), 523–7.

Burrard, G. (1934) *The Identification of Firearms and Forensic Ballistics*, Butler & Tanner Ltd, London.

Crime Laboratory Information System (CLIS) (1998) *General Rifling Characteristics File*, US Department of Justice, Federal Bureau of Investigation, Washington, DC, USA.

Crocell Hot Dip Strippable Coating, Croda Application Chemical Ltd, Doncaster, England.

DeFrance, C.S. and Van Arsdale, M.D. (2003) Validation study of electrochemical rifling. *AFTE Journal*, **35** (1), 35–7.

Evett, I.W. (1996) Expert evidence and forensic misconceptions of the nature of exact science. *Science and Justice*, **36** (2), 118–22.

Garrison, D.H. (1995) Examining auto body penetration in the reconstruction of vehicle shootings. *AFTE Journal*, **27**, 209–12, July.

Haag, L. (1975) Bullet ricochet: an empirical study and a device for measuring ricochet angle, *AFTE Journal*, **7** (3), 44–51.

Haag, L.C. (1987) The measurement of bullet deflection by intervening objects and a study of bullet behaviour after impact. *AFTE Journal*, **19** (4), 382–7, October.

Hall, E. (1983) Bullet markings from consecutively rifled shilen DGA barrels. *AFTE Journal*, **15** (1), 33–53.

Harper, W.W. (1993) The behaviour of bullets fired through glass. *Journal of Criminal Law, Criminology and Police Science*, **29** (1938), 718.

Hartline, P.C., Abraham, G. and Rowe, W.F. (1982) Study of shotgun ricochet from steel surfaces. *Journal of Forensic Sciences*, **27** (1982), 506–12.

Jauhari, M. (1969) Bullet ricochet from metal plates. *Journal of Criminal Law, Criminology and Police Science*, **60** (3), 387–3.

Kind, S.S., Wigmore, R., Whitehead, P.H. and Loxley, D.S. (1979) Terminology of forensic science. *Journal of Forensic Sciences*, **19** (3), 189–91.

Kingston, D.R. (1970) The Law of Probabilities and the Credibility of Witnesses and Evidence. *Journal of Forensic Science*. **15** (1), 18–27

Krcma, V. (1966) Fluted and annular grooved barrel chambers in firearms. *Journal of Forensic Sciences, JFSCA*, **41** (3), 407–17.

Mathews, J. (1962) U.S. Department of Justice. Federal Bureau of Investigation. NCIC. Criminalistics Laboratory Information System (CLIS) Operating Manual. 2001–2002.

McConnell, M.P., Triplett, G.M. and Rowe, W.F. (1981) A study of shotgun pellet ricochet. *Journal of Forensic Sciences*, **26** (4), 699–709.

Meyers, C.R. (1987) Objective v subjective boondoggle. *Association of Firearms and Toolmark Examiners Journal*, **19** (1), 24–30.

Pike, J.F. (1988) Electrochemical machining, a new barrel-making process. *AFTE Journal*, **20** (4), 396–403.

Rathman, G.A. (1987) Bullet ricochet and assorted phenomena. *AFTE Journal*, **19** (4), 374–81.

Rathman, G.A. (1993) Bullet impact damage and trajectory through auto glass. *AFTE Journal*, **25**, 79–86.

Salferstein, R. (1982) *Forensic Science Handbook*, Prentice-Hall Inc., New Jersey, USA.

Thornton, J.I. and Cashman, P.J. (1986) The effect of tempered glass on bullet trajectory. *Journal of Forensic Sciences*, **31**, 743–46.

Uchiyama, T. (1988) A criterion for landmark identification, automatic comparison model of land marks and a criterion for landmark identification using rare marks. *AFTE Journal*, **20** (3), 252–9.

Uchiyama, T. (1993) Automated land mark identification. *AFTE Journal*, **25** (3), 172–96, July.

Walls, H.G. (1968) *Forensic Science*, Sweet & Maxwell, UK.

Further Reading

Association of Firearms and Toolmark Examiners Glossary.

Greener, W.W. (2003) *The Gun*, Bonanza Books, New York, NY, USA (reprint).

Krcma, V. (1996) Fluted and annular grooved chambers in firearms. *Journal of Forensic Sciences, JFSVA*, **41** (3).

Mathews, J. (1962) *Firearms Identification*, **I**, University of Wisconsin Press, Madison, USA.

Rodney, J.C. (1998) Fluted chamber markings on fired cases. Presented at the 29th Annual Training Seminar, Tampa, FL, USA, July, 1998.

5

Range of Firing Estimations and Bullet Hole Examinations

5.1 Introduction

On the discharge of a firearm, a large volume of 'smoke' or, more correctly, gunshot residue (GSR), often also called firearms discharge residue (FDR), is discharged at high velocity from the muzzle. This FDR consists of a mixture of unburnt and partially burnt propellant, amorphous sooty material, a mixture of incandescent gases, primer discharge residues and, depending on the type of bullet used, volatilized lead from the base of the bullet.

Of these components, the primer residues form only a minute part of these FDRs. This component is, however, of fundamental importance in determining whether a person has fired or has been in the vicinity of a weapon being fired. This aspect will be fully dealt within Chapter 6 on 'Gunshot Residue Examination'.

As the bullet passes through any material, some of the surface of the bullet will be rubbed off the bullet onto the margins of the bullet hole. As the bullet has to physically push apart the structure of the material to gain entry, more of the lead or jacket material will be rubbed off the bullet on the entry side of the material than on the exit side. Chemical tests, especially when dealing with jacketed bullets, can often be inconclusive as to which side of a garment the bullet entry hole is situated. Examination, using the scanning electron microscope (SEM), of a simple adhesive lift taken from the periphery of each side of the hole in the material will quickly reveal which side of the hole has the greater quantity of bullet material and is thus the entry hole.

Handbook of Firearms and Ballistics: Second Edition   Brian J. Heard
© 2008 John Wiley & Sons, Ltd.

5.2   The Use of X-ray Photography

The use of X-rays in the investigation of gunshot wounds can be invaluable to the forensic investigator for a variety of reasons and can help to:

1. determine whether part or all of the bullet is still within the body;
2. locate the exact position of the bullet;
3. locate and determine the type and calibre of bullet where the bullet cannot be surgically removed;
4. determine the bullet path;
5. determine the position of all the pellets and wads in shotgun wounds prior to surgery.

In numerous cases that I have dealt with, a laborious and time-consuming dissection could have been prevented by taking a simple body X-ray to determine the position of the bullet and in fact whether it is still in the body.

5.2.1   Case example

This concerned a Hong Kong fisherman who had been illegally fishing in the waters off Vietnam. A Vietnamese gunboat gave chase and when the fisherman refused to stop, the gunboat crew opened fire with a number of AK47s and a 12.7 mm DShK heavy machine gun.

The fishing boat took numerous hits from both the AK47s and the DShK. In addition, the captain was hit with a 7.62×39 mm bullet and died almost immediately. Another member of the crew took over the control of the boat and continued the attempted escape from the gunboat. At some point, the fishing boat reached international waters and the gunboat gave up the chase.

To preserve the body, the crew put it in the ice hold, along with catch, and brought it back to Hong Kong for burial.

At the post mortem (PM) examination, it could be seen that the front of the body, which had been next to the ice, was perfectly preserved, whilst the rear was black and in a state of decomposition. It was also noted that there was only one bullet wound visible, which was in the centre chest area. This, the pathologist insisted, was the entry wound, and the bullet must still be inside the body. I had other opinions as I was convinced that the wound was from the bullet exiting and was not an entry hole. One does not, however, argue with Hong Kong pathologists.

No X-ray equipment was forthcoming, and an extremely messy and tedious dissection of the body commenced. This included the entire torso, both legs and arms. Despite this, no bullet was found. At the end of this dissection, the body was turned onto its front and it was noticed that the thick, suntanned and now blackened outer layer of the skin on the back of the body had separated from the underlying layers and was quite mobile.

When this outer layer of skin was stretched back into its correct location, a bullet entry hole was located just to the right of the midline. This had been completely covered by the wrinkled-up layer of skin. The bullet had obviously entered the back of the body, passed straight through the body and exited from the front. A simple X-ray of the body would have shown the wound track and the complete absence of any missile.

5.2.2   Estimation of calibre from X-rays

Whilst X-rays can be used to accurately locate a missile, they cannot be used to precisely measure the calibre of a missile as all X-ray images, by virtue of the way they are taken, are magnified to some degree. As the distance from X-ray plate to the missile increases, so does this magnification effect.

These problems can be offset by taking two X-ray photographs of the body, one face on and one side on. These can then be used to estimate the depth of the missile in the body. A number of bullets of different calibres can then be placed alongside the body at a suitable position and then X-rayed (Figures 5.1–5.3) to estimate the bullet calibre.

Alternatively, a micrometer, with its jaws open to a set measurement, can be placed in the appropriate position (Figure 5.4) and can be used to estimate the calibre.

The only way an X-ray can be used to directly estimate a bullet's calibre without the foregoing use of two X-rays taken at 90° to each other is to compare the size of the bullet's shadow on the X-ray alongside several bullets of known

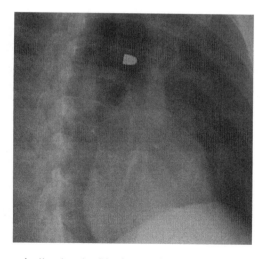

Figure 5.1 Bullet deep in the body. Photograph reproduced by permission of Evan Thompson.

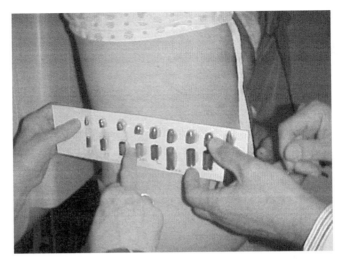

Figure 5.2 Bullets being placed in an appropriate position. Photograph reproduced by permission of Evan Thompson.

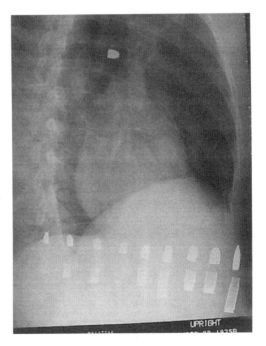

Figure 5.3 Bullet calibre comparison. Photograph reproduced by permission of Evan Thompson.

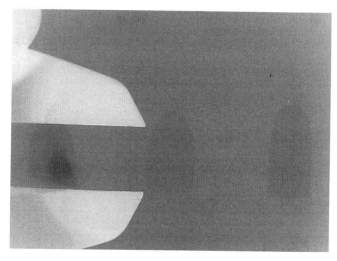

Figure 5.4 Example of how a micrometer can be used to estimate a bullet's calibre.

calibre. Whatever bullet calibre is closest in size to that on the X-ray must be the largest calibre of bullet that the bullet in the body can possibly be. For example, if the image is the same size as a 0.25″ calibre bullet, then the bullet in the body must be of a smaller calibre than 0.25″.

5.2.3 Case example

An interesting case involved the identification of missile holes in a vast 18 ft diameter table which was reputed to be that of King Arthur, a fifth century King of England (Biddle, 2000).

The table had been hanging on the wall of the great banqueting hall at Winchester Castle, Hampshire, and it was not until it was taken down for restoration that the missile holes were located.

An examination of the table's surface found there to be a total of 45 complete penetrations. X-ray photographs revealed a further five missiles still embedded in the thick central supporting beams. Unfortunately, I was prohibited from removing any of these (Figure 5.5 and 5.6).

Using side-on X-rays, it was possible to determine the exact depth of the missiles and thus their calibre which ranged from 0.6 to 0.9″. It was also noted that the missiles were very irregular in shape, suggesting that they were probably not cast in the conventional way.

In the early part of the seventeenth century, the military in England were armed with a wide variety of weapons ranging from 0.5 to 1.0″. The foot soldier was nearly always armed with a simple smooth-bore matchlock musket and the

Figure 5.5 King Arthur's Round Table (diagrams and photograph of the Winchester Round Table by courtesy of Prof. Martin Biddle).

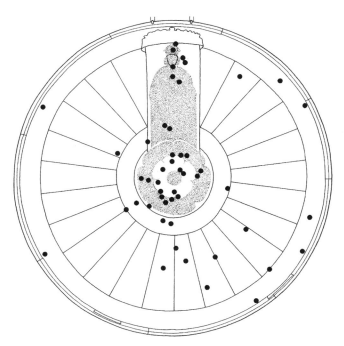

Figure 5.6 Missile entry holes in table. Diagram by courtesy of Prof. Martin Biddle.

cavalryman with a wheel-lock pistol or carbine. The missiles used in these weapons were rarely cast and usually, especially in times of battle, just lumps of lead which were simply hammered into a rough shape and size to fit the bore of the weapon. This situation was standardized by an order of 1673 where the calibre of service muskets was fixed at 12 bores (0.729″).

If the damage to the table was inflicted by military troops, then this probably took place before the last quarter of the seventeenth century as witnessed by the size and type of the missiles.

Historical records revealed that the castle was taken by Oliver Cromwell's parliamentary forces in 1642. The castle and town were regained by the King in 1643 but was taken again by parliamentary forces directly under Cromwell's command in 1645.

The trajectories of the missiles were found by comparing the positions of the entry and exit holes and side-on X-rays of the large beams under the table.

Whilst the resulting bullet trajectories would appear somewhat confusing, historical records do show the position of the dining table in the Great Hall. From this, it can be ascertained that the majority of the shots were fired from either side of the table, whilst those directed at the image of King Arthur came from the head of the table, possibly even fired by Cromwell himself (Figure 5.7).

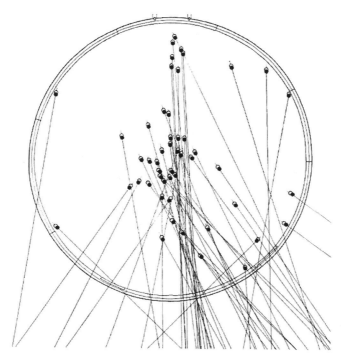

Figure 5.7 Trajectories from entry and exit holes. Diagram by courtesy of Prof. Martin Biddle.

Obviously, the missile holes had nothing to do with King Arthur and eventually, the table was dated, via dendrochronology, to the fourteenth century.

5.2.4   Case example

Another illustrative case on the use of X-ray photographs concerns the case of an old man who dropped dead on the streets of Hong Kong. There were no suspicious circumstances, but to ensure that no pacemakers or anything else was present in the body that could cause problems with the cremation, a standard X-ray was taken. It was at this stage that the shadow of a bullet was seen next to the spine.

At the PM, no obvious bullet could be found, but on excavating some calcified material surrounding the spine, a rifle bullet was discovered. No rifling marks were present on the bullet and the jacket material was so thin that it flaked off like tissue paper at the lightest touch.

A close examination of the old man's skin revealed a very old and almost imperceptible puckered wound inside the navel. This was obviously the bullet entry hole, but it had very long ago healed into scar tissue.

The bullet was identified as a 7.7 mm Arisaka rifle bullet which had obviously been fired at the old man when he was much younger during the 1941–1945 Japanese occupation of Hong Kong – a case of attempted murder by the Japanese military discovered over 50 years too late.

In penetrating wounds, the presence of lead fragments in the wound track would normally rule out a fully jacketed bullet. However, the opposite is not always true as a plain lead or hollow-point bullet need not necessarily expand and/or fragment on entering tissue.

One of the most characteristic X-ray photographs is that from a high-velocity soft-pointed hunting bullet. In such an X-ray, a snowstorm of lead fragments will be seen along the wound track.

One area where X-rays can be confusing is with Winchester Silvertip ammunition. These bullets have a jacket material made of aluminium (rather than the standard copper alloy), which readily separates from the core when entering the body. Being made of aluminium, the jacket does not show up on X-rays and it can easily be missed. As the core will exhibit class characteristics impressed through the jacket during its passage through the bore, this can be mistaken for a plain lead bullet with rifling marks impressed upon it.

Fibre, and very occasionally plastic, shotgun wads can often be seen on X-ray photographs despite the fact that they contain no metallic elements which would be opaque to X-rays. The reason for this is that they can pick up lead deposits from previous shots as they pass through the barrel. These are visualized on the photograph as faint opaque circles. With the move towards more 'eco-friendly' cartridges made of paper, a corrodible base and felt wads, these could be seen more often in the future.

A possible area of confusion over the missile and number of shots fired could arise over Winchester 0.25″ acp cartridge loaded with a hollow-point bullet. The cavity of this bullet contains either a steel or lead ball which is intended to ensure expansion of the bullet in this low-powered round. Rarely does the bullet expand on striking a body and the ball simply falls out of the cavity, resulting in what appears to be two missiles on the X-ray.

5.3   Range of Firing Estimations for Pistols and Rifles

At close range, up to 2 ft (60 cm) in a handgun and 6 ft (approximately 2 m) in a rifle, the impact of these discharge residues on the target enables the range of firing to be accurately determined. However, when the muzzle of the weapon is in very tight contact with the skin, these discharge residues may be completely absent. The wound, due to the lack of discharge residues and its appearance, is in fact often mistaken for the exit rather than for the entry hole.

In this situation, the discharge residues follow the bullet into the tissue, often leaving no trace round the margins of the wound. In areas of the body where the skin and subcutaneous tissue cover bone, that is, the skull, scapula or sternum, the gases become trapped between the subcutaneous tissue and the bone. The gases expand with extreme rapidity and immediately attempt to exit from the same hole through which they entered. As the gases now form an exceedingly large volume, the only way they can exit is by bursting back out through the tissue surrounding the bullet entry hole. This results in a gaping *stellate tear* with blood, tissue and often bone being ejected some distance backwards towards the firer.

Whilst stellate tearing is generally only seen where the skin covers bone, it can also be observed in areas of high subcutaneous fat deposition, i.e., round the midriff, or where the underlying tissue consists of rigid muscle, that is, pectoral or upper thigh region. In these cases, the gases become trapped in the subcutaneous fat, which occurs between the surface skin and underlying muscle. This is relatively uncommon and when it does arise, the stellate tearing is far less pronounced.

The degree of stellate tearing depends upon the volume of gas produced and the firmness with which the weapon is held against the skin. Thus, a 0.32″ ACP held loosely against the temple would probably cause very little stellate tearing, whilst a 12-bore shotgun held tightly against the pectoral muscle would produce massive tearing.

Without careful examination, a poorly defined stellate wound can easily be mistaken for an exit wound. To correctly identify the wound, it is necessary to excise the wound when partially burnt, and unburnt propellant particles should be easily located within the tissues. The identification of the range of firing as tight contact can then be made.

At ranges greater than tight contact, the impact of the components of the discharge residues on the target can be used to accurately determine the range at which the shot was fired.

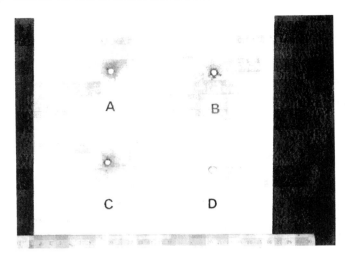

Figure 5.8 Discharge residue patterns for the same ammunition at (a) 1; (b) 2; (c) 4; (d) 6in.

The method employed for the detection of these components is generally a simple visual examination under a low-powered microscope. The observed distribution of these FDR particles can then be compared to test-fired samples (Figure 5.8).

It should be stressed that the test firings must be made with exactly the same ammunition and in the same type of weapon with the same barrel length. Different types of ammunition can give vastly variable discharge residue patterns. Likewise, the longer the barrel, the more complete the burning of the propellant and the fewer discharge residues.

It is also advantageous when conducting the range of firing estimations to select a target material as similar as possible to that under examination. It is of little use trying to compare, for example, test patterns made on a smooth material made from a man-made fibre with those on a thick woolly material. Likewise, for range of firing estimations on skin, much more meaningful results will be obtained if tests are carried out on pig skin rather than on a fine-weave sheet of cotton.

The appearance of the discharge residue components will vary depending on the range, weapon type, barrel length, propellant type and ammunition used (Figures 5.9 and 5.10). These observed effects can conveniently be split into three main groups.

5.3.1 Scorching

This is caused by the incandescent gases as they emerge from the muzzle of the weapon. Although they initially leave the barrel at a temperature of around

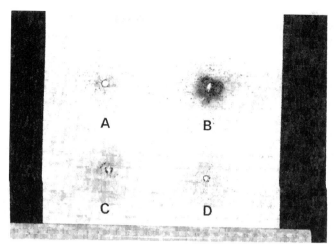

Figure 5.9 Discharge residue deposits for various types of ammunition at the same range: (a) Winchester; (b) Sellior and Bellot; (c) Norma; (d) Rem UHC.

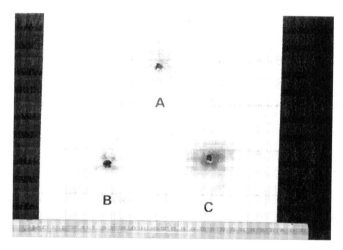

Figure 5.10 Discharge residue patterns for the same ammunition fired at the same range through different barrel lengths: (a) 6 in. barrel; (b) 4 in. barrel; (c) 2 in. barrel.

2000 °C, they rapidly cool and at a distance of no more than an inch, their scorching effect will be insignificant. The affected area is also very localized being no more than a $\frac{1}{4}$ inch round the periphery of the bullet entry hole.

The scorching effect of these gases is generally not visible on skin due to its high water content. Even when scorching is present, it is often difficult to discern beneath the amorphous sooty layer which occurs at short ranges.

Hair can exhibit a scorching effect, being generally identifiable by the crinkled nature of the individual hairs. Similarly, the finer fibres encountered in materials made from wool display the effects of scorching much more readily. The fibres are often shrivelled up to a fraction of their normal length and are completely blackened.

In man-made fibres, the effect is very pronounced with the ends of the fibres being melted into globules. This, however, must not be confused with the surface finish applied to many of the cheaper man-made fabrics. This finish is called 'pilling' and is accomplished by quickly running a hot gas flame over the surface of the fabric. This causes the ends of the individual fibres to melt into globules, which makes the fabric much harder wearing. It is these globules that can be easily mistaken for the scorching effect of the discharge gases. The potential confusion can easily be overcome by examining fibres from remote areas of the garment.

The degree of scorching is also dependent upon:

- *Surface condition of the target.* If it is wet, the degree of scorching will be very much reduced.
- *Powder type.* Double-based propellants, for example, burn much hotter than single-based propellants.
- *Pressure produced.* A high-pressure cartridge, such as a magnum, will produce a correspondingly higher degree of scorching than a non-magnum cartridge due to the higher temperature of the gases produced.
- *Weight of propellant.* The greater the weight of propellant, the greater the volume of gases produced. Thus, a rifle calibre will produce far more scorching than the same calibre in a pistol cartridge.

5.3.2 Blackening

This is caused by carbonaceous material in the discharge residues mainly resulting from incomplete combustion of the propellant. It can also result from excessive quantities of bullet lubricant or even the bitumen sealant used between the bullet and cartridge case. It is composed mainly of amorphous carbon, although fine particles of partially burnt propellant can also be present.

This effect really begins where scorching finishes and can be up to 10 in. (25 cm) from the muzzle in rifles and 5 in. (12.5 cm) in pistols.

The weight of the propellant obviously affects the degree of blackening in the same way as scorching, that is, the greater the charge, the greater the blackening. The effects of pressure and propellant are, however, exactly the opposite. A lower pressure means less efficient combustion, which gives rise to a greater proportion of carbonaceous materials. Likewise, the lower the temperature of burning, the less efficient the propellant.

The blackening is only a light surface coating and is very easily removed with water or by rubbing with a cloth. Hospital blankets and rain are particularly efficient at removing this type of discharge residue. The absence of blackening should not, therefore, be considered conclusive proof as to the range of firing. Blackening is often more obvious to the naked eye than it is through a low-powered microscope.

5.3.3 Unburnt and partially burnt propellant particles

Being much heavier than the carbonaceous material, the propellant particles can be found on the target at much greater distances. With low-powered microscopy, these particles can be located on the target at ranges up to 30″ for a handgun and to over 48″ for a rifle. With 30″ being the approximate arm length for an adult, the presence or absence of propellant particles can be extremely important in determining the sequence of events in a shooting case.

Factors influencing the quantity of this particulate matter found on the target are very similar to those for carbonaceous material. Basically, the more efficient the cartridge and the longer the length of the barrel, the fewer the propellant particles that will be discharged from the muzzle.

Unlike carbonaceous material, the propellant particles adhere much more strongly to fabrics. Often, the particles will melt the fabric and weld themselves into place.

With skin, the particles will, at very close range, often enter the epidermal layer and take the form of 'tattooing', which is all but impossible to remove.

5.3.4 Extended range of fire estimations

By using a SEM to examine adhesive lifts taken from the surface surrounding the bullet entry hole, the range of firing can be estimated up to a distance of 16 ft (5 m). This type of examination is, however, concerned with the search for the metallic components of the primer residues and not burnt and unburnt propellant particles.

This is a very specialized technique and will be covered at greater length in Chapter 6.

5.3.5 Range of firing estimation on badly decomposed bodies (B.J. Heard, unpublished paper)

Estimating the range of firing on a badly decomposed body can, unless a shotgun has been used, prove to be extremely difficult. The putrefying tissue either masks the presence of residues or they are removed as the outer layers of skin slough off.

A case where this problem was of considerable importance involved the shooting and subsequent dismembering of a young insurance sales woman.

After being shot and then dismembered, the body parts were placed into several black plastic bags and dumped on a hillside. The ambient temperature was in excess of 35 °C, and in the 2 days that it took for the body to be discovered, the body had become severely decomposed.

An examination of the head revealed the presence of two bullet entry holes of approximately 0.22″ calibre (Figures 5.11 and 5.12). It was noted that the skin surrounding one of these bullet entry holes was a mushy khaki, whilst the other had the normal blackened appearance of decomposing skin.

Inside the skull were found two severely damaged home-made 0.22″ calibre lead missiles. A microscopic examination of these missiles did not reveal the presence of any rifling and what stria were present showed them to have been fired from either a double-barrelled weapon or two different weapons.

A suspect was eventually arrested and in his flat was found a double-barrelled, muzzle-loading blank pistol which had been converted to fire 0.22″ ammunition (Figure 5.13). Both barrels of this pistol had been recently fired. A microscopic comparison of missiles fired from the pistol with those recovered from the victim's head showed them both to have been fired from the converted pistol.

The pistol had a single, non-selective trigger which was somewhat prone to firing both barrels together. It was thus necessary to determine the range of firing for both shots to eliminate any defence of accidental discharge during a struggle.

It was assumed that the difference in appearance of the two bullet entry holes could have something to do with one being closer than the other and that the

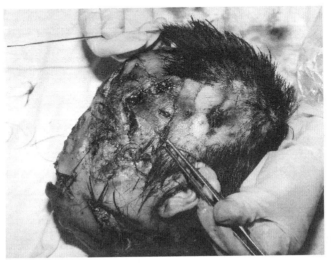

Figure 5.11 Skull showing area of discolouration.

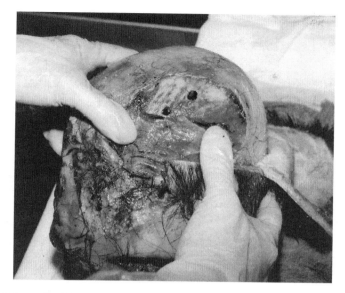

Figure 5.12 Skin pulled back revealing two missile entry holes.

Figure 5.13 Converted, 0.22″ calibre, muzzle-loading blank pistol.

residues from the closer shot were having some effect on the rate of decomposition of the surrounding skin.

A number of pieces of pig skin were shot at various ranges with exactly the same weapon and ammunition as that used in the crime. The skin was then sealed in black plastic bags of exactly the same type as the body parts were wrapped up in. The bags were then placed on the roof top of police headquarters and opened at half-day intervals. It was found that the pappy khaki colouration to the skin could be exactly duplicated in the pig skin. The effect was then duplicated in human skin.

These tests showed that the weapon was fired at a distance of about 2 in. from the head and then at a distance in excess of 12 in., thus disproving the defence of accidental discharge during a struggle for the weapon. It was not possible to determine the sequence in which the shots were fired.

5.3.6 Bullet wipe marks

Bullet lubricant, bullet/case mouth sealant and gases, which have squeezed past the bullet on its passage through the bore, leave the outside of the bullet coated with a layer of black sooty material. As the bullet passes through an object, whether it be cloth, skin or some solid object, this black material is deposited on the periphery of the bullet entry hole. This black ring is often referred to as the 'bullet wipe' and, where no discharge residues are present, it is a very useful identifier of the bullet entry hole.

The quantity of material left on the 'bullet wipe' mark is dependent on the quantity of carbonaceous material picked up by the bullet during its passage through the bore. Assuming that the first shot fired was through a clean unfouled barrel, the bullet wipe mark should be easily distinguishable from the second bullet which had been fired through the barrel fouled by the first bullet. In this instance, the first bullet wipe mark will contain less carbonaceous material and grease than the second and will appear much fainter than the one from the second shot. In cases where multiple shots have been fired, it is thus possible to determine with a reasonable degree of accuracy which was the first shot to strike the target.

5.3.7 Brief glossary

Blackening	Fine carbonaceous material in the discharge residues.
Bullet wipe mark	Mixture of bullet lubricant, mouth sealant and carbonaceous material picked up by the bullet whilst travelling down the bore, which is deposited on any material through which it passes.
GSR or FDR	GSR (gunshot residue) or FDR (firearms discharge residue) Mixture of unburnt and partially burnt propellant, amorphous sooty material, incandescent gases and primer discharge residues which issue from a weapon during firing.
Scorching	Close-range effect of hot gases emerging from the muzzle of a fired weapon.

5.4 Chemical Tests for Range of Firing Estimations and Bullet Entry/Exit Hole Identification

5.4.1 Introduction

In any well-funded laboratory, chemical spot tests for bullet entry/exit hole determination are generally a thing of the past. The vast majority of chemical tests used for such purposes can be carried out with a far higher degree of precision by use of the SEM.

Range of firing estimations are normally carried out by visually estimating the density of partially burnt propellant particles on the surface being examined. In handguns, the maximum range that these particles can be seen, even when using a microscope, is about 24 in. (60 cm). The presence of primer discharge residues can, however, be picked up with a SEM at ranges of 15 ft (5 m) or more.

The process is very laborious and involves taking tapings from control firings at a set distance, usually 4 in. (10 cm) from the bullet hole. From these tapings, a GSR particle density is calculated for each range. These particle densities are then compared to tapings taken from the garment in question and a range of firing estimation obtained.

As the GSR distribution will be different for each type of ammunition/barrel length combination, it is essential that these parameters are known before range of fire estimations can be calculated from the GSR particle density distribution tables. This technique does, however, enable range of fire estimations to be made at distances which cannot be accomplished by any other method.

5.4.2 Chemical tests for range of firing estimations

In cases where a SEM is not available, the tests described below can still be used. Great caution should be used with the interpretation of any results obtained from these tests as none of them is specific. At best, the results could be presumptive and at worst, only indicative.

Sodium rhodizonate test. The most valuable of the available spot tests is the sodium rhodizonate test for lead. This test is a rapid and very cheap method for determining, in those cases where a microscopic examination is ambiguous, the entry and exit holes.

The test relies on the specificity of this reagent, in acidic conditions, to give a positive reaction to lead. It also relies on the bullet being either plain lead or, if it is a jacketed bullet, having picked up some lead primer residues on its passage through the bore.

When passing through cloth, the residues or some of the bullet lead will be transferred from the bullet to the impact side of the target. Thus, if we are dealing with a bullet which has completely penetrated a body, the outside surface of the bullet entry hole on the outer garment will give a positive reaction to lead as will the inside surface of the bullet exit hole.

The test is carried out by firmly pressing a clean filter paper, which has been lightly moistened with 0.1 N hydrochloric acid (HCl), over the bullet hole. The filter paper is then dried using a hot air blower and carefully spotted with a saturated solution of sodium rhodizonate in water. The filter paper will eventually take on an orange colour from the sodium rhodizonate. The filter paper is then warmed once again with the air blower, but not dried. The solution of 0.1 N HCl is then lightly spotted, or preferably sprayed, onto the paper until the orange colour disappears. If there are any lead particles present, they will remain as a purple colouration.

The sodium rhodizonate test can also be used for the detection of barium, although it is not as sensitive as when used for lead.

This test can be used in conjunction with the test for lead, giving a more specific identifier of GSR.

Method.   After spotting with the 0.1 N HCl solution and noting or photographing any purple-coloured spots, hold the filter paper over a solution of 880 ammonia solution. This will, with care, place the filter paper into a mildly alkaline condition (preferably about pH 8). This will remove the purple colouration due to lead and place it in a condition where the sodium rhodizonate will react with any barium present to give a red/brown colouration.

Alternatively, the filter paper can be spotted with dilute ammonia solution, but this tends to dilute the result, leading to difficulties in identifying the colour change.

Walker test for nitrites.   This is used for the detection of nitrites in the partially burnt and unburnt propellants. On darkly coloured clothing, the test can indicate the distribution of such particles, thus enabling the range of firing to be estimated.

The test uses the slightly sticky, gelatinous surface layer of desensitized photographic paper to pick up the particles from the cloth. Any nitrites present are then converted to a diazo dye compound. These diazo compounds are, depending on what chemicals are used, brightly coloured red/orange dyes which can easily be seen and photographed.

The technique is as follows:

- Desensitize a sheet of photographic paper in hypo fixer.
- Immerse the paper in a solution of 5% 2-naphthylamine-4,8-disulphonic acid. Dry in air.
- Place a cloth wetted with 20% acetic acid under the clothing under test. Place the photographic paper on top and cover this with a piece of dry cloth. Apply pressure with a hot iron set at 'warm' for 5 min.

- Any bright red spots which appear indicate the presence of nitrite compounds.

It should be noted that many compounds other than nitrocellulose propellants can give a positive reaction, for example, urine, face powder, fertilizers.

Greiss test. This is identical to the Walker test except for the main reagent which is naphthylamine instead of 2-naphthylamine-4,8-disulphonic acid. This reagent gives orange spots. Once again, this test is mainly used for detection of propellant particles in range of firing estimations.

Marshall test. Using the desensitized photographic paper, soak it in 0.5% solution sulphanilic acid for 10 min, then dry. Soak this in a 0.5% solution of N-α naphthyl-ethylenediamine hydrochloride in methanol for 2 min then dry. Place a cloth wetted with 20% acetic acid under the clothing under test. Place the photographic paper on top and cover this with a piece of dry cloth. Apply pressure with a hot iron set at 'warm' for 5 min. A positive for nitrites will appear as purple spots on a purple background. Rinse in warm water to remove background colour. If this is then rinsed in methanol, the spots will turn orange. Once again, this test is mainly used for detection of propellant particles in range of firing estimations.

Tewari test. Dissolve 1 g of antazoline hydrochloride (2-N-benzylanilinomethyliminazoline hydrochloride) in 50 mL of water. Slowly add 45 mL of concentrated HCl. Stir until the white precipitate dissolves. Soak a filter paper in acetone and press on target. Air dry and spray heavily with the prepared antazoline solution. Nitrite compounds will register a positive reaction as deep yellow spots. This test is mainly used for range of firing estimations by visualization of propellant particles.

Lunge reagent. This was the original 'dermal nitrite test' used for the proof of firing a weapon.
Originally, the reagent consisted of a 0.25% solution of diphenybenzidine in concentrated sulphuric acid. This reagent was sprayed onto paraffin casts of the suspect's hands, and any nitrite particles present, which include nitrocellulose, would give a deep blue colouration.
Diphenybenzidine is, however, very carcinogenic and has been replaced with diphenyamine, which also gives a deep blue colouration to nitrites.
The problem with this test is that so many everyday chemicals, for example, fertilizer, urine, make-up, etc., can give a positive reaction with this reagent that it is no longer used for the identification of GSRs on hands.

Harrison and giliroy reagent. Whilst this reagent is really intended for the identification of GSR on hand swabs, it can be used just as well for range of firing estimations once the particles have been removed from the garment.

Use the photographic paper method of lifting the residues from the clothing, but use dilute HCl instead of acetic acid. Dry, then spray with a 10% solution of triphenylmethylarsonium iodide in alcohol. An orange colouration is positive for antimony. Dry and spray with a saturated solution of sodium rhodizonate. Red spots are positive for barium or lead. Dry and spray with dilute HCl. Purple spots are positive for lead. If the spots are then exposed to a 35% ammonia solution, any particles containing barium will give a red colouration.

Dithiooxamide (DTO) test.   As previously explained, sodium rhodizonate can be successfully utilized for the identification of bullet entry and exit holes caused by plain lead or semi-jacketed bullets. However, in the case of fully jacketed bullets, the only lead that is likely to be present around the bullet entry hole is from the priming compound. This is often of an insufficient quantity to produce a positive result.

DTO will, however, detect copper and nickel, and can be utilized for the determination of bullet entry and exit holes for fully jacketed gilding metal (Cu/Zn) and cupro nickel (Cu/Ni) bullets. It can also detect the presence of cobalt, although this is currently of no significance in forensic firearms examination.

With DTO, copper produces a very dark-green colouration, nickel a pink to violet colouration and cobalt a brown colouration. The presence of blood can, however, give a false negative result.

The reagent must be freshly prepared from 0.2 g of DTO in 100 mL of ethanol. The ammonium hydroxide is 20 mL of ammonium hydroxide in 50 mL of distilled water.

A filter paper moistened with the ammonium hydroxide is pressed onto the bullet hole. Gentle heat via a hair dryer can be applied, which will enhance the transfer.

Place three drops of the DTO solution to the area in contact with the bullet hole.

A dark greenish/gray reaction constitutes a positive reaction for copper.

A blue/violet colouration constitutes a positive reaction for nickel.

5.4.3   Range of firing estimations for non-toxic, non-lead primers

In general, it has been noted that when estimating the range of firing from discharge residue dispersion, the results from non-toxic primers do not tally with results from lead based primers (Gundry and Rockoff). This is probably due to the quantity of partially combusted materials present as well as the higher organic content of non-toxic primer compositions. The fact that lead has a high specific gravity might also be a contributing factor.

In very general terms, the spread of discharge residues from non-toxic primers will be less than that from lead-based primers, and the range at which they can be detected will be correspondingly shorter. As an example, if a GSR spread of 3 in. is witnessed around the bullet entry hole, with a lead-based primer, this will indicate a range (depending upon the barrel length, calibre and ammunition used) of 16 in., whilst a Sintox round under the same conditions will indicate a range of 13 in.

As there are so many different non-toxic compositions in use, range of firing estimations must be made with exactly the same ammunition as that used in the case under review.

A complicating factor is that non-lead-based primer compositions can give what appears to be a positive reaction with sodium rhodizonate. This is probably due to the presence of barium which, in a mildly alkaline (pH 8) solution, gives a red/brown colouration, whilst lead gives a purple colouration in mildly acid (pH 2.8) conditions. If the correct pH is not selected, the test results can, to the inexperienced, be confusing.

5.4.4 Range of firing estimations on heavily bloodstained garments

Whilst it may be possible to still see, under low-power microscopy, the unburnt propellant particles, the sooty deposit from close-range discharges may be completely obscured by the blood.

In instances such as these, the only recourse is to use infrared (IR) photography. By use of various filters and different wavelengths of IR, the colour of the garment and the bloodstaining can be eliminated, leaving the sooty deposit. This can then be photographed, using IR-sensitive film, and compared to test firings in the normal way.

A case example which adequately illustrates the use of IR photography of bloodstained clothing involved the fatal shooting of a suspected drug peddler by a police officer. The officer claimed that the suspect came running towards him with a knife and he had no option but to open fire. A witness, however, said that the officer grabbed hold of the deceased's vest, pulled him towards the gun and then shot him.

On examination of the vest worn by the deceased, it was found that the bloodstaining round the bullet entry site was too heavy for visual range of fire estimations to be carried out. By using IR photography, it was possible, however, to completely eliminate the interfering bloodstaining, allowing the sooty discharge residues to be easily seen. Reconstruction showed that at the time of firing, the range from muzzle to vest was no more than 2 in. and that one side of the vest had been closer to the gun than the other. This agreed with the story of the witness showing that the officer had grabbed the vest, pulling the suspect towards him (Figure 5.14 and 5.15).

Visualization of propellant particles on bloodstained garments. Even with heavily bloodstained garments, it should be possible to locate, microscopically,

(a)

(b)

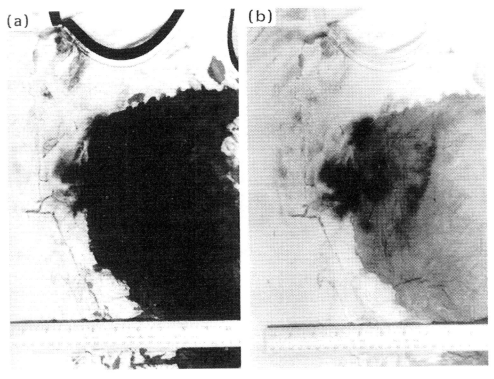

Figure 5.14 (a) T-shirt from deceased under normal lighting with heavy bloodstaining obscuring sooty discharge residues; (b) T-shirt under infrared lighting which eliminates the bloodstaining, thus allowing the sooty discharge residues to be seen.

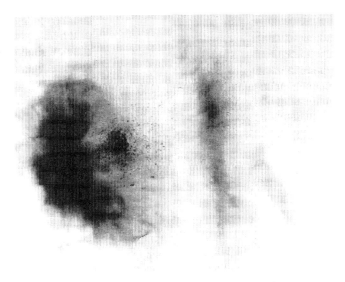

Figure 5.15 Sooty discharge residue distribution reconstructed by having muzzle of revolver in light contact with T-shirt whilst pulling the vest towards the firer with the left hand.

partially burnt propellant particles. The problem is that it is difficult to obtain an accurate picture of the distribution of these particles.

There is, however, a simple method of overcoming this problem without recourse to elaborate and time-consuming chemical tests.

The position of each particle, located under a low-powered microscope, is indicated by sticking a pin through the garment and into the backing board. By viewing, or even better by photographing, the garment from directly above, the pin heads can clearly be seen against the bloodstaining. This can then be used to directly compare with test firings as previously mentioned.

5.5 Range of Firing Estimations for Shotguns

5.5.1 Introduction

As shotguns fire cartridges loaded with pellets, rather than a single missile, the range of firing can be estimated with considerable accuracy up to 20 or 30 yd. This estimation relies on the fact that the pellets do not fly through the air as a single cohesive mass, but begin to disperse as soon as they leave the muzzle. This dispersion is caused by air pressure within the pellet mass, forcing them apart. This action continues throughout the range of the pellets.

One common misconception is that the distance, in inches, from the centre of the pattern to the point where the wads hit the target gives the range in yards. This is totally untrue and should never be used for estimation of range of firing.

Another misconception is that in heavy rain, the pellets will be disrupted by the rain drops. Once again, this has, for all practical purposes, been found to be false due to the relative weight and velocity of the pellets compared to that of raindrops.

5.5.2 Degree of shot dispersion

The degree of dispersion of the shot is dependent on many factors, the most important of which are:

- cartridge pressure;
- wad type;
- barrel choke;
- barrel length.

Cartridge type.   The higher the pressure generated by the cartridge, the more the shot will be disrupted as it emerges from the barrel by the following gases. Whilst this effect is largely offset by the wads used in modern cartridges, it is a factor which does affect the dispersion of the shot.

Wad type.   The wadding in traditional shotgun cartridges consisted of an over-powder wad, a series of filler wads and an overshot wad.

The over-powder wad was intended to act as a gas seal to prevent the high-pressure gases from escaping up into the shot column during firing. The filler wads were to cushion the shot against the rapid acceleration during its progress down the barrel, and the over-shot wad was to retain the shot in the cartridge case.

This construction did, however, suffer from a number of drawbacks. On firing, hot gases could escape passing the over-powder and filler wads into the shot charge. This could result in pellets becoming partially melted and fused together. Likewise, the filler wads did not provide sufficient cushioning of the shot to prevent distortion due to inter-shot contact or, in extreme cases, cold-welding together small clumps of shot due to pressures produced.

Also, during the passage of the shot through the barrel, severe distortion could occur through contact with the inside surface of the bore. Shot which had become so distorted would not fly in a predictable manner resulting in distorted and enlarged patterns.

Modern wads tend to be of the plastic cup type with an integral shock absorber and gas seal. The shock absorber consists of a semi-collapsible section which very effectively cushions the shot column at the moment of acceleration. The integral plastic cup protects the shot during its passage through the bore, and the plastic gas seal prevents the leakage of hot gases into the shot column.

Cartridges loaded with this type of one-piece wad (mono wad) will give a much more controlled spread of shot than one loaded with the old-type wad column (Figures 5.16–5.17).

Case example: cold-welding of shot.   An example of how shot, unprotected by a modern cup-type mono-wad system, can become cold-welded involved the jilted boyfriend of a girl who was a very keen horse rider. The ex-boyfriend was so upset that he decided to teach the girl a lesson. Hiding in a clump of trees close to a bridle path where the girl normally went riding, the ex-boy friend lay in wait with a 0.410″ shotgun loaded with very fine (dust) shot. His plan was to fire at the horse, which would feel the prick of the dust shot, and bolt, thus 'teaching the girl a lesson'. Unfortunately, the dust shot cold-welded and came out of the barrel as a solid lump and instead of hitting the horse went straight through the neck of the girl, virtually decapitating her.

Barrel choke.   Except for a few very unusual weapons, shotguns have smooth-bored barrels. Most sporting weapons have a constriction applied to the muzzle

A. Overcharge card wad
B. Undershot wad
C. Overshot wad
D. Cushion wads
E Shot column
F. Rollover crimp
G. Propellant
H. Base wad

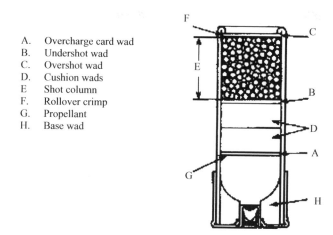

Figure 5.16 Shotgun cartridge.

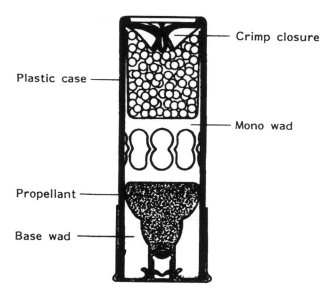

Figure 5.17 Modern shotgun cartridge loaded with a mono wad.

end of the weapon's bore to control the spread of the shot. This constriction is called 'choke'.

As the column of shot passes through this choked part of the barrel, the diameter of the shot column is reduced, thus elongating its length. This reduction in diameter results in the outer layers of shot in the column being given an inward acceleration. This inward acceleration delays the spreading of the shot once it leaves the barrel, thus reducing its degree of dispersion.

The tighter the degree of restriction, the tighter the pattern of shot at the target. The usual degrees of choke are called full, three-quarters, half, quarter, improved cylinder and true cylinder. The degree of constriction is irrespective of the bore of the weapon; thus, all full-choked barrels have a constriction of 0.004″, all half-choked barrels 0.002″, improved cylinder 0.0005″ and true cylinder no restriction at all.

One important thing to notice from these figures is that all bores should give the same spread of shot with a given 'choke' at a given distance. The only variation being that as there is less shot in a 0.410″ bore cartridge than a 12-bore cartridge, the density of shot at the target will be less.

The degree of choke is based upon the percentage of the total pellets in a cartridge which will be in a 30″ circle at any given range.

The following tables (Tables 5.1 and 5.2) show the effect of choke on pattern measured by percentage of shot in a 30″ circle and the *spread* of shot at various ranges for cartridges loaded with mono wads.

The *spread* of shot is the diameter of a circle which contains the majority of the shot charge at any given range. Factors such as irregularly shaped shot, shot which has contacted irregularities in the bore, pellets which become embedded in the wads, and so on, can all give rise to what are called 'flyers'. These flyers are pellets which do not fly true with the rest of the charge, falling outside the main body of shot at the target. Deciding which pellets constitute flyers and should thus be excluded from the main spread requires much experience with the examination of shot patterns and is something which just cannot be explained in a book (Figure 5.18).

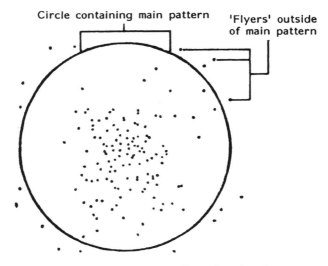

Figure 5.18 Example of a shotgun pellet pattern showing flyers.

Table 5.1 Showing the percentage of total pellets in a 30″ circle for various chokes.

Barrel choke	Range in yards							
	20	25	30	35	40	45	50	55
True cylinder	80	69	60	49	40	33	27	22
Improved	92	82	72	60	50	41	33	27
Quarter	100	87	77	65	55	46	38	30
Half	100	94	83	71	60	50	41	33
Three-quarters	100	100	91	77	65	55	46	37
Full	100	100	100	84	70	59	49	40

Table 5.2 Showing spread of shot, in inches, for various chokes.

Barrel choke	Range in yards						
	10	15	20	25	30	35	40
True cylinder	20	26	32	38	44	51	58
Improved	15	20	26	32	38	44	51
Quarter	13	18	23	29	35	41	48
Half	12	16	21	26	32	38	45
Three-quarters	10	14	18	23	29	35	42
Full	9	12	16	21	27	33	40

Using the above table and the one following, it is possible to determine the actual number of pellets in a 30″ circle in any of the six borings of a gun at the stated ranges (Table 5.3).

Example: Number of pellets striking within a 30″ circle at 40 yd for a $\frac{1}{2}$ choked barrel with a charge of $1\frac{1}{16}$ oz no. 6 shot. Total pellets in $1\frac{1}{16}$ oz shot is 287. This is multiplied by 60 (% in circle at 40 yd) divided by 100 = 172.

Barrel length.   Shortening the barrel by sawing off the muzzle end does have some effect on the spread of shot. It is, however, not as great as popular tradition has it.

What effect exists, however, is mainly due to the high-pressure gases disrupting the shot column as it exits from the barrel.

Shotgun propellants are very fast-burning, giving rise to a very sharp rise in pressure during the first few moments of ignition. In full-length barrels, the overall pressure within the barrel drops very considerably as the shot nears the muzzle and the volume of gas between the over-powder wad and the standing breech of the weapon increases.

As the barrel is progressively shortened, the pressure being exerted on the base of the shot column as it exits the barrel becomes progressively greater.

Table 5.3 Actual number of pellets stoking within a 30″ circle.

| Weight of shot (oz) | Number of pellets in shot load | | | | | |
| | Shot size | | | | | |
	3	4	5	6	7	8
$1\frac{5}{8}$	228	276	358	439	552	732
$1\frac{1}{2}$	210	255	330	405	510	675
$1\frac{1}{4}$	175	213	275	338	425	562
$1\frac{3}{16}$	160	202	261	321	404	534
$1\frac{1}{8}$	157	191	248	304	383	506
$1\frac{1}{16}$	149	181	234	287	361	478
1	140	170	220	270	340	450
$\frac{15}{16}$	131	159	206	253	319	422
$\frac{7}{8}$	122	149	193	236	298	394
$\frac{13}{16}$	113	138	179	219	276	366
$\frac{5}{8}$	87	106	138	169	212	282
$\frac{9}{16}$	78	96	124	152	191	254
$\frac{7}{16}$	61	75	97	118	149	187
$\frac{5}{16}$	44	53	69	84	106	141

These pressures can lead to a destabilization of the shot column and a 'blown' pattern. This effect can be identified by an irregular shot pattern and a larger spread than would normally be expected.

The effect is much less than popular tradition would have us believe and is only marginally greater than that for a full-length cylinder bored barrel.

5.5.3   Summary

As can be seen from the above, the discharge residue exiting from the muzzle of the weapon can provide extremely useful information in respect to the range of firing. At close ranges, up to 2 ft (60 cm) in handguns and 6 ft (2 m) in rifles, estimations can be made as to the range of firing. If the weapon and ammunition type are known, an accuracy of + or − 2 in. (5 cm) can be obtained.

This is normally carried out by direct visual examination of the target material. On heavily bloodstained or dark clothing which might camouflage the presence of the discharge residues, IR photography or chemical methods can be used to visualize the residues.

At greater ranges, the SEM can detect sub-microscopic particles of primer residues which can give range estimations up to 6 or more feet (2 m), but with a much lower accuracy.

With shotgun ammunition, the spread of shot can provide range of firing estimations with reasonable accuracy up to the maximum range.

References

Biddle, M. (2000) *King Arthur's Round Table*, Boydell Press, ISBN 0-85115-626-6.

Gundry, R. and Rockoff, I. *Comparison of Gunshot Residue Patterns from Lead-Based and Lead-Free Primer Ammunition*, http://www.gwu.edu/.

Further Reading

Di Maio, V.J.M. (1985) *Gunshot Wounds, Practical Aspects of Firearms, Ballistics, and Forensic Techniques*, Elsevier.

Fatteh, A. (1976) *Medicolegal Investigation of Gunshot Wounds*, J.B. Lippincott Co.

Greener, W.W. *The Gun and Its Development, Ninth Edition*, Bonanza Books NY, 1910. Bonanza Books (reprint), New York.

Hatcher, J.S. (1935) *Firearms Investigation, Identification and Evidence*, Small Arms Technical Publishing Co; Marines, NC, USA.

6

Gunshot Residue Examination

6.1 Introduction

When attempting to prove that a person has fired a weapon, the detection of *gunshot residues* (GSRs) on the hands of a suspect can be of great significance. The use of the *scanning electron microscope* (SEM) for this is probably the most important advance in the field of forensic firearms examination since the invention of the comparison microscope.

It is important, however, that one has an overview of the history of the subject to place the significance of this advance into its true perspective and the shortcomings of some of the other methods which are still in use today.

6.2 Formation of Discharge Residue

When a weapon is fired, a great volume of incandescent (circa 2000 °C) gaseous material is produced. This gaseous material is mainly the combustion products from the propellant and consists of carbon dioxide, carbon monoxide, water as steam and oxides of nitrogen. In amongst this vast cloud of gases are also partially burnt and unburnt propellant particles and combustion products from the priming compound. These solid particles are collectively called *GSR* particles. Less frequently, they are also referred to as *firearms discharge residues*.

One of the most important aspects concerning primer discharge residues is the mechanism of their formation. The importance of this will become

Handbook of Firearms and Ballistics: Second Edition   Brian J. Heard
© 2008 John Wiley & Sons, Ltd.

clear in the section dealing with the identification of GSR particles using the SEM.

At the moment the firing pin strikes the primer and the priming compounds violently explode, the temperature in the primer cap rises to approximately 2500 °C. The metallic components in the residue are volatilized and emerge from the primer pocket as vapour. This cloud of vapourized metallic components rapidly condenses, forming exceedingly small spherical and spheroidal particles in the size range 0.1–5 μ, where $1 \mu = 1 \times 10^{-6}$ meters. As the vapours produced within the primer pocket are tightly confined, the resulting spheroidal particles will contain various combinations of the elements present. Some will obviously only contain one element, some two and others all the metallic elements present. It is the particles which contain all the elements, together with their morphology, which makes them unique to GSR.

6.3 Distribution of GSR Particles

During the firing of a handgun, the vast majority of these GSR particles exit, at great velocity, from the muzzle of the weapon and are projected away from the firer. In *self-loading pistols,* some of the remainder escapes from the ejection port to settle on the hand holding the weapon. In *revolvers,* the particles escape from the gap between the rear of the barrel and the front of the cylinder. Whilst this gap is somewhat further forward than the ejection port in self-loading pistols, the gases are at a substantially higher pressure and still settle on the firing hand.

In *rifles* and *shotguns,* the situation is a little different. If the weapon is of the self-loading variety, then gases will escape from the ejection port as with a self-loading pistol. In this case, residues could be deposited on the hands of the firer depending on the position of the ejection port. If, however, the weapon is of the bolt action or locked breech, as in a normal break-barrel-action shotgun, then there will be virtually no gas escape from the breech end of the barrel until the action is manually opened. In this case, the deposition of GSR on the hands of the firer will only occur if the action is opened immediately after firing.

Apart from the GSR particles which escape from the muzzle and breech end of the weapon, some are also left in the fired cartridge case and in the barrel and chamber of the weapon.

The vast majority of the GSR particles produced during the firing of a cartridge consist of partially burnt and unburnt propellant particles which are mainly organic in nature. The rest consist of the metallic compounds left over from the discharged priming compound. In addition to these, some particles of plain lead, which have volatilized from the base of the bullet, or copper and zinc particles from the inside surface of the cartridge case, are also often found amongst the GSR particles.

6.4 Identification of GSR Particles

6.4.1 Organic components

The quantity of organic compounds left over from the burning of the propellant is obviously vast in comparison to those from the priming compound. As a result, early attempts at detecting GSRs were directed towards the recovery and identification of the organic components.

These included the identification of nitrites and nitrates in partially burnt propellant particles using chemical spot tests.

One very popular test was the *Walker test* (Walker, 1940), which used desensitized photographic paper as a medium to pick up and retain the particles. After picking up the particles, they were then visualized using a chemical spot test for the nitrites present. The technique was, however, mainly intended for recovery of GSR particles from clothes and was of little use in discovering whether a person had fired a weapon.

The technique was quite long and was conducted as follows:

- Desensitize a sheet of photographic paper by removing the silver halides with 'hypo' photographic fixer.

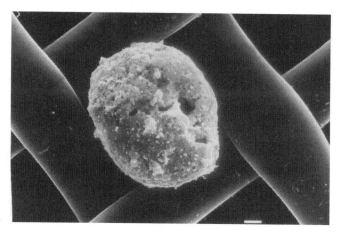

Figure 6.1 Large gunshot residue particle. Scale bar = 0.5 μ.

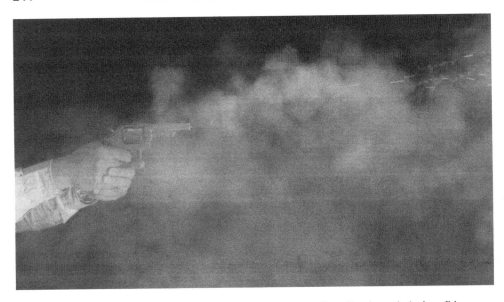

Figure 6.2 Photograph of discharge residue surrounding the hand during firing.

- After drying, immerse the paper in a solution of 5% 2-naphthylamine 4,8 disulphonic acid and dry.
- Place a cloth wetted with 20% acetic acid under the object to be tested. Place the photographic paper on top and press with a hot iron. This softens up the gel coating of the photographic paper to enable it to pick up any GSR particles.
- Any bright red spots which appear are diazo compounds indicating the presence of nitrites.

Despite its complex nature, the test was very efficient at picking up partially burnt propellant particles from clothing for range of firing estimations.

The *Greiss*, *Marshall* and *Tewari tests* were merely variations on the Walker test using different chemicals to produce other coloured diazo compounds.

Probably the most infamous test was the *dermal nitrate* or *paraffin test*, which was first introduced by Teodoro Gonzalez of the Mexico City police laboratory in 1933. This involved the taking of a cast of the back of the suspect's hand using hot paraffin wax. When cooled and set, the wax was peeled off along with any imbedded GSR particles. The cast was then sprayed with *Lunge reagent*, which is a 0.25% solution of diphenylbenzidine in concentrated sulphuric acid. Later variations of the test used diphenylamine in concentrated sulphuric acid. Both these reagents gave a deep blue colouration with nitrates from the partially burnt and unburnt propellant particles.

Unlike the Walker, Greiss and Marshall tests, which merely indicated the presence of these particles on the hands, the paraffin test gave a distribution pattern for the particles. As particles are only deposited on the back of the hand during firing, the palm being wrapped round the weapon's grip and thus protected, the presence of these particles only on the back of the hands is highly indicative of a person having fired a weapon.

Whilst the test gave good information regarding the distribution of these particles, the test itself was only indicative of nitrates. Fertilizer, rust, face powder, sugar, paint, even urine were also found to give a positive reaction to the Lunge reagent.

In 1935, the FBI indicated that the test was not specific and cautioned against its further use (FBI Law Enforcement Bulletin 4, 1935; 9, 1940).

Thin layer and *gas chromatography* were also used at this time to detect the nitrocellulose component of propellants. Whilst these were quite successful, nitrocellulose is not a desirable analyte for GSR analysis due to its presence in many consumer products such as nail polish, wood finishes, paints and even the surface of playing cards.

Gas chromatography and high-pressure liquid chromatography have also been used (Andrasko, 1992) for the identification of propellant particles. As the identification of propellant particles is less specific than that of the primer discharge residues, such methods have found little favour.

6.4.2 Inorganic or metallic component identification

In 1959, Harrison and Gillroy developed a test for the identification of lead, barium and antimony, the main metallic components of primer discharge residues (see Section 2.5, primer compositions).

In this test, the back and palm of each hand (a total of four swabs) are vigorously rubbed with a swab moistened with dilute hydrochloric acid. This physically removes any GSR particles and places them into an acidic environment. The swab is then dried and treated with a solution of triphenylmethylarsonium iodide. Any orange spots would indicate the presence of antimony. After drying, a solution of sodium rhodizonate was added. Any red spots indicate barium which, if on the addition of dilute hydrochloric acid turn purple, indicate the presence of lead.

The great advantage of this test over the dermal nitrate test was the low incidence of false positives. Its shortcomings, however, included a relatively low sensitivity and the fact that it only showed the presence of the individual elements on the hands. What was required was to show the presence of all three elements in discrete particles as occurs in GSR particles. Merely identifying the presence of the individual elements leaves open the interpretation as to whether they originated from general environmental and occupational contaminants or from the discharge of a firearm.

In 1966, the use of *neutron activation analysis (NAA)* for the identification of GSR was reported (Ruch *et al.*, 1964). In this, the samples are placed in a nuclear reactor and bombarded with neutrons making the various elements present radioactive. By analyzing the energy distribution and intensity of the radioactive emissions, it is possible to identify the elements present and the amount of each. This is a highly sensitive method of analysis for most elements, but it is, of course, not applicable to lead, the main component of GSR. Another problem is that not everybody has a convenient nuclear reactor.

In 1970, Bashinki, Davis and Young of the Oakland Police Laboratory, USA, reported on the use of *sodium rhodizonate* for the detection of GSR. This test is only useful for the identification of lead and barium, but because of its sensitivity and simplicity, it is still a commonly used test. Whilst it is of little use in determining whether a person has fired a gun, it is still very useful for range of firing estimations on dark clothing and identification of entry and exit holes in clothing. In this test, the area to be examined is rubbed with a swab in slightly acidic (pH 2.8) conditions. The swab is then partially dried (with hot air and not an *infrared* (IR) hot lamp as this destroys the test). The swab is then lightly sprayed with a saturated solution of sodium rhodizonate in water. Any deep purple-coloured spots indicate lead. The swab is then partially dried and lightly sprayed with dilute hydrochloric acid. Purple spots remaining confirm the presence of lead. If the swab is then placed into an alkaline condition, that is, by exposing it to the fumes of 880 ammonia solution, any pink/orange spots which develop indicate the presence of barium.

In 1972, a technique was reported for the analysis of GSR by *atomic absorption spectroscopy (AAS)* (Green and Sauve, 1973). Atomic absorbtion derives its name from the fact that the atoms of an element will absorb light at a wavelength which is particular to that element. Also, the quantity of light absorbed is proportional to the quantity of that element present.

Basically, a solution of the chemical under test is aspirated into a flame which is sufficiently hot to vapourize the element into its free atoms. If light of the appropriate wavelength is shone through the flame, a portion of the light will be absorbed by the free atoms present. It is the wavelength of the light absorbed which identifies the element present and the quantity of light absorbed which reveals the quantity of the element.

Heated graphite tubes were later used instead of a flame as this was found to give a greatly enhanced sensitivity. This technique was called *flameless atomic absorption spectroscopy (FAAS)*.

Whilst this technique is an extremely sensitive and accurate analytical technique for lead, barium and antimony, it still lacks the specificity required. The results only show that the three elements are present; it cannot show that they are all in a single particle. As such, the elements could be environmental contaminants picked up separately, that is, antimony as a surficant on most fibres to give them lustre, barium from face make-up powders and lead from battery terminals, or a hundred and one other sources.

Many other techniques have been tried, including *proton-induced X-ray emission* (Panigahi *et al.*, 1982), *anodic stripping voltammetry* (Brihaye, Machiroux and Gillain, 1982) and *Auger electron microscopy* (Hellmiss, 1987). For one reason or another, none ever gained any great deal of credibility.

The most which can be said for any of the above tests is that they provide presumptive evidence for the presence of GSR particles.

6.5   The Use of the SEM for GSR Detection

The most successful technique to date for the analysis of GSR particles is without a doubt the *scanning electron microscope with an energy-dispersive X-ray analyzer (SEM-EDX)*.

Basically, the SEM is a microscope which uses a beam of electrons to visualize the object under observation rather than visible light as in a conventional optical microscope. As the beam of electrons is focused by a series of magnets rather than glass lenses, the control is infinitely finer. The electron beam scans the sample in a TV-type raster pattern which is picked up, after reflection, by a video camera. The image is then manipulated electronically and the result visualized on a high-definition monitor.

With a depth of field in the region of 200 times greater than an optical microscope and an extremely high resolution, magnifications in excess of $1\,000\,000\times$ are possible. In addition, on striking the sample, the electrons give up some of their energy to the elements present and this energy is then re-emitted as X-rays, the wavelength of which is particular to the elements present. These X-rays are analyzed via the EDX for wavelength and intensity, and a qualitative and quantitative analysis of the object under examination can be obtained.

With most of the other techniques which have been used for GSR analysis, the sample is destroyed during its examination. With the SEM-EDX, however, the sample is virtually unaffected by the analysis and can be re-examined, if necessary, many times.

Probably the earliest researches into the use of the SEM-EDX for GSR analysis were carried out in the Metropolitan Police Forensic Laboratory, New Scotland Yard, England around 1968. It was not, however, until 1978 that their first paper was published as a Met. Lab. Report by Dr Robin Keeley. This was a general introduction to electron microscopy with GSR examination forming only a small part. It did, however, lay down the basic techniques for the collection, examination and identification of GSR tapings taken from the hands of suspects.

In 1977, Metracardi and Kilty of the FBI laboratory produced an extensive paper (Matricardi and Kilty, 1977) on the subject. Without doubt, the most extensive work on the subject is by Wolton, Nesbitt, Calloway, Loper and Jones (Wolten *et al.*, 1978). This is a contract paper sponsored under the Law Enforcement Administration, and its findings probably did more to advance this subject than any other. The paper is in three parts and covers everything from primer compositions, particle formation, distribution during firing, collection, analysis, and interpretation to environmental considerations.

Other papers followed in profusion (Wallace and Quinlan, 1984; Zeichner *et al.*, 1989; DeGaetano, 1992; Zeichner, Levin and Dvorachek, 1992; Gunaratnam and Himber, 1994), all of which have added more to the science. The basic techniques for obtaining the samples and examining them on the SEM have, however, remained the same.

6.6 Sample Collection

The methodology for sample collection for GSR analysis is simplicity itself. The most commonly used technique uses a 1×1 cm strip of double-sided adhesive tape stuck onto a thin acetate strip. The acetate strip allows the adhesive surface to be conveniently manipulated without any fear of contact with the sampler's hands. One of these tapes is used to take samples from each of the four areas as illustrated in Figure 6.3. During the taking of the samples, the skin must be stretched as much as possible to ensure that any GSR particles which may be hidden within the folds of the skin or inside the hair follicles are removed.

It is important to cover the sampled area at least three times even if the adhesive has lost its tackiness. The adhesive is quite soft and particles can still be pressed into the surface even if there is no discernable stickiness left. It is also important to be consistent in the number of times the area is covered to ensure consistency, for interpretation of the results.

6.6.1 Alternative sampling technique

Whilst a 1×1 cm square of double-sided adhesive tape on a strip of acetate is an effective and cheap way of collecting samples for GSR examination, it does have a number of disadvantages. Of these, the most serious is the requirement for carbon coating and the concomitant possibility of contamination.

This carbon coating must be applied to prevent the sample charging whilst it is being scanned by the SEM electron beam. It is an essential stage in the sample preparation when using this type of sampling technique and cannot be skipped.

For carbon coating, the sample must go through the following procedures:

1. removal of acetate strip containing sample from protective tube;

2. removing the 1×1 cm sample from the acetate strip;

3. sticking the sample onto a SEM stub with double-sided tape;

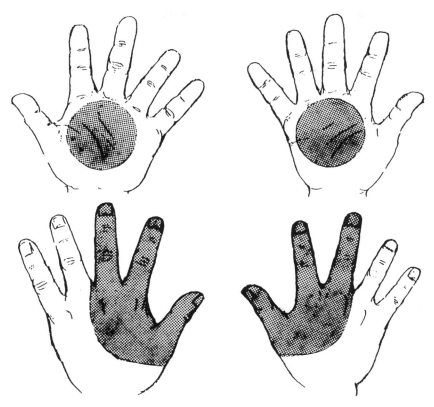

Figure 6.3 Diagram of areas of the hand to be taped for gunshot residue recovery.

4. placing the stub in a multiple stub holder for coating;
5. sputter coating the sample in a near vacuum;
6. re-pressurizing the coater to ambient conditions;
7. transfer of the sample from the coater to the SEM.

Each and every step involves the possible contamination of the sample with the two most serious being:

1. placing the sample alongside other samples and, more seriously, control GSR samples in the sputter coater whilst air is drawn across the sample as the coating chamber is evacuated;
2. re-pressurizing the coater chamber where a large volume of outside, potentially contaminated, air is drawn across the sample.

This whole process can, however, be simplified and the number of procedures where the sample is exposed to the outside air reduced to an absolute minimum. This involves the use of pre-carbon-coated adhesive discs.

These adhesive discs are similar to double-sided tape but the adhesive material, which is specially formulated for SEM use, is pre-impregnated with carbon dust. This completely eliminates the requirement for carbon coating of the sample.

These discs are available from SEM supply companies who can pre-apply these to SEM stubs. These stubs are then individually placed in clean sealed SEM stub tubes under ultra-clean conditions. These tubes have special stub holders in the cap which enable the tube to be simply removed from the cap for sampling. Once the tube is replaced over the cap, it self-seals, preventing any chance of the sample being tampered with.

With this sampling technique, the tube is simply taken off the cap, the adhesive disc dabbed over the relevant part of the hand and then replaced back in the tube.

When it comes to the SEM examination, the SEM stub is removed from the cap with a pair of SEM stub tweezers and transferred to the SEM stub holder and into the SEM chamber. It can then be directly examined in the SEM without any further treatment.

If the hands are wet, they should be allowed to dry naturally. Blow-drying the hands must not be used since it will remove all GSR particles. Sampling from areas of the hand covered with blood should be avoided at all costs; the imaging technique used during the search for the particles (backscattered imaging) is completely overloaded by the iron content of haemoglobin in blood.

It is extremely important that any chance of contamination is avoided. There will, in all probability, be only a few particles of GSR deposited on the hands after firing a round of ammunition. Contamination by a single particle of stray GSR from the sampler would be extremely difficult to detect and could easily be construed as a false positive result.

If the sampler has any contact at all with firearms, he should, before taking the samples, change his clothes, shower and wash his hair thoroughly. During the taking of samples, disposable gloves, boiler suit and hair cover should also be worn. This should be done even if the sampler has had no contact with a weapon. These disposable clothes and gloves should be changed for each suspect examined. It should also be stressed that if the suspect has to be handcuffed, disposable nylon restraints should be used rather than the police issue handcuffs, which may well have been contaminated either from range courses or the gun the officer might be wearing. A control blank taping should also be submitted with the samples. The tapings should be placed in individual bottles and sealed. The individual bottles should be placed in sealed bags and the sealed bags placed in another sealed bag.

To give a rather extreme example of how easy it is to contaminate GSR samples, during conversations with the firearms examiners at a particular laboratory, it was discovered that all their shooting incidents were with 0.22″ weapons. The officers were also proud to point out that they had never had one negative case with respect to GSR and that they always found lead, barium, antimony and aluminium on their hand tapings. This was a little surprising as the vast majority of 0.22″ priming compounds contain only lead and barium. It transpired that the officers, who did all the sampling themselves, were also firearms instructors firing anything up to 200 rounds a day. The ammunition they fired, surprisingly enough, contained lead, barium, antimony and aluminium in the primer.

6.7   GSR Retention

GSR particles deposited on the hands as a result of firing are not stuck there by some 'magic' glue-like property. Neither are they imbedded in the skin. They are merely lying on the surface of the skin. They are, therefore, readily removed by everyday activities.

If there is anything in their favour for being retained on the surface of the skin, it is their exceedingly small size. Being in the range of 0.1–$5\,\mu$ ($1\,\mu = 1 \times 10^{-6}$ meters), they readily become trapped in the microscopic folds of the skin or drop down into hair follicles. Even so, for all practical purposes, all GSR particles will be removed from the hands by everyday activities within 3 hours or, at the very most, 4 hours of a weapon being fired.

Washing the hands will immediately remove all the GSR particles. Great care should also be taken if a suspect requests to be allowed to go to the toilet as urine is also very effective at removing GSR particles.

Likewise, if the suspect requires medical treatment and is covered in a rough hospital blanket, the GSR particles will also be immediately removed.

Insertion of drips into the back of the hand by the hospital should also be discouraged as the insertion point is usually scrubbed with a disinfectant. The medical profession are usually more than willing to assist, and other sites for drip needles are easily located.

If it is raining or the suspect is sweating heavily at the time of firing, the result will, once again, be negative.

In the case of a deceased person, the problem of removal of GSR particles by everyday activities is not relevant. Assuming the GSR particles are not removed by some external means, they should remain on the hands of the deceased indefinitely. If, however, the body had been placed in the mortuary refrigerator, the skin does become clammy and it is very difficult to take the samples. If possible, it is preferable to take the GSR tapings from the body at the scene.

6.8   Conservation of GSR Particles on the Hands

On arrest, every attempt should be made to preserve what residues may be on the hands and to prevent any contamination until the samples can be taken. The

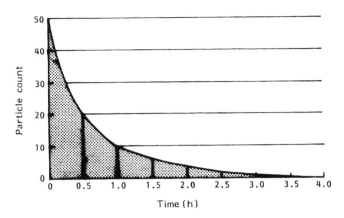

Figure 6.4 Gunshot residue retention on the hands.

only way to do this is to cover each hand either with a paper bag or a large clean envelope. Being porous, the paper bags will reduce sweating and the likelihood for either contamination or the accidental or deliberate removal of GSR particles.

Attempts at conserving any GSR particles which may be on the hands by placing them in polyethylene bags is very detrimental to recovery rates. The problem here is that the hands sweat profusely in the bags and any residues which may be present will very soon end up in the bottom of the bag. There is also a problem with static electricity attracting the particles from the hands onto the surface of the bag.

6.9   GSR Distribution on the Hands

When interpreting GSR distribution results from a SEM analysis of the four tapings taken from the hands, the following points must be considered.

(a) The gases issuing from the muzzle are projected at great velocity away from the firer. Unless there is a very strong wind blowing towards the firer, these GSR-containing gases will not be deposited on the hands.

(b) The gases issuing from the breech end of the barrel, whether it is a revolver or a self-loading pistol, are of much lower velocity. Unless the non-firing hand is held within a few inches of the gun during firing, these gases will only be deposited on the back of the firing hand.

(c) The palm of the firing hand will be protected from the deposition of any GSR particles during firing as it is wrapped round the grip.

(d) In a weapon which has been fired, both the muzzle and breech end of the barrel will be contaminated with GSR. Handling these areas of a fired weapon will deposit GSR particles on the palms of the hands.

(e) Immediately after firing a weapon, the GSR distribution pattern on the hands will be fairly predictable. With time, however, there will be some redistribution of particles over the hands. It is the interpretations of the GSR distribution vs. time patterns which are difficult.

Bearing in mind the above, there are four basic GSR distribution patterns which may be encountered. These are as follows:

1. *GSR particles found only on the taping taken from the back of the right (or left if the person is left-handed) hand.* This is highly indicative of the person having fired a weapon in that hand.

2. *GSR particles found only on the tapings taken from the backs of both hands.* This is highly indicative that the person fired the weapon in one hand whilst supporting the firing hand with the other.

3. *GSR particles found on all four tapings.* This would indicate that the person was standing in front of a weapon when it was fired and was enveloped in the large cloud of gases emanating from the muzzle of the weapon. The person could have been either an innocent bystander or part of the gang carrying out the robbery.

4. *GSR particles only on the tapings taken from the palms of both hands.* This could indicate that the person had merely handled a weapon which had been recently fired.

When considering these interpretations, it must be kept in mind that the longer the elapsed time between the firing incident and the taking of the tapings, the greater the redistribution of particles. As the elapsed time increases, greater emphasis must be placed on the interpretation of indicative GSR particle distribution and the indicative GSR/confirmed GSR particle ratio. This interpretation is purely a matter of experience.

6.9.1   Interpretation of results

Merely looking for particles on hand tapings which match, in elemental composition, those taken from a control cartridge case is simply not enough.

Not all primer residue particles formed during the firing of a weapon will contain all the elements present in the original primer mix. If a standard primer composition of lead styphnate, barium nitrate and antimony sulphide is taken, then only particles which contain lead (Pb), *barium* (Ba) and antimony (Sb) can be positively identified as being GSR particles. There will, however, be a very much larger number of *indicative GSR particles* formed at the same time. These indicative GSR particles can contain PB/Sb, Pb/Ba or Ba/Sb. Other particles of *indeterminate origin* will also be present, which contain only Pb, Ba or Sb.

There will be, depending on the ammunition type and make, a very approximate relationship between the ratios of these confirmed GSR particles and indicative GSR particles. If the bullet is plain lead, there will also be a distinct GSR/Pb ratio from lead volatilized from the base of the bullet.

The ratio of plain lead particles to GSR particles (in ammunition containing a plain lead bullet) will be higher at the muzzle than at the breech end of the barrel. This can be accounted for by (i) the hot gases emerging from the muzzle having had longer to volatilize the lead from the base of the bullet than those emerging from the breech and (ii) the fact that particles of lead are torn off the sides of the bullet as it passes down the rifling.

This can be extremely useful when determining whether particles found on a suspect's hands were from actually firing a weapon or whether they were from merely being in front of the weapon, possibly as an innocent bystander, when it was fired.

As an example, at the breech end of the barrel, Winchester 0.38" Special calibre plain lead ammunition has a ratio of approximately 15 plain lead particles to every confirmed GSR particle, whilst at the muzzle, this will be in excess of 35 plain lead particles to every GSR particle.

These ratios are only very approximate and can only be obtained from controlled test firings. Likewise, they are only of use in ammunition which is plain lead, that is, non-jacketed.

The situation with fully jacketed ammunition is similar, but the Pb/GSR ratio is much lower due to the smaller area of lead which is exposed. Some interpretation of the Pb/GSR ratios at the breech can be made, but it is much more difficult. In this situation, it is probably better to search for Cu/Zn particles which may have been stripped from the bullet jacket by the rifling. These particles should only be present in the residues issuing from the muzzle.

6.9.2   Minimum requirements for a positive result

One major question when interpreting GSR results concerns the minimum number of GSR particles which constitute a positive result.

If the necessity for associated particle identification is taken into consideration, then the answer must be one. However, the fact that the above ratios for confirmed GSR to indicative GSR particles is one based on averages when a number, much larger than one, of confirmed particles are present must not be forgotten. For example, if the ratio were 1 : 5 for breech emitted particles where there are 50 positive GSR particles, then the possibility for there being only one positive GSR particle with no associated particles is high.

Several papers (DeGaetano and Siegel, 1991; ASTM E1588, 1993; Singer *et al.*, 1996) have investigated the common laboratory practice for the threshold limit for a positive finding of GSR on hand tapings. The results are varied with most coming out in the 1–2 region.

In practice, the situation is a little more complex. If, for example, one is in an area where the police force is issued with ammunition containing Pb, Ba, Sb and Al and the criminals are using ammunition containing Hg, Sn, K and Cl, the finding of only one Hg, Sn, K and Cl particle on the hands of a suspect would have far more significance than if both the criminals and the police were using Pb-, Sb-, Ba-, Al-based ammunition.

In the author's laboratory, even though the GSR in ammunition issued to the police and that used by the criminals is radically different, the benchmark of a minimum of two confirmed GSR particles, together with associated particles, is considered the absolute lowest limit for a positive result.

6.10 Identification of Type of Ammunition, Country of Origin from GSR Analysis

Modern centre fire ammunition from Western countries, that is, Europe, America, Sweden, Australia and New Zealand, and so on, all contain a very similar priming composition, the basic elements found being Pb, Ba and Sb with calcium silicide and/or powdered glass giving *silicon* (Si). With so little variation, it is therefore very difficult to make any differentiation between calibres and origin.

Aluminium (Al), or sometimes *magnesium* (Mg), is also often added to increase the temperature and burn time of the flame produced. This is usually found in the higher-pressure cartridges, that is, 9 mm PB, 0.357″ Magnum and +P cartridges. This can sometimes be useful in identifying the type of ammunition fired.

A case illustrating this involved a very large and determined gang of heavily armed robbers who, after robbing a bank of several tens of millions of dollars, became involved in a running shoot-out through the streets. At one point, an innocent bystander turned a corner and was shot in the head by one of the culprits. The bullet was a 0.357″ Magnum, and GSR found on the base of the bullet contained Pb, Ba, Sb, Si and Al. This was the only round of 0.357″ Magnum fired during the chase, the rest being 0.38″ Special, none of which contained Al in the GSR.

Sometime later, a number of string gloves were found on a hillside along with some of the stolen money and guns. It was easy to determine from GSR found in the cloth material of the gloves which was used to fire the 0.357″ Magnum round and it was easy to determine which of the guns had fired the fatal bullet. Luckily, the glove which had the GSR containing the Al on it also had some blood from where the wearer had cut his hand on some glass. Eventually, the suspects were located, and it was just a matter of blood grouping them to determine who had been wearing the glove which was used to fire the fatal shot.

Centre fire ammunition from what was previously called the Warsaw Pact countries, that is, Russia, Poland, Czechoslovakia, Hungary, Romania, as well as China and Korea tend to have a completely different primer composition. Generally speaking, the priming compounds are much more corrosive than those found elsewhere in the world.

The basic elements found in these priming compounds are:

- mercury (Hg);
- tin (Sn);
- antimony (Sb);
- phosphorous (P);
- potassium (K);
- sodium (Na);
- silicon (Si) and
- calcium (Ca).

Other compounds occasionally encountered include:

- lead (Pb);
- barium (Ba);
- silver (Ag);
- zinc (Zn);
- copper (Cu);
- magnesium (Mg);
- aluminium (Al) and
- lanthanum/cerium/iron (basically lighter flint).

It is this great diversity of elements which, in some circumstances, enables the identification of calibre, country of origin and sometimes even a factory code from the GSR composition.

6.11   Environmental Contaminants

When interpreting GSR/Pb ratios, great care should be exercised to correctly identify particles containing lead and *bromine* (Br). These particles are found in the emissions from car exhausts and come from the ethylene dibromide which is used to remove the lead used in the petrol anti-knock compound, lead tetraethyl.

Likewise, barium is also utilized in face powders and a filler in paper. In these situations, it is nearly always associated with sulphur (S) and should be readily identified.

With modern non-corrosive ammunition, it is very rare to find sulphur in a priming compound. In 7.62×25 mm and 7.62×39 mm ammunition, however, barium and sulphur are often found together in the priming compound and confusion can arise.

Lead is alloyed with antimony in battery plates and type metal. It is also alloyed with tin and/or antimony in solder. This is a common contaminant especially with anyone working in the printing or car repair trade.

Antimony is also used as its oxide as a fire retardant in cotton and polyester blend fibres.

Zirconium and titanium (used in lead-free primer compounds) is used as fluoro-complexes in the treatment of wool.

6.12 Sources of Elements Commonly Found in Lead-Based GSRs

6.12.1 Lead alloys (Table 6.1)

Table 6.1 A list of some common lead alloys.

Alloy	Uses
Pb–Sb	Tank linings, coils, pumps, valves, lead lined pipes, car storage batteries, collapsible tubes, bullets, lead shot, insoluble anodes.
Cu–Pb–Sb	Type metals, bearings, special casting alloys
Ca–Pb	Grids of industrial storage batteries, tape to separate double glazing panes
Cu–Pb	Car and aircraft bearings and bushings
Ag–Pb	Solders, insoluble anode in electro winning of Zn, manganese refining
Te–Pb	Pipe and sheet in chemical installations
Sn–Pb	Solders (tin cars, circuit boards), manufacture of car radiators, heat exchangers, car industry (covering welded body sections), corrosive protective coatings on steel and copper, gaskets, metal furniture, gutter piping and fittings, roof flashing, coating on steel and copper electronic components.
Sn–Sb–Pb	Sleeve bearings, casting alloys, slush castings, journal bearings (railway freight cars)
Pb–Sn–Bi–Cd	Sprinkler systems, foundry patterns, moulds, died and punches, chucks, cores, mandrills, low-temperature solders.

6.12.2   Lead compounds (Table 6.2)

Table 6.2 A list of some common compounds containing lead.

Compound	Use
Lead arsenates	Insecticides
Lead azides	Explosives, priming compounds
Lead borate	Glazes, enamels on pottery, porcelain, chinawork, drier in paints
Basic lead carbonates	Exterior paints, ceramic glazes and enamels
Lead chromates	Paint pigments
Lead silichromates	Paint pigments
Lead cyanamide	Anti-rust paints
Lead 2-ethylhexoate	Driers, metallic soap
Lead fluorosilicate	Electrolyte in electrolytic refining of lead
Lead formate	Manufacture of specialized rubber compounds
Tetrabasic lead fumarate	Heat stabilizer for plastisols, records, electric insulation, vulcanization reagent
Lead chloride	Laboratory drying agent
Lead lineolate	Driers, metallic soaps
Lead maleate	Vulcanizing agent for chlorosulphonated polyethylene
Lead molybdate	Anti-corrosive paint pigment
Lead Nitrate	Match industry, pyrotechnics
Lead oleates	Metallic soap
Lead monoxide	Litharge – ceramic industry, manufacture of glasses, glazes, vitreous enamels, oil refining, insecticides
Trilead tetroxide	Storage batteries, paints, ceramic industry, lubricants, petroleum, rubber
Lead dioxide	Manufacture of dyes, chemical, matches, pyrotechnics, rubber substitutes, polysulphide polymers
Lead seleride	In IR detectors
Lead silicates	Glass, ceramics, high temp dry lubricant
Lead stannate	Manufacture of ceramic and electronic bodies
Lead sulphate	Paint pigments, stabilizers for vinyl and other plastics, lead storage battery
Lead sulphide	Semiconductors, photoelectric cells, photosensitive resistor circuits
Lead tellate	Driers, metallic soaps
Lead telluride	Semiconductors, IR detection, heat-sensing instruments
Lead thiocyanate	Matches, explosives, priming compounds
Lead thiosuphfate	Vulcanizing rubber, deposition of lead mirrors
Lead tungstate	Pigment
Lead zirconate	Ferroelectric characteristics, memory devices for computers
Tetraalkyllead	Gasoline industry, organomercury fungicides

IR, infrared.

6.12.3 Antimony (Table 6.3)

Table 6.3 A list of some common compounnds containing atrtinary.

Compound	Use
Pure Sb	Ornamental applications
Sb alloys	Type metal, battery grids, bearing metal, cable covering, sheet and pipe, plumbers solder, pewter, Britannia metal, bullets, shrapnel
Antimony oxide	Flame retardant, glasses, ceramics, vitreous enamels, opacifier
Antimony fluoride	Mordant in dyeing
Antimony chloride	Catalyst and mordant in calico dyeing
Antimony sulphide	Fireworks, matches, priming compounds
Tartar emetic	Medicines, insecticide, mordant in dyeing

6.12.4 Barium (Table 6.4)

Table 6.4 A list of some common compounds containing barium.

Compound	Use
Barium carbonate	Ceramic industry, optical glasses, flux, steel carburizing, paper industry
Barium sulphate	Paper industry
Barium Ferrite	Inexpensive magnetic materials
Barium chloride	Blanc fix for photographic paper, leather and cloth, case hardening, heat treating baths
Barium nitrate	Pyrotechnics, green flares, tracer bullets, primers, detonators
Barium sulphate	Barium meal X-rays, anti-diarrhoeal and demulcent powder, manufacture of linoleum, oilcloth, storage battery, rubber, cosmetics face powder, paint and pigments, oil well treatment, paint filler
Barium titanate	Transducer crystal used in sonar equipment, record pick-up cartridge and other electronic equipment

6.13 Extending the Recovery Period for GSR

GSR particles will, as stated earlier, rapidly be lost from the surface of the hands through everyday activities. Within 3 hours, 4 hours at the absolute most, all GSR particles will have been lost from the hands.

In the search for alternative sampling sites where these particles might be retained for longer periods, the face, hair, cuffs of jackets and the front of any clothing worn have been examined.

Whilst some of these areas showed promise, they all suffered from the same problem, that is, the GSR vented from the breech end of a pistol is of low velocity and as such, particles can only be found on the surfaces immediately surrounding the breech of the weapon, that is, the hands. The likelihood of any GSR particles being found on any of these alternative sites, unless a strong wind is blowing towards the firer, is therefore extremely small.

It has been found (B.J. Heard, unpublished work), however, that on putting the hand into a trouser pocket, GSR particles are transferred from the back of the hand onto the inside surfaces of the pocket. With time, these particles gravitate to the bottom of the pocket and become trapped within the folds of material and general pocket fluff and debris which accumulate in this area. The particles are protected so well by this debris that they are not affected by repeated washing and dry cleaning of the trousers. GSR particles have been recovered up to 16 months after a shooting incident (Figures 6.5–6.7).

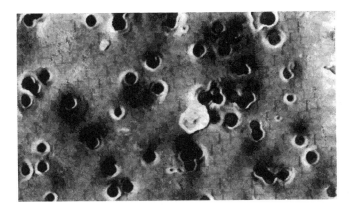

Figure 6.5 Gunshot residue particle on filter membrane.

Figure 6.6 Gunshot residue particle on plasma-ashed taping.

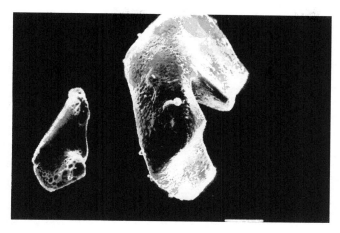

Figure 6.7 Photomicrograph of propellant particle with adhering gunshot residue particle recovered from dent in sign.

Recovery of GSR particles from the inside of a pocket is somewhat problematical as they are associated with large quantities of organic and inorganic material. This debris not only makes efficient recovery difficult, but it also interferes with the SEM examination.

Using a vacuuming system has been suggested, but recovery rates were found, by the author, to be unacceptably low. Picking up the debris with an adhesive (a high-molecular-weight polyisobutylene) covered metal disc, then dissolving the adhesive material from the disc in an organic solvent has been tried with some success. (Wallace, 1984) In this system, the debris-covered adhesive is removed from the disc by dissolving in a suitable solvent. The resulting solution, with suspended debris, is then passed through a two-stage filter system. The first filter, which is generally of about 100μ pore size, is to filter out the general debris. The second, of pore size 0.5 or 1μ and of the nucleopore type, collects any GSR particles which are present. Whilst the vacuum and solvents used tend to result in the GSR particles losing their distinctive morphology, it does leave a fairly clean sample for examination. The potential for GSR loss is, once again, quite high.

A much better recovery rate can be obtained by lifting the debris from the pocket with a 1.5×1.5 cm taping and by removing the excess organic debris by treatment in a low-temperature oxygen plasma asher.

The plasma asher 'burns' off the organic debris by way of a highly reactive form of oxygen at a temperature not much higher than ambient. By careful manipulation of the oxygen plasma, it is possible to remove virtually all of the general organic debris without touching the adhesive material on the strip (Figure 6.6).

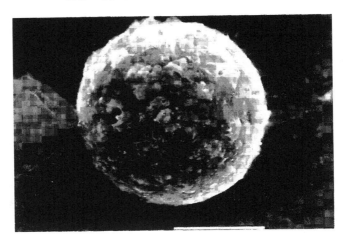

Figure 6.8 Gunshot residue particle on propellant particle recovered from sign.

A case which illustrates the use of GSR in the investigation of crime incidents and the recovery of particles from trouser pockets involved a jewellery shop robbery in the central district of Hong Kong.

During the robbery, an armed robber was posted outside the shop as a lookout. A police constable on patrol duties happened to notice that something was amiss and started to run towards the scene of the incident. At this stage, the lookout fired a shot at the officer which luckily missed. Whilst the officer dived for cover, the robbers threw a hand grenade into the street to deter any would-be followers and then made good their escape in a waiting car.

An examination of the scene did not reveal the presence of any fired bullets, cartridge cases or identifiable bullet damage to the area. As a result, there was some doubt as to whether a shot was fired at the constable. An examination of the road traffic sign under which the officer was standing when the alleged shot was fired did reveal an unidentifiable dent. Much to the consternation of the transport department, the portion of the sign containing the dent was cut out for further examination.

A microscopic examination of the damage showed that it was not typical of a normal bullet strike mark. A taping was, however, taken from the dented area and examined under the SEM.

This examination revealed the presence of microscopic fragments of steel with a thin copper coating along with some smears of lead. Also on the taping was found a microscopic fragment of partially burnt propellant with a perfect sphere of GSR attached.

An EDX analysis of the sphere showed it to contain mercury, tin, antimony, potassium, chlorine and phosphorous: a GSR composition of the type associated with 7.62×25 mm ammunition but unlike anything in the GSR database.

The presence of steel with a coating in copper would suggest a $7.62 \times 25\,mm$ bullet, probably of Chinese origin. The presence of lead together with the partially burnt propellant particle indicated that the bullet had been travelling backwards at the time it hit the sign. This could have been caused by the bullet having been fired through an unrifled barrel, indicating a home-made weapon.

Some 8 months later, a suspect was arrested and in his flat was found a home-made $7.62 \times 25\,mm$ calibre weapon. Tapings taken from the barrel showed the last round to have been fired contained exactly the same GSR composition as that found on the sign. This taping also showed that the last bullet fired had a copper-coated steel jacket.

A search through the suspect's clothes revealed a pair of trousers fitting the description of those worn by the lookout at the robbery. Tapings taken from inside the pockets of these trousers revealed the presence of three particles of GSR which also possessed exactly the same composition as those on the sign and inside the barrel of the home-made weapon.

Whilst the GSR results were insufficient to convict on their own, they did form very strong supportive evidence.

6.13.1   Case example: the Jill Dando murder

In April 1999, Jill Dando, a highly respected TV news reader, was found dead outside her home. Death was caused by a single contact shot to the head from a 9 mm PB pistol. Almost a year later, a suspect, Barry George, was arrested and charged with her murder.

The evidence against Barry George was almost entirely circumstantial and based around his interest in toy replica firearms, a history of stalking and the fact that he was seen in the vicinity on the day of the shooting. This last piece of circumstantial evidence was, however, largely discounted as he lived in a street quite close to where the victim lived.

The only forensic evidence was a single spherical particle of GSR in the pocket of one of his coats (Figure 6.9).

The found the particle contained lead, barium, antimony and aluminium, the same as that found around the fatal wound. There has never been mention of any associated/indicative particles being found.

During the trial, the prosecution said that the spherical particle found in Barry George's coat pocket provided 'compelling' evidence of guilt.

In July 2001, Barry George was found guilty by a 10–1 majority and was sentenced to life imprisonment.

In July 2002, George lost an appeal against an unsafe conviction and in December 2002, the Final Court of Appeal once again refused an application for appeal.

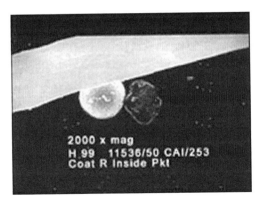

Figure 6.9 GSR particle from the evidence against Barry George in the Jill Dando case.

In June 2007, the Criminal Cases Review Board granted George the right to appeal on the grounds that conviction on little more than a single particle was unsafe.

It transpired that the coat on which the particle had been recovered had been placed on a dummy at the police photographic section. It was accepted by the photographic section that this dummy could well have been contaminated with GSR from other exhibits.

It was also noted that at the time of the murder, the police were also using ammunition which contained lead, barium, antimony and aluminium in the primer.

Three appeal judges decided his murder conviction at the Old Bailey in July 2001 was unsafe as the jury had been misled about the significance of a single microscopic speck of GSR found on the lining of an inside pocket of his overcoat.

Lawyers for George argued in the appeal hearing that the Crown had advanced the speck as significant evidence of his guilt, but now scientists, including the principal forensic witness for the prosecution, accepted its evidential value was 'neutral.'

In essence, the experts now agreed the single speck was 'no more likely to have come from a gun fired by George than from any other, non-incriminating source', and in August 2008, the conviction was overturned on appeal.

How many particles the Metropolitan Police Forensic Science Services Laboratory now consider relevant and whether they require the indicative/associated ratios to be correct before a positive result is reported is unclear.

This case does, however, illustrate the importance of a requirement for a number of GSR particles greater than one to be necessary and for the indicative/associated particle ratio to be taken into consideration.

In all cases examined by the author (B.J. Heard, unpublished paper) involving the transfer of GSR from the hands or from the discharge of a weapon to the clothes, there has always been associated/indicative particles present in approximately the correct ratio.

6.13.2 Search parameters for GSR particles

Manual searching for GSR particles is an extremely manpower intensive undertaking to say nothing of it being exceedingly tedious. Even under the best of circumstances, the search of a 1.0 cm diameter GSR sample stub for 0.5 μ particles of GSR can take six or more hours.

Most SEM systems now have fast, fully automated, search routines, but even these can still take three or more hours per sample. Considering that two samples must be taken from each hand and one blank control for each suspect, the time involved to process each case can be prohibitive. However, by using some simple statistical data and the elimination of certain types of particle, the search can, even with a fast automated scanning routine, be reduced dramatically with even 30 min or less being possible.

All automated systems now come with a particle recognition system where the elemental composition of expected particles is logged into a database. Once a particle is identified as having a significantly strong backscattered electron image to warrant further investigation, it is very briefly scanned and its composition is compared with the database. If the particle's composition matches one in the database, it is then subjected to a much longer scan and the result logged in for future reference. This, however, all takes time, and many particles of no significance are scanned and recorded to no end whatsoever. By eliminating the full scan of those particles of no relevance, significant savings in SEM run-time can be achieved.

To this end, most automated search routines can easily be set up to eliminate the long scan of non-relevant particles or to 'flag up' certain other particles which require further investigation.

A list of generally accepted particle classifications would include:

SnSbBaPb	positive GSR
SbBaPb	positive GSR
SbSnPb	positive GSR
SbSnBa	positive GSR
SnBaPb	positive GSR
SbBa	indicative
SbPb	indicative
BaPb	indicative
SbSn	indicative
Sr	indicative
Pb	indicative

Sb	environmental
CuZn	environmental/bullet jacket material
Ni	environmental
Sn	environmental
Au	environmental
Lighter flint	environmental
Fe	environmental
Cu	environmental

6.13.3   Particles to be flagged for further investigation

The first to be flagged up relates to **particle size.** No GSR particle above 20 μm should ever be present on the hands. Any particle of a size greater than this will fall off almost immediately. In over 4000 examined hand lifts, no particle of this size has ever been detected. If a particle of this size is encountered, it should be viewed with great suspicion.

Perfectly spherical particles of GSR should also be viewed with suspicion and appropriately 'flagged'. GSR particles are invariably spheroidal, but rarely spherical. Cases have been examined where a fired cartridge case has been held over a stub and shaken to produce a positive result. These fortunately very rare instances are easily identified by the number of spherical particles associated with very large, amorphous, partially burnt propellant particles coated with spherical GSR particles. In one published paper, the imprint of a cartridge case mouth could clearly been seen on the stub of a sample allegedly taken from a suspect. Large numbers of perfectly spherical and amorphous GSR particles were, not unsurprisingly, located on the stub!

6.13.4   Particles to be eliminated from further investigation

Particles containing only barium can be ignored. Whilst there is some possibility of barium from a standard Pb, Ba, Sb, primer being present alone, it is far more probable that it will be a contaminant $BaSO_4$ particle from paper or even ladies' make-up.

Large, absolutely spherical particles in the region of 5 μm or more containing cerium, lanthanum, iron and aluminium can be ignored as these are invariably **mischmetal** from cigarette lighter flints. Mischmetal is an alloy of rare earth metals containing approximately 50% cerium and 45% lanthanum, with small amounts of neodymium, praseodymium, iron and aluminium. Mischmetal gives an extremely strong backscattered electron detector signal and should not be confused with that from a GSR particle.

Spherical particles containing iron, aluminium and silicon ranging in size from 0.5 to 100 μm can be ignored. These particles are **boiler fly ash** and contain silicon (SiO_2), aluminium (Al_2O_3) and iron (Fe_2O_3) and, like mischmetal, give a strong backscattered electron detector signal.

Antimony is, for some unknown reason, very rarely encountered alone as a GSR indicative particle. Once again, if a pure antimony particle is located, it is most probably a contaminant.

Particles containing Pb and Sn. These are invariably from type metal or plumber's solder. Plumbing solder is another material that is also available in non-toxic form and nowadays contains tin, copper, silver and sometimes bismuth, indium, zinc, antimony and other metals in varying amounts.

In some areas where camping is a popular pastime, spherical particles of **thorium** are sometimes located on the hands. These are from the mantles used in gas or paraffin-powered light sources. Being spherical and of a high atomic number, they give a very strong backscattered electron signal. Any particle containing thorium should be ignored.

6.13.5 Statistical elimination of potentially negative samples

The small number of GSR particles present on most samples would, by itself, rule out any search routines based on the probability of the presence of a positive particle. However, if indicative GSR particles (also called associated GSR particles) are taken into account, such an elimination process becomes a distinct possibility.

Indicative particles in a standard Pb-, Ba-, Sb-type primer would include Pb, Pb/Sb, Pb/Ba and Ba/Sb particles; plain Ba and Sb particles can be ignored as previously explained. If Al, Mg, Ca and/or Si are added into the equation, the number of possible indicative particle types becomes far greater.

For non-toxic, or the decidedly toxic $7.62 \times 17\,mm$, $7.62 \times 25\,mm$, $7.62 \times 39\,mm$ and 9 mm MAK, priming compositions, the potential variation in metallic elements can be huge. When dealing with these types of priming composition, the search and exclusion routines will have to be set up for each ammunition type.

The $7.62 \times 17\,mm$, $7.62 \times 25\,mm$, $7.62 \times 39\,mm$ and 9 mm MAK ammunition has been described as 'decidedly toxic' due to the general use of Mercury (Hg), normally as the fulminate, in its composition.

When dealing with GSR from this ammunition, the volatility of mercury should be kept in mind. Over time, the mercury evaporates from the GSR particles, eventually disappearing altogether. This is very dependent on ambient conditions and can be as little as a few months to several years.

If a GSR Outstanding Crime Index is maintained, something which is entirely possible when dealing with Eastern European, Russian and Chinese ammunition, stored case GSR samples cannot be relied upon to have the same elemental composition as when first examined due to this problem with mercury.

However, if the standard Pb, Ba, Sb primer composition is taken as an example to classify a particle as being positive GSR, it would have to contain all three elements, that is, Pb, Ba and Sb in one particle.

As previously explained, indicative particles in a standard Pb-, Ba-, Sb-type primer would include Pb, Pb/Sb, Pb/Ba and Ba/Sb particles.

The ratio of positive to indicative particles can vary widely between different makes and, particularly, type of ammunition. With a plain lead bullet and a Pb, Sb, Ba primer, the positive/indicative ratio would be in the region of 1 : 40 or even more. For this example, however, a jacketed hollow-point bullet with a positive to indicative particle ratio of 1 : 10 will be used.

For this example, it can be assumed that there are 200 fields to be examined on the sample stub.

If the baseline for a positive GSR result is taken as being two positive particles, then there should be at least 20 indicative particles present on the stub. Hence, one in every 10 fields should contain an indicative particle. If no indicative particles are located in the first 10 fields examined, then potentially, there are no positive particles on the sample stub.

Statistically, however, this is a very small number to base any predictive finding of a positive GSR particle. The number of fields examined before a sample stub can be eliminated can, therefore, be doubled, or even trebled. Even by trebling the number of fields examined, the sample search time will still be significantly reduced when compared to the time taken to search the whole of the stub.

If after searching half of the stub, no positive particles and less than 10 indicative particles have been located. Statistically, there is little likelihood of finding a sufficient additional number of indicative and positive particles in the second half to satisfy the 1 : 10 positive/indicative GSR particle ratio as well as the threshold two positive GSR particles for a positive result.

If 10 or more indicative particles are located in the first half of the stub, the whole stub must be searched as there is still a statistically significant chance of satisfying the requirement for a positive result.

The foregoing is, however, only a guide, and each laboratory must decide on its own criteria for continuing or abandoning the search of a stub.

References

Andrasko, J. (1992) Characterisation of smokeless powder flakes from fired cartridge cases and from discharge patterns on clothing. *Journal of Forensic Sciences*, 37, 1030.

ASTM E1588 (1993) *Standard Guide for the Analysis of GSR by SEM/EDX*, American National Standards Institute, Philadelphia, PA, USA.

Brihaye, C., Machiroux, R. and Gillain, G. (1982) GSR detection by anodic stripping voltammetry. *Forensic Science International*, **20**.

DeGaetano, D. (1992) A comparison of three techniques developed for the sampling and analysis of GSR by SEM/EDX. *Journal of Forensic Sciences*, **37**, 281.

DeGaetano, D. and Siegel, J.A. (1990) Survey of GSR analysis in forensic science laboratories. *Journal of Forensic Sciences*, **35**, 1087–1095.

Federal Bureau of Investigation (1935) *FBI Law Enforcement Bulletin*, **4** (10).

Federal Bureau of Investigation (1940) *FBI Law Enforcement Bulletin*, **9**.

Green, A.L. and Sauve, J.P. (1973) *The Analysis of GSR by Atomic Absorbtion Spectrometry*.

Gunaratnam, L. and Himber, K. (1994) The identification of GSR from lead-free sintox ammunition. *Journal of Forensic Sciences*, **39**, 532–536.

Harrison, H.C. and Gillroy, R. (1959) Firearms discharge residues. *Journal of Forensic Sciences*, **4**, 184–199.

Hellmiss, G. (1987) Investigation of GSR by Auger electron microscopy. *Journal of Forensic Sciences*, **32**, 747–760.

Matricardi, V.R. and Kilty, W. (1977) Detection of GSR particles on the hands of the firer. *Journal of Forensic Sciences*, **22**, 725–728.

Panigrahi, P.K., Varier, K.M., Sen, P. and Mehta, D. (1982) Application of PIXE for GSR analysis. *Journal of Forensic Sciences*, **27**, 330.

Ruch, R.R., Buchanan, J.D., Guinn, V.P., Bellanca, S.C. and Pinker, R.H. (1964) Neutron activation analysis in scientific crime detection. *Journal of Forensic Science*, **9** (1), 119–133.

Singer, R.L., Davis, D. and Houck, M.M. (1996) A survey of GSR analysis methods. *Journal of Forensic Sciences*, **41** (2), 195–198.

Walker, J.T. (1940) Bullet holes and chermical residues in shooting cases. *Journal of Crime Law and Criminology*, **31**, 497–452.

Wallace, J. (1981) Northern Ireland Forensic Science Laboratory Methods Manual.

Wallace, J.S. and Quinlan, S. (1984) Discharge residues from cartridge operated fixing tools. *Journal of Forensic Sciences*, **24** (5), 495–508.

Wolten, G.M., Nesbitt, R.S., Calloway, A.R., Loper, G.L. and Jones, P.F. (1978) *Final report on particle analysis for GSR Detection*. ATR-77 (7915)-3, Aerospace Corp., El Segundo, CA, USA.

Zeichner, A., Foner, H.A., Dvorachek, M., Bergman, P. and Levin, N. (1989) Concentration techniques for the detection of GSR by **SEM/EDX**. *Journal of Forensic Sciences*, **34** (2), 312–320.

Zeichner, A., Levin, N. and Dvorachek, M. (1992) GSR particles formed by using ammunition that have mercury fulminate based primers. *Journal of Forensic Sciences*, **37**, 1567.

7

Gun-Handling Tests

7.1 Introduction

In armed robbery incidents where no shot has been fired, it is often necessary to demonstrate a link between the suspect and a recovered weapon. As GSR particles will not be present on the hands, the only way this can be effected is through the detection of any metal traces which may have been transferred from the weapon to the hands.

The quantity of metal traces transferred from the weapon to the hand is extremely small and probably below the threshold for analytical detection by conventional instrumental methods. Even if the quantity of metal were sufficient to perform an analysis, the only information available would be that there were traces of iron (or aluminium, if it were an aluminium-framed weapon) on the palm of the hands. This would be of little or no evidential value whatsoever.

Due to the very characteristic shape of a weapon, the way it is held in the hand and the fact that large portions of it are covered by non-metallic materials in the form of the grip plates, the signature from the metal traces left on the hands should be readily identifiable as that of a firearm.

Visualization of the metallic traces left on the hands using trace metal detection (TMD) sprays is a very easy technique and one that can return dramatic results.

Probably the first recorded instance of the use of TMD sprays was during the Vietnam War. During this action, it was often necessary to differentiate between innocent farmers going to work in the morning and V-C guerillas who had been

Handbook of Firearms and Ballistics: Second Edition   Brian J. Heard
© 2008 John Wiley & Sons, Ltd.

out at night with their AK47 assault rifles. A simple spray test (US Govt Printing Office, 1972; Stevens and Messler, 1974) was developed which would visualize, under ultraviolet (UV) light, a number of different metals. The reagent used in this spray was a 0.2% solution of 8-hydroxyquinoline in isopropyl alcohol. This reagent reacts with iron to give a bright blue fluorescence under UV light. Many other metals also react with this reagent including aluminium, lead, zinc and copper, some of which fluoresce and some of which adsorb the UV light.

Whilst this test is very sensitive and it is quite easy to distinguish between various metals, the results can be very confusing. The outline of a weapon might be overlaid with that from an aluminium door handle, and the nickel and copper from handling small change. There is also the problem of carrying round a large UV light cabinet to enable the result to be seen and special photographic equipment to record it.

Another reagent, ferrozine or 3-(2-pyridyl)-5,6-diphenyl-1,2,4-triazine-p,p′-disulphonic acid, disodium salt trihydrate (also known as PDT) (Goldman and Thornton, 1976), was found to be far superior to the 8-hydroxyquinoline and not to require a UV light box for visualization.

In this test, the reagent was made up as a saturated (0.2%) solution in methanol which was simply sprayed onto the hands, a positive reaction to iron being visualized as a deep magenta colour. This colour results from the formation of a bidentate ligand with any ferrous Fe(II) traces which may be present.

The iron which is transferred from a weapon to the hands is, however, predominately in the ferric, Fe(III), form, which does not give a reaction with ferrozine. It has been found (Lee, 1986) that by adding 1% ascorbic acid to the ferrozine solution, the Fe(III) is effectively reduced to the Fe(II) state, thus increasing the sensitivity by six- or sevenfold.

It has been suggested that a buffer be used in addition to the ascorbic acid. Whilst the buffer can help in the elimination of interfering metal traces, the extra spray has been found to dilute the results rather than to enhance them.

Figure 7.1 Grooved trigger of 1911A1 Colt 0.45″ ACP pistol.

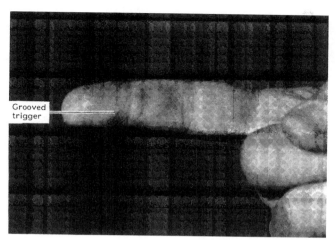

Figure 7.2 Trigger finger after spraying with ferrozine.

Figure 7.3 Back strap of 1911A1 Colt 0.45″ ACP pistol.

Of the other metallic elements which give a colour reaction with ferrozine, only Cu(II) and Al(III) are of note. They are, however, of little significance as Cu(II) gives only a weak golden brown colouration and Al(III), which does give a similar colour to Fe(II), is so insensitive that a positive reaction can only be obtained in a test tube at untypically high concentrations.

Recent advances (B.J. Heard and Dr C.M. Lau,[1] unpublished paper) in the use of ferrozine spray include the use of the base chemical rather than the sodium salt. The advantages of this over the sodium salt include a much greater

[1] HK Government Laboratory.

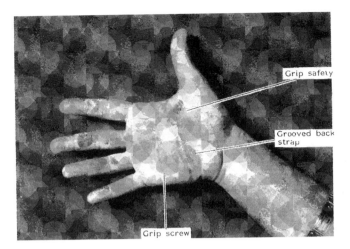

Figure 7.4 Palm of hand after spraying with ferrozine.

sensitivity and the ability to make solutions in excess of 0.2% strength. The higher-strength solutions mean that less of the spray has to be applied, thus reducing the tendency for the result to diffuse by running over the hand. The solution is also made up in ethanol rather than methanol, which is quite poisonous.

The use of 2-nitroso-1-naphthol (Kokocinski, Brundage and Nicol, 1980) has been suggested as an alternative to ferrozine, but this gives coloured complexes with iron, copper, zinc and silver. As a result, it has gained little support.

7.2   Methodology for Ferrozine Use

Unlike GSR particles, which are merely lying on the surface of the skin, Fe(II) traces transferred to the hands through holding an iron object appear to be absorbed into the skin. As such, they are not easily removed and are often detectable with the ferrozine spray 8 hours or more after an incident.

This is a fairly simple test to apply, but a background knowledge of the influencing factors will assist in obtaining the best from it. Following are a few considerations one should bear in mind.

As the coloured complex formed is soluble in the ethanol used to make up the reagent, the results will run if too much reagent is applied at one time. Far better results will be obtained with several light applications of the spray, allowing each to dry before applying the next.

The reaction between Fe(II) and ferrozine is catalyzed by short-wave UV light. In a dark office at night with only strip lighting or with very weak transfers, the result can take an hour or more to develop. A simple hand-held UV source will be sufficient to speed up and enhance the development of the reaction.

Weak reactions, even when using the UV light source as a catalyst, can take anything up to an hour to develop. Additional light sprays of the reagent, exposure to UV light and some patience will be required for light transfers or when the elapsed time approaches 8 hours.

This test is mutually compatible with the taping of hands for GSR. The taping must be completed before the ferrozine spray is started. If the weapon has a slightly rusty surface, it is possible to obtain a positive reaction from cotton gloves. Painted or plated weapons will not give a positive reaction to the test. Neither will aluminium-framed weapons or stainless steel weapons. A conventional blue or 'Parkerized' (phosphated) finish to the weapon will not affect the test.

Black and white film does not appear to be very sensitive to the magenta part of the spectrum. Photography of the results should be carried out with colour film, preferably with a green background for added contrast.

If it was raining during the holding of the weapon, the test will always return a negative result. The reason for this is unknown.

If the hands are damp due to nervous sweat, a light application of a hot air blower will assist. The hot air blower should also be applied between applications of the spray. This will not only speed up the reaction, but it will also stop the reagent from running over the hand and spoiling the result.

Washing the hands with soap and water will only remove about 50% of the transfer. It appears that once the transfer has been made, the skin has a greater affinity for the metal traces than water.

The hands must never be placed in plastic bags to conserve any transfer. As soon as the hands start to sweat, the results spread over the entire hand and the result will be meaningless.

Protect the hands with paper bags and do not restrain the hands with steel handcuffs. Likewise, do not place the suspect in a cell with steel bars. Neither should the suspect be allowed to urinate on his hands. Whilst this does not remove all of the Fe(III) traces from the hands, it does place the hand in an acidic state which interferes with the bidentate ligand formation.

If the hands of a deceased have to be tested, never allow the body to be placed in the refrigerator before carrying out the test. Once the body has cooled down below ambient temperature, it is impossible to obtain a positive result even if the hands are reheated. The reason for this is unknown.

7.3 Case Notes

It is interesting to note that in all cases of suicide with a revolver which have been examined by the author, there has been a very distinctive positive reaction on the pad of the right thumb. It is assumed that there is some trepidation over committing the act and that the hammer has been cocked and uncocked several times (Figure 7.5).

This test is not exclusive to firearms and will give a positive with any iron object. Spanners, car jacks, crowbars, and so on can all give a positive reaction. A case example of how useful this can be involved a breaking and entering case where a row of shops had the front door locks drilled out. A suspect was spotted

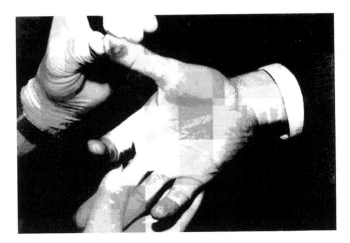

Figure 7.5 Positive ferrozine reaction on pad of thumb in suicide case.

in the act of drilling a door lock and when approached, he fled, leaving his equipment behind. This equipment consisted of a motorcycle starter motor with a drill chuck attached to the spindle. This was driven by a battery held in a shoulder bag. A suspect was eventually located some 4 hours later, and when his hands were sprayed with the ferrozine reagent, a perfect imprint of the castellated chuck was observed. He denied all knowledge of the burglary incidents, passing the chuck mark off as from a drill at his home. Fortunately, the chuck on the starter motor had half of one of the castellations missing, which matched perfectly with that on his hand.

Another very positive case concerned the use of a stolen police weapon in a shooting incident. The suspect denied all knowledge until a ferrozine test revealed traces of the serial number of the weapon, which had been stamped on the back strap of the gun, on the palm of his hand.

References

Goldman, G.L. and Thornton, J.I. (1976) A new Trace Ferrous Metal Detection Reagent. *Journal of Forensic Science*, **21** (3), 625–628.

Kokocinski, C.W., Brundage, D.J. and Nicol, J.D. (1980) A Study of the Use of 2-Nitroso-1-Naphthol as a Trace Metal Detection Reagent. *Journal of Forensic Sciences*, **25** (4).

Lee, G.-W. (1986) The Detection of Iron Traces on Hands by Ferrozine Sprays: A Report on the Sensitivity and Interference of the Method and Recommended Procedure in Forensic Science Investigation. *Journal of Forensic Sciences*, **31** (3).

Stevens, J.M. and Messler, H. (1974) The Trace Metal Detection Technique (TMDT): A Report Outlining a Procedure for Photographing Results in Color, and Some Factors Influencing the Results in Controlled Laboratory Tests. *Journal of Forensic Sciences*, **19** (3), 496–503.

US Govt Printing Office (1972) *US Government Printing Office Publication*.

8

Restoration of Erased Numbers

8.1   Introduction

When a weapon is located, either as part of a crime or merely as a recovered item, it is often advantageous to determine the origin of the weapon.

The make and model can normally be determined from the weapon's physical characteristics. Its history, that is, when and to whom the factory originally shipped the weapon and the chain of ownership, can only be obtained from the serial number.

8.2   Methods Used for Removal of Serial Numbers

It is often the case that stolen weapons will have the serial number obliterated in an attempt to hide the weapon's origin. Methods of obliteration generally fall into the following categories:

8.2.1   Filing or grinding

This is simply removing the number by hand filing or grinding with a high-speed carborundum grinding wheel. This is often followed by polishing and then over-stamping with a new number.

Handbook of Firearms and Ballistics: Second Edition   Brian J. Heard
© 2008 John Wiley & Sons, Ltd.

8.2.2   Peening

This merely involves the hammering of the surface with a round punch to completely hide the number.

8.2.3   Over-stamping

Over-stamping is simply stamping a new number over the old. For numbers with curved surfaces, that is, 2, 3, 5, 6, 9 and 0, the 8 stamp is the one most often chosen. For numbers with straight surfaces, that is, 1 and 7, the 4 stamp is the obvious choice. Serial numbers with a preponderance of '8' or '4' numbers should be treated with suspicion.

8.2.4   Centre punching

Centre punching is obliterating the whole numbered surface with a pointed punch.

8.2.5   Drilling

Drilling is completely removing the number and the surrounding metal with a drill. The hole left is usually filled up with either lead solder or weld material.

8.2.6   Welding

Welding is heating the surface until the metal flows with either an oxy-acetylene welder or an arc welder.

8.3   Theory behind Number Restoration

All metals are polycrystalline in structure, that is, they are composed of irregularly shaped crystals or grains. These form when the molten metal cools to the point of solidification. By regulating the cooling of the metal during manufacture, the size of the grains or crystals are controlled, thus affecting the mechanical properties of the metal.

When a number is stamped into metal, the crystalline structure surrounding the stamped number is distorted and the grain structure is compressed. This effectively reduces the size of the grain or crystal size of the metal altering its physical and mechanical characteristics.

As a result of this altered crystalline structure, the metal will, in the immediate area surrounding the stamped number, exhibit altered hardness, strength, magnetic, electrical and chemical properties. Beyond the immediate area surrounding the stamped number, this effect becomes too dissipated to have any effect.

The depth of metal affected by the compressed crystalline structure will be dependent upon the metal and the force applied to the punch.

It is by these means that the original serial number may be redeveloped and made visible (Figure 8.1).

If the surface is filed or ground down until the number has just been removed, the new surface will still contain an area of altered crystalline structure that, if correctly treated, can be revealed. This area of altered crystalline structure will conform to the outline of the obliterated number.

This altered area of crystalline structure can be revealed by the action of a suitable etching reagent which will show the change in crystalline structure from a compressed to a non-compressed area.

Likewise, if a magnetic field is applied to the metal, the compressed crystalline structure will behave in a slightly different way from the uncompressed area. This difference can be visualized by the use of finely divided iron dust.

8.4 Non-recoverable Methods of Number Removal

Of the methods used to remove the punched serial number, only drilling and welding will permanently remove all recoverable traces of the original number.

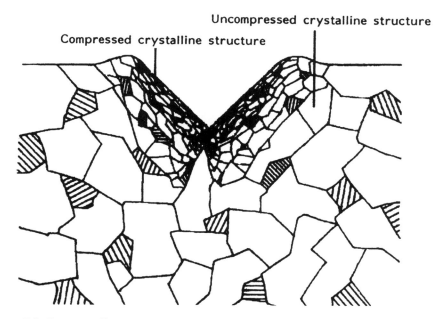

Figure 8.1 Cross-sectional view of deformation of crystalline structure of metal by stamping.

With drilling, unless it is very superficial, the altered crystalline structure will be removed and so will any recoverable traces of the number.

Centre punching can, depending upon the area of the serial number covered and the force applied to the punch, make it extremely difficult to interpret any restored number. The problem here is that the centre punching will alter the crystalline structure itself. Any restoration performed will restore the centre punching marks as well as the serial number. One overlaid upon the other results in an extremely confusing pattern of marks to decipher.

Applying an oxy-acetylene torch or arc welder until the metal flows will also permanently remove all traces of the crystalline structure. In this case, the metal is being re-melted and the crystalline structure allowed to reform into a completely new and uniform pattern on cooling. Thus, the original crystalline structure together with the altered crystalline pattern formed by punching will have been completely lost.

8.5   Practice of Number Restoration

8.5.1   Surface preparation

As the surface must be treated to reveal the crystalline structure of the metal, it is necessary to polish the surface as a preliminary step to the recovery process. This is best accomplished by first removing all scratches and other gross marks with fine emery paper. This is followed by a final polishing to a mirror-like finish with jeweller's rouge or 'flour paper'.

After polishing, the surface must be degreased and cleaned with chloroform or acetone.

8.6   Chemical Methods of Restoration

The general technique of chemical etching is essentially the same for all metals, although different chemical formulae will have to be used for each.

Basically, the reagent is applied to the polished area with a cotton wool swab, with a rubbing action. After approximately 1 min, the reagent is rinsed off with acetone and viewed.

The number should begin to appear as a shadow which is often best viewed with oblique lighting. If nothing appears after 1 min, the process is repeated for consecutive intervals of 2, 5 then 10 min for a total of 2 hours.

The application of sufficient heat to make the surface hot enough to just be able to touch not only speeds up the development, but also appears to enhance the result.

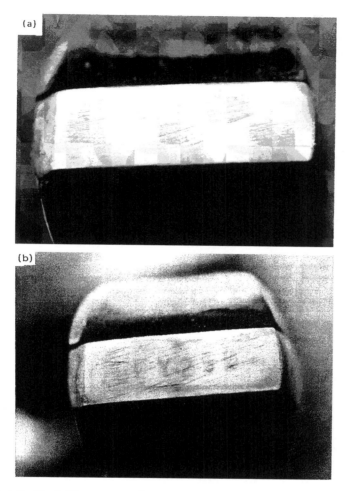

Figure 8.2 (a) Smith & Wesson revolver showing surface where serial number has been erased; (b) Smith & Wesson revolver showing restored number by chemical etching.

8.7   Reagents Used for Various Metals

The list of etching agents for various metals is endless. Nickoll's book on forensic science (Nickolls, 1956) lists a number; Hatcher, Jury and Weller (1957) recommend Fry's reagent as does Mathews (1962); and a number of very useful reagents are listed in the *Journal of the Institute of Metals*, No. 1915, Vol. XIII.

Probably the most authoritative work on the subject was carried out under a NASA contract (NASA Lewis Research Center, 1978). This work lists a very large number of reagents and covers all aspects of number restoration.

Some of the more popular reagents follow:

8.7.1   Iron and steel

1. Fry's reagent:

   90 g cupric chloride

   120 ml hydrochloric acid

   100 ml water

   After applying the solution as described above, the area is washed with acetone and then treated with a 15% solution of nitric acid. The process is repeated until a number develops.

2. 5 g cupric chloride

   40 ml hydrochloric acid

   25 ml ethyl alcohol

   30 ml water

3. 5 g ferric chloride

   50 ml hydrochloric acid

   100 ml water

4. saturated solution of picric acid in ethyl alcohol

5. 40 g chromic acid

   50 ml water

6. 1% nitric acid in water

Of these, probably the most widely used and successful is Fry's reagent.

8.7.2   Aluminium and aluminium alloys

1. Villela's reagent is probably the best reagent, but it is extremely dangerous.

   – 30 ml glycerine

   – 20 ml hydrofluoric acid

   – ml nitric acid

2. The Hume–Rothery reagent is not quite as efficient as Villela's reagent, but it is much safer.

   – 200 g cupric chloride

   – 5 ml hydrochloric acid

   – 1000 ml water

Fry's reagent can also be used on aluminium and its alloys, but care has to be taken as the reaction is a little rapid.

8.7.3 Zinc and zinc/aluminium alloys

Fifty percent hydrochloric acid followed by 50% nitric acid

8.7.4 Brass

1. 40 g cupric chloride
   150 ml hydrochloric acid
   50 ml water
2. 19 g ferric chloride
   6 ml hydrochloric acid
   100 ml water

8.8 Electrolytic Methods of Restoration

Electropolishing is a process where the specimen is made the anode in an electrochemical cell. When a current is applied, minute irregularities in the surface are dissolved, leaving a highly polished surface.

As the electrical properties of the stamped area are minutely altered due to the compressed crystalline structure, the dissolution of the compressed area will be different from that in the non-compressed area. This was first developed about 25 years ago (Arai and Shegio, 1953) and has proved to be a successful method for serial number restoration.

In this method, the specimen is made the anode, and a cotton swab containing the electrolytic solution becomes the cathode. An external variable DC voltage is applied and adjusted to be just greater than the minimum voltage necessary for the current to flow. This is called the *critical voltage*. For steel, the critical voltage is approximately 6 V, for brass 7 V and aluminium 7.5 V.

8.9 Reagents Used

8.9.1 Steel

1. 1 g cupric sulphate
   15 ml sulphuric acid
   1 g gelatin
   500 ml water
2. 5 g cupric ammonium chloride
   50 ml hydrochloric acid
   50 ml water

8.9.2 Aluminium

1. 17% sulphuric acid;
2. 2% fluoroboric acid.

8.10 Ultrasonic Cavitation for Restoration

Cavitation is the formation of vapour bubbles in a liquid due to a very localized reduction in pressure. This can be observed in high-speed motor boat propellers where a stream of bubbles is created. The phenomenon is very similar to boiling where bubbles of vapour are formed due to a localized increase in temperature.

Any metal object which is subjected to this cavitational effect will be surface etched. In pumps, high-speed propellers and pipes carrying high-velocity liquids, this can be extremely troublesome. Under controlled conditions, this surface etching can, however, be used for the restoration of erased serial numbers (Young, 1974).

8.10.1 Method

If a high frequency electrical current (commonly 20 kHz) is delivered via a piezoelectric transducer, the electrical current will be transformed into mechanical vibrations of the same frequency. If these mechanical vibrations are introduced into water, either directly via a probe or through some secondary method, then vibrational cavitation, called *ultrasonic cavitation,* of the water will occur.

The specimen is simply placed in the stream of cavitation bubbles. Visualization of the erased number occurs as a result of the cavitation, removing less metal from the stamped area than the non-stamped area. This is probably due to the stamped area becoming 'work-hardened' due to compression of the crystalline structure. This 'work-hardened' area, being more resilient than the surrounding area, is more resistant to cavitation.

The method has the advantages of being applicable to all metals and not to require the treatment with any chemical reagents.

8.11 Magnetic Particle Method for Restoration

A standard method for the visualization of minute flaws or cracks in ferro-metallic objects (Betz, 1967) is to magnetize the object then to spray it with magnetic particle dust. Any flaws or cracks in the metal are indicated by an accumulation of the magnetic particles. Once again, this is due to a change in the crystalline structure of the metal around the crack or flaw, giving rise to an altered magnetic property.

The magnetic particle dust is available commercially either as a suspension in oil or water, or as a dry powder.

Application of this process for the restoration of erased numbers is a standard method and has been the subject of a number of papers(FBI Law Enforcement Bulletin, 1950; Wolfer and Lee, 1960).

The great advantage of this method is that it is non-destructive. It may, therefore, be tried before attempting other more damaging techniques of restoration.

8.11.1   Method

The easiest way of applying this technique is to attach a large horseshoe magnet to the object, with the erased area between the poles. The area is then sprayed with the magnetic dust and any excess gently blown off.

Experience has shown that the most efficient method of applying the magnet dust is with a spray can, with the dust suspended in an oil suspension. These oil-based suspensions are available either coloured or with a fluorescent marker, both of which are very efficient.

The method will only work with ferro-magnetic metals as the material must become temporarily magnetized. Stainless steel, although non-magnetic, can sometimes work with this method. It is believed that when stamped, the stainless steel work-hardens and becomes slightly magnetic. This faint magnetic property in an area which is non-magnetic is often sufficient for a restoration.

8.12   Other Methods of Restoration

Heating with an oxyacetylene torch to *heat tint* the surface has been reported (Katterwe, 1956) as has heating the object in an inert atmosphere, called *heat etching*. Neither technique has found any degree of favour.

Cooling the object until water vapour frost forms on the surface has also been reported (Cook, 1975). This has not proved all that successful a method.

Electroplating, the opposite of electro-etching, has also been suggested, but once again, it is rarely successful.

Other more esoteric methods under review or development include:

- electrolytic etching;
- hardness profile measurements;
- relief polishing;
- X-rays (transmission);

- X-rays (reflection);
- scanning acoustic microscopy and
- electron channelling contrast (Treptow, 1978; Polk and Giessen, 1989; Katterwe, 1994, 1996, 2003a, b, 2004, 2006a & b; Pohl *et al.*, 1995; Feyer, Pohl and Katterwe, 2002; Katterwe and Weimar, 2006).

Of all the above methods, the most simple and most efficient has been found to be chemical etching. It is quick, simple, does not require any expensive or bulky equipment, and the results can easily be photographed. Of all the reagents, Fry's is probably the best for steel. It can also be used, with care, on virtually any other metal.

8.13   Laser-Etched Serial Numbers and Bar Codes and Their Restoration

8.13.1   Laser-etched serial numbers

In the late 1990s, Hecker and Koch (H&K), at their Nottingham-based factory, were laser etching serial numbers onto their HK MP5 weapons. Whilst the etching process did not give rise to any crystalline structure deformation as in a normal stamped serial number, the heating process produced by the laser was quite considerable and did lead to a change in surface features. This phenomenon is called the 'heat-affected zone'. Whilst the effect is small, the number can, with care, be restored via normal acid etching processes applicable to the material under examination.

8.13.2   Laser-etched bar codes

Laser-etched bar codes, as seen on the Smith & Wesson Sigma pistols, are somewhat different as the amount of material removed is very small and the heat-affected zone is much shallower. As such, restoration is far more difficult. Acid etching is, once again, the most efficient method, but far less aggressive chemicals must be used (Klees, 2002; Malikowski, 2004).

Laser-etched bar codes are also under consideration in the United Kingdom, Europe, Australia and New Zealand, and will become far more prevalent in the future.

8.13.3   Laser etching of serial numbers on the firing pin

Laser-etched serial numbers on the firing pin and/or the breech face is a much more recent addition to this technique, which has now reached the point of being mandatory in parts of the United States (Figure 8.3).

Figure 8.3 Firing pin impression with laser-etched serial number.

California was the first state to pass the micro-stamping legislation. Massachusetts and Rhode Island has introduced similar legislation, and the Maryland Police Department is promoting consideration as well. It is intended that in the United States legislation be introduced to require micro-stamping on a federal level.

The United Kingdom, Europe and Australasia are also looking into this technique.

Whilst the marks are easily removed with a file, they are generally engraved on at least two parts of the firearm (firing pin and standing breech) and require disassembly of the weapon to remove them all.

It remains to be seen how long the laser-etched marks remain on the firing pin, although Neuman Micro Technologies Inc. of New Hampshire does report that the serial number is still present after 30 000 cycles.

8.13.4 Bar codes laser etched inside the barrel

Laser-etched bar codes inside the muzzle of the weapon (US Patent 6462302 and many others) which are transferred onto a fired bullet are also under consideration.

The bar code would be transferred to the bullet on firing and could be read with a specialized peripheral bar code scanner. The bar code would include the serial number of the weapon, its make and model as well as the owner's name and address (Coffey, 2002, Rifled Weapon Barrel Engraver and Scanner Intellectual Property Organisation).

Once again, the life expectancy of such a bar code in a very hostile environment would be the biggest drawback to the implementation of such technology.

In addition, most bullets recovered from crime scenes tend to be damaged to some extent. The likelihood of recovering an intact bar code from such would appear to be problematical.

Removing such a bar code would be very difficult without severely damaging the barrel. Restoring it would be even more difficult, if not impossible.

References

Arai and Shegio (1953) The application of electrolytic polishing to restore erased numbers on metals. *Journal of Criminology*, **34**.

Betz, C.E. (1967) *Principles of Magnetic Particle Testing*, Magnaflux Co., Chicago, IL, USA.

Coffey, V. (2002) Laser Focus World.

Cook, C.W. (1975) Restoration of obliterated stamped markings on metal, AFTE Conference Paper.

Federal Bureau of Investigation (1950) Metallurgy vs Crime. *FBI Law Enforcement Bulletin*, **19** (11), 8.

Federal Bureau of Investigation (1956) Restoration of obliterated markings on metal. *FBI Law Enforcement Bulletin*, **25** (7), 13.

Feyer, M., Pohl, M. and Katterwe, H. (2002) *Proceedings ENFSI EWG Marks Berlin*, pp. 23–31.

Hatcher, J.S., Jury, F.J. and Weller, J. (1957) *Firearms Investigation, Identification and Evidence*, Stackpole & Co., Harrisburg, PA, USA.

Katterwe, H. (1994) Serial number restoration in metals and polymers. *Journal of the Forensic Science Society*, **34**, 11–16.

Katterwe, H. (1996) Modern approaches for the examination of toolmarks and other surface marks. *Forensic Science Review*, **8**, 45–72.

Katterwe, H. (2003a) Polymerphysical aspects of serial number recovery. *Forensic Science International*, **347**.

Katterwe, H. (2003b) Serial number restoration in metals and polymers. *Wiedersichtbarmachungsmethoden*, Bundeskriminalamt.

Katterwe, H. (2004) *Practical Metallography*, **41**, 286–95.

Katterwe, H. (2006a) Restoration of serial numbers, in *Stolen-Recovered Vehicles* (eds E. Stauffer and M. Bonfanti).

Katterwe, H. (2006b) Serial number restoration in metals & polymers, in *Bundeskriminalamt, Forensic Science Institute, Materials Technology*, D-65173, Wiesbaden/Germany.

Katterwe, H. and Weimar, B. (2006) Proceedings German Marks Meeting Bremen.

Klees, G.S. (2002) Restoration of obliterated laser-etched firearm identifiers. *AFTE Journal*, **34** (3).

Malikowski, S.G. (2004) Restoration of obliterated serial numbers and barcode. *AFTE Journal*, **36** (2).

Mathews, J.H. (1962) *Firearms Identification*, Vol. 1, University of Wisconsin Press, Madison, WI, USA.

NASA Lewis Research Center (1978) NASA contract report CR–I 35322, in *Handbook of Methods for the Restoration of Obliterated Serial Numbers*, NASA Lewis Research Center, Cleveland, OH, USA.

Nickolls, L.C. (1956) *The Scientific Investigation of Crime*, Butterworth & Co., London.

Pohl, M., Katterwe, H., Feyer, M. and Illenseer, O. (1995) *Practical Metallography*, **26**, 405–13.

Polk, D. and Giessen, B. (1989) *AFTE Journal*, **21**, 174–81.

Rifled Weapon Barrel Engraver and Scanner Intellectual Property Organisation (2002) *WO/2002/of Obliterated Serial Numbers*, NASA Lewis Research Center, Ohio, USA.

Treptow, R.S. (1978) Methods for the restoration of obliterated serial numbers.

Wolfer, D.A. and Lee, W.J. (1960) Application of magnetic principles to the restoration of serial numbers. *Journal of Criminal Law, Criminology and Police Science*, **50**, 519–20.

Young, S.G. (1974) Restoration of obliterated serial numbers by ultrasonically induced cavitation in water. *Journal of Forensic Sciences*, **19** (4), 820–35.

Further Reading

Mathews, J.H. (1962) *Firearms Identification*, Vol. I, University of Wisconsin Press, USA.

Nickolls, L.C. (1956) *The Scientific Investigation of Crime*, Butterworth & Co., London.

Treptow, R. (1978) *Handbook of Methods for the Restoration of Obliterated Serial Numbers*, NASA Lewis Research Center, Ohio, USA.

Walls, H.J. (1968) *Forensic Science*, Sweet & Maxwell Ltd., London.

9
Qualifying the Expert and Cross-Examination Questions

9.1 Introduction

As a consequence of advances in analytical technology and limitations on the way in which suspect interrogation is carried out, there has been an increasing necessity for the courts of law to rely on expert testimony. Scientific proof has therefore become a necessity in reconstructing the sequence of events at a crime scene. Such 'scientific proof' covers a large range of disciplines varying in value from the indisputable to that of very dubious value.

Data obtained in a forensic laboratory has no meaning or worth until presented to a court of law. It is the expert witness who must serve as the vehicle to effectively present this scientific data to the court in a manner understandable to the layman.

Unfortunately, it is often the interface between the lawyer and the expert which breaks down, leaving the court with a somewhat myopic view of the evidence available. This lack of intelligible dialogue with the expert will often result in both the defence and prosecution failing to fully utilize the testimony of the expert to their best advantage.

At times, it is the lawyer's lack of scientific knowledge which is at fault, and at others, it is the expert's inability to present his testimony in a clear and precise manner.

It must be stated that it is not the role of the defence, or for that matter the prosecution, to verbally batter the expert into submission. This could easily destroy a perfectly well-qualified expert's career and alienate the court towards the lawyer concerned. What is required is for the lawyer to qualify the expert,

Handbook of Firearms and Ballistics: Second Edition   Brian J. Heard
© 2008 John Wiley & Sons, Ltd.

seek out the relevance of his experience and qualifications to the matter in question and then delve into the probative value of the evidence tendered.

The following questions are suggested as a starting point for the lawyer. It would also serve as a pointer to the trainee forensic expert as to what questions could arise. The list is directed towards the forensic firearms examiner, but with modification, many of the topics are equally well suited to other disciplines.

It should be taken as nothing other than a series of questions which could arise and a possible response. Apart from the opening few questions regarding a witness' background and qualifications, there is no case thread to follow.

9.1.1   Qualifying the expert

Qualifying the expert is becoming increasingly important as there are, unfortunately, a growing number of so-called defence 'experts' who have little or no knowledge of the scientific disciplines in which they are giving evidence.

To counter this, there are an increasing number of professional associations offering 'accreditation' in various forensic fields. This is a very good starting point as far as the forensic profession is concerned, and some of the qualifications are very highly regarded. There are, however, a number of less reputable bodies offering accreditation for a fee or at best, an extremely simple written examination. Academic and professional qualifications should, therefore, be carefully examined.

Q1.   What are your academic qualifications and how do they relate to your profession as a firearms and toolmark examiner?

A1.   In reply, it should be stated that whilst in the past it was considered that as firearms and toolmark examinations tended to be more technically than academically orientated, experience plus a good secondary education was often acceptable. Nowadays, however, a good university degree is a basic requirement. Specialized post-degree qualification in firearms and toolmark examination from an accredited university, the Association of Firearms and Toolmark Examiners (AFTE) or the British Forensic Science Society (FSS) should also be held.

Q2.   What are your professional qualifications?

A2.   This should include information on training periods, subject matter covered, attachments to other forensic organizations, papers written for professional organizations, and so on.

Q3.   Do you hold accreditation from any professional forensic body? If not, why?

A3.   In the reply, it should be stated that many of the professional forensic associations now offer accreditation, some of which carry post-degree status. One should, however, be aware of those offered by small colleges and available through mail order or correspondence courses. These are often very elementary, and any competent examiner will look upon their value as dubious.

Two of the best professional qualifications are the British FSS qualification in Forensic Firearms and Toolmark Examination and AFTE's Certification in Firearms, Toolmark and Gunshot Residue (GSR) Examination.

9.2   General Background Questions

Q4.   What is ballistics?

A4.   This should not include any reference to forensic firearms examination unless it is to note that it is often misrepresented as 'forensic ballistics'.

Ballistics includes **internal ballistics,** which is the behaviour of a missile within the barrel, **external ballistics,** what course the missile takes from the muzzle to the target, and **terminal ballistics,** the bullet's effect on the target. These matters seldom have any relevance to forensic firearms examination.

Q5.   What is the make model and calibre of the evidence weapon?

A5.   One must be equipped with sufficient background information to answer general questions on the evidence weapon, for example, weight of weapon, magazine capacity, materials it is made from, introduction dates and model variations. If the questioning strays outside of that which the examiner feels comfortable, then the stock answer 'I can look up the reference for that particular question should you so deem it necessary' should be utilized.

Q6.   When you say that this gun is . . . calibre, what do you mean?

A6.   A good knowledge of the fact that the calibre is often only indicative of the bore diameter is a prerequisite for court testimony. Cross reference Section 2.2.

Q7.   By examining a fired bullet, can you tell the exact manufacturer of the weapon and its model?

A7.   Possible, but of little significance.

The Crime Laboratory Information System (CLIS) file on General Rifling Characteristics (Crime Laboratory Information System) gives thousands of land/groove widths, and it is possible, though time consuming, to determine the make and model of a weapon from these measurements. It is, however, of little real value in the investigation of a crime.

J. Howard Mathews' *Firearms Identification* Vol. I also has quite an extensive, although nowadays outdated, list of rifling characteristics.

Q8.   Have you measured the pitch (rifling pitch, The distance the projectile must move along a rifled bore to make one revolution. Usually expressed as 'one turn in x inches (or millimetres)') of the rifling on this bullet/in the bore of the weapon concerned?

A8.   Possible, but of absolutely no use in the investigation of a crime. It would also be worth explaining what exactly 'pitch' means, that is, the rifling rate of twist and how it is measured. Cross reference Section 4.2.

Q9.   Did you measure the width of the lands and grooves on this bullet?

A9.   With a graticule in the eyepiece of a microscope, it is quite easy to obtain these measurements. Once again, these measurements are of little or no importance. It is the microscopic comparison which determines whether a bullet was fired from a particular weapon, not the physical dimensions of the lands and grooves.

9.3   Comparison Microscopy

Q10.   What is a photomicrograph and did you take one in respect to this case?

A10.   A photomicrograph is simply a photograph taken under the magnification of a microscope. It could be a simple photomicrograph or a comparison photomicrograph. The answer should be 'Yes, I took a/several representative photographs for my own reference, but not specifically for court purposes.

Q11.   Why not? Was this an attempt to deny some important knowledge to the court?

A11.   Simply put, it takes years of experience to become a competent comparison microscopist. It is thus totally unrealistic to expect members of the court to become instant experts and to be able to interpret the significance of a comparison photomicrograph from a single print. At best, a photograph of a match will be illustrative, at worst, totally misleading.

In addition, a photomicrograph only shows a small portion of any match obtained. To obtain a photographic representation of the whole circumference of a bullet, thus illustrating the concordance between the two, would require hundreds of photographs.

Despite this, some jurisdictions do require the production of photomicrographs. In these instances, the examiner should make clear to the court the limitation of this type of evidence.

Most, if not all, comparison microscopes are now fitted with a video camera and video recorder which can simplify the matter considerably. If the court demands this type of photographic evidence, a video recording of the match is the only real way of demonstrating how the positive comparison was made.

As an alternative, the examiner could offer the court access to a comparison microscope. In this way, it will be possible for the judge and jury to see the match at first hand and to have a clearer idea as to the problems involved. Under no circumstances should the witness tell the court or give it the impression that 'I am the expert, believe me.'

Q12. A question as to the expert's experience with either a pantoscopic camera or a peripheral camera could follow this.

A12. These merely take low-magnification photographs of the circumference of a bullet and are totally unsuitable for comparing the micro stria. It is also unlikely that a modern laboratory would have one of these cameras.

Q13. Can you see the marks that you are using to prove that the bullet came from the gun in question?

A13. Only gross marks will be visible to the naked eye and it would be impossible to even contemplate making a comparison from these. Having said that, I have observed 'expert witnesses' demonstrating to a court how a comparison was made using a simple hand lens.

Q14. How much magnification do you require?

A14. Between 25 and 80 times as a general rule.

Q15. If you don't use enough magnification, you cannot see all the detail. Is that correct?

A15. Yes, but further qualification is required as per the following question.

Q16. But if you use too much, you lose sight of the small details?

A16. A nonsense question but one which can easily trip the unwary. Basically, you require enough magnification to see the fine detail produced on the bullet by manufacturing defects in the barrel. This is generally accepted as being about 40× magnification. Once the magnification rises above 100×, stria made by dirt dust and general debris in the bore becomes visible. This is obviously of no significance, but at this magnification, this very fine stria becomes readily visible and interferes with the overall picture.

Q17. Is it not true that even on a positive match there are many non-matching stria?

A17. This is true, and it is by experience alone that the examiner is able to determine which are relevant and which are non-relevant stria (see A19 and A20). Non-relevant stria would include those made by debris in the bore, microscopic traces of corrosion and fragments of the bullet being torn off by the rifling and becoming trapped between the barrel and the bore of the weapon. The variation in these micro stria could be illustrated by taking photographs of consecutively fired bullets. This could help to demystify the concepts of comparison microscopy by reducing the subjectivity of the process and increasing the objectivity, that is, scientific aspects, as much as possible. Reference should be made to the PhD thesis by Dr J. Hamby on matching and non-matching stria.

Q18.   When you are comparing the rifling on a bullet, how much agreement do you require before you can identify a bullet having come from a particular weapon?

A18.   An amount that exceeds the best known non-match. See Section 4.6.

Q19.   How much agreement is required?

A19.   A non-quantifiable amount and one that must be determined by the individual examiner based on his experience. This is not to say 'I am the expert believe me' and qualification (Section 4.6 and A20 below) is required.

Q20.   What is the standard amount of agreement required by other firearms examiners?

A20.   No real standard, but experience of other firearms examiners' work has shown that the 'mind's eye' criteria used is fairly consistent. Every forensic firearms laboratory should be part of an external proficiency review programme American Society of Crime Laboratory Directors Laboratory Accreditation Board (ASCLD LAB) or similar) for stria matching. There should also be an internal proficiency programme. The results of these should be readily available should they be required by the court.

Q21.   Would you expect to find some matching stria between bullets known to have been made by different weapons?

A21.   The answer is yes, but with the proviso that with the thousands of stria in any bullet comparison, there are bound to be a number of accidentally matching stria. It is the experience of the examiner that enables him to determine which matching stria are relevant and which are accidental.

Q22.   Have you ever deliberately compared bullets from different weapons to determine the best known non-match?

A22.   The answer here must be a resounding 'yes'; otherwise, it would not have been possible for the examiner to formulate a criteria for a 'best known non-match'.

Q23.   If a barrel is rusty, doesn't each bullet fired through it change its characteristics?

A23.   Depends upon the degree of rusting. Light rusting will have little effect on the characteristic stria, whilst heavy rusting could make it impossible to match successive bullets.

Q24.   Could you compare and match the first and the one hundredth bullet fired through the same barrel?

A24.   As long as the barrel had not been damaged by rusting or some other external influence, for example, cleaning with a steel rod, heavy use of steel wool, the answer to this must be 'most definitely yes'. This type of comparison should form part of every firearms examiner's training.

Q25.   Is it not true that two guns of the same make and model will impart the same characteristics on bullets fired through them?

A25.   Class characteristics will be the same, that is, calibre, number, direction and angle of twist, groove profile, groove depth will be the same. The individual characteristics will not. See Section 4.4.

Q26.   Would you agree that the matching of bullets is not an 'exact science' such as fingerprint examination, which requires 16 points of similarity?

A26.   This should be answered along the lines of
        'I do not understand the term 'exact science'; possibly you could elaborate. If you are inferring that 16 points of similarity constitutes an 'exactness', then why not 15, 17 or 63? There being no logical, rational or statistical justification to the selection of the number 16, it cannot, therefore, be inferred as endowing some magic quality of an 'exact science' to the subject.'
        'With striation matches, there are often hundreds, if not thousands, of concording points which constitute a positive identification. That these matching lines are not counted or assigned an arbitrary number makes this type of examination no less of an exact science than fingerprints.'

9.4 GSRs

Q27.   Who took the GSR samples in this case?

A27.   Ideally, they should have been taken by the officer on the stand, and he should be able to account for any possibility of contamination. If not, then it will be necessary to call to the stand the scene of crime officer who did take the samples.

Q28.   What precautions did you take to prevent any contamination of the exhibits?

A28.   Preferably, the expert giving evidence has no day-to-day contact with firearms. If not, he would have to demonstrate that every precaution had been taken to prevent any contamination from himself. This would, at the very least, involve showering, washing hair, changing clothes, using disposable gloves and disposable coveralls with hair cover. Control tapings would have to be taken from himself and the disposable gloves before taping the suspect. Gloves and, preferably, coveralls must be changed for each subject taped.

Q29.   How do you know that the tapings were not tampered with before being examined via the scanning electron microscope (SEM)?

A29.   It should be standard procedure to examine the tapings under low power in the SEM before they are scanned. If any tampering has taken place, then the added residues will be visible as particles lying on the top of the tape. Anything picked up from the hands will be impressed into the tape's surface. Once again, this is only learnt by experience and deliberately making control false positive samples.

Q30.   What steps have been taken, at the collection point and within the laboratory, to ensure that any chance of contamination has been eliminated?

A30.   Disposable gloves and coveralls with hair cover must be used when taking samples from a suspect or dead body. The bags in which these items were stored must be kept in a sealed bag for future examination should questionable results occur or defence counsel requests it. It should also be laboratory practice to randomly examine used gloves and coveralls as part of contamination review procedures.

Q31.   Laboratory procedure should be questioned as to the possibility for environmental contamination.

A31.   Ideally, no one working with weapons should have access to the SEM preparation and examination room. The room should also be positively pressurized to minimize ingress of contamination. There should also be a vestibule in which one dons the anti-contamination suits and shoes prior to entering the SEM room. This should be at a lower pressure than the SEM room, but higher than outside.

Q32.   Is there a firing range within half a mile?

A32.   An irrelevant question if all of the above precautions have been taken. Having said that, the answer must be available.

Q33.   Does anybody in the immediate vicinity of where the samples are examined have any connection with firearms?

A33.   A very valid question. Ideally, the SEM operator should be a qualified and practicing firearms examiner as he will have the experience and background knowledge, as well as up-to-date information on ammunition developments, to recognize the relevance of any ambiguous or questionable results. He will also be able to interpret those results and, via his knowledge, be able to explain their relevance to the court. There is, however, every possibility of such an operator bringing contamination to the SEM room. If this is the case, the operator will have to demonstrate that every possible precaution has been taken to ensure that contamination has been eliminated.

As part of this daily control, samples from the SEM bench and preparation areas must be taken and scanned for contamination as a prerequisite. In addition, the following should be considered as an absolute minimum:

1. Ensure that any SEM work is carried out before entering any other part of the laboratory.

2. Wash hair prior to entering the SEM room.

3. Prior to entering the SEM room, strip off all clothes and put on disposable anti-contamination suit with hair cover, gloves and shoe covers.

4. Complete all tasks in the SEM room in one sitting to reduce the number of exits and entries to an absolute minimum. If it is necessary to leave the SEM room, dispose of the anti-contamination kit and put on a new set prior to entering the SEM room again.

Q35. Where were the bags obtained that were used to protect the hands of the suspect?

A35. Often, these are merely envelopes taken from police station supplies, or even worse, plastic bags, and are thus very susceptible to contamination. This contamination could come from either a range within the station or from officers who carry or use weapons.

The inside and outside of these bags or envelopes should be control taped before use to determine whether they have been contaminated.

Ideally, these should be paper bags obtained from an outside source. These should be randomly taped and examined in the SEM for any possible signs of contamination. The results of these examinations must be retained for court purposes.

GSR sample kits should be made up by an outside contractor. These should contain surgical gloves, plastic restraints, disposable coveralls, disposable shoe covers, five sampling tubes and an instruction leaflet.

Q36. How were the suspect's hands secured whilst he was awaiting the taking of the tapings?

A36. If they were handcuffed, there is a very real possibility of GSR particles being transferred from the cuffs to the hands of the suspect. Research has shown (B.J. Heard, unpublished paper) that during range courses, an officer's clothes, baton, handcuffs and holster will become heavily contaminated with GSR particles. The GSR particles remain in the handcuff pouch and when the handcuffs are used, these particles will be transferred to the hands of an arrested person. Only plastic cable ties (see A35) should be used as restraints. These can be supplied to police stations in sealed plastic bags.

Q37. How can you be sure that the particles found were in fact from the firing of a weapon and not environmental or other contamination?

A37. Knowledge will have to be shown of GSR/indicative GSR particle ratios as well as GSR particle/lead particle ratios and how they relate to the case statistics.

Q38.   What do you consider to be a minimum number of GSR particles for a positive result and how did you decide on that number?

A38.   One is the minimum number, but this would have to be backed up with the relevant GSR particle/lead particle and GSR/indicative particle ratios. As a general rule, two particles, with the aforementioned ratios, is generally considered the minimum requirement for a positive finding.

9.5 Ferrozine Test

Q39.   How do you know that the results obtained from this test were not caused by a kitchen knife, or a knife fork and spoon?

A39.   Firstly, most kitchen utensils are made from stainless steel or are nickel or chromium plated, none of which gives a positive result to this test. In addition, this whole test relies on the interpretation of the visualized marks on the hands. The examiner will, therefore, have to prove beyond reasonable doubt that the marks observed were those from a weapon and not something accidental such as a pry bar or a car jack.

Personally, I always carry a spray can of ferrozine with me when giving such evidence. A member of the court, jury or even the judge himself can then be asked to hold the object in question and then to have his or her hands sprayed. A highly effective technique.

Q40.   What other metals give a positive reaction to this test?

A40.   The examiner should have knowledge of the interfering metals in this test and how to differentiate between copper and iron. He should also be aware, as any forensic chemist should, of the chemical processes involved, that is, bidentate ligand formation with ferrous ions.

Q41.   How many times did you spray the suspect's hands?

A41.   A stock question to catch out the unwary. This is a qualitative test, not quantitative, and the number of times the hand is sprayed or the quantity of reagent applied to the hands has no bearing on the result.

9.6 Standard of Review: 'Daubert Trilogy'

The Daubert standard is a legal precedent set in 1993 by the Supreme Court of the United States regarding the admissibility of expert witnesses' testimony during legal proceedings (Daubert v. Merrell Dow Pharmaceuticals, 509 US 579 (1993)).

A Daubert motion is a motion, raised before or during trial, to exclude the presentation of unqualified evidence to the jury. This is usually used to exclude the testimony of an expert witness who has no such expertise or who used questionable methods to obtain the information.

In Daubert, the Supreme Court held that federal trial judges are the 'gatekeepers' of scientific evidence. Under the Daubert standard, the trial judges must evaluate proffered expert witnesses to determine whether their testimony is both 'relevant' and 'reliable', a two-pronged test of admissibility.

The relevancy prong. The relevancy of a testimony refers to whether or not the expert's evidence 'fits' the facts of the case. For example, you may invite an astronomer to tell the jury if it had been a full moon on the night of a crime. However, the astronomer would not be allowed to testify if the fact that the moon was full was not relevant to the issue at hand in the trial.

The reliability prong. The Supreme Court explained that in order for expert testimony to be considered reliable, the expert must have derived his or her conclusions from the scientific method (Daubert v. Merrell Dow Pharmaceuticals, Inc. (1993) 509 US 579, 589) The Court offered 'general observations' of whether proffered evidence was based on the scientific method, although the list was not intended to be used as an exacting checklist:

A third prong, empirical testing, is also taken into account.

Empirical testing:

1. The theory or technique must be falsifiable, refutable and testable.

2. Subjected to peer review and publication.

3. Known or potential error rate and the existence and maintenance of standards concerning its operation.

4. Whether the theory and technique is generally accepted by a relevant scientific community.

Although trial judges have always had the authority to exclude inappropriate testimony, previous to Daubert, trial courts often preferred to let juries hear evidence proffered by both sides.

Once certain evidence has been excluded by a Daubert motion because it fails to meet the relevancy and reliability standard, it will likely be challenged when introduced again in another trial. Even though a Daubert motion is not binding to other courts of law, if something has been found not trustworthy, other judges may choose to follow that precedent.

The Daubert decision was heralded by many observers as one of the most important Supreme Court decisions of the last century imparting crucial legal reforms to reduce the volume of what has disparagingly been labelled junk science in the court room.

Many of these individuals were convinced by Peter Huber's 1991 book *Galileo's Revenge: Junk Science in the Courtroom*, which argued that numerous product liability and toxic tort verdicts were unjustly made on the basis of junk science. According to Huber, junk science in the courts threatened not only justice but the workings of the American economy. This threat rested on two premises:

1. Juries are not competent to recognize flaws in scientific testimony, especially toxic tort or product liability suits where decisions on causation rested on complex scientific issues and

2. The result of junk science is the issuance of awards that deter manufacturers from introducing worthwhile products into the marketplace out of fear of unwarranted tort liability for injuries their products have not caused.

By requiring experts to provide relevant opinions grounded in reliable methodology, proponents of Daubert were satisfied that these standards would result in a fair and rational resolution of the scientific and technological issues which lie at the heart of product liability adjudication.

To summarize, five cardinal points Daubert asks from every new technique to be admissible in court are:

1. Has the technique been tested in actual field conditions (and not just in a laboratory) (For example, fingerprinting has been extensively tested and verified not only in laboratory conditions, but even in actual criminal cases. So it is admissible. Polygraphy, on the other hand, has been well tested in laboratories but not so well tested in field conditions.)?

2. Has the technique been subject to peer review and publication?

3. What is the known or potential rate of error? Is it zero, or low enough to be close to zero?

4. Do standards exist for the control of the technique's operation?

5. Has the technique been generally accepted within the relevant scientific community?

The Supreme Court explicitly cautioned that the Daubert list should not be regarded by judges as 'a definitive checklist or test . . .'. Yet in practice, many judges regularly exclude scientific evidence when they, assuming the role of 'amateur scientist', determine it to be lacking on even a single Daubert point, instead of assessing the totality of such evidence.

References

Crime Laboratory Information System, US Department of Justice, Federal Bureau of Investigation, Washington, DC 20535.

Huber, Peter W. (1991) *Galileo's Revenge: Junk Science in the Courtroom*, Basic Books. ISBN 0-465-02623-0.

Further Reading

Papers and articles providing further reading on qualifying the expert witness include:

Berger, M.A. (2005) What has a decade of Daubert wrought (PDF). *American Journal of Public Health*, 95 (S1), S59. Retrieved on 2006-07-12.

Dixon, L. and Gill. B. (2002) *Changes in the Standards for Admitting Expert Evidence in Federal Civil Cases Since the Daubert Decision*, RAND Institute for Civil Justice Santa Monica, CA.

Gatowski, S.I., Dobbin, S.A., Richardson, J.T., Ginsburg, G.P., Merlino, M.L. and Dahir, V. (2001) Asking the gatekeepers: a national survey of judges on judging expert evidence in a post-Daubert world. *Law and Human Behavior*, **25** (5), 433–58.

Gottesman, M. (Fall 1998). For barefoot to Daubert to joiner: triple play or double error? *Arizona Law Review*, **40**, 753.

Hodge, E. and Blackburn, B. (1979) The firearms/toolmark examiner in court 21:2. *Association of Firearms and Toolmark Examiners Journal*, 11 232, 238 (1989) [first published 1979].

Jasanoff, S. (2005) Law's knowledge: science for justice in legal settings. *American Journal of Public Health*, **95** (S1), S49–568.

Melnick, R. (2005) A Daubert motion: a legal strategy to exclude essential scientific evidence in toxic tort litigation. *American Journal of Public Health*, **95** (S1), S30.

Moenssens, A.A., Moses, R.E. and Inbau, F.E. (1965) *Scientific Evidence in Criminal Cases*, Foundation Press, Evanston, IL, USA.

Moss, R. (1970) Scientific proof in criminal cases, a Texas lawyer's guide. *Association of Firearms and Toolmark Newsletter*, 10.

Murdock, J. (1992) Some suggested court questions to test criteria for identification qualifications. *Association of Firearms and Toolmark Examiners Journal*, 24.

Neufeld, P. (2005) The (near) irrelevance of daubert to criminal justice and some suggestions for reform. *American Journal of Public Health*, **95** (S1), S107.

Owen, D.G. (2002) A decade of Daubert. *Denver University Law Review*, **80**, 345.

Risinger, D.M. (2000) Navigating expert reliability: are criminal standards of certainty being left on the dock? *Albany Law Review*, **64** (1), 2000.

Rothman, K.J. and Greenland, S. (2005) Causation and causal inference in epidemiology. *American Journal of Public Health*, **95** (S1), S144.

10

Classification of Firearm-Related Death

The manner of death from firearm injuries can be classified as homicide, suicide, accident or undetermined.

Unfortunately, there is no single characteristic appearance, position or type of gunshot wound that defines the exact manner of death. Such a determination requires analysis of multiple pieces of evidence, including the scene investigation, the examination of the body, ballistics evidence, trace metal detection on the hands, analysis for gunshot residue (GSR) and interviews of persons involved with the decedent and the scene of death.

The presence of multiple entrance wounds may not exclude suicide. Kohlmeier, McMahan and DiMaio (2001) have analyzed 1704 suicidal firearms deaths and determined the characteristics of those injuries.

The type of weapon used was a revolver in 49.8%, an automatic pistol in 19.5%, a rifle in 30.0% and some other firearm in 0.7%.

The site of the entrance wound involved the head in 83.7% of cases, the chest in 14.0%, the abdomen in 1.9% and a combination of sites in 0.4%. The table below identifies the site of the entrance wound by type of weapon used in suicidal firearms deaths (Table 10.1):

In the above series, contact wounds were found in 97.9%, near contact in 2.0% and a combination of these or an unknown range in the remainder.

GSR deposition (Chapter 6) will, in many cases, be only indicative in determining the exact cause of death. Deposition of residues only on the palms of the hands being indicative of them being held up in self-preservation, whilst in those cases where it is located on the back of either one or both hands, it is indicative that the person fired the weapon.

Handbook of Firearms and Ballistics: Second Edition   Brian J. Heard
© 2008 John Wiley & Sons, Ltd.

Table 10.1 Sites of suicidal firearms deaths and the type of weapon used.

Site	Handgun (%)	Rifle (%)	Shotgun (%)
Right temple	50.0	22.9	9.3
Left temple	5.8	3.3	3.7
Mouth	14.5	24.3	31.7
Forehead	5.9	15.7	8.1
Under chin	2.4	9.1	10.6
Back of head	3.6	3.8	1.2
Chest	13.2	15.7	19.9
Abdomen	1.4	1.9	5.6
Other	3.2	3.3	9.9

GSR deposition is extremely difficult to fake convincingly and any competent electron microscopist specializing in GSR interpretation should easily be able to spot any such attempt.

In the few cases I have dealt with where such an attempt has been made, it has been easily identifiable by:

- the size of the GSR particles (where they have been shaken out of a fired cartridge case);
- their morphology (predominantly spherical with large, amorphous, partially burnt propellant particles covered in GSR particles);
- incorrect positive/indicative GSR ratios;
- the presence of large quantities of semi-burnt propellant particles, once again shaken out of a fired cartridge case.

The deciding factor, when taken in the light of GSR deposition, can often be via trace metal detection with either (3-2(2-pyridyl)-5,6-diphenyl-1,2,4-triazine-p,p'-disulphonic acid, disodium salt trihydrate (PDT) or ferrozine (Chapter 7). With Trace Metal Detection (TMD) results being even more difficult to fake than GSR deposition, this is crucial in deciding the true nature of the crime.

The problem with attempting to fake a TMD result is that

- Sweat is crucial in the transfer of iron in its ferric (Fe^{+++}) form.
- Dead bodies do not sweat and, as any that may be present at the time of death soon evaporates, it is extremely difficult to effect any substantial transfer. This is especially so once the body starts to cool down.
- The transfer requires a conscious and sustained pressure upon the weapon, which is all but impossible to convincingly recreate with a dead body.

In addition to the above, in every case of suicide involving a revolver that I have dealt with, there has always been a very positive result on the thumb of

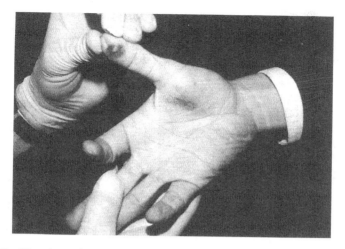

Figure 10.1 Positive ferrozine reaction on pad of thumb in suicide case.

the deceased. This, I can only conclude, results from some trepidation over committing the act and the hammer has been cocked and uncocked several times before the weapon is eventually fired (Figure 10.1).

In the realms of accidental death, there are too many variables to list here. Personally, however, I have never encountered a case in which accidental death was caused during the cleaning of a firearm. Naturally, this does not exclude the possibility of such an event.

Whilst it is of little more than academic interest, the following table shows the ratio of violent deaths vs. suicides for various countries (Table 10.2).

10.1 Multiple-Shot Suicides

Multiple-shot suicides engender controversy due to the misconception that it is impossible to inflict more than one gunshot upon oneself. Tied in with this mistaken belief of instant incapacity are fallacies such as 'the impact of the bullet would send you reeling backwards', 'the gun would fly out of your hand', and so on.

Incapacitation can be divided into three major groups:

1. **Instant incapacitation.** This can only result from a cessation in the functioning of the central nervous system via direct disruption of brain stem tissue.

2. **Rapid incapacitation.** This can be achieved via massive bleeding from the heart, the thoracic aorta, the pulmonary artery or other major vein or artery. This can take 5 min or more.

3. **Delayed incapacitation.** This can result from damage to other major organs, that is, the lungs, kidney, liver. With such damage to the internal organs, total incapacitation can take a considerable period of time.

Table 10.2 International violent death rate table (death rates are per 10000).

Country	Year	Population	Total homicide	Firearm homicide	Total suicide	Firearm suicide	% Households with guns
Estonia	1994	1 499 257	28.21	8.07	40.95	3.13	n/a
Hungary	1994	10 245 677	3.53	0.23	35.38	0.88	n/a
Slovenia	1994	1 989 477	2.01	0.35	31.16	2.51	n/a
Finland[a]	1994	5 088 333	3.24	0.86	27.26	5.78	23.2
Brazil	1993	160 737 000	19.04	10.58	3.46	0.73	n/a
Denmark	1993	5 189 378	1.21	0.23	22.13	2.25	n/a
Austria	1994	8 029 717	1.17	0.42	22.12	4.06	n/a
Switzerland[b]	1994	7 021 000	1.32	0.58	21.28	5.61	27.2
France	1994	57 915 450	1.12	0.44	20.79	5.14	22.6
Mexico	1994	90 011 259	17.58	9.88	2.89	0.91	n/a
Belgium	1990	9 967 387	1.41	0.60	19.04	2.56	16.6
Portugal	1994	5,138,600	2.98	1.28	14.83	1.28	n/a
United States[c]	1993	257 783 004	5.70	3.72	12.06	7.35	39.0
Japan	1994	124 069 000	0.62	0.02	16.72	0.04	n/a
Sweden	1993	8 718 571	1.30	0.18	15.75	2.09	15.1
Germany	1994	81 338 093	1.17	0.22	15.64	1.17	8.9
Taiwan	1996	21 979 444	8.12	0.97	6.88	0.12	n/a
Singapore	1994	2 930 200	1.71	0.07	14.06	0.17	n/a
Canada	1992	28 120 065	2.16	0.76	13.19	3.72	29.1
Mauritius	1993	1 062 810	2.35	0	12.98	0.09	n/a
Argentina	1994	34 179 000	4.51	2.11	6.71	3.05	n/a
Norway	1993	4 324 815	0.97	0.30	13.64	3.95	32.0
N. Ireland	1994	1 641 711	6.09	5.24	8.41	1.34	8.4
Australia	1994	17 838 401	1.86	0.44	12.65	2.35	19.4
New Zealand	1993	3 458 850	1.47	0.17	12.81	2.14	22.3
Scotland	1994	5 132 400	2.24	0.19	12.16	0.31	4.7
Hong Kong	1993	5 919 000	1.23	0.12	10.29	0.07	Nil
Netherlands	1994	15 382 830	1.11	0.36	10.10	0.31	1.9
South Korea	1994	44 453 179	1.62	0.04	9.48	0.02	n/a
Ireland	1991	3 525 719	0.62	0.03	9.81	0.94	n/a
Italy	1992	56 764 854	2.25	1.66	8.00	1.11	16.0
England/ Wales	1992	51 429 000	1.41	0.11	7.68	0.33	4.7
Israel	1993	5 261 700	2.32	0.72	7.05	1.84	n/a
Spain	1993	39 086 079	0.95	0.21	7.77	0.43	13.1
Greece	1994	10 426 289	1.14	0.59	3.40	0.84	n/a
Kuwait	1995	1 684 529	1.01	0.36	1.66	0.06	n/a

[a] The United Nations International Study on Firearm Regulation reports Finland's gun ownership rate at 50% of households.
[b] Percent households with guns includes all army personnel.
[c] Total homicide rate and firearm homicide rates are for 1999, FBI Uniform Crime Report (1999).

Whilst multiple-shot suicides are uncommon, they are by no means rare. Of the cases I have dealt with, one involved an Australian who shot himself in the back seven times with a 0.22″ calibre rifle, a police officer who shot himself once in the mouth and then through the roof of the mouth with a 0.410″ bolt-action shotgun, and another police officer who shot himself five times in the chest with a 0.38″ Smith & Wesson calibre revolver. All of these cases were conclusively shown to be suicide with no external influences.

Betz, Peschel and Eisenmenger (1994) states that of 117 gunshot suicides, seven showed more than one gunshot wound. Two of these were unusual in that the second shot was fired directly into the first wound.

Hudson (1981) reports that from 7895 gunshot deaths, 3522 were suicides. Of these, 58 (0.7%) were multi-shot suicides.

Introna and Smialek (1989) reports than in 6 years at the Office of the Chief Medical Examiner, nine cases of multiple-shot suicide were examined with each victim suffering three to five gunshot wounds. No preferential sites for the wounds were of significance.

In conclusion, one must approach any such case with severe scepticism, and every avenue of investigation must be thoroughly examined before reaching a decision as to the exact circumstances leading up to the death.

References

Betz, P., Peschel, O. and Eisenmenger, W. (1994) Suicidal gunshot wounds – site and characteristics. *Archiv fur Kriminologie*, **193**(3–4), 65–71.

Federal Bureau of Investigation (1999) *FBI Uniform Crime Report*.

Hudson, P. (1981) Multishot firearms suicide. Examination of 58 cases. *American Journal of Forensic Medicine and Pathology*, **2**(3), 239–42.

Introna, F. and Smialek, J.E. (1989) Suicide from multiple gunshot wounds. *American Journal of Forensic Medicine and Pathology*, **10**(4), 275–84.

Kohlmeier, R.E., McMahan, C.A., DiMaio, V.J.M. (2001) Suicide by firearms. *American Journal of Forensic Medicine and Pathology*, **22**, 337–40.

11
Glossary

ACP	Abbreviation for Automatic Colt Pistol. Used to designate calibres designed for use in Colt self-loading pistols.
Action	The mechanism of a firearm.
Action, Blow Forward	A design for a semi-automatic firearm wherein the breech-block is stationary and the barrel moves forward by gas pressure to open and eject the cartridge and re-cycle the action.
Action, Blowback	A design found in semi-automatic and automatic firearms where the inertia of some component, usually supplemented with a spring, is the main locking force and no mechanical locking of the breech occurs.
Action, Bolt	A firearm in which the breech closure is in line with the bore at all times; manually reciprocated to load, unload and cock, and is locked in place by breech bolt lugs engaging abutments usually in the receiver. There are two principle types of bolt actions, that is, the turn bolt and the straight-pull type.
Action, Box Lock	A design in which the hammer and hammer springs are located within the frame and the trigger assembly is in the lower tang. Generally only found in rifles and shotguns.
Action, Delayed Blowback	An action which utilizes a mechanical means in conjunction with bolt mass to gain additional delay prior to bolt opening. Also called retarded blowback.

Handbook of Firearms and Ballistics: Second Edition   Brian J. Heard
© 2008 John Wiley & Sons, Ltd.

Action, Double	A handgun mechanism in which a single pull of the trigger first cocks and then releases the hammer.
Action, Dropping Block	An action in which the breechblock moves vertically, or nearly so, inside of the receiver walls. Also called a falling block.
Action, Hinged Frame	A design wherein the barrel(s), one or more being either smooth or rifled, is pivoted on the frame. When the action is open, the barrel may pivot up or down or sideways for loading or unloading. When the action is closed, the breech of the barrels swings against the standing breech. Opening is normally accomplished by movement of a top or side lever.
Action, Lever	A design wherein the breech mechanism is cycled by an external lever generally below the receiver.
Action, Locked Breech	Any action wherein the breech bolt is locked to the barrel or receiver, through a portion or all of the recoiling motion.
Action, Open Breech	A type of action wherein the breech bolt is held open until the trigger is pulled. Example: Sten SMG.
Action, Pump	A firearm which features a moveable forearm which is manually actuated in motion parallel to the barrel. Forearm motion is transmitted to a breech bolt assembly which performs all the functions of the firing cycle assigned to it by the design. This type of action is prevalent in rimfire rifles and shotguns and to a lesser extent in centre fire rifles. Also known as slide action or trombone action.
Action, Top Break	A design in which the barrel or barrels are connected to the frame by a hinge pin below the barrels. Upon release of the locking mechanism, usually by a top, side or under-lever, the barrel or barrels rotate around the hinge pin away from the standing breech.
Action, Turn Bolt	A bolt-action firearm on which it is necessary to rotate the bolt handle upwards for unlocking before it can be pulled to the rear. Similarly, it is necessary to rotate the bolt handle downwards after closing to lock the firearm and to enable the gun to be fired.
Action, Underlever	The same as a top break mechanism except that the lever that unlocks the firearm, allowing the barrels to pivot and expose the breech, is located below the trigger guard or forms the trigger guard.
Air Gun	A weapon using compressed air to propel the missile. Usually, this is achieved by a spring-powered piston.

Ammunition	Bulleted ammunition consists of a cartridge case, propellant, priming compound and missile.
	Blank ammunition is the same but with the omission of the bullet.
Ammunition, Ball	A military term to designate ammunition with a fully jacketed bullet.
Ammunition, Small Arms	A military term to designate ammunition with a calibre of less than 1 in.
Angle of Departure	The angle of elevation of the barrel from the horizontal.
Annulus	The space between the primer cup and the primer pocket.
Antimony (Sb)	A white metal which, when alloyed with lead, increases its hardness.
Antimony Sulphide	Common additive to modern priming compounds which acts as a fuel to increase the burning time of the mixture.
Anvil	Metallic component of a primer cup against which the priming compound is crushed by the firing pin. In a **Boxer** primer, the anvil constitutes part of the primer cup; in a **Berdan** primer, it is part of the cartridge case. For diagrams, see Chapter 2.2.
AP	Abbreviation for armour-piercing bullet. In this type of ammunition, there is usually a hard tungsten core to the bullet.
Assault Rifle	Generally a compact military weapon firing a centre fire cartridge of a power below that of a rifle cartridge but above that used in sub-machine guns.
Atomic Absorption (AA)	A method of qualitative and quantitative analysis often used in GSR examinations. Atomic absorption derives it name from the fact that the atoms of an element will absorb light at a wavelength which is particular to that element. If an element is introduced into a flame through which light of an appropriate wavelength is shone, a portion of the light will be absorbed by the free atoms present. It is the wavelength of the light absorbed which identifies the element present and the quantity of light absorbed which reveals the quantity of the element present.
Auto-loading	See self-loading.
Automatic	Often misused term for 'semi-automatic' or 'self-loading'. When correctly applied to a pistol, or rifle, it signifies a

weapon whereby the action will continue to operate, that is, automatically, until the finger is removed from the trigger or the magazine is empty.

Axis (Bullet)	The centre line through a bullet about which it rotates.
Backlash	The continuing rearward movement of the trigger after the firing pin or hammer has been released to fire the weapon.
Backstrap	The portion of a pistol's frame which forms the rear of the grip.
Ball Burnishing	A method of applying a mirror-like finish to the tops of the lands in a rifled barrel by forcing a hardened steel ball down the bore.
Ball Powder	Spherical propellant introduced by Winchester Western in 1933.
Ballistic Coefficient	The ratio of the sectional density of the bullet to its form factor. This gives a numerical factor showing the rate of deceleration of a missile due to air resistance.
Ballistics	The study of a missile's movement from the time of cartridge ignition until it reaches the target. Often wrongly confused with forensic firearms examination.
Ballistics, Exterior	The study of the flight of a missile from the moment it leaves the barrel until it reaches the target.
Ballistics, Interior	The study of what happens between the moment the firing pin strikes the primer until the missile leaves the barrel.
Ballistics, Terminal	The study of the effect the missile has on the target.
Barium Nitrate	A component of most priming compounds which supplies oxygen to the reaction.
Barrel	The tube in a firearm through which the missile is projected. Can be rifled or smooth bored.
Barrel Pressure	An extremely thick-walled barrel with a pressure measuring device. To measure the pressure produced during the firing of a cartridge.
Barrel Swaging	The process of manufacturing the rifling in a barrel by either squeezing on hammering the barrel onto a negative form of the rifling.
Battery	When the standing breech of a weapon is in correct alignment with the rear of the barrel ready for firing.
Battery Cup	A flanged metal cup used in shotgun cartridge primers.
BB	Designation for shotgun pellets having a diameter of 0.16″. Also used for steel balls used in air guns of 0.175″ diameter.

BB Cap	A very short 0.22″ rimfire cartridge with a round ball. Very popular at the turn of the century for use in indoor gallery shooting.
Bearing Surface	The portion of a bullet which comes into contact with the rifling.
Bent	A step in the hammer into which the sear is held engaged under spring tension until withdrawn by pulling the trigger. In American terminology often referred to as the **Sear Notch.**
Berdan Primer	See Primer, Berdan.
Black Powder	A mechanical mixture of potassium nitrate, sulphur and charcoal.
Blank	See Cartridge, Blank.
Blish Action	A blowback system using a phosphor bronze 'H'-shaped block sliding in angled slots. Originally designed for the Thompson sub-machine gun but is of dubious value.
Blowback Action	In self-loading or fully automatic weapons which use the rearward force of the cartridge case on the standing breech to cycle the weapon.
Blowback, Delayed	Also referred to as Retarded Action. A firearms action incorporating some form of mechanism to delay the opening of the action until the internal pressures have fallen to a safe level.
Boat-tail Bullet	See Bullet, Boat-tail.
Bolt Action	The type of breech closure which is accomplished by the longitudinal movement of a bolt. The actual locking movement can be 'turn bolt', 'straight pull' or 'camming bolt'.
Bolt Face	See Breech Face.
Bolt Handle	The extension from the bolt by which it is operated.
Bolt Head	The forward part of the bolt including the breech (or bolt) face.
Bore	English term to designate the size of a shotgun bore. Based on the number of round lead balls of the same diameter as the barrel which weigh 1 lb. Thus, a 12-bore barrel has the same diameter as a ball of lead weighing $\frac{1}{12}$ lb .
Bore	The inside of the barrel.
Bore Diameter	The inside diameter of the barrel measured across the tops of the barrel lands or across a circle formed by the lands if there is an uneven number.

Bottleneck Cartridge	See Cartridge, Bottleneck.
Boxer Primer	See Primer, Boxer.
Breech	The rear of the barrel where the cartridge is inserted.
Breechblock	The moveable part of a firearm which seals the breech.
Breech Face	The part of the breechblock or breech bolt which is in contact with the head of the cartridge during firing.
Breech Face Markings	A negative impression of the breech face marks which are impressed onto the head of a cartridge case during firing.
Breech Plug	The metal plug which seals the breech end of a muzzle-loading weapon.
Breech Pressure	Incorrect terminology for **Chamber Pressure**. Chamber pressure is the pressure produced in the chamber during firing.
Breech, Standing	It is that part of a revolver's frame which supports the cartridge head during firing.
Buckshot	An American term designating shotgun pellets ranging in size from 0.2 to 0.36″ diameter.
Buffer	A granular substance, nowadays generally polyethylene, used in shotgun cartridges to protect the shot from distortion during firing.
Bullet	A non-spherical missile for use in rifled barrels.
Bullet, Armour Piercing (AP)	A bullet designed to penetrate metal. Generally with a core of tungsten but can be any hardened metal.
Bullet, Boat-tail	Bullet with a tapered base to reduce drag.
Bullet, Cast	Plain lead bullet formed by pouring molten lead into a mould.
Bullet, Coated	Lead bullet with a surface coating of a harder metal to reduce metal fouling in the bore. Generally either copper or brass.
Bullet, Copper Washed	Generally steel-jacketed bullets bullet which have received a coat of copper to reduce corrosion.
Bullet Core	The inner portion of a jacketed bullet, usually plain lead.
Bullet Drop	The fall of a bullet during its flight due to gravity.
Bullet, Dum-Dum	Soft-nosed 0.303″ bullets produced in 1894 by the Indian Dum-Dum Armoury. A term often wrongly applied to hollow-point bullets.
Bullet Engraving	The impressed rifling on a bullet.
Bullet, Frangible	A bullet designed to break up on impact with a hard surface to minimize ricochet. Can be made from brass or tungsten dust in epoxy resin or compressed iron dust.

Bullet, Full Metal Jacket (FMJ)	A bullet which has a lead core covered with a hard metal jacket leaving only the base exposed. The jacket can be of almost any material, although brass and steel are the most common. Also referred to as full metal case, fully jacketed and ball ammunition.
Bullet, Gallery	Frangible 0.22″ bullet made from compressed iron filings.
Bullet Groove	The portion of the bullet engraved by the raised part of the barrel's rifling. When viewing a cross section of a fired bullet, the bullet grooves will be the parts on the bearing surface of the bullet which are depressed.
Bullet, Gas Check	Small brass cup which fits onto the base of plain lead bullets to reduce metal fouling in the bore.
Bullet, Hollow-Point	A bullet with a cavity in the nose to assist in expansion when striking tissue.
Bullet, Incendiary	A military bullet with a chemical compound in the nose which ignites on impact.
Bullet Jacket	The metal covering to a jacketed bullet.
Bullet Jump	The distance a bullet must travel from the cartridge case until it reaches the rifling. In self-loading pistols and rifles, this is generally very small, but in revolvers, the distance from the cylinder to the rifling in the barrel can be appreciable.
Bullet, Land	The portion of the bullet **not** engraved by the raised part of the rifling in the bore of the weapon. When viewing a cross section of a fired bullet, the bullet lands will be the parts on the bearing surface of the bullet which are standing proud of the rest.
Bullet Ogive	The curved forward part of a bullet's nose.
Bullet Recovery System	A system for the undamaged recovery of test-fired bullets for examination under a microscope. High-grade cotton wool and water are the most commonly used mediums.
Bullet, Semi-jacketed Hollow-Point	Bullet with a partial jacket which exposes a hollow-pointed nose.
Bullet, Semi-wadcutter	A bullet primarily for target use which has a truncated cone nose shape.
Bullet, Soft-Point	Jacketed bullet with the lead core at the nose exposed.
Bullet Spin	The rotation motion of a bullet imparted by the rifling.
Bullet, Swaged	A bullet which has been made by compressing a plug of plain lead into a die.

Bullet, Tracer	Bullet, usually military, with a small pellet of brightly burning compound in the base which permits its trajectory to be viewed. Can be day or night tracer.
Bullet Trap	A means of stopping a bullet when recovery is not the object. Can be an angled steel plate, sand, telephone books, etc.
Bullet, Truncated Cone	Conical-shaped nose rather than the conventional ogival shape.
Bullet, Wadcutter	A bullet with a flat nose intended to cleanly cut a clean hole in the paper target when target shooting.
Bullet Wipe	The discoloured area surrounding a bullet hole caused by bullet lubricant and discharge residues wiped off the bullet surface. Can be useful in determining the bullet entry/exit hole.
Butt	The bottom part of a handgun grip or the rear of the stock in a long arm.
Button Rifling	See Rifling, Button.
Calcium Silicide	A common component of priming compounds which acts as a fuel.
Calibre (Caliber)	In weapons, the approximate diameter of the inside of the bore across the tops of the rifling lands.
	In ammunition, the approximate diameter of the missile.
Cannelure	A groove round the bearing surface of a bullet for either crimping the mouth of the cartridge case or to hold bullet lubricant.
Cup, Percussion	Small metallic cup containing a priming compound. Used with percussion muzzle-loading weapons as an ignition system for the propellant.
Carbine	A short-barrelled rifle, originally intended for mounted troops.
Cartridge	An imprecise term usually referring to a single, live, unfired, round of ammunition comprising missile, cartridge case, propellant and primer. The correct term is, however, a **Round** of ammunition.
Cartridge, Blank	A round of ammunition, without a missile, which is intended to make a large report on firing.
Cartridge, Bottleneck	A cartridge case with main diameter steeply stepping down to a case mouth of a smaller diameter.

Cartridge Case	Refers to the ammunition case and primer and does not include the bullet. Can be either a 'fired cartridge case' or a 'live cartridge case'. A 'live cartridge case' has a live, unfired primer, but there is no propellant or bullet present.
Cartridge Case, Centre Fire	A cartridge case that has the primer contained in a small metal cup placed in a receptacle in the centre of the head of the cartridge case.
Cartridge Case, Belted	A cartridge case which has an extra band of metal ahead of the extractor groove. Intended to give extra support to the base of the cartridge in high-power Magnums.
Cartridge Case Mouth	The open end of a cartridge into which the bullet would be seated.
Cartridge Case, Rebated	This is a cartridge case which has a rim diameter which is less than the diameter of the cartridge case. The designation used in the metric system is 'RB'. This type of cartridge case configuration tends to be reserved for high-powered cannon ammunition.
Cartridge Case, Rimless	This is a cartridge case in which the case head diameter is the same as the case body and there is, for extraction purposes, a groove around the case body just in front of the flange. There is generally no letter system to designate this cartridge base type. Self-loading pistols are almost invariably designed for use with semi-rimmed or rimless ammunition.
Cartridge Case, Rimmed	A cartridge case having a flanged head that is larger in diameter than the body of the cartridge case.
Cartridge Case, Semi-rimmed	A cartridge case having a case head flange only slightly larger than the case body.
Cartridge, Cook-Off	The ignition of a cartridge due to overheating. This generally happens above 350 °C and it is the priming compound which ignites first, not the propellant.
Cartridge, Drill/Dummy	A cartridge which cannot be fired, usually used for demonstration purposes.
Cartridge NATO	A designation for military ammunition conforming to NATO (North Atlantic Treaty Organisation) standards. Usually 9 mm Parabellum and 7.62 × 51 mm.
Cartridge Proof	Special high-pressure cartridges used for proofing commercial weapons.
Cartridge, Rimfire	A flanged cartridge with the priming compound in the hollow rim.

Caseless Ammunition	Ammunition which has the propellant and primer moulded round the bullet and thus requiring no cartridge case.
CB Cap	A very short, low-powered cartridge, generally 0.22″ calibre, with a conical-shaped bullet.
Chamber	The portion of the rear end of the barrel which receives and supports the cartridge. In a revolver, the chambers are not part of the barrel, but are bored in the revolving cylinder behind the barrel.
Chamber, Fluted	A chamber which has longitudinal grooves cut in the wall to assist in extraction.
Chamber Marks	Individual microscopic marks present on the chamber walls as a result of manufacturing.
Chamber Throat	The area in a chamber immediately in front of the case mouth which leads the bullet into the rifling. Also called **Leade** or **Forcing Cone**.
Charger	A clip containing rounds of ammunition as a means of rapidly reloading a magazine. Also called **Clip** or **Stripper Clip**.
Choke	A constriction near the muzzle of a shotgun to reduce the spread of shot. A fully choked barrel, whatever its bore, will have a restriction of 0.04″.
Chronograph	A device to measure the velocity of missiles. Basically, it consists of two photoelectric detectors connected to a microsecond clock. As the missile passes over the first detector, it starts the clock and when it passes over the second, it stops the clock. By knowing the separation of the detectors and the time taken, the velocity can be calculated.
Cock	To place a firing mechanism under spring tension. In flint-lock weapons, this was the spring-loaded vice used to hold the flint.
Coefficient of Form	A numerical term indicating the profile of a missile.
Comparison Microscope	Basically the bottom half of two normal microscopes connected by an optical bridge to one set of eye pieces. This allows the comparison of two objects simultaneously.
Copper Units of Pressure (CUP)	A means of comparing the degree of compression of copper cylinders to pounds pressure produced. See **Crusher Gauge**.
Compensator	A device attached to or integral with the muzzle of a weapon to divert some of the combustion gases in an upward direction to counter recoil.

Crane	The part of a solid frame revolver on which the cylinder is swung out to load and unload. Also called a **Yoke.**
Crimp	The bevelling of the top of a cartridge case to hold the projectile in place. In shotgun cartridges, a portion of the top of the cartridge case will be folded over top to achieve the same purposes.
Critical Angle	The angle of elevation of the barrel at which maximum range is obtained.
Crusher Gauge	A means of measuring the pressure produced in a barrel. Achieved by venting some of the gases off and allowing them to act on a piston to crush a cylinder of metal of known hardness. The degree of crushing will give an indication of the pressure produced.
Cylinder	The rotating part of a revolver which contains the chambers.
Cylinder Gap	The gap between the end of the barrel and the front of the cylinder.
Cylinder Stop	A metal peg which locates with **cut-outs** in the exterior of the cylinder. This stops the cylinder rotation in the correct position to align the chamber and bore.
Cylinder Stop Cut-Out	Grooves cut into the external surface of the cylinder into which the cylinder stop engages to ensure correct alignment of chamber and barrel. Also called **Bolt Notch** or **Cylinder Stop Notch.**
Damascus	An obsolete barrel-making process involving the hot welding together of steel and iron wires which are then wound round a mandril and hot welded into a tube.
Dermal Nitrate Test	The treatment of paraffin wax casts of the hands with a solution of diphenylamine in concentrated sulphuric acid. This reagent visualizes propellant particles, that is, oxidizing agents, as deep purple-coloured spots. Also gives positive reactions to urine, face powder, fertilizer, weed killer, etc. Unreliable and no longer used. Also known as **Paraffin Wax Test.**
Detonate	Term used with explosives meaning to explode with sudden violence. Propellants do not detonate under normal circumstances, but merely rapidly burn.
Discharge	The firing of a weapon.
Double Action	A method of operating a revolver whereby a single long and relatively heavy pull on the trigger rotates the cylinder,

cocks the hammer then drops it all in one action. Some self-loading pistols also have a double-action trigger mechanism where a long pull on the trigger cocks the hammer then drops it to fire the weapon.

Double Base Powder	A propellant containing both nitrocellulose and nitroglycerine.
Drilling	A three-barrelled long arm containing a combination of smooth and rifled barrels.
Driving Edge	The driving edge of the rifling on a fired bullet with a right twist is the left edge of the rifling groove. Also called the **Leading Edge**.
Dum-Dum Bullet	Soft-point 0.303″ calibre rifle bullets made by the Dum-Dum Armoury in India. Hollow-point bullets are often wrongly called dum-dum bullets.
Ejection	The act of expelling a fired cartridge case from a weapon.
Ejection Port	The opening in the receiver or slide of a self-loading or automatic weapon through which the fired cartridge case is ejected.
Ejector	Generally a small pin which the cartridge case strikes when it has been pulled out of the chamber by the extractor.
Ejector Marks	Marks left on the base of a fired or sometimes unfired cartridge case by the ejector.
Energy	The capacity of an object to do work. Generally expressed in joules or foot pound.
Energy, Muzzle	The energy of the projectile at the muzzle. Normally measured over a short distance from a few feet in front of the muzzle.
Escutcheon	Small metal plate on a weapon displaying the company name.
Express Cartridge	A rifle calibre cartridge of higher than normal velocity.
Exterior Ballistics	The study of a missile from the muzzle to the target.
Extractor	A spring-loaded claw attached to the bolt or breechblock which engages in the extractor groove as the breech is closed. When the breech is opened the extractor claw extracts the cartridge from the chamber.
Extractor Groove	The groove in a cartridge just forward of the cartridge head into which the extractor engages.
Extractor Mark	The mark left in the extractor groove of a cartridge.

Feed Ramp	A sloping surface at the breech end of the chamber of magazine fed weapons which guides the cartridge from the magazine into the chamber.
Firearms Identification	A discipline of forensic science concerned with the forensic examination of arms and ammunition. Often wrongly referred to as ballistics examination.
Firing Pin	The part of the mechanism which strikes the primer to fire the cartridge.
Firing Pin Drag Marks	Marks caused by the firing pin dragging across the primer during the extraction purposes.
Firing Pin Impression	The mark left on the primer of a fired cartridge case by the firing pin.
Flash Hole	The hole connecting the primer pocket to the main body of the cartridge case which allows the flash from the primer to reach the propellant charge.
Flash Suppressor	A muzzle attachment designed to reduce the muzzle flash produced on firing. Generally only on military weapons.
Flechette	Small dart-like nail generally loaded as multiple projectiles in shotgun and rifle cartridges.
Full Auto	A designation for fully automatic fire.
Full Cock	The position of the hammer when the weapon is in the position ready to fire.
Fulminate of Mercury	High explosive compound used in primers.
Gas Operated	An automatic or semi-automatic weapon in which the propellant gases are used to operate the mechanism.
Gauge	An American term for the bore of a shotgun. Based on the number of round lead balls of the same diameter as the barrel which weighs 1 lb. Thus, a 12-bore barrel has the same diameter as a ball of lead weighing $\frac{1}{12}$ lb.
Gilding Metal	Copper/zinc alloys used for bullet jackets. Generally in the region 90–95% copper and 5–10% zinc.
Grain	Avoirdupois measurement of weight with 7000 gr equalling 1 lb. Generally used in American and English measurements relating to ammunition components.
Grease Groove	Cannelure used to hold bullet lubricant.
Greiss test	Chemical spot test for nitrites.
Grip	In handguns, the part of the weapon held by the hand and in long arms, the piece of stock to the rear of the trigger.

Grip Safety	A safety mechanism on some weapons which prevent the weapon being fired unless the weapon is tightly held.
Groove	See Rifling.
Gun Cotton	Another name for nitrocellulose.
Gunpowder	The generic name for black powder.
Gunshot Residues (GSRs)	The residues emanating from a fired weapon. These include primer residues and propellant residues.
Half Cock	The hammer position when it is held in an intermediate, and deep bent, and cannot be released by pulling the trigger.
Hammer	The component of a firearm which provides the force on the firing pin to discharge the primer.
Hammer Block	A safety mechanism which blocks the hammer from reaching the firing pin.
Hand	The lever which engages in the **Ratchet** at the rear of the cylinder which rotates it to bring a fresh cartridge in line with the firing pin. Also called **Cylinder Pawl.**
Handgun	Weapon designed to be fired in the hand.
Hand-loading	The process of assembling ammunition from cartridge case, primer, propellant and primer.
Hangfire	When a cartridge fails to fire immediately after the firing pin strikes the primer.
Headspace	The distance from the face of the closed breech to the surface in the chamber on which the cartridge rests. It is basically the distance the cartridge case is allowed to stretch during firing.
Ignition Time	The time from firing pin contact with the primer until the bullet begins to move out of the cartridge.
In Battery	When the breech mechanism is in the closed position ready to fire.
Incendiary Bullet	Bullet containing a chemical compound in the nose which ignites on striking a hard object.
Inside Lubricated Bullet	One in which the bullet lubricant is held within a cannelure which is situated inside of the cartridge case.
Individual Characteristics	Those marks produced during manufacture or subsequently due to corrosion, mistreatment, etc. which are individual to that weapon and none other.
Interior Ballistics	The study of what happens between the moment the firing pin strikes the primer until the missile leaves the barrel.

Land, Bullet	The portion of the bullet **not** engraved by the raised part of the rifling in the bore of the weapon. When viewing a cross section of a fired bullet, the bullet lands will be the parts on the bearing surface of the bullet which are standing proud of the rest.
Land, Rifling	The raised portion between the grooves in a rifled bore.
Lead Azide	A highly explosive chemical used in priming compounds.
Lead Styphnate (also sometimes referred to as Lead styphenate)	A highly explosive chemical used in priming compounds. (Lead 2,4,6-trimifroresor-cindte $C_6HN_3'C_8Pb$).
Leading	The accumulation of lead in the bore of a weapon, generally through insufficient bullet lubricant or a very rough bore.
Load, Duplex	A round of ammunition containing two projectiles.
	A round of ammunition containing two different types of propellant powder.
Loading Density	The ratio of case volume to propellant volume.
Long Recoil	A mechanism, designed to reduce recoil, in which the barrel and bolt recoil to the rear locked together. At the fullest extent of the recoil, the barrel unlocks from the breech and moves forward. When fully forward, the breech moves forward, feeding the next cartridge into the chamber.
Long Rifle	Designation for one type of 0.22″ calibre rimfire cartridges.
Lubaloy	Winchester Western trade name for a very thin coating of copper applied to plain lead bullets. Now only seen on 0.22″ calibre rimfire ammunition.
Magazine	Spring-loaded container for cartridges; can be box, drum, rotary or tubular.
Magazine Safety	A safety device found on some semi-automatic pistols which prevents the weapon from being fired unless a magazine has been inserted.
Magnum	Designation for a cartridge which is larger, contains a heavier missile or produces a larger velocity than the standard round.
Mainspring	The spring in the lockwork which produces the power for the hammer or striker.
Marshall's Reagent	Reagent used in the Greiss test as a spot test for nitrites in GSR.
Maximum Range	The maximum range obtainable when firing a weapon at the optimum angle. This angle is generally between 30° and 45°.

Metal Fouling	Lead or jacket material stripped from the bullet and deposited in the bore of the weapon leading to inaccuracy and in extreme cases, bullets stuck in the bore. Generally caused by either lack of lubrication or a very rough bore.
Metal Patched Bullet	Another name for fully jacketed bullet.
Microphotograph	Misnomer for photomicrograph, that is, a photograph taken through a microscope.
Microscopic Comparison	The comparison of two items under a comparison microscope.
Minute of Angle	$\frac{1}{60}$ of 1°. A minute of angle at 100 yds equals 1.047″. Thus, if the sights of a rifle are set 1 min off centre, then at a range of 100 yd, the bullet will strike the target 1.047″ off centre.
Misfire	The failure of the primer to ignite or the primer to ignite the propellant.
Muzzle	The end of the barrel from which the bullet emerges.
Muzzle Brake	A device fitted to the muzzle end of the barrel which vents the high-pressure gases produced on firing in an upward direction to reduce recoil.
Muzzle Crown	A slight counter boring of the muzzle end of the bore primarily to protect the rifling.
Muzzle Energy	The kinetic energy of the missile as it leaves the muzzle.
Muzzle Flash	The flash caused by incandescent gases as they emerge from the muzzle of a fired weapon.
Muzzle Loader	A weapon in which the propellant and missile are loaded from the muzzle end of the barrel.
Nipple	A hollow cone-shaped tube inserted into the breech end of a muzzle loader onto which is placed a percussion cap. When the cap is struck by the hammer, the flame so produced travels down the hollow nipple and into the propellant igniting it.
Nitrocellulose	Nitrated cellulose of any form but generally cotton wool. The primary ingredient of modern propellants.
Nitroglycerine	Nitrated glycerine. By itself a high explosive, but when dissolved in nitrocellulose becomes stable and produces an extremely efficient propellant.
Obturation	The sealing of the chamber due to the expansion of the cartridge case due to the high pressures produced.
	Also, the sealing of the bore of a weapon due to the expansion (upset) of the bullet due to the high pressures produced.

Outside Lubricated Bullet	A bullet in which the bullet lubricant is in a cannelure situated outside of the cartridge case. Generally, only 0.22″ rimfire ammunition has this type of lubrication system.
Over-Powder Wad	A thin card-like disc placed over the propellant to seal the bore.
Overshot Wad	A thin card-like disc placed over the shot to retain it in place.
Pantascopic Camera	A camera designed to photograph the circumference of a bullet. Also called a **Peripheral Camera** or a **Balliscan Camera**.
Parabellum	Latin meaning 'for war'. Designation for military pistol cartridges, in particular 7.65 mm Parabellum and 9 mm Parabellum.
Paraffin Test	See Dermal Nitrate Test.
Pellet	General name for air gun ammunition.
Pen Gun	A weapon disguised to look like a pen. Usually 0.22″ calibre.
Percussion Cap	Small metal cap containing a priming compound for use with muzzle-loading percussion weapons.
Piezoelectric Pressure Measurement	Method of measuring breech pressures using a quartz crystal which, when compressed, gives out a small electric charge. As the charge is proportional to the pressure applied, accurate breech pressure measurements may be obtained.
Pistol	Basically a handgun.
	When using English terminology, a weapon can be a self-loading pistol, a revolving pistol or a single-shot pistol.
	Using American terminology, a pistol is generally either a self-loading pistol or a single-shot pistol.
Polygonal Rifling	Rifling grooves which have a rounded rather than a sharp-edged profile.
Potassium Nitrate	Component of black powder which supplies oxygen for the burning.
Powder	Common term for propellant.
Powder, Ball	Propellant in spherical balls. Introduced by Winchester Western in 1933.
Powder, Black	Mechanical mixture of potassium nitrate, sulphur and charcoal.
Powder, Blank	A very fast-burning powder designed for use in blank cartridges.

Powder, Double-Based	Propellant consisting of nitrocellulose dissolved in nitroglycerine.
Powder, Semi-smokeless	An obsolete propellant consisting of a mixture of nitrocellulose and black powder.
Powder, Single-Based	Propellant consisting only of nitrocellulose.
Powder, Smokeless	Basically a modern propellant, either single or double based, which produces far less smoke than black powder.
Pressure barrel	A very heavy barrel fitted with a pressure measuring device to measure the pressure during firing.
Primer	The ignition system for the propellant.
Primer, Battery Cup	Type of primer container used in shotgun ammunition which serves as a holder for the primer components.
Primer, Berdan	A plain cup containing only the priming compound and a foil covering. In this system, the anvil is integral with the cartridge case. An American design used mainly in military ammunition.
Primer, Boxer	A self-contained priming system consisting of priming compound, anvil and foil cover in a primer cup. British design and used almost exclusively in commercial ammunition.
Primer, Corrosive	A priming mixture the residues of which tend to corrode the bore.
Primer Pocket	Cavity in the centre of the head of a cartridge case into which fits the primer cap.
Primer Residues	The residues from the discharge of a primer, usually referred to as GSR (Gunshot Residues). Sometimes also called FDR (Firarms Discharge Residues).
Primer, Rimfire	A priming system where the priming compound is held in the hollow rim of flanged ammunition. Generally, only 0.22″ calibre rimfire ammunition is available nowadays.
Primer Setback	When the primer cap moves partially out of its pocket during firing.
Proof Mark	A stamp applied to a weapon to show that it has passed a test showing that it is capable of firing cartridges of commercial pressure.
Propellant	In firearms, the chemical compound or mixture of chemical compounds which, when ignited, produce a high volume of gases. These gases are used to propel a missile from the barrel of a weapon.
Pump Action	A type of breech closure which is accomplished through an operating rod attached to a moveable fore-end. This

fore-end is moved back and forward to open and close the action. Also called **Slide Action**.

Pyrodex	Modern substitute for black powder.
Range	An area for the firing of weapons.
	The distance between firearm and target.
Range, Effective	The maximum range which a projectile could be expected to produce a lethal wound. A very subjective measurement.
Range, Maximum	The maximum distance a missile will reach when fired at its optimum angle of elevation. This angle is usually between 35° and 45°.
Ratchet	A notched area at the rear of the cylinder of a revolver which causes the cylinder to rotate when moved by the hand.
Rate of Twist	The distance over which the rifling completes one turn.
Receiver	The basic part of the firearm which houses the action and breech and to which the barrel and butt stock are assembled.
Recoil	The rearward motion of the weapon as a result of firing.
Recoil Shield	The plate at the rear of the cylinder of a revolver which supports the cartridge during firing.
Recoil Spring	The large spring which controls the rearward movement of the slide during the firing stage and returns the slide to battery.
Reload	A cartridge which has been assembled, often non-commercially, from cartridge case, primer, propellant and bullet. Usually, the cartridge case has already been fired and is not new.
Revolver	A handgun having a series of chambers in a cylinder mounted in line with the barrel. A mechanism revolves the cylinder that the chambers are successively aligned with the bore. Only the chamber which is, at any one time, in line with the bore is fired.
Ricochet	A bullet which has struck an object and glanced off.
Rifling	The spiral cut into the bore to impart a spinning motion to the bullet. Normally, the rifling is composed of 'Lands' and 'Grooves'. The lands are the parts of the bore left standing after the grooves have been cut away.
Rifling Pitch	The distance the projectile must move along a rifled bore to make one revolution. Usually expressed as 'one turn in x inches (or millimetres).'

Sabot	A lightweight carrier for a small calibre projectile allowing it to be fired in a larger-calibre bore.
Safety	A mechanism designed to prevent accidental discharge of a firearm.
Scanning Electron Microscope (SEM)	A very sophisticated microscope using electrons to visualize the object rather than light. It is capable of magnifications in excess of 1 000 000 times. With an **Energy-Dispersive X-ray Analyzer (EDX)**, attachment is also capable of non-destructively analyzing the object under view.
Sear	A part of the mechanism which connects with the bent to keep the action in the cocked position until released by the trigger.
Sectional Density	The ratio of the bullet weight to its cross-sectional area.
Self-loader/Semi-automatic	A repeating firearm requiring a separate pull of the trigger for each shot fired. After manually loading the first round from the magazine, the weapon will use the energy of discharge to eject the fired cartridge and to load a new cartridge from the magazine into the barrel ready for firing.
Shot	Spherical pellets, generally of lead, loaded into shotgun cartridges.
Shot, Steel	A replacement for lead shot in shotgun cartridges.
Silencer	A device attached to the muzzle of a weapon to reduce the report of firing. Due to the gases escaping from the gap between the cylinder and barrel, this type of device is of little use in revolvers. Likewise, if the bullet is travelling faster than the speed of sound, the supersonic crack will not be reduced.
Skid Marks	As a bullet travels from the cylinder of a revolver to the rifling in the barrel, it has considerable forward velocity but no rotational velocity. As it hits the rifling, it takes some short period of time for it to catch up giving rise to a widening of the land impression marks. These are called skid marks.
Sodium Rhodizonate	A chemical used as a spot test for lead.
Spalling	Material dislodged from the face opposite the strike face by the impact of a missile.
Striations (Stria)	Longitudinal marks caused by imperfections in the tool making them. These are by their nature individual to that tool and none other.

Swaging	The process of manufacturing the rifling in a barrel by either squeezing the barrel onto a negative form of the rifling.
Tattooing	Marks on the skin caused by the close-range impact of propellant particles.
Terminal Ballistics	The effect a missile has on the target.
Terminal Velocity	The maximum velocity obtainable by a falling object in free air.
Trace Metal Detection	A chemical spray test to reveal traces of metal which may have been transferred to a hand through the holding of a metallic object.
Tracer Bullet	Bullet, usually military, with a small pellet of brightly burning compound in the base which permits its trajectory to be viewed; can be day or night tracer.
Trajectory	The curved path of a bullet from muzzle to target due to the gravitational effects on the bullet.
Transfer Bar	A bar which, when the trigger is pulled, interposes itself between the hammer and firing pin, thus allowing the weapon to be fired.
Trigger	That part of the mechanism which, when manually pulled, causes the firearm to fire.
Trigger Guard	A curved piece of metal protecting the trigger from being accidentally pulled.
Trigger Pull	That pressure required on the trigger to fire the weapon.
Twist, Direction Of	The direction in which the rifling spirals.
Ultraviolet Light (UV)	That part of the spectrum of light beyond violet and before X-rays.
Velocity	The speed of a missile.
Velocity, Terminal	The maximum velocity attainable by a free-falling object in air.
Wad	A card, felt or plastic sealing device in a shotgun cartridge. Generally, **Over-Powder, Cushion Wad, Undershot and Overshot.**
Wadcutter Bullet	A bullet with a flat nose to neatly cut the paper in target shooting.
Walker Test	A spot test for nitrites in GSR.
Yaw, Bullet	The spiral movement of the bullet about its axis before it settles down to stable gyroscopically stable flight.

Appendix 1   Important dates in the History of Firearms from 1247

Event	Date
The first record of the actual use of gunpowder in Europe is a statement by Bishop Albertus Magnus in 1280 that it was used at the Siege of Seville in 1247.	1247
Roger Bacon gives an account of gunpowder in his Opus Majus (Actually, his account was written in cryptic form. See T. *Explosives* (Pelican Books, 1942)).	1267
Hand cannon had appeared in the field of battle during the reign of Edward III.	1364
Handguns were known in Italy in 1397, and in England they appear to have been used as early as 1375.	1375
The first mechanical device for firing the handgun made its appearance.	1424
We hear of armour being penetrated by bullets and the handgun showing signs of becoming a weapon capable of rudimentary precision.	1425
Henry VII organized the corps of Yeomen of the Guard, half of whom were to carry bows and arrows while the other half were equipped with harquebuses. This represents the first introduction of firearms as an official weapon of the Royal Guard.	1485
Rifling was invented.	1498
The first wheel lock or 'rose lock' was invented somewhere about this date.	1509

Handbook of Firearms and Ballistics: Second Edition   Brian J. Heard
© 2008 John Wiley & Sons, Ltd.

Event	Date
Firearms were recognized as hunting arms as early as 1515, and a book (*Balleates Mosetuetas y Areabuces Pablo del Fucar*, Naples, 1535) on sporting firearms appeared in 1535.	1535
Rifled arms have been made since 1540.	1540
The hair trigger was a German invention of about 1540.	1540
The invention of the typical Spanish lock is attributed by some writers to Simon Macuarte the Second, about 1560.	1560
The snaphaunce lock, the forerunner of the true flintlock, was invented about, or considerably earlier than 1580.	1580
The standard flintlock gun came in.	1630
The London Gunmakers' Company initiated proofs when it was first incorporated, but it is not clear whether private proofs or a trade proof house common to the Company was used (a crowned A was given as the mark).	1637
The screw or cannon barrel pistol came in probably prior to 1640.	1640
The bayonet was introduced by the French; it was a long narrow blade with a wooden plug handle and was simply dropped into the muzzle of the musket.	1640
The London Gunmakers' Company enjoyed powers which enabled them to enforce proof when the second charter was granted in 1672.	1672
A ring attachment was added to the bayonet so that it no longer served as a muzzle plug.	1680
The earliest known English breech-loading rifle was made by Willmore, who was apprenticed to Foad in 1689.	1689
The 'Brown Bess' was known in Ireland as a 'King's Arm' from its use by William at the Battle of the Boyne.	1690
The whole English army was equipped with flintlocks.	1690
Snaphaunces continued to be made on the Continent until about 1700.	1700
In the reign of Queen Anne, the 'Brown Bess' was known as the 'Queen's Arm' in Ireland.	1702–1714
The socket bayonet had appeared and was adopted in the British service.	1710
The letters G.R. were adopted as a mark in the reign of George I (1714–1727), but successive Georges did not add any variant.	1714–1830

Event	Date
The broad arrow as a sign of government property was adopted during the reign of George I, and the word TOWER was marked on the lock plate of many of these arms.	1714–1727
The French established their 'Manufacturers Royales' at Charleville, St. Etienne and Maubeuge.	1718
The large box lock type of pistol made its appearance.	1730
A few hammerless flintlock sporting guns were made by Stanislaus Paczelt, of Prague in Bohemia.	1730
The use of pistols for duelling purposes became general as the practice of carrying the rapier or small sword died out between 1750 and 1765.	1750–1765
The duelling pistol was entirely unknown until about 1760.	1760
Note: Meetings were fought with horse pistols prior to this date. The horse pistol showed a marked development into the true duelling pistol from 1760 to 1775.	1760–1775
Double shotguns were rather peculiar arms, usually of the under- and over-revolving barrel type until about 1760.	1760
Duelling pistols became officially standardized weapons, then it was laid down that they should be 9 or 10 in. barrelled, smooth bore flintlocks of 1 in. bore, carrying a ball of 48 to the pound.	1777
The top rib in double-barrelled guns appeared.	1780
Spring bayonets are common on blunderbusses and pistols of the period subsequent to the date of the patent (John Waters, Pat. No. 1284).	1781
The first patent for single trigger locks for double arms (James Templeman, Pat. No. 1707) was in 1789.	1789
Single trigger pistols, with side-by-side, and also under- and over-barrels, were made by Egg.	1789
The acorn pattern trigger guard extension toward the barrel used up to about 1790.	1790
Joseph Manton's first patent (no. 1865) introduces the 'break-off' breech, into which the barrel fits with a lump instead of being secured by a tang and screw as previously used.	1792
The swivel ramrod attached to the piece by a stirrup appeared.	1800
The 'First Baker Rifle' was issued.	1800
The half-stocked pistol with the lower rib beneath the barrel fitted to carry the ramrod came in.	1800

Event	Date
The 'Second Baker Rifle' was introduced.	1807
Alexander Forsyth patented the detonating or percussion principle.	1807
The first serious military breech loader was an American invention, Colonel John H. Hall's patent. This was made first as a flintlock, then as percussion, and is the first breech loader officially adopted by any army. The flintlocks were made until 1832, the percussion model from 1831.	1811
The copper percussion cap is not definitely alluded to in the patent records until 1823, but appears to have been invented about 1814–1816.	1814–1816
The saw handle was very popular, both in flint and percussion pistols.	1815–1825
The true flintlock revolver is the very rare weapon made by Collier.	1820
Flints were converted to percussion cap, and the flint principle lost favour.	1820
The percussion cap came into general use on private arms.	1826
The Delvigne (French) service rifle was invented.	1826
The 'Third Baker Rifle' was issued.	1830
The back action lock made its appearance.	1830
The Robert rifle was invented by Robert, a gunsmith of Paris.	1831
The percussion cap system of ignition was in common use before it was adopted for the service weapon. It was tested at Woolwich in 1843.	1843
Coach pistols supplied to the guard of public stage coaches are extremely rare, but were made with flintlocks and brass lock plates until 1835.	1835
Percussion cap locks fitted with a pierced platinum disc below the nipple gradually fell into disuse and are seldom found in arms subsequent to 1835.	1835
Colt claims the ratchet motion, locking the cylinder and centre fire position of the nipples as particular points of his specification.	1835
Colt did not know that the revolving principle was an old European idea until he visited England in 1835.	1835
The Enfield percussion carbine – 0.65 in. calibre with hinged spring triangular bayonet folding below the barrel was made for Constabulary service.	1835
Dreys released the first needle fire rifle.	1836

Event	Date
The true pinfire cartridge emerged.	1840
It was not until 1840 that we definitely found a breech-loading needle gun cartridge patented (Wm. Bush, Pat. No. 8513).	1840
The Brunswick rifle superseded the Baker model.	1840
Duelling declined in England after 1840.	1840
The period of decadence of duelling was noticeable for the production of rather short-barrelled pistols.	1840–1850
A few service arms were converted to the percussion cap system in 1839, and it was officially adopted in 1842.	1842
The service percussion musket was mainly experimental until 1844.	1844
A double-barrelled 26 in. barrel, 0.67 in. calibre arm was issued for constabulary use.	1845
The Prussians concentrated on experiments with the needle gun in 1844, and it was used in the war of 1848.	1848
The shotgun or fowling piece began its separation from the musket in the latter half of the 18th century and divorce was completed by 1850.	1850
The Minie (English) service rifle was introduced.	1850
Minie's patent for the self-expanding bullet was purchased and adopted by the British Government for the Enfield rifle.	1851
Muzzle loading was so unassailably established we do not find a single breech-loading cartridge weapon shown by a British firm at the Great Exhibition of 1851.	1851
Colt delivered a lecture on Colt revolvers before the Institute of Civil Engineers during his visit to London in 1851.	1851
Charles Lancaster brought out his central fire under lever gun with extractor and the first true centre fire cartridge.	1852
Colt procured a factory at Thames, Bank, Pimlico, London, and produced replicas of his standard pistols marked on the barrel 'Address Col. Colt, London'.	1853–1857
The Pritchett bullet, a plain lead cylindroconoidal plug with a shallow base depression, was selected as the best type of bullet for the new Enfield rifle.	1853
Note: Later, this was superseded by the Enfield bullet.	
During the Crimean War, 25 000 Enfield rifles were made in America. This war was the last war in which all combatants used muzzle loaders.	1854–1856

Event	Date
There never was an official British State-maintained arms factory until the government established Enfield as a government factory when the Birmingham gunmakers struck for higher wages in the middle of the Crimean War.	1855
Whitworth rifles were produced.	1857
Duelling continued in India to the date of the Mutiny.	1857–1858
The first recorded European revolver for central fire cartridges appears to be that patented by Perrin and Delmas in 1859.	1859
The first effective and widely used magazine repeater was undoubtedly the Spencer carbine, patented in the United States in 1860.	1860
Tyler F. Henry brought out the Henry rifle.	1860
In the American Civil War, both breech and muzzle loader were used.	1860–1865
Breech loaders were coming into general use by 1861.	1861
The first central fire repeater appears to have been Ball's carbine made by the Lamson Arms Co., Windsor, Vermont, USA in 1863.	1863
For all practical purposes, metallic cartridges were not widely introduced until 1863–1864.	1863–1864
The first cartridge repeater shotgun appears to have been the Roper of 1866.	1866
The Snider service rifle was issued.	1866
The Henry was merged into the Winchester.	1866
Claims have been made for an American origin for choke boring, but these have never been proved, and there is no doubt that it was the invention of Pape of Newcastle in 1866.	1866
Duels were fought in Ireland until as late as 1868.	1868
The Martini–Henry rifle was issued.	1869
The first European magazine military arm was the Swiss Vetterli rifle of 1869–1871.	1869–1871
In 1866, the Chassepot was authorized and all branches of the French army were equipped with the weapon by 1870.	1870
The Franco-German War was almost entirely a breech-loading affair.	1870–1871
The first true hammerless gun appears to have been that of Murcott in 1871–1871.	1871–1871
The first bolt action military repeater seems to be the Edge rifle (Pat. No. 3643) of 1874–1875.	1874–1875

Event	Date
First double action revolver.	1877
Lee patented his box magazine.	1879
The French adopted the Lebel rifle.	1886
The Gras–Kropatschek rifle was issued for the French Marine.	1886–1887
Winchester repeating shotguns were first introduced.	1887
The Maxim was officially adopted in the army as a machine gun.	1887
The Lee–Metford rifle was adopted by Great Britain.	1888
The first self-loading weapon to appear on the market was the Borchardt pistol in 1893.	1893
The Bergmann pistol appeared.	1894
The first Mannlicher self-loading pistol was introduced.	1894
The Mauser combination self-loading pistol or carbine, the wooden holster serving as a stock attachment was introduced.	1898
The Browning self-loading pistol of 0.32 in. calibre, made its appearance.	1898
The Webley Fosberry 0.455 self-loading revolver was introduced.	1901
All self-loading pistols were of small bore until 1903.	1903
The Winchester Firearms Company brought out the first widely sold self-loading rifle.	1903
The Webley self-loading 0.455 in. pistol was adopted for the British Navy.	1905
German 9 mm PB Luger introduced.	1908
Broom-handled 7.63 mm Military Mauser introduced.	1912
Browning 9 mm PB HP introduced.	1935
British 0.303 Bren MG.	1936
German MG42 7.92 × 57 mm introduced.	1938
British Lanchester 9 mm PB sub-machine gun introduced.	1940
British Sten Mk I 9 mm PB smg introduced.	1941
Thompson M1 0.45ACP smg introduced.	1942
Kalashnikov AK47 7.62 × 39 mm assault rifle.	1947
Israeli 9 mm PB Uzi smg introduced.	1953
British Sterling 9 mm PB smg introduced.	1953
Chinese 7.62 × 25 mm Type 54 introduced. This is a direct copy of the Russian TT.	1954
0.44 Remington Magnum introduced.	1955
Chinese Type 58 7.62 × 39 mm assault rifle introduced. This is an exact copy of the Russian AK47.	1956

Event	Date
0.454 Casull Cartridge introduced.	1959
Czechoslovakian 7.65 mm ACP Skorpion introduced.	1960
H&K MP5 9 mm PB introduced.	1965
Beretta 92 introduced.	1976
Steyr–Manlicher AUG 5.56×45 or 7.62×51 mm NATO.	1978
Israeli 0.257 Magnum Desert Eagle introduced.	1982
Glock 17 9 mm PB introduced.	1983
Barrett M82A1 0.50 Browning long range sniping rifle introduced.	1983
Enfield L85A1 5.56×45 mm NATO introduced.	1985
Israeli 0.50 Action Express Desert Eagle introduced.	1991

Appendix 2   GSR results for Chinese and USSR ammunition

6.72 × 25 mm GSR Results

Headstamp	GSR results											
	Pb	Sb	Sn	Ba	Hg	Al	Fe	Cu	K	Cl	S	Other
11 55		X	X						X	X	X	
11 57		X	X						X	X	X	
11 58		X	X						X	X	X	
11 62		X	X						X	X	X	(2)
11 62		X	X		X				X	X	X	(3)
11 63	X	X	X						X	X	X	
11 64		X	X		X				X	X	X	
11 64		X	X		X					X	X	
11 65		X							X	X	X	
11 65		X	X						X	X	X	(2)
11 69		X	X						X	X	X	
11 71		X	X				X	X	X	X	X	
11 76		X	X		X				X	X	X	
11 77		X	X		X				X	X	X	(4)
11 82		X	X		X						X	
11 83		X	X		X				X	X	X	(2)
11 83		X	X		X				X	X	X	Ag, Cl
11 83		X	X								X	(3)
11 84		X	X		X				X	X	X	(5)
11 85	X	X	X	X		X						
11 85		X	X		X				X	X	X	(3)
11 88		X	X		X				X	X	X	
38 43		X	X	X	X				X	X	X	
38 44	X	X	X		X				X	X	X	

Handbook of Firearms and Ballistics: Second Edition   Brian J. Heard
© 2008 John Wiley & Sons, Ltd.

6.72 × 25 mm **GSR Results** (cont.)

Headstamp	GSR results										
38 45		X	X					X	X	X	
38 78	X	X	X	X	X			X	X		
38 N		X	X			X	X	X	X	X	
70 57		X				X	X				X
70 59		X	X			X	X			X	X
38 6 46*		X	X	X				X	X	X	
270*49*		X	X					X	X	X	
270*46 III		X	X			X		X	X	X	
710*45 IV	X	X	X	X		X	X	X	X	X	
1113*45		X	X			X	X	X	X	X	
539 = <49>		X	X			X					X
547 44	X	X	X			X		X	X	X	
TT 57		X	X			X		X	X	X	
T T 85		X	X					X	X	X	
21 32 17 53		X	X					X	X	X	
21 32 20 53		X						X	X	X	
34 2 21		X	X					X	X	X	
*3*50		X	X			X		X	X	X	
*3*50		X	X			X	X	X	X	X	
*3>44		X	X								X
21 51		X	X			X		X	X	X	
21 52		X	X			X		X	X	X	
21 52		X	X					X	X	X	
21 67		X	X					X	X	X	
21 67		X	X					X	X	X	
21 68		X	X					X	X	X	
21 69		X	X					X	X	X	
21 70	X	X	X			X		X	X	X	
21 73	X	X	X	X				X	X	X	
21 89		X	X				X	X	X	X	
22 52		X	X			X		X	X	X	(4)
22 52		X	X					X	X	X	
22 54		X	X					X	X	X	(2)
22 54		X	X			X		X	X	X	
22 69	X	X	X					X	X	X	As
343 53		X	X					X	X	X	
53 343 33		X				X		X	X	X	
343 54		X	X			X		X	X	X	

6.72×25 mm GSR Results (cont.)

Headstamp				GSR results									
343 54	X	X	X		X					X	X	X		
343 54		X	X		X					X	X	X		
54 4 21	X	X								X	X	X		
54 5 21		X	X		X					X	X	X		
54 5 21		X	X		X					X	X	X	Si	
54 3 21		X	X		X					X	X	X		
54 2 21		X	X		X					X	X	X		(2)
52 2 21		X	X							X	X	X		
54 17 21		X	X		X		X			X	X	X		
54 54		X	X		X					X	X	X		
801 33		X	X				X	X	X	X	X			
04 57	X	X	X	X	X					X	X	X	Ca, Si	
Headstamp	Pb	Sb	Sn	Ba	Hg	Al	Fe	Cu	K	Cl	S	Other		

N.B. If conflicting results have been obtained for cartridges with the same headstamp, the number in brackets indicates the number of samples with that composition.

Other Chinese GSR results.

Headstamp	GSR results											
7.62 × 17 mm GSR analysis results												
	Pb	Sb	Sn	Ba	Hg	Al	Fe	Cu	K	Cl	S	Other
301 83		X	X		X				X	X	X	
3084		X	X		X				X	X		
9 mm MAKAROV GSR analysis results												
81 83		X	X		X				X	X	X	(2)
38 73		X	X		X				X	X	X	
38 79		X	X		X				X	X	X	
39 71		X	X		X				X	X	X	
21 68	X	X	X	X	X				X	X	X	
21 69		X	X		X				X	X	X	(2)
21 73	X	X	X	X					X	X	X	
04 72		X	X						X	X	X	
7.62 × 39 mm GSR analysis results												
21 65		X	X		X				X	X	X	
23 68	X	X		X								Mg
31 65	X	X	X	X					X	X	X	
<270>51		X	X		X				X	X	X	
60 60	X	X	X	X	X				X	X	X	
661 65		X	X		X					X	X	(2)
661 71		X	X						X	X	X	
947 75	X	X	X		X					X	X	Cr
9661 67	X	X	X		X				X	X	X	
bxn 85 (Blank)	X	X						X	X	X		P
9 mm Parabellum results												
L 9 × 19 Y 9x (Commercial)	X		X		X							Si
L 9 × 19 Y9X (Military)	X		X		X							Si
Other calibres of Chinese ammunition												
0.22 LR CJ	X		X									
12 Bore Elephant	X	X	X	X		X						

Appendix 3 Primer content of some cartridge-operated nail guns

Nail gun	Cartridge manufacturer	Primer content
With piston		
Obo SG75	Societe Outifix (Gevelot)	Pb, Sb, Ba
Hilti DX400B	Dynamit Nobel	Pb, Ba
Hilti DX450	Dynamit Nobel	Pb, Ba
Pistonless		
Ucan CT333	Eley, UK	Pb, Ba
Omark 823	Omark USA	Pb, Ba
Ramset	Winchester Eley Australia	Pb, Ba

Handbook of Firearms and Ballistics: Second Edition   Brian J. Heard
© 2008 John Wiley & Sons, Ltd.

Appendix 4 Commercial and General Abbreviations for Bullet Configurations

ACC: Accelerator – sub-calibre bullet fitted into conventional cartridge with a plastic sabot.

ACP: Automatic Colt Pistol. Used as a designation for cartridges designed specifically for self-loading pistol cartridges (i.e. 0.380 ACP, 0.45 ACP). Can also be in lower case (i.e. 0.380 acp or 0.45 acp).

AP: Armour-piercing bullet usually with a tungsten core.

API: Armour-piercing incendiary. As above but with the addition of an incendiary pellet in the nose.

BBWC: Bevel base wad cutter.

BRPT: Bronze point. Bronze insert in tip improves trajectory, velocity and energy transfer at extreme ranges. Tip expands rapidly when driven back through bullet.

BT: Boat tail.

CL: Core-Lokt. A Remington bullet with the core bonded to the jacket. Also has a progressively tapered jacket which initiates and controls expansion.

CP: Copper-plated. Lead bullet dipped in copper; reduces lead fouling and is cheaper than copper coating.

EFMJ: Expanding full-metal jacket. Federal's answer to areas with restrictions on hollow points. A regular full-metal-jacket bullet but with a rubber tip to the lead core. The tip of the jacket is grooved which collapses on striking the target producing petal-like expansion and delivers energy without over-penetration.

Handbook of Firearms and Ballistics: Second Edition   Brian J. Heard
© 2008 John Wiley & Sons, Ltd.

ENCAP: Encapsulated. A bullet completely encapsulated with a metal jacket, usually by electroplating. Intended to reduce environmental lead contamination in training ranges.

EP: Expanding point. Winchester developed bullet to assist expansion in small-calibre hollow-point bullets (i.e. 0.25 ACP). The hollow point has a round lead ball inserted into the hollow-point cavity to assist in feeding and expansion on striking target.

ERBT: Extended-range boat tail. Long-range bullet by Remington.

Exp: Express cartridge. Used on high-powered sporting rifle cartridges to designate a higher velocity and kinetic energy than the standard calibre. Initially used with the additional prefix "nitro" to distinguish between black powder and nitrocellulose-based propellants.

FMJ: Full-metal jacket. Jacketed bullet with lead core exposed at base.

FMJE: Full-metal-jacket encapsulated. Like FMJ but also has the base covered and does not expose any of the lead core.

FNSP: Flat-nose soft point. Similar to the FPJ but has lead-exposed point that expands on impact.

FP: Flat-pointed bullet.

FPJ: Flat-point jacketed. Full-metal-jacketed bullet with a flat point. Most 0.40 S&W and 0.30–30 Winchester rounds have this design. The 0.30–30 Winchester has a tubular magazine and uses a flat-point bullet to prevent accidental detonation of one round by the tip of another during recoil.

FRAN: Frangible. Prevents ricochet by breaking apart on contact. Usually made from lead, iron or tungsten dust bonded with hard wax or an epoxy resin. Originally used in fairground mini-range ammunition to prevent ricochet or penetration of the target. Has recently been developed for air marshals to avoid over-penetration and ricochet aboard airplanes. Metal dust other than lead is used in non-toxic ammunition for use in indoor ranges (see chapter on non-toxic ammunition).

GCK: Gas check. Metallic cup or disc is attached to bottom of lead-alloy bullet. Decreases gas blow-by, increases velocity and reduces lead fouling.

GDHP: Gold dot hollow point. Speer's hollow-point bullet with jacket bonded to lead core to prevent separation and to control expansion and penetration.

GS: Golden Saber. Remington-designed controlled expansion bullet.

GS: Grand Slam. Speer's design for hunting big game. Jacket is 45% bigger at base to prevent rollback and to retain the bullet's weight. Internal jacket flutes ensure proper expansion. Bullet's core is a ternary (three-part) alloy, which is poured into jacket at 900 °F to prevent jacket slippage.

H&H: Holland and Holland cartridge designed for the company for their high-powered sporting rifles.

HSHK: Hydra-Shok. Federal's handgun defence bullet. Unique centre-post design delivers controlled expansion. Notched jacket transfers energy efficiently and penetrates barriers while retaining stopping power.

JHC: Jacketed hollow cavity. Jacketed bullet with hole in tip to promote expansion on impact. More often designated JHP (i.e. jacketed hollow point).

KTW: A metal-penetrating round. Originally made of sintered tungsten and later hardened brass coated with green-coloured polytetraphcoroethylene (PTFE). Only sold to law enforcement agencies.

LHP: Lead hollow point.

LRN: Lead round nose.

LSWC: Lead semi-wadcutter.

LSWC-GC: Lead semi-wadcutter gas checked.

LWC: Lead wadcutter. Bullet with completely flat nose to cut clean hole through paper targets.

LTC: Lead truncated cone. Conical-shaped bullet with flat point.

MC: Metal cased. Jacketed bullet.

Mag: Magnum, to specify cartridges of a higher power that standard (i.e. 0.41 Rem Mag., 0.44 Mag).

MK: MatchKing. Bullets made to exact tolerances by Sierra for target shooting.

MOLY: Moly-coated. Bullet is coated with molybdenum disulphide to reduce friction and to increase velocity.

NBT: Nosler ballistic tip. Nosler developed this bullet with a polycarbonate tip that protects the bullet from damage in the magazine resulting from recoil. The tip also stabilizes the bullet for long-range shooting and insures reliable expansion when the bullet hits its target.

NP: Nosler partition. Has two lead cores separated by bullet jacket. Top part of jacket is thin and promotes expansion of bullet. Bottom part of bullet has thicker jacket that retains bullet's weight, stops fragmentation and increases penetration.

Nyclad: Federal's bullet totally coated with black nylon to reduce friction and to reduce lead pollution in ranges.

PB: 9×19 mm and 7.65×19 mm cartridges with Latin designation Parabellum (i.e. for war).

PEP: Positive expanding point. Winchester bullet for maximum impact on medium-size game.

PG: Partition Gold. Winchester's proprietary design delivers expansion and penetration on medium- and large-size game at wide range of impact velocities. Rear core is hard lead alloy, locked in place with a heel crimp to prevent core slippage and to maximize penetration. Patented steel cup reinforces, prevents core distortion at high-impact velocities.

PL: Power-Lokt: Remington's small-game bullet produces benchrest-level accuracy. Copper jacket is electrolytically bonded to lead core.

+P: "Plus P" (10–15% over-pressure). High-pressure cartridge for use in standard weapon where greater power is required.

+P+: "Plus P Plus" (20–25% over-pressure). As above but even more powerful. Only recommended for weapons with a strong frame and usually only sold to law enforcement agencies.

PP: Power-point-jacketed soft nose from Winchester delivers maximum energy on impact. Notches around jacket's mouth improve upset and ensure uniform, rapid expansion.

PSP: Pointed soft point. Pointed bullet retains velocity over long ranges. Soft nose initiates rapid bullet expansion. Jacket and core toughness vary according to calibre and weight of bullet.

PTHP: Platinum-tipped hollow point. A Winchester design for handgun hunters.

PWC: Pointed wad cutter. Lubricated solid lead with pointed nose. Formed by swaging process with sharp shoulder for clean hole punching in paper targets.

RN: Round nose. Ogival nose shape to bullet.

RNFP: Round-nose flat point. As above but with flat point to ogive.

RNL: Round-nosed lead. Plain lead bullet with ogive-shaped bullet.

S&W: Designation for cartridges designed specifically for Smith and Wesson designed weapons (i.e. 0.38 S&W revolver).

SBK: Sierra BlitzKing. Used for varmint hunting; has plastic tip inserted into bullet cavity, which expands on impact.

SFS: Supreme fail safe. Hollow-point bullet with lead core and steel insert. Delivers controlled expansion, deeper penetration and bullet weight retention.

SLD: Solid. Rifle bullet usually made from copper, bronze or brass alloy, but not lead. For thick-skinned game (i.e. buffalo, elephant).

SMP: Semi-pointed.

SP: Soft point. Jacketed bullet with exposed lead tip.

SP: Spire point. Long sharp-pointed bullet.

SPTZ: Spitzer. Pointed bullet.

ST: Silver Tip: Winchester trade name for bullet with an alloy aerodynamic tip.

SWC: Semi-wadcutter. Intermediate between a wadcutter and a round-nosed bullet.

SPCL: Soft-point Core-Lokt. Locks progressively heavier jacketed mid-section to lead core, preventing separation. Stays together on impact, expands in a controlled manner and mushrooms uniformly.

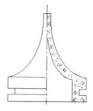

Figure 4.A.1 Tres Haute Vitesse bullet.

SPT: Spitzer. Pointed bullet normally used in modern military rifles.

SST: Super Shock Tipped. Hornady's design incorporates a pointed polymer tip that improves ballistic coefficient and increases velocity, accuracy and down-range power. Specially designed jacket grips and controls expanding core, allowing maximum expansion while retaining mass and momentum.

SXT: Supreme Expansion Technology. Winchester's personal protection bullet. Designed with reverse tapered jacket, has uniform expansion, greater accuracy and reliable firearm functioning.

TAP: Tactical Application Police. Designed by Hornady specifically for law enforcement. Heavier bullet weight and polymer tip provide rapid expansion and excellent barrier penetration (without over-penetration).

TC: Truncated cone. Similar to an inverted cone, but with the top chopped off.

TCHP: Truncated cone hollow point. Same as truncated cone but with a hole in top to promote expansion in target.

THV: Tres Haute Vitesse. French for 'very high velocity'. Very light weight and thin spire pointed bullet made, usually, from a bronze alloy. High speed and design result in not only huge wound cavities, but also good metal and bullet resistant vest (BRV) penetrative capabilities (Figure 4.A.1).

TMJ: Total metal jacket. Same as full-metal jacket, except base is also jacketed.

TMWC: Target-Master wad cutter. Wad cutter bullets made to highest tolerances to achieve best accuracy possible.

V-MAX: Varmint Express Ballistic Tip. Hornady's ballistic-tip varmint bullet has a polymer insert that aids in rapid expansion once bullet hits target.

WC: Wadcutter: Essentially a round-nosed bullet without the round nose. Gives a sharp edge for cutting clean holes in the target when target shooting.

XTP: Extreme Terminal Performance. Hornady bullet designed for controlled expansion at wide range of handgun velocities. Bullet's jacket and core expansion rates are the same, reducing separation and increasing trauma in target.

Z BULLET: Zinc alloy bullet made in various configurations by National Bullet Co.

Appendix 5 Trade Names

A.A	Trade name of Azanza y Arrizabalaga, Spain Manufactured copies of cheap Belgian pistols
Acme	Trade name of spur trigger revolvers made by Hopkins & Allen about 1885
Acme Arms	Used by J.Stevens Arms Co. about 1882
Acme Hammerless	Used by Hulbert Bros on Hopkins & Allen revolvers about 1893
Adams Patent Small Arms Co, London.	Manufacturer of Adams designed firearms 1864–1892
Aetna	Spur trigger revolvers made by Harrington and Richardson about 1876
Ajax Army	On revolvers sold by Meacham & Co. 1880
Alamo	On revolvers sold by Stoeger from W. Germany
Allen	Trade name on revolvers made by Hopkins & Allen
Alpine Industries	Makers of M1 carbines 1962–1965
Robert Adams	London gunmaker 1809–1890 patented the first successful double-action revolver in 1851. His revolvers were used during the Crimean War, the Indian Mutiny, the US Civil War, and the Anglo-Zulu War.
AM	Abbreviation on Italian military arms meaning Air Force

Handbook of Firearms and Ballistics: Second Edition   Brian J. Heard
© 2008 John Wiley & Sons, Ltd.

American International	Importers in Salt Lake City, Utah (Mormons?) of 0.22 RF calibre machine guns notably the AR180
Amadeo	Trade name of Barthelet D. Amadeo of Eibar, Spain
	Manufactured copy of 'Galand', calibre 11 mm, marked 'Privilegiado A.P.E.G. Eibar'
Anciens Establissments Pieper	Bayard pistols from 1907 to 1939
Anschutz, Bruno	German manufacturer of sporting arms 1919–1926
Arizmendi	Trade name of F Arizmendi y Goenaga of Eibar, Spain
	Manufactured copied of Belgian pistols as well as their own design
Arminius	Trade name of Friederich Pickert pre-World War II (WWII) probably manufactured in East Germany. Now made by Weihrauch
Astra	Astra-Unceta y Cia. Formed in 1908 in Eibar. Moved to Guernica 1913. In 1926 name changed to Unceta y Cia and in 1953 to Astra Unceta y Cia
Auto Ordinance Corp	Developers of the Thompson smg. New York City about 1920
Baby Russian	Model name used by H. Kolb and Sedgeley on small revolvers
Martin Bascaran	Made Spanish copies of cheap Belgian pistols 1919–1927
Baltimore Arms Co.	Maker of hammerless shotguns 1895–1902
Bauer Firearms	Manufacturer of pocket pistols, 1972–1984 Fraser, MI, USA
Beeman Airguns	Founded in 1972 and sold to S/R Industries of Maryland in 1993
Beretta, Pietro	Italian manufacturer of shotguns, rifles and pistols back to 1680
Bernadelli, Vincenzo	Italian manufacturer of sporting arms since 1865
Bicycle	Trade name on revolvers made by Harrison & Richardson
Isaac Blisset	Leadenhall Street, London, England 1822–1845. Double-barrelled side lock hammer shotguns
Bolumburu Gregorio	Belgian manufacturer of cheap-quality self-loading pistols 1917–1923
Boy's Choice	Trade name used on revolvers from Hood Firearms about 1873

John Brown	John Brown, a silversmith and gunsmith worked at Lincolns Inn Fields, 1805–1808. Very high-quality flintlock pistols
Bulldog & British Bulldog	Trade name on revolvers made by Forehand & Wadsworth about 1871–1890
Cadet	Trade name on revolvers sold by Maltby & Curtis 1876–1910
CETME	Centro de Estudios Tecnicos de Materiales Especiales of Madrid Spain. Name of military rifle made between 1958 and 1982
Cogswell & Harrison	Gunmakers in London 1770 to date and 1924–1938 in Paris
Cow Boy	Trade name of Fabrication Francaise
Colt, London	Factory opened in January 1853 and was located at Pimlico on the bank of the river Thames, London. Over the next 3 years, it produced a total of 11 000 Model 1849 Pocket revolvers and 42 000 Model 1851 revolvers. There were also some 700 third Model Dragoons with parts made in Hartford and assembled in London.
Colt, USA	Founded in 1847. Among the most famous products from Colt are the Walker Colt used by the Texas Rangers and the Single Action Army. Later well-known Colt revolvers include the Colt Python and Colt Anaconda. John Browning also worked for Colt for a time, and came up with the Colt M1900 pistol, leading to numerous pistol designs including the famous Colt M1911
Crown Jewel	Trade name used on pistols by Norwich Falls Pistol Co. 1881–1887
Cumberland Arms	Trade name used by Grey & Dudley Hardware Nashville, USA
CZ	Trade name of Ceska Zbrojovka 1919 to date
Daisy	Trade name on revolvers from Bacon Arms Co 1864–1891
Daly Arms Co.	Revolver maker in New York 1890
Dan Wesson	Revolver manufacturer bought by CZ in late 1980s
Georges Henry Daw	British percussion gunmaker in the 1850s
Destroyer Carbines	Spanish police carbines made by Gaztanaga y Cia, Eibar 1926 and more recently by Ayra Duria S.A. of Eibar
Detonics	Manufacturer of pistols in Seattle, USA 1964 to present
Dreadnaught	Trademark used by Hopkins and Allen 1984

Dreyse	Trade name of Rheinische Metallwaren und Maschinenfabrik. Needle gun in 1836
DWM	Abbreviation for Deutsche Waffen und munitionsfabriken
Eastern	Trade name used by Stevens Arms Co.
Egg, Henry W, Joseph and Durs.	1 Piccadilly, London. 1851–1880, makers of fine flintlock pistols, shotguns and rifles
EIG	Importer of cheap firearms into the US from Italy between 1950 and 1970
Electrique	Trade name used on electrically fired guns made by SMFM 1963
El Gamo	Originated in 1880s, when known as Antonio Casas, S.A. making various lead products. 1945 specialized in air gun pellets then high-quality air rifles and pistols
EM-GE	Trade name on blank/tear gas/flare guns made by Moritz & Gerstenberger (before 1939) or Gerstenberger & Eberwein (after 1939).
Empire State	Trade name on revolvers, double- and single-barrelled shotguns made by Meriden Firearms Co. 1895–1918
Enfield	Royal Small Arms Factory (RSAF), Enfield, has produced British military rifles and muskets since 1804. It was built on the instructions of the Board of Ordnance on marsh land at Enfield Lock, on the banks of the River Lea, round about the end of the Napoleonic War. It was privatized in 1984 along with a number of Royal Ordnance Factories to become part of Royal Ordnance Plc, which was later bought by British Aerospace (BAe), who closed the site in 1988.
Estrella	Trade name of Bonifacio Echeverria. Started business in 1905. In 1919, Bonifacio formally registered the Star trade name, and all subsequent weapons were marked as such.
Excel	Trade name used by Iver Johnson
FAB	Trade name used by Rohn on revolvers
Fabrica Nacional De Armas Mexico	Began production of weapons before World War I (WWI). Manufacturing H&K G3 rifles since 1980 for the Mexican army
Federal Arms	Used by Sears Roebuck on revolvers made by Meriden Arms
F.I.E.	Firearms Import and Export Co., Miami, Florida. Manufacturers and importers of cartridge and black powder weapons

Finladia Firearms	Tikka Arms, Finland
Finnish Lion	Target rifles made by Valmet of Finland
FMG	Fab de Material de Guerra Ejercito of Santiago, Chile
FN	Fabrique National d'Arms de Guerre, herstal, Belgium from 1889 to date. Manufacturers of sporting and military arms. Noted for Browning designed weapons
Forjas Taurus	Manufacturer of Taurus branded revolvers. Taurus produced its first revolver, the Model 38101SO, in 1941.
Fortuna Werke	Current manufacturer of sporting arms in Suhl, Germany
Frommer	Fegyveres Gepygar Resvenytarsasag, Budapest. Later Femaru Fegyver-es Gepyar. Manufacturer of the Fromer STOP a long recoil 0.32 pistol.
Frontier Bulldog	Trade name on Fab d'Armes de Guerre.
FS	On grip of Fromer Stop pistols
Galesi	Trade name of Industria Armi Galesi pistols. Founded in 1910. They began to produce pistols in 1914, following Italy's entry into WWI. The first design was a 6.35 mm blowback design based on the Browning 1906.
Game Getter	Trade name on Marble Arms
Geco	August Genshaw, only manufactures ammunition now
Golden Eagle	Trade name on guns made by Nikko Arms Co., Japan
Grant, Stevens and Sons	Makers of sporting arms in London, England 1841 until merged with C. Lancaster and Lang and Hussey to form Joseph Lang and Co.
W.W. Greener	In 1829, William Greener had been working in London for Manton, a prominent gunmaker, returned to his hometown of Newcastle and founded the W. Greener company. In November 1844, he moved his business to Birmingham. During the period of 1845–1858, W. Greener was appointed to make guns for the Prince Consort. Money obtained from supplying South Africa with two-groove rifles enabled the company to erect a factory on 'Rifle Hill', Aston, in 1859. This was around the time when the firm really began to prosper. Mr Greener was a firm believer in the concept of muzzle loaders and refused to make any breech loaders. Hence, his son, William Wellington Greener, struck out a line of his own (the W.W. Greener company) and produced his first breech loader in 1864. When William Greener died in 1869, the two companies were amalgamated together as the W.W. Greener Company, and carried on by William Wellington Greener.

Guardian	Trade name on revolvers made by Bacon Arms Co.
Haenel, C.G. Waffen Und Fahrradfabrik	Manufacturers of sporting and military firearms from 1840 to 1945 when it became Ernst Thalman Werk, VEB.
Haerens To Jhus	Marking on Bayard/Bergman pistols made by Anciens Etablissments Pieper under Danish contract.
Halcon	Trade name on 0.22 rifles of Metalurgica Centro in Argentina
James Hall	Birmingham, UK 1820-33. Manufacturer of fine flintlock pistols
Hammerli	Lenzburg, Switzerland from 1921 to date. Makers of high-quality target pistols and rifles
Harrington and Richardson	Worcester, Mass, US since 1874 now in Gardener Mass. Manufacturers of sporting and military arms
Hartford Arms	Manufacturers of handguns in Hartfort, CT from 1929. Purchased by High Standard in 1932
Herculese	Trade name used by J. Steven Arms Co. on shotguns
Holland and & Holland	98 New Bond St, London. 1835 to present. Manufacturers of the finest quality shoguns and rifles.
Hopkins and Allen	Established in Norwich, CT in 1868 taken over by Marlin-Rockwell in 1917 now owned by Numrich Arms Co. Made all types of sporting arms but best known for their early revolvers
H&R	Abbreviation for Harrington and Richardson
Husqvarna	Trade name for Husqvarna Vapenfabrik Akiebolak, makers of a wide range of firearms since 1867 in Jonkoping, Sweden
HW	Abbreviation and trade name on Herman Weirauch Sportenwaffenfabrik. On revolvers made in West Germany
Hi Standard	CT, USA. In 1932, Hi Standard, a drilling company purchased the Hartford Arms and Equipment Company and began making 0.22 calibre target pistols. Company closed in 1984. Reopened in 1993 in Houston, Texas
Hy Score Arms Co.	One of the largest American air gunmakers. Began production in 1948 copying a British air pistol design where the piston encircles the barrel
IAB SpA	Manufacturer of reproduction black powder and cartridge replica weapons in Italy
IAG	Abbreviation for Industria Armi Galesi on self-loading pistols

IBM	Abbreviation for International Business Machines. Made M1 carbines during WWII at Poughkeepsie, NY
ICI	After the First World War, many of the UK ammunition and explosives manufacturers were brought together under Nobel Explosives to become Nobel Industries, which was a founding element of Imperial Chemical Industries Ltd (ICI) in 1926. Kynoch, along with names such as Eley, became brands of subsidiaries. With general downturn in ammunition requirements, the sidelines in sporting cartridges were discontinued by Imperial Metal Industries (IMI), of which ICI was part, in 1970. IMI became independent of ICI in 1977, still producing rimfire and shotgun cartridges for the sporting markets. The more economically viable production of shotgun and rimfire ammunition continued. The Ammunition Division was incorporated separately as Eley Limited in 1983.
I.M.I.	Abbreviation for Israeli Military Industries, Tel Aviv, Israel
Indian Arms Co.	Current manufacturer of pistols in Detroit, MI
Industria Armi Galesi	Manufacturer of pistols in Collebeato, Italy since 1914
Inglis, John Co	WWII manufacturer of Browning HP 9 mm PB pistols and Bren M/Gs in Toronto Canada.
Ingram	Trade name on smg made by Police Ordinance of LA and Military Armament Co. of GA, USA
Ingram Gordon	In 1964, Gordon Ingram designed the M10 smg in 0.45 acp. Also produced M11 in 9 mm PB
Inland	Division of General Motors made M-1 Carbines during WWII
Interarms	Manufacturers of sporting arms since 1954
Irwin-Pedersen	Manufacturer of M-I Carbines, Grand Rapids. None accepted for service use, although some were re-tooled by Saginaw and put into service.
Ithaca Gun Co	Manufacturer of sporting arms in Ithaca, NY
Iver Johnson Arms & Cycle Works	Started as Johnson, Bye & Co in 1871 at Worcester Mass. In 1883 became Iver Johnson and changed to current name in 1884. In 1891 moved to Finchburg, MA, USA
Jackson Hole Rifles	Manufacturer of take-down rifles about 1972
Jaga	Used by Frantisek Dusek on Czechoslovakian pistols

Jager, Franz & Co	Gunmakers in Suhl, Germany from 1923 to 1929
Jeffrey W & Son	Manufacturer of high-quality sporting and military arms in Plymouth England. 1866–1929
J.G.A.	Trade name of J.G. Anschutz
J-9	Trade name used by Zavodi Crevena Zastava of Belgrade, Yugoslavia
Johnson-Tucker Firearms	Made MI type carbines in St Louis, US about 1965
Just, Joseph	Manufacturer of sporting arms in Ferlach, Austria 1919–1939
K.G.F.	Abbreviation for Koenigliche Gewehrfabrik of Potsdam, Germany
Killdeer	Trade name on single-shot rifles made by Western Arms Co. 1910
Kimball	In 1958, the J. Kimball Arms Co. went into business (and out of business quite shortly) producing a 0.30 carbine caliber pistol that closely resembled a slightly scaled-up High Standard Field King
Knockabout	Trade name on Mod311 shotguns made by Stevens Arms Co.
Kodiak Manufacturing Co.	North Haven, CT, USA manufacturer of rifles and shotguns about 1965
Koishigawa	See Kokura Arsel Japan
Kokura Arsenal	Tokyo, Japan from about 1900 until end of WWII. Originally named Koishigawa
Kolibri	Trade name used by Georg Grabner, Austria. The 2 mm Kolibri (also known as the 2.7 mm Kolibri Car Pistol or 2.7 x 9 mm Kolibri) is the smallest commercially available centerfire cartridge patented in 1910 and introduced in 1914 by Franz Pfannl, an Austrian watchmaker, with financial support from Georg Grabner. It was designed to accompany the Kolibri semi-auto pistol or single-shot pistol, both marketed as self-defence weapon.
Kongsberg	Government arms manufacturer in Kongsberg, Norway
Krico	Trade name used by Kreigeskorte of Stuttgart-Hedelfingen West Germany on current sporting arms
Krieghoff, heinrich	Manufacturer of military and sporting arms from 1929 to 1945 in Suhl, Germany and from 1945 until present in Ulm, Germany

Kruschitz	Trade name on custom arms made in Vienna about 1956
K.T.G.	Shotgun manufacturer in Hitachi, Japan.
La Industria Orbea	Trade name of Orbea Hermanos, Eibar, Spain
Lancaster, Charles & Co.	London England 1867–1900 successor to Charles William Lancaster. Best known for the manufacture of very high-quality sporting rifles and big game hunting pistols. Merged with Stephen Grant & Sons and Lang and Hussey in 1900 to become Joseph Lang & Co. Ltd.
Lang, Joseph & Co.	See above
Lefever Sons & Co	Started in Syraccuse in 1976 and in 1926 purchased by Ithaca Gun Co.
Le Francais	Trade name of Mre. Francais d'Armes et Cycles. Manufacturer of a tip-up barrel 0.32 acp pistol
L&H Gun Co.	Manufactured military style firearms with surplus parts 1972–1974 in San Antonio Texas. Purchased by Springfield Armoury
Liliput pistol	The 4.25 mm Liliput pistol is one of the smallest semi-automatic handguns made (the Kolibri is generally considered the smallest). The Liliput was manufactured by Waffenfabrik August Menz in Suhl, Germany from approximately 1920 to 1927.
Lithgow	Royal Australian Small Arms Factory, NSW Australia making military arms. From 1959 until the early 1990s, the Australians used the British L-1A1 (licensed to the Australian company of the Lithgow Small Arms Factory) as their standard personal weapon, when it was replaced by the F-88 (the Australian designation for the Steyr AUG)
Llama	Llama firearms are produced by the firm of Gabilondo y Cia located in Elgoibar, Spain. In 1931, Gabilonda Y Cia decided to do its part in revitalizing the reputation of the lagging Spanish firearms industry. To this end, they began making almost exact copies of the Colt/Browning M1911 design. The name Llama (pronounced Yama) was chosen for this line of pistols to separate it from earlier production of 'Ruby style' pistols of WWI vintage. The Ruby pistols did not have the quality control they needed and as a result earned a very bad reputation for Spanish firearms and Gabilondo y Cia. The new line of Llama pistols was produced in 9 mm Long, 0.38 ACP and 0.45 ACP.

Long Branch	Canadian Arsenals Ltd of Long Branch, Ontario. Manufacturer of military arms
Lovell Arms Co.	1840–1891, Boston, MA, USA. Became J.P. Lovell & Sons about 1870. Possibly absorbed by Ivor Johnson in 1868 but allowed to operate under its own name
Luger	Trade name of Stoeger Industries. Used on P08 pistols and copies which are sold by Stoeger.
Lynx	Trade name on revolvers made in South Africa
M.A.B.	Abbreviation for Mre. D'Armes Automatiques Bayone. Manufacturer since 1921 of automatic pistols based on the Browning mechanism. Used during WWII by German forces (some models exist with German marks) and also by the French army. Now used as surplus pistols for the French police.
M.A.C.	Abbreviation for Military Armaments Corp. Manufacturer of M10 and M11 smg.
Mamba	Trade name on pistols made by Relay Products of Johannesburg, South Africa
Mannlicher-Schoenauer	Trade name on rifles made by Daimler Puch of Steyr, Austria used on rotary magazine bolt action rifle adopted by both the Greek and Austrian Armies in 1903
Joseph Manton	From 1760 to 1835 was a much celebrated British gunsmith who was to revolutionize sport shooting, vastly improve the quality of weapons and father the modern artillery shell
Manufrance	Trade name for Mre. Francais d'Armes et Cycles
Manurhin	Trade name for Manufacture de Machines du Haut-Rhin, France who at the end of the WWII started producing Walther handguns (PP, PPk and P38) They produced the M73 pistol for the French police, but it was too expensive to manufacture in numbers. In order to produce a more affordable handgun, Manurhin signed an agreement with Sturm Ruger using Ruger's investment casting technology and know-how. They did also start the production of a new revolver. It was called the M-88. This revolver kept the cylinder and barrel of the MR-73, but the frame was the one from the Ruger Security Six. The French police was then issued this gun.
Marble Arms Manufacturing	From 1898 to 1908 manufacturing the 'Game Getter' rifles and shotguns
Marksman	Trade name on rifles made by H. Pieper of Liege about 1900

Marlin Firearms	1870 established as J.M. Marlin. In 1881 became Marlin Firearms Co. in 1915 Marlin Rockwell and in 1926 Marlin Firearms Co again. Made sporting and military rifles and shotguns.
Mars	Long recoil, very high-powered pistol designed by Gabbett–Fairfax and made by Webley and Scott in Birmingham, England between 1895–1915 available in 8.5 mm, 9 mm and 0.45 (both long and short chambering),
Marson, Samuel & Co	Manufacturer of sporting and military arms in Birmingham, England 1840 on.
Martini Henry	The Martini–Henry (also known as the Peabody–Martini–Henry) was a breech-loading lever-actuated rifle adopted by the British, combining an action worked on by Friedrich von Martini (based on the Peabody rifle developed by Henry Peabody), with the rifled barrel designed by Scotsman Alexander Henry. It first entered service in 1871 replacing the Snider-Enfield, and variants were used throughout the British Empire for 30 years. It was the first British service rifle that was a true breech-loading rifle using metallic cartridges.
Mathiew Arms Co	Manufacturer of rifles in Oakland, CA, USA, 1950–1963
Mauser Werke AG.	Established 1864, manufacturer of sporting and military rifles. Their designs were built for the German armed forces, and have been exported and licensed to a number of countries in the later nineteenth and early twentieth century, as well as being a popular civilian firearm. In the late twentieth century, Mauser continued making sporting and hunting rifles. In the 1990s, it became a subsidiary of Rheinmetall. Mauser Jagdwaffen GmbH was split off and continues making rifles.
Melior	Trade name on pistols made by Robar et Cie
Mikros	Trade name of Mre. D'Armes des Pyrenees on pistols from 1934 to 1939 and 1958 to date
Minneapolis Firearms Co.	Made palm pistols about 1891
MKE	Trade name of Kirikkale Tufek Fb. Turkey. Used on Walther PP copies
Charles Moore	London, England from 1820 to 1843, produced fine quality pistols

Mossberg O.F. & Sons	Manufacturer of sporting arms from 1892 Oscar F. Mossberg and 1919 O.F. Mossberg
Nagoya	Japanese military weapon plant to 1948
National Postal Meter	Manufactured M-1 carbines
New Nambu	On copies of Colt M1911A1 made in Japan by Shin Chau Kogyo of Tokyo
Newton Arms Co.	Made rifles in Buffalo, NY from 1914. Closed in 1918 and reorganized in 1918 as Newton Rifle Co. Finished trading in 1931
Nitro Proof/Special	Used on shotguns made by J. Stevens Co.
Niva	Trade name of Kohout & Spol on Czechoslovakian pistols
Norinco, China	The China North Industries Corporation official English name Norinco, manufactures vehicles (trucks, cars and motorcycles), machinery, optical-electronic products, oil field equipment, chemicals, light industrial products, explosives and blast materials, civil and military firearms and ammunition, etc. Norinco is also known outside of China for its high-tech defence products, many of which are adaptations of Soviet equipment. Norinco produces precision strike systems, amphibious assault weapons and equipment, long-range suppression weapon systems, anti-aircraft & anti-missile systems, information and night vision products, high-effect destruction systems, fuel air bombs, anti-terrorism and anti-riot equipment and small arms.
North American Arms Co.	Quebec Canada manufacturer of 1911A1 pistols
Numrich Arms Co.	West Hurley, NY. Current manufacturers of sporting and black powder arms, machine guns and parts. Present owners of Auto Ordinance and Hopkins and Allen
NWM	Abbreviation of Nederlandische Wapenen Munitiefabrik in Holland. Sporting and military arms to present
Oak Leak	Trade name of J. Stevens Arms Co on shotguns
Ojanguran Y Vidosa	Hangun manufacturer in Eibar, Spain, 1922–1938
Orbea	Orbea Hermanos, manufacturer of handguns in Eibar Spain, 1916–1922
Omnipol	Czechoslovakian arms export organization in Prague

Owen	The Owen Machine Carbine, was an Australian submachine gun designed by Evelyn (Evo) Owen in 1939. The Owen was the only Australian-designed service firearm of WWII and was the main submachine gun used by the Australian Army during the war
Oy Tikkakoski	Rifle manufacturer in Tikkakoski, Finland from 1963. Used trade names Tikka and Ithaca LSA
Pancor Corporation	Produced the Pancor Jackhammer a bore, gas-operated automatic weapon. It is one of very few fully automatic shotguns, and although patented in 1987, it never entered full-scale production
Paragon	Trade name used by Hokins and Allen on revolvers about 1886
Parker Bros	Meriden Mass, US 1868, produced shotguns until taken over by Remington Arms in 1934
Parker-Hale	Parker Hale Ltd. was a UK firearms, air rifle and firearms accessory manufacturer, located in Petersfield, Hampshire. It was purchased by John Rothery Wholesale Ltd in late 2000 and ceased firearm production, although cleaning kits and accessories continue to be produced. The company had over 115 years of history and produced pistols, rifles, air guns and accessories of varying sorts.
Parkhurst, William	Arms maker in Bristol, England about 1923
Pedersen Custom Guns	Division of O.F. Mossberg & Sons
Perfection Automatic Revolver	Trade name used by Forehand Arms Co, about 1890
Perla	Trade name used on Czechoslovakian pistols
Phoenix Arms Co	Makers of pocket pistols, Lowell, MA, USA, about 1920
Pieper, Henri	Liege, Belgium from 1884–1907 when company became Ancions Etablisments Pieper
Pinkerton	Used by Gaspar Arizaga, Spain on pistols
Poly Tech	PolyTech Arms Corp in association with Norinco, China produce commercial weapons. The PolyTech has been imported in both pre and post ban variations until the 1998 importation bans. Many people like the gun and say that is the best Chinese AK imported in to the United States.

PZK	Abbreviation for Posumavska Zbrojovka
Quackenbush	Henry Quackenbush manufacturer of rifles and air guns in Herkimer, NY about 1880. Dennis Quackenbush started making large bore air guns suitable for big game hunting 1992
Quality Hardware and Machine	Made M-1 carbines in Chicago, USA
R.A.	Abbreviation of Trade name Republic Arms, gunmakers in Johannesburg, SA
RA	Abbreviation on Italian military arms meaning Regia Aeronautica (Air Force)
Radom	Polish VIS M35 9 mm PB pistol
Ralock	Used by BSA, Birmingham, England on rotating block self-loading 0.22 calibre rifles
Ranger Arms	Rifle maker in Texas, USA 1972 on
Retzola	The Retolaza brothers, of Belgium, made their appearance in about 1890, with the inevitable imitation of 'Velo-Dog' type revolvers. Had strong links with gunsmiths in Eibar Spain. Continued to build automatics at low prices until the US Civil War
RE	Abbreviation on Italian military arms meaning Regia Esercito (Royal Army)
Remington Arms	Establishedin 1816 by Eliphalet Remington. In 1831 became E. Remington & Sons. In 1888 became Remington Arms Co. 1910 Remington Arms UMC Co and finally in 1925 again Remington Arms Co.
RG	Abbreviation for Rohm Gesellschaft on West German guns
Rheinmetall	Trademark of Rheinische Metallwaren Fabrik
Riverside Arms Co	Trade name used by Stevens Arms & Tool Co.
Robar et de Kirhove	Arms maker in Liege until 1958
Robin Hood	Trade name used by Hood Firearms Co about 1882
Rochester Defence Co	Made M-1 carbines during WWII
Romanski	Current manufacturer of target arms in Obendorf, Germany.
Rossi, Maedeo S.A.	Began manufacture in 1889 and continues to date making high-quality shotguns, rifles and revolvers

Rubi	Cheap-quality revolvers and self-loading pistols
Ruby	The semi-automatic 0.32 acp Ruby pistol is best known as a French WWI sidearm, the *Pistolet Automatique de 7.65 millim. genre 'Ruby'*. It was closely modelled after the Browning M1903 by Belgian Fabrique Nationale de Herstal, and was produced primarily by the Spanish Gabilondo y Urresti-Eibar firm (the official 'Gabilondo Ruby').
RWS	Abbreviation of Rheinische Westfalische Sprengstoff. Ammunition makers since 1931
Sarasqueta, Victor	Sporting arms manufacturer in Eibar Spain from 1934
Sarsilmaz	Turkish arms manufacturer established by Abdüllatif in 1880. Produces weapons and equipment for the Turkish military.
Sauer, J. P. & Sohn	J.P. Sauer & Sohn GmbH, established in 1751, is the oldest gun manufacturer in Germany manufacturing high-quality shotguns, rifles and pistols
Sears	Trade name on weapons made for Sears, Roebuck & Co.
SFM	Abbreviation for Societie Francaise des Muntions de Chasse of St Etienne, France. Notable for its THV high-velocity ammunition.
Sharps Arms Co.	Manufacturer of replica Sharps rifles in 1969 until purchased by Colt in 1970.
Simplex	The Bergmann Simplex Pistol was a German semi-automatic pistol produced from 1901 to 1914 and was chambered for the 9 mm Bergmann cartridge.
SMFM	French manufacturer of electrically fired weapons 1965
Spencer Arms	Windsor, CT, USA, makers of repeating shotguns
Spencer rifle	Designed by Christopher Spencer in 1860. It was a magazine-fed, lever-operated rifle chambered for the 0.56–56 rimfire cartridge.
Springfield	US Govt armoury in Springfield, MA, USA from 1782
Springfield Arms	Sporting arms manufacturers in Springfield, MA since 1850. Now part of Savage Arms Co.
Squibman	Trade name on arms made by Squires Bingham of the Philippines. 1930 on
S&S	Trade name of J.P. Sauer & Sohn
Standard Arms Co.	Manufacturere of rifles in Wilmington, Del. US 1909–1912

Star	Trade name of Bonafacio Echeverria, Spain. Pistols and revolvers
J. Stevens Arms and Tool Co.	Established in 1864, absorbed by Page-Lewis Arms in 1926 then by Savage Arms Co in 1936
Sterling Arms	Manufacturers of pistols and rifles. Established 1968
Stoeger Industries	Manufacturer since 1924 of good quality shotguns of all types
Swift Rifle	Manufacturer of military arms in London about 1943, most notably the military Swift Training Rifle
Tanque	Trade name of guns made by Ojanguren y Vidosa, Spain
Taurus	Trade name of Forjas Taurus of Brazil. Manufactures high-quality revolvers and pistols
TDA	Trade name of Thermodynamic Systems revolvers
Techni-Mec	Trade name of shotguns made by Fabbrica d'Armi di Isidoro Rizzini of Bresica, Italy. Founded in 1971 by Guido Rizzini and his brothers. Makers of high-quality shotguns
Terrible	Trade name on pistols made by Hijos de Calixto Arrizabalaga
TGE	Abbreviation of Tokyo Gas and Electric, used on Baby nambu pistols
Tikka	Trade name on high-quality rifles made by Oy Tikkakoski, Finland
Titan	Trade name on pistols imported into the United States from Bresica Italy. Now made in US by FIE
Tokagypt	Trade name on 9mm copy of TT3 for Egyptian Arms by femaru Fegyver es Gepgyar of Hungary
Tokarev	Russian TT33 7.62 × 25 mm pistol
Tulsky Oruzheiny Zavod	Russian manufacturers of high-quality shotguns
Uberto	Current manufacturer of sporting arms in Ponte Zanano, Italy. Best known for their reproduction Colt single-action revolvers.
UD42	The United Defense M42 was an American submachine gun in WWII. It was produced from 1942 to 1943 by United Defense Supply Corp. for possible issue as a replacement for the Thompson submachine gun and was used by agents of the Office of Strategic Services (OSS). Made in both 9 mm Luger Parabellum and 0.45 ACP prototypes, the 9 mm version was the only one to ever see widespread production.

UMC	Abbreviation for Union Metallic Cartridge Co. Ammunition makers
Union Firearms	Toledo, OH, USA. From 1903 until purchased by Ithaca. Manufacturer of shotguns and revolvers
Unique	Trade name used by C.S. Shattuck on revolvers around 1882
Unique	Tadename used by Mre. D'Armes des Pyrenees, France
United States Arms Corp.	Manufactures of revolvers in Riverhead NY since 1976
Universal Sporting Goods	Manufacturer in WWII of M-I carbines
US Arms and Cutlery	Rochester NY. Manufacturer of knife pistols about 1875
US & S	Abbreviation for Union Switch & Signal of Swissvale, US on 1911A1 pistols made in 1943
US Small Arms Co	Chicago about 1917 manufactured knife pistols
Valtion Kivaari Tehdas	Finnish state rifle factory. Made Lahti pistol in 1935
Valmet	Manufactures rifles for Finnish Defence Forces
Våpensmia	Manufacturer of NM149 sniper rifle for the Norwegian Army based on the M98 bolt action
VB	Abbreviation for Vincenzo Bernadelli on pistols
Vestpocket	Trade name found on revolvers marked Rosco Arms Co.
Vincenzo Bernadelli	Manufacturer of fine shotguns, rifles and pistols since 1721
Voere	Current sporting arms manufacturer in Kufstein, Austria
Volcanic Rifle	In 1854, Horace Smith and Daniel Wesson began manufacturing a lever-action magazine-fed pistol called the Volcanic. In 1856, it was joined by the Volcanic Repeating Rifle. They were built in their plant at Norwich, USA
Vyatskie Polyany Machine-Building Plant 'Molot'	Russian manufacturers of target rifles and shotguns
Walam	Trade name on copies of Walther PP made by Femaru Fegyver es Gepgyar in Budapest, Hungary
Walther, Carl	Manufacturer of sporting and military arms since 1886 in Zella-Mehlis, Germany until 1945, now in Ulm, Germany

Weatherby	Weatherby, Inc. is an American gun manufacturer founded in 1945 by Roy Weatherby. The company is best known for its high-powered magnum cartridges, such as the 0.257 Weatherby Magnum and the 0.460 Weatherby Magnum. Company headquarters is in the northern San Luis Obispo County town of Paso Robles, CA
Webley	The Webley Revolver (also known/referred to as the Webley Break-Top Revolver or Webley Self-Extracting Revolver) was, in various marks, the standard issue service pistol for the armed forces of the United Kingdom, the British Empire and the Commonwealth from 1887 until 1963.
Webley & Scott	Webley and Scott is an arms manufacturer based in Birmingham, England. Webley produced handguns and long guns from 1834. The company ceased to manufacture firearms in 1979 and now produces air pistols and air rifles
Westley Richards	Westley Richards is one of the oldest surviving traditional English gunmakers. It was founded in 1812 by William Westley Richards. Over the years invented some of the most widely used inventions, like the Anson & Deeley box-lock action and the Droplock which equals in status James Purdey's self-opening and Holland & Holland's removable locks
Weihrauch	Weihrauch & Weihrauch GmbH & Co. KG is a German manufacturer of target and sporting air rifles and air pistols. The company also manufactures a small range of cartridge rifles and pistols. In North America, they are often distributed under the 'Beeman' brand name. Weihrauch air rifles have a reputation for being rugged and solidly built, but heavy; an accessorized HW 77 can weigh as much as 10 lb
Wesson Firearms	Manufacturers of shotguns in Springfield, MA 1864–1868
Wesson, Dan	Daniel B. Wesson, who founded Wesson Firearms Co., Inc. in 1968 was the great grandson of D.B. Wesson, co-founder of Smith & Wesson. Dan Wesson produces innovative revolver and pistols of very high quality. In the 1980s, Dan Wesson Arms began to produce revolvers chambered for the 0.357, 0.375 and 0.445 SuperMag cartridges. In 2000, they added 0.414 Supermag, and 0.460 Rowland.

Westley Richards is one of the oldest surviving traditional English gunmakers. It was founded in 1812 by William Westley Richards. Over the years invented some of the most widely used inventions, like the Anson & Deeley box-lock action and the Droplock which equals in status James Purdey's self-opening and Holland & Holland's removable locks.

William Powell & Son, Ltd	Since 1812, William Powell & Son, Ltd has made exclusive shotguns in Birmingham, England
Winchester Repeating Arms Co.	New Haven, CT, USA, 1857 to date. In 1857, Oliver Winchester reorganized the Volcanic Repeating Arms Co. into the New Haven Arms Co and in 1866, it became the Winchester Repeating Arms Co. In 1869 absorbed Fogerty Repeating Rifle Co. and American Rifle Co., the Spencer Repeating Arms Co. in 1870 and Adrionack Arms in 1874.
WRA	Abbreviation for Winchester Repeating Arms
XL	Trade name used by Hopkins & Allen 1883
XXX Standard	Trade name used on revolvers by J.M. Marlin 1877
Yamamoto Firearms	Current manufacturer of shotguns in Kochi, Japan
Teodoro Ybarzábal	Belgian manufacturer of 9 mm Galand type revolvers
Young America	Trade name on revolvers made by Harrington & Richardson about 1900
Zabala	Spanish manufacturer of shotguns
Zastava Arms.	Serbian arms manufacturer Zastava Arms makes clones of the Russian AK-47 Kalashnikov
Zigana	Turkish manufactured 9 mm PB pistol
Zoli, Antonio	Manufacturer of shotguns in Bresica, Italy
Z-M Weapons	Z-M Weapons is a firearm design and manufacturing firm based in Bernardston, MA. The company specializes in the AR-15, M16 and its own LR-300 rifle.

Appendix 6 Gun Marks

Gun marks can include proof marks, but for this chapter, they are restricted to manufacturer's marks, inspector's marks and arsenal marks.

There are many thousand of these and it would take several books to even begin to list them. They do, however, form a very valuable aid to the forensic firearms examiner as they can give information as to a weapon's age, history, country of origin and manufacturing factory.

In addition to gun marks, there are thousands of **trade names** which can reveal similar details to that of gun marks. As with gun marks, to list all the trade names is beyond the scope of this book.

Some examples of both gun marks and trade names are listed for general reference purposes (Figure 6.A.1).

Probably the most authoritive book available on these subjects is *Gunmarks* by David Byron.

Other useful books would include:

- *English, Irish and Scottish Firearms Makers: Middle Sixteenth Century to the End of the Nineteenth Century* by A Merwyn Carey;
- *American Firearms Makers: When, Where, and What They Made from the Colonial period to the End of the Nineteenth Century* by A. Merwyn Carey;
- *Arms Makers of Colonial America* by James B. Whisker and
- *Firearms Identification* I, II and III by J. Howard Mathews.

Handbook of Firearms and Ballistics: Second Edition   Brian J. Heard
© 2008 John Wiley & Sons, Ltd.

Lions

	Trademark on Danish Madsen machine guns		Relay products of Johannesburg, SA, trademark on Mamba pistols
	Aguirre y Aranzabal of Eibar Spain Trademark on shotguns and rifles		Trademark on pistols by Harrison & Richardson revolvers

Birds

	Mre. Liegeoise d'Armes a Feu of Liege, Belgium trademark		US Springfield Armoury, inspector's mark on 1911 pistols
	Gebruder Merkel of Sujhl, Germany, trademark on rifles and shotguns		On WWII German Nazi pistols

Crests

	Ethiopian crest		Bulgarian Crest
	Argentinean crest		B.S.A. of Birmingham, England trademark
	Armi Famars, Brescia, Italy Trademark on		Herter's Inc of Waseca, US trademark
	Shotguns		
	Iver Johnson, Fitchburg, US Trademark on shotguns		Stevens Arms and Tool Co., USA on butt plates

Figure 6.A.1 Examples of gun marks.

Geometric Designs

	Tula Weapons Factory, Russia Commercial trademark		Russian gripmark on pistols
	Gerstenberger u Eberwein, W. Germany Gripmark on revolvers		Harrington and Richardson, MA., USA gripmark on revolvers
	Japanese, Kokura Arsenal mark 1928-1935	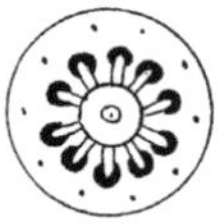	Meridian Firearms Company of CT, US. Gripmark on revolvers

In Borders

	Marlin Firearms Co., CT, USA gripmark on revolvers	MAFLAN	Israeli mark on arms for export
I M I	Israeli mark on arms for export	 SLAVIA	Vilimec of Kdyne, Czechoslovakia gripmark

In Circles

	U.S. Inspection Mark of W. Penfold on M1911 Pistols		Trocaola, Aranabal y Cia of Eibar, Spain Revolver gripmark
	Ceska Zbrojovka of Czechoslovakia grip mark		Sears Roebuck & Co. Grip mark on revolvers
	Smith & Wesson of Springfield, MA., USA Trademark on revolvers and self-loading pistols		J.P. Sauer & Sohn Trademark on pistols

Figure 6.A.1 Continued

Appendix 7 Powder Burn Rate

This powder burn rate chart is by no means a complete list of powders available and is intended for reference only (Table 7.A.1).

Powders may move up and down the list as new powders become available or as other powders are discontinued.

Powder burn rates can and do change from batch to batch, or as manufacturers change product specifications.

No. 1 on this chart is the fastest powder, with powders becoming progressively slower as you move down the list to No. 173.

Table 7.A.1 Powder burn rate chart.

	Slowest burning				
1.	R-1 (Norma)	59.	HS-7 (Hodgdon)	117.	Varget (Hodgdon)
2.	N310 (Vihtavuori)	60.	Blue Dot (Alliant)	118.	5000 (Vectan)
3.	Titewad (Hodgdon)	61.	571 (Winchester)	119.	AR2208 (ADI)
4.	AS- 30N (ADI)	62.	N105 (Vihtavuori)	120.	4064 (IMR)
5.	Nitro 100 (Accurate)	63.	No. 9 (Accurate)	121.	4064 XMR (Accurate)
6.	Bullseye (Alliant)	64.	Enforcer (Ramshot)	122.	2520 (Accurate)
7.	Solo 1000 (Accurate)	65.	4100 (Scot)	123.	4320 (IMR)
8.	Red Diamond (Scot)	66.	Steel (Alliant)	124.	N203 (Norma)
9.	AS (Vectan)	67.	2400 (Alliant)	125.	N140 (Vihtavuori)
10.	Red Dot (Alliant)	68.	N110 (Vihtavuori)	126.	N540 (Vihtavuori)

Handbook of Firearms and Ballistics: Second Edition   Brian J. Heard
© 2008 John Wiley & Sons, Ltd.

Table 7.A.1 Continued

Slowest burning

11. Promo (Alliant)	69. Lil Gun (Hodgdon)	127. 2700 (Accurate)
12. Titegroup (Hodgdon)	70. R123 (Norma)	128. Big Game (Ramshot)
13. No. 2 (Accurate)	71. H110 (Hodgdon)	129. Reloader 15 (Alliant)
14. American Select (Alliant)	72. 296 (Winchester)	130. H380 (Hodgdon)
15. AA Plus (Winchester)	73. AR2205 (ADI)	131. 760 (Winchester)
16. Clays (Hodgdon)	74. SR-4759 (IMR)	132. Brig 4351 (Scot)
17. N320 (Vihtavuori)	75. N120 (Vihtavuori)	133. H414 (Hodgdon)
18. Competition (Ramshot)	76. 4227 (IMR)	134. N150 (Vihtavuori)
19. Royal D (Scot)	77. H4227 (Hodgdon)	135. N550 (Vihtavuori)
20. WST (Winchester)	78. 5744 XMR (Accurate)	136. 4350 XMR (Accurate)
21. AP- 50N (ADI)	79. 410 (Alliant)	137. 4350 (IMR)
22. HP38 (Hodgdon)	80. N130 (Vihtavuori)	138. 7000 (Vectan)
23. AO (Vectan)	81. SP-3 (Vectan)	139. AR2209 (ADI)
24. 452AA (Winchester)	82. 680 (Winchester)	140. H4350 (Hodgdon)
25. 453 (Scot)	83. N200 (Norma)	141. N204 (Norma)
26. 231 (Winchester)	84. 1680 (Accurate)	142. Hunter (Ramshot)
27. Zip (Ramshot)	85. AR2207 (ADI)	143. Reloader 19 (Alliant)
28. 700X (IMR)	86. H4198 (Hodgdon)	144. N160 (Vihtavuori)
29. Green Dot (Alliant)	87. N133 (Vihtavuori)	145. N560 (Vihtavuori)
30. AS- 50N (ADI)	88. 4198 (IMR)	146. 4831 (IMR)
31. International Clays (Hodgdon)	89. BM1 (ADI)	147. Brig 4831 (Scot)
32. 473AA (Winchester)	90. Brig 4197 (Scot)	148. AR2213SC (ADI)
33. HS-5 (Hodgdon)	91. 2015 XMR (Accurate)	149. N205 (Norma)
34. WSL (Winchester)	92. Brig 3032 (Scot)	150. 3100 XMR (Accurate)
35. Unique (Alliant)	93. Reloader 7 (Alliant)	151. WMR (Winchester)
36. Universal Clays (Hodgdon)	94. 3031 (IMR)	152. H4831 (Hodgdon)
37. N330 (Vihtavuori)	95. Benchmark (Hodgdon)	153. MRP (Norma)
38. AP- 70N (ADI)	96. BM2 (ADI)	154. Reloader 22 (Alliant)
39. Power Pistol (Alliant)	97. N201 (Norma)	155. 785 (Winchester)
40. SR-7625 (IMR)	98. Brig 322 (Scot)	156. H450 (Hodgdon)
41. HS-6 (Hodgdon)	99. AR2219 (ADI)	157. Mag Pro (Accurate)
42. Silhouette (Ramshot)	100. H322 (Hodgdon)	158. N165 (Vihtavuori)

Table 7.A.1 Continued

	Slowest burning				
43.	WAP (Winchester)	101.	X-Terminator (Ramshot)	159.	WXR (Winchester)
44.	N340 (Vihtavuori)	102.	2230 (Accurate)	160.	7828 (IMR)
45.	540 (Winchester)	103.	748 (Winchester)	161.	8700 (Accurate)
46.	Herco (Alliant)	104.	Reloader 10X (Alliant)	162.	H1000 (Hodgdon)
47.	WSF (Winchester)	105.	BLC-2 (Hodgdon)	163.	AR2217 (ADI)
48.	SR-4756 (IMR)	106.	AR2206 (ADI)	164.	Magnum (Ramshot)
49.	AP- 100 (ADI)	107.	2460 (Accurate)	165.	Reloader 25 (Alliant)
50.	Solo 1250 (Accurate)	108.	H335 (Hodgdon)	166.	AR2225 (ADI)
51.	3N37 (Vihtavuori)	109.	TAC (Ramshot)	167.	Retumbo (Hodgdon)
52.	800X (IMR)	110.	H4895 (Hodgdon)	168.	H870 (Hodgdon)
53.	No. 7 (Accurate)	111.	2495 XMR (Accurate)	169.	N170 (Vihtavuori)
54.	Longshot (Hodgdon)	112.	AR2206H (ADI)	170.	24N41 (Vihtavuori)
55.	Solo 1500 (Scot)	113.	Reloader 12 (Alliant)	171.	50 BMG (Hodgdon)
56.	True Blue (Ramshot)	114.	4895 (IMR)	172.	AR2218 (ADI)
57.	N350 (Vihtavuori)	115.	Brig 4065 (Scot)	173.	20N29 (Vihtavuori)

Appendix 8 Hearing Loss

Hearing loss amongst firearms examiners is a major problem. Those regularly firing sawn-off 12-bore shotguns and high-powered military or hunting rifles are particularly at risk, for no matter what hearing protection is utilized, each shot will produce some permanent damage.

Before delving further into this subject, some background information on how the inner ear works is appropriate.

How We Hear

Sound waves enter the outer ear and travel through a narrow passageway called the ear canal, which leads to the eardrum.

The eardrum vibrates from the incoming sound waves and sends these vibrations to three tiny bones in the middle ear. These bones are called the malleus, incus and stapes.

The bones in the middle ear amplify, or increase, the sound and send the vibrations to the snail-shaped cochlea, or inner ear. The cochlea is a fluid-filled organ with an elastic membrane that runs down its length and divides the cochlea into an upper and lower part. This membrane is called the 'basilar' membrane because it serves as the base, or ground floor, on which key hearing structures sit.

The vibrations cause the fluid inside the cochlea to ripple, and a travelling wave forms along the basilar membrane. This motion causes bristly structures on top of the hair cells to bump up against an overlying membrane and to deflect to one side.

Handbook of Firearms and Ballistics: Second Edition   Brian J. Heard
© 2008 John Wiley & Sons, Ltd.

Table 8.A.1 Some reference sound levels.

Approximate decibel level	Example
0	Faintest sound heard by human ear
30	Whisper, quiet library
60	Normal conversation, sewing machine, typewriter
90	Lawnmower, shop tools, truck traffic
100	Chainsaw, pneumatic drill, snowmobile
115	Sandblasting, loud rock concert, auto horn
140	Jet engine; noise causes pain and even brief exposure injures unprotected ears; considered to be the threshold of pain

As the bristles, or stereocilia, move, pore-like channels on their surface open up. This allows certain chemicals to rush in that generate an electrical signal.

The auditory nerve carries the signal to the brain, which translates it into a 'sound' that we recognize and understand.

Hair cells near the base of the cochlea detect higher-pitched sounds, such as a cellphone ringing. Those nearer the apex, or centremost point, detect lower-pitched sounds, such as a large dog barking.

It is these hair cells at the base of the cochlea which receive most damage by high-frequency and high-volume sounds, such as the discharge of a firearm. Damage to these hair cells is irreversible and results in a permanent loss of hearing.

After exposure to excessive levels of high-frequency sound, a ringing in the ears, tinnitus, can also be experienced. This can, likewise, be permanent.

Frequency

Pitch is measured in frequency of sound vibrations (cycles) per second, called hertz (Hz). A low pitch such as a deep voice or a tuba makes fewer vibrations per second than a high voice or violin. The higher the pitch of the sound, the higher the frequency.

Generally, noise-induced hearing loss occurs at a pitch of about 2,000–4,000 Hz.

Young children, who generally have the best hearing, can often distinguish sounds from about 20 Hz, such as the lowest note on a large pipe organ, to 20,000 Hz, such as the high shrill of a dog whistle that many people are unable to hear.

Human speech, which ranges from 300 to 4,000 Hz, sounds louder to most people than noises at very high or very low frequencies. When hearing impairment begins, the high frequencies are often lost first, which is why people with

Table 8.A.2 Centre fire pistol data.

	dB
0.25 ACP	155
0.32 Long	152
0.32 ACP	153
0.380	157
9 mm	159
0.38 S&W	153
0.38 Spl	156
0.357 Magnum	165
0.41 Magnum	163
0.44 Spl	155
0.45 ACP	157

hearing loss often have difficulty hearing the high-pitched voices of women and children.

Loss of high-frequency hearing also can distort sound, so that speech is difficult to understand even though it can be heard. Hearing-impaired people often have difficulty detecting differences between certain words that sound alike, especially words that contain S, F, SH, CH, H, or soft C, sounds, because the sound of these consonants is in a much higher frequency range than vowels and other consonants.

Hearing Loss

It is generally accepted that a continuous noise level of 85 db (decibels) is the maximum safe level for long-term exposure to steady noise level within the frequency range of about 600–1,200 Hz. The very brief gunfire noises are another matter.

Leading hearing specialists stipulate that about 150 db is the maximum peak limit for gunfire noises without impairment of speech perception and 140 db maximum without impairment of good hearing of music and the like.

It should be noted that decibels are a logarithmic scale and that the sound energy doubles with each 3 db increase.

Below are listed data describing peak sound pressure levels produced by firearms of various calibres. With the introduction of muzzle breaks and porting, the risks of hearing loss dramatically increase (Tables 8.A.2–10.4).

Dr. Krammer[1] states that the damage caused by one shot from a 0.357 Magnum pistol, which can expose a shooter to 165 dB for 2 ms, is equivalent to over 40 h in a noisy workplace.

[1] Dr Krammer, Ball State University, Muncie, Indiana, USA.

Table 8.A.3 Shotgun noise data.

	dB
0.410-Bore 28″ barrel	150
26″ Barrel	150
18″ Barrel	156
20-Gauge 28″ barrel	152
22″ Barrel	154
12-Gauge 28″ barrel	151
26″ Barrel	156
18″ Barrel	161
12″ Barrel	168
8″ Barrel	172

Table 8.A.4 Centre fire rifle data.

	dB
0.223, 18″ Barrel	155
0.243 in 22″ barrel	155
0.30–30 in 20″ barrel	156
7 mm Magnum in 20″ barrel	157
0.308 in 24″ barrel	156
0.30–06 in 24″ barrel	158
0.30–06 in 18″ barrel	163
0.375 18″ Barrel	162
0.375 18″ Barrel with muzzle brake	170

Hearing Protectors

Hearing protection devices decrease the intensity of sound that reaches the eardrum. They come in two basic forms: earplugs and earmuffs.

Properly fitted earplugs or muffs reduce noise 15–30 dB. The better earplugs and muffs are approximately equal in sound reduction, although earplugs are better for low-frequency noise and earmuffs for high-frequency noise.

Simultaneous use of earplugs and muffs usually adds 10–15 dB more protection than either used alone. Combined use should be considered when noise exceeds 105 dB. Note that for such situations, it may be that there is no type of hearing protection that will stop a very loud noise from causing permanent damage.

Types Available

Expandable foam plugs

These plugs are made of a formable material designed to expand and conform to the shape of each person's ear canal. Basically, they are rolled flat, inserted into the ear and then allowed to expand to form a tight fit. They are simple and highly effective, but only intended for single use due to contamination by ear wax.

Pre-moulded, reusable plugs

Pre-moulded plugs are made from silicone, plastic or rubber and are manufactured as either 'one-size-fits-most' or are available in several sizes. Many premoulded plugs are available in sizes for small, medium or large ear canals.

It should be noted that a person may need a different size plug for each ear. The plugs should seal the ear canal without being uncomfortable. This takes trial and error of the various sizes. These can be custom made for an individual.

Canal caps

Canal caps often resemble earplugs on a flexible plastic or metal band. The earplug tips of a canal cap may be a formable or pre-moulded material. Some have headbands that can be worn over the head, behind the neck or under the chin. Newer models have jointed bands increasing the ability to properly seal the earplug.

The main advantage that canal caps offer is convenience. Some people find the pressure from the bands uncomfortable. Not all canal caps have tips that adequately block all types of noise. Generally, the canal cap tips that resemble stand-alone ear canal caps appear to block the most noise.

Earmuffs

Earmuffs come in many models designed to fit most people. They work to block out noise by completely covering the outer ear. Muffs can be 'low profile' with small ear cups or large to hold extra materials for use in extreme noise. Some muffs also include electronic components to help users communicate but block impulsive noises when they reach a certain threshold.

Workers who have heavy beards or sideburns or who wear glasses may find it difficult to get good protection from earmuffs. The hair and the arms of the glasses break the seal that the earmuff cushions make around the ear.

Fine fibreglass wool

Originally marketed by Bilsom, this is an extremely fine grade of fibreglass wool which is rolled up and pushed into the ear canal. Whilst it is extremely effective, concerns have been aired over the practice of placing fibreglass, no matter how fine, into such a sensitive area. This may no longer be available.

Miscellaneous Devices

Manufacturers are receptive to comments from hearing protection users. This has led to the development of new devices that are hybrids of the traditional types of hearing protectors.

Because many people like the comfort of foam plugs but do not want to roll them in dirty environments, a plug is now available that is essentially a foam tip on a stem. This plug is inserted in the same way as a pre-moulded plug but without rolling the foam.

Cotton wool/rolled-up paper

This is often used but of very little use as an attenuation of only around 7 dB can be achieved, likewise for bullets or cartridge cases pushed into the ear canal.

Extreme Conditions

For those situations where extreme noise pollution is anticipated, such as when firing multiple shots from sawn-off 12-bore shotguns, additional precautions have to be taken.

The problem with extremely high impulse sound is that it is also transmitted to the inner ear via the facial bones and the teeth. Whilst some attenuation may occur due to tissue and muscle, damage to the hearing can still be caused. The use of a Makralon face shield to deflect the sound, lining the ear muff with additional layers of foam and wearing ear plugs will, if all used together, significantly reduce the risk.

Further Reading

Christiansson, B.A.C. and Wintzell, K.A. (1995) *An audiological survey of officers at an infantry regiment. Scandinavian Audiology*, **22**, 147–52.

Paul, D.R., Chai-lip and Marcus, T. (1979) *Hearing in military personnel. Annals of the Academy of Medicine*, **8** (2).

Pelausa, E., Abel, S. and Dempsey, I. (1995) *Prevention of hearing loss in the Canadian military. Journal of Otolaryngology*, **24** (5), 271–80.

Wenselman, L., Henderson, D. *et al.* (1995) *Effects of Noise Exposure Race and Years of Service on Hearing in U.S. Army Soldiers Ear and Hearing*, Williams and Wilkins, Ear Hear, Aug 1995 **16** (4) 382–91.

Ylikoski, M. and Ylikoski, J. (1994) Hearing loss and Handicap of professional soldiers exposed to gun fire noise. Scand J Work Envion Health, **20** (2) 93–100.

Appendix 9 General Firearms Values Conversion Table

To convert from	To	Multiply by
ft/s	m/s	0.0508
ft/s	miles/h	0.6818
m/s	ft/min	196.85039
m/s	ft/s	3.2808399
ft lb	erg	1.35582×10^7
ft lb	J	1.35582
ft lb	kg m	0.138255
J (Int)	ft lb	0.737684
J (Int)	ft lb	23.73428
Gravitational constant	cm (s×s)	980.621
Gravitational constant	ft (s×s)	32.1725

Handbook of Firearms and Ballistics: Second Edition   Brian J. Heard
© 2008 John Wiley & Sons, Ltd.

Length

To convert from	To	Multiply by
cm	ft	0.0328
cm	in.	0.3937
dm	in.	3.937
ft	cm	30.48
ft	dm	3.048
ft	m	0.3048
in.	cm	2.54
in.	mm	25.4
km	ft	3280.8
km	m	1000
km	miles	0.62137
km	yd	1093.6
m	in.	39.3701
m	km	0.001
m	miles, nautical, British	0.0005396
m	miles, statute	0.000621
m	mm	1000
m	mμ	1×10^{9}
μ	cm	0.0001
μ	in.	3.9370079×10^{-5}
m	yd	1.0936
miles	km	1.6093
miles	m	1609.3
mm	in.	0.03937
mm	parsec	3.2408×10^{-20}
yd	cm	91.44
yd	m	0.9144

Weight

To convert from	To	Multiply by
g	drams (troy)	0.2572
g	drams (avoirdupois)	0.5644
g	gr	15.432
g	kg	0.001
g	µg	1×10^6
g	mg	1000
g	oz (troy)	0.03215
g	oz (avoirdupois)	0.03527
g	lb (troy)	0.00268
g	lb (avoirdupois)	0.002205
g	t (metric)	1×10^{-6}
g	drams (apothecary or troy)	257.21
kg	drams (avoirdupois)	564.38
kg	gr	15432.36
kg	g	1000
kg	oz (apothecary or troy)	32.1507
kg	oz (avoirdupois)	35.27396
kg	lb (apothecary or troy)	267923
kg	lb (avoirdupois)	2.20462
kg	t (long)	0.00098
kg	t (metric)	0.001
kg	t (short)	0.001102
oz (avoirdupois)	drams (apothecary or troy)	7.2917
oz (avoirdupois)	drams (avoirdupois)	16
oz (avoirdupois)	gr	437.5
oz (avoirdupois)	g	28.3495
oz (avoirdupois)	lb (apothecary or troy)	0.07596
oz (avoirdupois)	lb (avoirdupois)	0.0625
lb (avoirdupois)	drams (apothecary or troy)	116.667
lb (avoirdupois)	drams (avoirdupois)	256
lb (avoirdupois)	gr	7000
lb (avoirdupois)	g	453.59
lb (avoirdupois)	kg	0.4536
lb (avoirdupois)	oz (apothecary or troy)	14.583
lb (avoirdupois)	oz (avoirdupois)	16
lb (avoirdupois)	lb (apothecary or troy)	1.21528
lb (avoirdupois)	scruples (apothecary)	350
lb (avoirdupois)	t (long)	0.0004464
lb (avoirdupois)	t (metric)	0.0004536
lb (avoirdupois)	t (short)	0.0005

Index

Handbook of Firearms and Ballistics: Second Edition Brian J. Heard
© 2008 John Wiley & Sons, Ltd.

Printed in the USA/Agawam, MA
August 7, 2013